A REVOLUTION IN FRAGMENTS

A REVO LUTION

IN FRAG MENTS

Traversing Scales of
Justice, Ideology,
and Practice
in Bolivia

MARK GOODALE

Duke University Press   Durham and London   2019

Printed and bound by CPI Group (UK) Ltd, Croydon, CR0 4YY
Designed by Drew Sisk
Typeset in Minion Pro, Folio Std and Italian Old Style MT Std
by Westchester Publishing Services

Library of Congress Cataloging-in-Publication Data
Names: Goodale, Mark, author.
Title: A revolution in fragments : traversing scales of justice, ideology, and
    practice in Bolivia / Mark Goodale.
Description: Durham : Duke University Press, 2019. | Includes bibliographical
    references and index.
Identifiers: LCCN 2019010892 (print) | LCCN 2019980376 (ebook)
ISBN 9781478005865 (hardcover)
ISBN 9781478006527 (paperback)
ISBN 9781478007234 (ebook)
Subjects: LCSH: Bolivia—Politics and government—2006- | Bolivia—History—
    21st century. | Bolivia—Social conditions—21st century. | Bolivia—Economic
    conditions—21st century. | Bolivia—Ethnic relations—Political aspects.
Classification: LCC F3327.G663 2019 (print) | LCC F3327 (ebook) | DDC 984.05/4—dc23
LC record available at https://lccn.loc.gov/2019010892
LC ebook record available at https://lccn.loc.gov/2019980376

Cover art: Art illustration of Evo Morales and Túpac Katari, from a political poster for
MAS (Movement toward Socialism). Design by Drew Sisk.

As always, for Isaiah, Dara, and Romana, in whose presence
"I acknowledge my life, my destiny."

———

Taqi kun sum puquñpataki. ("May everything produce well.")

—QUOTED IN Olivia Harris,
To Make the Earth Bear Fruit (2000)

Contents

PREFACE   ix

INTRODUCTION   Meaning and Crisis in Cosmic Time   1

1   Hearing Revolution in a Minor Key   33

2   Legal Cosmovisions   64

3   Opposition as a Cultural System:
    Myth, Embodiment, Violence   95

4   A Revolution without Revolutionaries:
    El proceso de cambio in a Trotskyized Country   134

5   The Unstable Assemblage of Law   166

6   And the Pututu Shall Sound   200

CONCLUSION   The Politics of Forever   234

NOTES   249

REFERENCES   265

INDEX   283

Preface

In October 1997, after a week of commemorations that "had a quasi-religious character," as a *New York Times* article put it, the remains of Che Guevara were interred on the grounds of a massive public monument, built in his honor, in the provincial capital of Santa Clara, Cuba. Santa Clara had been chosen by the Castro regime because it had been the site of a critical battle during the Cuban revolution, in which Guevara had led a decisive victory over government forces. Although Guevara had been executed in Bolivia in 1967 after the insurrection he fomented had been violently suppressed by a special Bolivian counterinsurgency unit trained and advised by U.S. military and CIA personnel, the location of his remains was not revealed until the mid-1990s. Retired Bolivian military officers led an international forensic team to a common grave near an airstrip in Vallegrande, where Guevara's skeleton was identified in part because it was the only one that lacked hands. Soon after his execution, his hands had been removed so that his body could be identified through his fingerprints. At some point during the intervening decades, these relics were supposedly acquired by the Castro government in Havana, where they were privately displayed on occasion to visiting luminaries at the Palace of the Revolution.

But what was fascinating about this moment in which the circle of Guevara's revolutionary martyrdom was finally, after thirty years, closed was the way in which it was experienced by average Cubans. Instead of understanding the symbolic importance of Guevara, and by extension the Cuban revolution, in terms of a unifying ideology of global class struggle and the dialectical rhythms of historical materialism, Cubans viewed the legacy of the heroic guerrilla leader in quite varied and vernacularized ways. The same *New York Times* article quotes an aging retiree, for whom the significance of Guevara lay in the simple fact that Guevara's deeds "drove a stake into the heart of the Batista tyranny." In other words, it was not the fact that Che helped steer Cuba on its glorious passage into communism that mattered. Instead, it was that he played a key role in overthrowing a brutal dictatorship that had preserved Cuba as a zone of economic plunder and a play-place for wealthy foreign tourists, gamblers, and the American mafia.

I kept this lesson in mind both during ethnographic research over nine years in Bolivia and during the writing of this book. In trying to come to terms with the meaning and significance of the period 2006–15 in Bolivia, a period variously described as revolutionary, reformist, crypto-neoliberal, and increasingly authoritarian, among others, it was this basic tension that recurred time and again—the tension between the politics of ideological "condensation," in Victor Turner's terms, and the centrifugal realities of everyday life. In a sense, the anthropological dilemma mirrored the social and political one: how to crystalize the analysis of the "process of change" in Bolivia in a way that was consistent with its ethnographic heterogeneity and ambiguity. The response, which I hope is sufficiently reflected in this book, was to conceive of the period 2006–15 in terms of the many and shifting fragments that came together, or were mobilized, or were resisted, at particular moments in time. Even more, the book tries to privilege the ways in which these fragmentary assemblages took on a prismatic quality, in which categories of ethnicity, gender, class, and political identity, among others, intersectionally shaped the quotidian experiences of "revolution" and its various afterlives.

———

Before I get to the many acknowledgments and expressions of gratitude, there are several points of methodological order that must be made. The first concerns the use of the past tense throughout the book. I decided early on to abandon the fraught ethnographic present, and this decision proved to be liberating. Ethically, the use of the ethnographic present is problematic, since it traffics in unacceptable tropes of cultural timelessness. Stylistically, it is also troubling, since it attempts to collapse the distance between the anthropologist-as-writer, reader, and whoever or whatever is being described in ways that confuse even as it harnesses the power of what Malinowski called the "ethnographer's magic." And historically, the use of the ethnographic present poses simple problems of descriptive accuracy. This was a particular concern in writing about ethnographic research conducted during different periods over nine years. By adopting the simple past tense throughout much of the book, I realized that I was also putting down the magician's wand, and, as a consequence, letting go of the tight grip of ethnographic authority. In the end, the use of the past tense seemed to be of a piece with an analytical approach to the period 2006–15 in Bolivia that underscored the fragmentary, the partial, and the prismatic.

Another important methodological point concerns the use of names. This is something I discussed with almost every interlocutor over nine years:

Do you want me to change your name? In almost every case, the answer was "no," and I couldn't think of a reason to disregard these express wishes on the matter. There are key exceptions: for example, when I discuss interviews with students and nonpublic figures, I routinely use pseudonyms. But these are exceptions that prove the general rule. Obviously, the use of pseudonyms would not have been possible for many of the figures who appear in the book, since they were (and many still are) well-known intellectuals, political leaders, jurists, and indigenous activists, among other official and semiofficial positions.

As will soon become clear, I make extensive use of ethnographic interviews throughout the book. This was a way to give priority to the voices of a wide range of Bolivians who played a role, in one way or another, during this extraordinary period in Bolivian history. Over nine years, I accumulated an enormous amount of data from interviews. For example, ethnographic interviews in 2008 and 2009 alone yielded almost five hundred pages of interview transcripts. Nevertheless, I was only able to use a fraction of the overall interview data in the book. I edited interviews—at times, extensively and liberally—for clarity and legibility after first translating them into English. In general, I tried to interpret and present extended interview passages in a way that would be easier to read without changing the narrative flow or interrupting the particularity of the exchange.

Beyond questions of methodology, there are a few broader issues that should be addressed. First, although ethnographic research over nine years in Bolivia was, as I explain in the introduction, regionally and historically wide-ranging, it was far from comprehensive. For example, in 2009, I returned to the region in which I had conducted doctoral fieldwork in the late 1990s, northern Potosí Department. This was more of a personal visit than a research trip. Yet even at the height of conflict over the new constitution in the major cities, life in and around Sacaca seemed to go on much as before, with certain subtle yet important changes, such as the fact that the town's leadership included a few members from some of the close-in rural hamlets. I imagine a version of this provincial story was true throughout the country; it is an important story, just not the one that forms the basis for this book.

And second, there are no doubt any number of glaring ethnographic gaps in the book, since they were not part of the underlying research. For example, although I conducted relatively attenuated research with Guaraní political leaders in Santa Cruz in 2015, I didn't feel sufficiently knowledgeable about lowland politics to incorporate this material into the book. Yet there is no question—as a number of recent volumes demonstrate—that from the TIPNIS conflict of 2011 to the ongoing marginalization of lowland indigenous interests

by the La Paz–centric MAS government, the "democratic and cultural revolution" of the period 2006–15 must be understood in relation to regional, linguistic, and cultural specificities. In addition, by empirically and theoretically
foregrounding justice, ideology, and practice as orienting scales for the project,
other areas were necessarily left aside. A particularly important absence in this
sense is obviously the place of economic processes and state planning, including resource exploitation and, increasingly, industrialization.

———

In acknowledging the vital role played in the project by different people, I have
decided to focus on the many Bolivians who collaborated, in one way or another, in the research, conceptual analysis, and writing. I am not able to acknowledge everyone who gave of their time and wisdom, but this book could
never have been written without a willingness to participate, even (or especially) critically, in the long-term research that forms the basis for the book.
Having said this, it is also true that by acknowledging these debts I do not mean
to associate anyone with particular arguments, observations, or anthropologi-
cal critiques, that is, beyond the associations that appear in the book itself.
For their collaboration, participation, and time, I acknowledge the following:
Virginia Aillón, Emilio Barea Medrano, Ricardo Calla, Mary Carrasco, Efrén
Choque Capuma, Frida Choque de Claros, Adolfo Colque Gutiérrez, Oswaldo
Cuevas Gaete, Carlos Dabdoub Arrien, Carlos Derpic Salazar, Erika Dueñas,
Carolina Floru, Gustavo Guzmán, Luis E. Huarachi Miranda, Martín Hurtado
Tovar, Delina Joffré Romandú, Gonz Jove, Julio Llanos Rojas, Sacha Llorenti,
Felipe Machaca Quispe, Ricardo Montero, Mónica Pacheco Sanjinés, René
Gonzalo Párraga Gallardo, Antonio Peredo Leigue, Miguel Pérez Quispe, José
Antonio Quiroga Trigo, David Ricalde, Luis Pedro Rodríguez Calvo, Cecilia
Salazar de la Torre, Hugo Siles Núñez del Prado, Luis Tapia, Virginia Tapia,
Leonardo Villafuente Philippsborn, Rolando Villena Villegas, and Fernanda
Wanderley.

Research and writing took place during the same years in which I served
as one of the editors for the long-term project that culminated (in 2018) in *The
Bolivia Reader: History, Culture, Politics*. Under the steady and indefatigable
hand of the project's lead editor, Sinclair Thomson, the volume took shape over
more than fifteen years and gave me the incomparable opportunity to learn
from a vast amount of diverse historical material, some of which I draw from
in the current book. At the same time, it was a privilege to collaborate with the
Reader's other editors: Xavier Albó, Rossana Barragán, and Seemin Qayum.

The slow development of the book's ethnographic and theoretical approaches took place in large part through invited lectures, seminars, and presentations rather than through earlier journal articles and book chapters. Each of these moments was a time to explore what seemed to be an always-emerging and evolving framework for understanding the period 2006–15 in Bolivia. These occasions were so valuable to me in large part because of the critical engagement of colleagues, students, and audience members, whose collective responses and recommendations became, over time, interwoven into my own long-term thinking about contemporary Bolivia. I express my heartfelt gratitude for having been given the chance to develop the project in this way at events at the following places: University of Oslo (Department of Anthropology, October 2006); Universidad de Antioquia (Department of Anthropology, March 2008); University of Pittsburgh (Department of Anthropology, September 2008); Stanford University (Center for Latin American Studies, April 2009); Rutgers University (Center for Latin American Studies and Department of Anthropology, October 2009); Cambridge University (Centre for Research in the Arts, Social Sciences and Humanities, January 2010); Catholic University of Leuven (European Commission and the Marie Curie Fellows program, March 2010); University of Wisconsin–Madison (Department of Anthropology, April 2010); International University College of Turin (October 2010); Max Planck Institute for Social Anthropology and Martin-Luther-Universität Halle-Wittenberg (Institute for Social Anthropology, October 2010); Northwestern University (Department of Anthropology and Rhetoric, and Public Culture Program, Department of Communication Studies, October 2011); University of Minnesota (School of Law, Institute for Advanced Studies, Human Rights Program, and Center for Holocaust and Genocide Studies, October 2013); University of Coimbra (Centre for Social Sciences, March 2014); Stanford University (Program on Human Rights; Center on Democracy, Development and the Rule of Law; Freeman Spogli Institute for International Studies, April 2014); London School of Economics (Department of Anthropology, May 2014); Martin-Luther-Universität Halle-Wittenberg (Institute for Social Anthropology, January 2016); University of Zurich (Department of Social Anthropology and Cultural Studies, November 2016); The Hebrew University of Jerusalem (Department of Sociology and Anthropology, January 2017); University of Cagliari (Faculty of Jurisprudence and the Institute for Advanced Studies, May 2017); and University of Helsinki (Helsinki Institute of Sustainability Science, Department of Anthropology, September 2018).

Research over nine years would obviously not have been possible without the generous assistance of a number of different foundations and institutions.

Major funding was provided by the Center for Global Studies and the Office of the Provost, George Mason University; the Wenner-Gren Foundation for Anthropological Research; the Cultural Anthropology Program of the U.S. National Science Foundation; and the Institute of Social Sciences and Office of the Dean, Faculty of Social and Political Sciences, University of Lausanne. Individuals at these various institutions whose support was fundamental in the research and writing of the book include Sara Cobb and Peter Stearns at George Mason University and Fabien Ohl, Nicky Le Feuvre, Daniel Oesch, Eléonore Lépinard, and Jean-Philippe Leresche at the University of Lausanne. More generally, I must express my deepest gratitude to colleagues, staff, and students in the Institute of Social Sciences and the Laboratory of Cultural and Social Anthropology (LACS) at the University of Lausanne, who have contributed to making the university a delightful and productive base from which to conduct research, write, and teach.

I am grateful for the participation of a number of graduate research assistants over the years. Adriana Salcedo performed a wide range of important tasks and was able to join me during field research in Bolivia, where she participated in interviews and observations, conducted data analysis, and later transcribed interviews. Michael Posse joined me during later fieldwork and also participated in interviews and observations, including the interviews with the members of the survivors' association with which I begin the book. Finally, Maya Avis conducted valuable bibliographic research during the drafting of the manuscript.

I would be remiss if I did not also thank the staff at the Hotel Calacoto in La Paz, which has welcomed me for extended periods of time since 2006. Several of the hotel's longtime staff members have become like old friends; it is a pleasure to see them each time I return to Bolivia, even as we remark on the way we all continue to age.

The process of publishing with Duke University Press has been rewarding at every stage. As is standard with the press, the book manuscript was subject to two distinct rounds of anonymous peer review, a level of scrutiny and revision that proved vital for the book's development. Gisela Fosado's early support for the book was critical, as was her wise counsel and guiding hand throughout the entire process. I must also thank Alejandra Mejía, who provided technical support and advice on different aspects of the manuscript.

As with other books I have published, this one too is formally dedicated to my family, Isaiah, Dara, and Romana. Their support and love is the glue that holds everything together and makes my life—professional and personal— possible. When I first began the project, Isaiah and Dara were little children;

now they are teenagers, both headstrong and filled with hope, their entire futures ahead of them. In a sense, this too was a lesson I kept in mind during the writing of this book. In considering the extraordinary, if contested, process of change in Bolivia during the period 2006–15, the danger is not that we will overestimate its significance, its implications, its revolutionary moments, however fragmentary. The real danger is that, in a cynical age marked by global inequality, political disenchantment, and enduring patriarchy, among other ills, we are losing the ability to even imagine better futures, let alone to recognize the fleeting signs of their appearance on the horizon.

Introduction   # MEANING AND CRISIS
IN COSMIC TIME

Even against the noise and perpetual movement
of La Paz's El Prado, the city's historic central bou-
levard, the structure was impossible to miss. It appeared in 2012 directly across from the building
that housed the various vice ministries and offices
of the Ministry of Justice. The structure was semi-
permanent, with wooden walls and a corrugated
metal roof. As was common throughout Bolivia, the
sheets of corrugated metal that constituted the roof
were held down by a dozen clay bricks. This shack
sat in the middle of El Prado's median strip, a long
and well-used pedestrian public space that featured

a series of statues, benches, and aging tile groundwork. The structure's outer walls were covered with posters and signs that proclaimed in large bright red and black letters: "18 Years of Dictatorship. How Many More Years of Injustice and Impunity? Plan Condor. Survivors of the Dictatorships." Various figures drawn on the posters held up signs that demanded "justice," "truth," and "reparations." And on the edge of one large poster, the faces from the rogues' gallery of Bolivian dictators stared down at passers-by: Barrientos, Banzer, Pereda, Natusch, and the worst of all, García Meza, the narcofascist *paceño* who worked closely with the Nazi war criminal Klaus Barbie, the "Butcher of Lyon," during García Meza's one-year reign of terror.

The shack on El Prado was constructed by members of a nationwide "platform" for survivors of the eighteen years of almost continual brutal oppression between 1964 and 1982, a period in which successive Bolivian dictatorships collaborated with both U.S. and regional economic, military, and intelligence interests as part of a hemispheric war against various movements that sought to challenge capitalist hegemony and conservative political rule. Nationwide, about five thousand people considered themselves survivors of the Bolivian dictatorships, although only about two hundred participated regularly in maintaining and occupying their unofficial headquarters on El Prado. Because the current government had ignored their demands for recognition and reparations, the local members of the survivors' organization decided to establish an open-ended vigil in which their stark presence across from the Ministry of Justice was meant as a quiet and dignified rebuke, a constant reminder to the thousands who passed daily that Bolivian history did not begin in 2006, the year Evo Morales and the Movement to Socialism (MAS) party took power.

Just outside the entrance, the survivors had placed a wooden table on which they had arranged various types of office equipment, including old computers, that had been warped and twisted by fire, a testament to the fact that their vigil on El Prado had been met on occasion by violence, harassment, and the constant threat of eviction by what they believed were plainclothes intelligence and police personnel acting on government orders to make life difficult and ultimately to break their resolve.

The inside of the structure was divided into three small areas: one that served as a kitchen in which simple meals were prepared; a second that contained piles of documents, legal files, photographs, and other evidence from the survivors' histories; and a third, a central space flanked by two long wooden benches. Here is where the survivors came and went during the day, where they sat with each other to trade small talk about ailments and personal travails, and where they kept a wary eye on a list of names that loomed over them. This was the list that recorded the *compañeros fallecidos en la vigilia*, the comrades who had died during the vigil on El Prado. In August 2015, there were thirteen names on the list, meaning thirteen survivors had died just since 2012. The collective health of the survivors on El Prado was extremely precarious. Most of them were in their late seventies and some were in their eighties. Because many of them had been tortured during the dictatorships, they suffered from lasting physical and psychological disabilities. And because some of them had also been miners in their youth, they were afflicted with advanced cases of silicosis and other lung diseases. Indeed, in a country whose life expectancy at birth was only around fifty years as late as 1980, it was something close to a miracle that any of the survivors—particularly those from the dictatorships of the 1960s—were still alive.

Although the survivors' organization did not have formal political status, one of its members had agreed to act as its spokesperson. Alejandro Mamani was a *dirigente* at the Colquiri mine in La Paz Department in the 1960s who was a leading advocate for anti-imperialist revolution among his fellow miners. He had been an enthusiastic supporter of Che Guevara right up until the moment the Argentinian revolutionary was cornered and executed in La Higuera in 1967 by Bolivian soldiers operating under the close supervision and assistance of the U.S. CIA and military advisers.

Mamani was seventy-seven years old, a quiet man who walked slowly with a slight limp that was the result of beatings he suffered during six separate periods of detention between 1965 and 1975. I asked him if he was willing to tell me what happened to him, and he reluctantly agreed. He sighed, looked around the room at the other survivors, and began.

———

The first time I was held was terrible, it was a terrible shock. I had received train-ing in ideology [during a trip to China in 1964], *but I wasn't prepared for what I saw and what happened to me when I was taken into custody by the military. Yes, I was in custody that first time for about a month. I was interrogated first for many days and then tortured. They pulled out the fingernails on this hand* [his right]. *After that, they tied me up against a wall and dripped water on my head all day. I couldn't move my head because they squeezed two boards on either side of it very tight, like this* [pushes his hands to his ears like a vise]. *Sometime after that, I can't say how long, they took a group of us to Lake Titicaca in a truck, but we were in boxes, like coffins. They stopped by the shore and they told us, from outside, that we were dead. Then I heard splashes. I waited, but then they loaded some of us back into the truck and drove us back to La Paz. I couldn't be sure which of our comrades were in those boxes, but they were gone.*

I asked him if he remembered his longest detention.

In 1969, they kept me for three months. I was sure they were finally going to kill me. That was the time I lost my finger [points to the middle finger on his left hand, which had been severed at the middle knuckle]. *I'll never forget his name, a sadistic guard named Álvaro Lanza* [not a pseudonym]. *They grabbed my hand and Lanza pulled out his bayonet. They held the hand down and Lanza started playing a game, like this* [makes gesture of poking quickly between his fingers].

Here Mamani put his face in his old hands to hide tears, but he quickly continued.

Lanza started going faster and faster and then the tip came down right in the middle of my finger and cut it off. Part of the finger was just there, with blood everywhere and this Lanza was laughing and laughing.

I asked him how his wife and children coped with these many periods of detention and torture, the constant threat that he would simply be disappeared one day.

During this same detention [in 1969], *they held me along with many other comrades in a torture center that was right next to the Parliament* [in Plaza Murillo]. *I will never forget what happened on Christmas Eve. They allowed the prisoners to go into home detention for several days to be with their families, but not me. Everyone was allowed a home detention except me. That night, they put me into a jeep and drove around and around the plaza. And there was my family, waiting for me, my wife and three children, sitting on a bench. After they had driven around the plaza very slowly about ten times, one of them said to me, "have a long look at your family, because this is the last time you are ever going to see them, carajo." And then they drove right back into the building.*

During three of my later detentions, they told my family I had died, but they wouldn't tell my wife anything more. Even today [2015], *almost fifty years later, she still suffers, she still has nightmares that I've been killed.*

———

So why begin in this way with Alejandro Mamani's heartrending account? Doing so allows me to introduce three implicit framing devices that reoccur throughout the book in the form of theoretical argument, historical observation, and a kind of ethnographic ethics. The first is the idea that the process of change in Bolivia was marked by the destabilizing manipulation of coevalness. As the German anthropologist Johannes Fabian (1983) showed, social and political power can be exercised by creating what he calls a chronological "cultural taxonomy" that establishes different possibilities and impossibilities for coexistence.

As we will see, from the preamble to the 2009 Bolivian constitution to the rhetoric of world-reversal or world-renewal associated with the concept of *Pachakuti*, the period of change in Bolivian history that underwent a profound turning point with the election of Evo Morales was shaped by a politics of allochrony—the reification of past, present, and future into categories that did certain kinds of public work. Even more, not all of these categories were equal. In particular, the MAS government mobilized—politically, ideologically, and symbolically—the cultural taxonomies associated with what the Indianist writer and guru Fausto Reinaga described as "cosmic time" (1978: 45).

Second, a politics of allochrony was only one expression of another key characteristic of the country's contested democratic and cultural revolution: the fact that change took place in terms of a series of inclusions and exclusions that were problematically, even paradoxically, justified within a broader ideological framework of pluralistic belonging. In this sense, the ethnography of post-2005 Bolivia revealed a social and discursive dynamic that has implications for other processes of profound transformation. In forming categories, even those that encompassed historically marginalized ethnic, regional, and class groups, others were at the same time excluded. To this extent, even a novel social rhetoric of inclusion and empowerment could function as well as a rhetoric of denial and disempowerment. This dialectical interplay had significant consequences during the period 2006–15 in Bolivia, as will be explored in depth throughout the book, but it evoked at a social, political, and legal level the basic insight about language formulated by the Spanish philosopher and essayist José Ortega y Gasset—to define is to exclude and negate.

Third, the life and experiences of Alejandro Mamani and the other members of the national platform of survivors of the dictatorships pointed to a calibrated pragmatism behind much of a process of change that was more typically marked off by the recognizably spectacular moments of public ritual and resistance. The members of the group themselves believed that their claims had been ignored by a government whose official commitment to socialism should have made it sympathetic to its comrades from early struggles not because of a disagreement over beliefs, but for actuarial reasons. As Mamani explained,

Well, it's simple, we are dying, the survivors. Look over there [points to the list on the wall]. *We had thirteen of our comrades die just since 2012.*

I asked him if he thought that was the reason the Morales government had done nothing to recognize or respond to their claims, including those for reparations.

Without a doubt, they are just waiting, waiting for us to die. Of course, we will all be dead soon, but we still have hope while we have life. And if they don't [recognize our claims] and give us the justice that we deserve, there is a greater danger that the past will be repeated.

The fact is that the survivors of the dictatorships faced unique and lasting forms of harm, since—as with Alejandro Mamani—many of them could not work for almost twenty years while they were persecuted, imprisoned, exiled, and blacklisted. This meant that what for many of them should have been their prime earning years as workers were simply erased, with corresponding reductions to pensions, social security benefits, and medical entitlements. Their claims for reparations from the Bolivian government involved massive payments to account for these vast and diverse economic losses. So, as Mamani put it, "although we are old men and women [and] still consider ourselves fighters against imperialism," the government preferred to let time render moot the claims for reparations of these aging and ailing ideological ancestors.

And finally, to begin with Alejandro Mamani's story of torture, persecution, and the eventual outlasting of the historical epoch that was determined to destroy him is to recognize, and perhaps even prioritize, that which was irreducible in the phenomenologies of suffering, resistance, sacrifice, hope, and disenchantment that constituted the lived realities of Bolivia's moment of "refoundation."[1] Or rather, it is to draw a distinction between what could be reduced to, or captured by, the act of ethnographic and critical analysis, and what could not. Although, at a certain level of reflection, there were lessons to be drawn from Mamani's experiences, it is important to acknowledge that there was another level that lay underneath, that Wittgensteinian bedrock where the meaning of experience begins and ends with the unique forms of life through which it is expressed. Thus, in the first instance, one had to simply *hear* Mamani tell his story of lying in a dark wooden box on the shores of Lake Titicaca moments away from being thrown into the frigid water without demanding anything more from the ethnographic encounter. A sensitivity to the problem of irreducibility shapes this book in different ways as much for ethical as for epistemological reasons.[2]

(NOT) MISSING THE REVOLUTION

Although I conducted the research for my first ethnographic study of Bolivia between 1998 and 1999, I did not finish the manuscript based on this research until early 2007. The conclusion to that book (Goodale 2008a) was an attempt to bridge the findings from a study of law, conflict, and human rights activism in the north of Potosí Department with rapidly changing events throughout the country following the election of Evo Morales, the formation of a constituent assembly to write a new constitution, and the emergence of a strong opposition based in the southern valleys and eastern lowlands of the country. Nevertheless, it was clear that the political, economic, and social context had shifted in ways that demanded renewed ethnographic attention.

At the same time, I was keenly aware of the kind of critique of Andean anthropology perhaps best represented by Orin Starn's 1991 article "Missing the Revolution," which argued that the methodological tradition of conducting village-based ethnohistorical and ethnographic research played a role in preventing scholars from fully appreciating the underlying political, economic, and ideological mobilizations that led to the rise of the Shining Path Maoist movement and the subsequent violence throughout the 1980s. Beyond the critique of a particular form of ethnographic research, Starn also argued that village-based Andeanist researchers were to varying degrees motivated by an Orientalist conception of highland peoples, one rooted in a set of romantic stereotypes about *lo andino*, the ideal Andean. Although Starn's critique (see also Starn 1994) was itself reductionist to a certain extent, painting, as it did, quite different kinds of research traditions and approaches with a broad brush, the basic thrust of his argument demanded serious consideration. Given the fact that my research experiences had been localized in an iconic region of rural highland Bolivia, how was I to conceive of a methodology that not only would not "miss the revolution," but would track its contours in a way that combined thick description with both a sense of national politics and an appreciation for the wider political economies within which Bolivia's revolution was taking shape?

Complicating the task even further was the fact that the process of refoundation in Bolivia was embedded in an emerging hybrid ideology that depended on much of the same kind of Orientalist imagery that Starn had associated critically with foreign scholars, with the exception that lo andino had been replaced by *lo indígena*, the ideal—and idealized—indigenous person. Thus, it was not possible to draw an easy analytical or ethnographic distinction between the political economic factors that were supposed to ground revolutionary mobilization from the base and the superstructural categories of identity that ultimately distracted attention from the root causes of inequality. In post-2005 Bolivia, the relationship between base and superstructure was being reconfigured.[3]

Finally, there was the problem of the ethnographer's dilemma. The sociocultural anthropologist must at a certain point justify an interpretation or a particular description through the epistemological elusiveness of ethnographic authority, a problematic form of justification that depends on a kind of anti-Popperian disregard for "reliability": I was the only anthropologist to observe something that will never appear in precisely that form, or with precisely that meaning, again. The legitimacy of an ethnographic account, therefore, is inseparable from, indeed even coextensive with, one's own knowledge and capacities. Given the importance of relationships to space and place in the formation of anthropological knowledge and capacities in this sense (see Gupta and Ferguson 1997), the dilemma is that the ethnographer risks sacrificing interpretive power the farther she gets from the spaces and places with which her knowledge and capacities are most closely linked.

In my case, the spaces and places that had grounded my formation were in the north of Potosí Department, a remote region of Bolivia's central highlands that for a series of cultural, historical, and geographical reasons remained at the very margins of national life. Yet while transformations at the national level were being reflected in important local changes, such as the appearance of new rural political parties like the Movimiento Originario Popular (Goodale 2006), the force of these local shifts was still relatively weak compared with the ferment and historic mobilizations in places like La Paz, Sucre, and Santa Cruz. Although the newspapers that arrived each day by bus in the provincial capital, Sacaca, carried headlines of regional unrest, constitution-making, and national economic restructuring, these epochal developments had little impact on the daily rhythms and concerns of the province's agro-pastoralists.

It was clear, therefore, that I needed to adopt a different methodology in order to capture these diffuse broader transformations while staying true to the ethnographic project, that is, the commitment to distance-near description, a sensitivity to the possibilities and perils of representation, and a heightened awareness of the importance of the quotidian in the face of ideological posturing. The prevailing model for the kind of translocal research I had in mind was multisited ethnography (see Marcus 1995, 1999). This approach had formed the foundation for a number of innovative studies in the mid-2000s, including Sally Engle Merry's 2006 account of the international system that was developed to monitor compliance with the Convention on the Elimination of All Forms of Discrimination against Women (CEDAW; see Merry 2006a).

Yet as I considered multisited ethnography as a framework for the study of Bolivia's unfolding process of change, it soon became apparent that the fit was not ideal. Multisited ethnography was not simply a way to describe what it means to conduct ethnographic research in multiple places. The essence of multisited ethnography was that it was a way to track the same process in different locations without losing the value of ethnographic immediacy. Merry's research, which examined CEDAW processes and actors in several countries from the national to the local level, as well as international institutions and governmental bodies, is in many ways a paradigmatic example of the value of multisited ethnographic research.

As I moved forward with planning in 2005 and 2006, however, I was not able to formulate the project in terms of a single or even several processes that could be followed in a similar way within Bolivia. The contested landscape of the early Morales years appeared to be too dynamic to be reduced to a series of sites at which isolated processes could be studied ethnographically. In addition, the project of transformation in Bolivia was being constituted in part through compressions, reframings, and distortions of what might be thought of as cultural space-time—that is, the overlaying of multiple idea-systems onto region, topography, and time itself, for example, through the emergence of the Pachakuti as an alternative temporality with charged political implications.[4]

What I settled on, therefore, was a form of research that took place between 2006 and 2015 that I conceptualized as a "multiscalar longitudinal ethnography." Rather than sites, scales were meant to capture key dimensions of the study that were partly defined relationally (see Xiang 2013).[5] Even more important, thinking of the research methodology in terms of scales allowed me to track the most important categories of compressions, reframings, and distortions along a relational continuum on which the "event" (Deleuze 1994; see also Kapferer 2015) and what Marc Bloch (1953) called "historical time" were closely intertwined. The most important scales of the study in this sense were those of *justice*, *ideology*, and *practice*.

If the project was multiscalar, it was also, importantly, longitudinal. The question of the relationship between synchronic and diachronic approaches to ethnographic research has long occupied anthropological theorists and historians. In addition to the epistemological and ethical dimensions to these debates, scholars such as Eleanor Leacock, Sidney Mintz, June Nash, and Eric Wolf brought a concern with global political economies to the problem of history in anthropology. In my case, although extended, multiyear fieldwork was a common marker of what anthropologists describe as "second projects," meaning the project that follows doctoral fieldwork, the research became longitudinal as a response to Bolivia's unstable unfolding history more than anything else.

What I was looking for with each passing fieldwork season, periods of research that took place for weeks and months in December and January and between June and August, was what I envisioned as an arc of interpretive coherence. Yet because historical conditions in Bolivia were changing so rapidly, at least until the end of 2011, it remained difficult to move forward with an interpretation of the process of refoundation with any level of confidence. Nevertheless, as the years of fieldwork stretched on, a certain ethnographic chronology started to emerge, one that included key changes *after* the tumultuous year of 2011. By the end of the 2015 fieldwork season, I felt that the outlines of an interpretive arc were clear enough to move from research to the process of book-length writing.

The kind of longitudinal ethnography that forms the basis for what follows is perhaps ultimately organic to the project itself. Yet without drawing out too many broader methodological lessons for other researchers confronting similar historical processes with similar intentions to deploy ethnography over time, it was clear, as much in retrospect as anything else, that as the *longue durée* slowly took shape, the interpretation somewhat paradoxically both deepened and became more diffuse. It deepened for likely more obvious reasons: sometime in 2012, the synchronic and diachronic dimensions of the project collapsed into each other; what emerged from thick description over many years became inseparable from the chronology of post-2005 Bolivia as I understood it.

Yet at the same time, the collapse of the synchronic into the diachronic destabilized what had been a relatively straightforward analytical framework, one in which the social, political, and legal forces of "revolution" in Bolivia were counterposed to those of "counterrevolution." Indeed, until the end of 2009, I continued to conduct research in terms of this dialectic. But with each passing year, interpretive coherence for the project became more and more defined by a kind of analytical ambiguity. The turning point came when I realized that the rough contours of this ambiguous vision of post-2005 Bolivia were not necessarily the result of a failure of imagination on my part, but were rather a reflection of ambiguities that were woven into the concepts, institutions, and practices that occupied much of my ethnographic attention, from the development of MAS's ideological program to the articulation of regional autonomy by anti-government activists in the lowlands.

This is not to say that the account of these analytical ambiguities, those partly my own and those partly constitutive of the process of refoundation in Bolivia itself, brings us any closer to a privileged perspective on the period 2006–15. Rather, it is perhaps more accurate to say that what appears here reflects a certain set of ethnographic truths, which are, as James Clifford (1986) classically argued, always inherently partial. Yet as Clifford also emphasized, only ethnographic truths that are both "serious" and "committed" are worth our collective consideration, and I am likewise content to make these the more general evaluative bases on which the book stakes its claims.

Finally, given that the nine-year research project was fundamentally concerned with questions of radical social change, redistribution, the politics of identity, inequality, and ethnic valorization, something should be said about my own subject position—and positioning—in the midst of these transformations. It is true that I began the research in 2006 in the full flush of enthusiasm for MAS's revolutionary ambitions. For someone who had been conducting research in Bolivia since 1996, someone bound to the country by both fictive kinship ties and a long-term professional commitment, the sight of Evo Morales performing an inauguration ritual at Tiwanaku attended by Aymara ritual specialists, or *yatiris*, was historically unprecedented and personally stirring. Like the first election of Daniel Ortega in 1984 during the Nicaraguan revolution, like the beginning of the Zapatista revolt against the Mexican state in 1994, and perhaps even like the coming to power of Salvador Allende in Chile in 1970, the inauguration of Morales in January 2006 seemed to represent a turning point that would lead to fundamental changes in Bolivia that were desperately needed: more equitable distribution of public resources across region, class, and ethnicity; greater investment in infrastructure; a redistribution of political power to the benefit of women, rural people, and workers; a direct challenge to the long history of U.S. interference in Bolivian affairs, a legacy that was only a more recent phase in centuries of resource exploitation and pillage during which Bolivia (and its earlier geopolitical iterations) served as what the Uruguayan writer Eduardo Galeano described as the "open veins of Latin America"; and, perhaps most important, the development of a viable alternative model of state-making, social and legal pluralism, and public ethics at a moment in historical time in which life in the post–Cold War was more and more being regulated by what James Ferguson (2006) called the "neoliberal world order."

Whether or not any of these fundamental changes took place in Bolivia after January 2006 is obviously a question that will be taken up, in different ways and with different answers, throughout this book. Yet over the course of nine years, my own orientation to the problems of revolution, resistance, empowerment, and disenchantment in Bolivia remained intentionally in the background. I did not take a stand, as I could have done based on the growing body of my research data, as either a supporter of the MAS revolution or as a critic of it. I did not write opinion pieces for *La Razón* or *El Deber*. I did not act as a consultant for government agencies or social justice organizations. I did not provide legal opinions or drafting advice during the Constituent Assembly of 2006–7. And I did not take part—as either organizer or participant—in the dozens of marches and public mobilizations that occurred during periods of research in La Paz, Sucre, and Santa Cruz.

In some ways, this orientation ran counter to much of the movement in anthropology toward what has variously been described as "engaged" or "activist" methodologies. In his insightful discussion of the various stakes involved in these debates, Daniel M. Goldstein (2012) argues that different forms of engagement by the anthropologist can be placed along a spectrum. At one end are self-understandings of research that envision it as a direct mechanism of "collaboration with an organized group in struggle for social justice" (2012: 35; quoting Charles Hale 2010). At the other end of the spectrum is the disciplinary self-understanding that seeks to broaden the conception of engagement to be maximally inclusive so that many forms of anthropological activity can be seen to have a purpose beyond the simple production and diffusion of knowledge. Citing Setha Low and Sally Engle Merry's important 2010 review of the topic, Goldstein explains that this broadest vision includes something for everyone: social and cultural critique; sharing, support, and empathy; knowledge exchange with research interlocutors; teaching and public communication; advocacy, that is, "using the language of policy to translate grievances to a wider public"; and activism, in the sense defined by Hale (Goldstein 2012: 38–39).

Yet Goldstein worries that the most expansive accounts of engaged anthropology run the risk of redundancy. As he puts it, "if nearly everything anthropologists do counts as engagement—baby-sitting at community gatherings, teaching our classes, writing about environmental degradation, and so on—then what is the point of naming a subset of the field 'engaged anthropology'?" (39). Apart from the problem of redundancy, Goldstein also flags the ethical dilemma in the movement toward a broad self-understanding of the discipline's obligation to influence the world beyond research: how to distinguish between forms of influence that are legitimate and forms that are not. Even if there is widespread agreement among anthropologists that forms of engagement that seek to reduce inequality, promote social justice, and alleviate social suffering, among others, are legitimate, and those that reinforce hegemony, support military and intelligence agencies, and perpetuate violent practices based on the politics of cultural difference, among others, are not, where are the more difficult lines to be drawn, and by whom? In many countries, most professional anthropologists are members of national associations that have the legal right to regulate the conduct of members through codes of ethics, but the dilemma of engaged anthropology goes well beyond a simple question of organizational self-regulation.

In Goldstein's own pathbreaking research on conflicts between security and rights in the periurban barrios of Cochabamba, Bolivia, he developed an innovative response to his subject position as a long-term researcher that was anchored in the pragmatics of his field site more than anything else. Partly as a way to fund his own summer research, Goldstein organized a university field school that required students to participate in service learning and local community development. These more practical activities led Goldstein to develop a local nongovernmental organization that responded to the needs of his interlocutors, friends, and community colleagues around the problem of access to justice. His many experiences with these forms of engagement were then combined with those from interviews, observations, and other techniques of ethnographic inquiry as the diverse sources for his 2012 study. As he puts it, "activism opens doors . . . engagement can be a critical component of the research process, one that makes rigorous research possible rather than obstructing it" (2012: 42, 46).

In my own case, it was a similar pragmatics that led me to something like the opposite set of methodological choices. Beginning in 2006, with each passing fieldwork season I broadened the scope of inquiry to include different institutions, different political parties, different regions, different social movements, different trade unions, and different social classes. Without pretending to an epistemologically and ethically unsustainable position of neutrality, it was clear that a certain detachment was the only basis on which I would be able to develop relations of trust and conduct ethnographic fieldwork among key actors and institutions within a national assemblage that was, at certain times, particularly in 2008 and 2009, on the brink of civil war. Although I did not conceive of it precisely in these terms at the time, it was only by pursuing a *dis*engaged and *non*collaborative anthropology that I was able, for example, to conduct ethnographic interviews in the same week with Evo Morales's closest adviser in the Palacio Quemado in La Paz and with leaders of Santa Cruz's radically anti-MAS and anti-Indian Unión Juvenil Cruceñista (UJC).

In the end, the uncertain and theoretically unmoored practice of disengaged anthropology had its limits, boundaries that themselves proved to be important points of ethnographic reference. In 2009, during the tense weeks leading up to the late-January national referendum on the new constitution, hundreds of indigenous community leaders came to La Paz to take part in assemblies organized by the Consejo Nacional de Ayllus y Markas del Qullasuyu, or CONAMAQ, the social movement most closely associated during these years with an ideology of indigenous militancy and anti-Western ethnic power.

The days when indigenous people could not enter the main plazas of La Paz for fear of being abused or racially tormented were long gone. Instead, hundreds of indigenous leaders with aspirations of becoming the *Jiliri Apu Mallku* or *Arquiri Apu Mallku*, accompanied by groups of community members and assistants, took the seat of government by storm, striding purposely up and down La Paz's clogged and precipitous streets to obtain documents and notarial stamps or to drink *mate de coca* in cafes, dressed in the uniform of the office and bearing staff and whip, a reminder that the occasional use of violence is part of their mandate.

When I entered one such assembly at a community hall in La Paz's Miraflores district, I was immediately struck by the sight of perhaps over three hundred indigenous community leaders separated into dozens of smaller groups of between eight and ten people, huddled together in strategy sessions. They had come from different communities, different *ayllus*,[6] different departments, and different ethnic groups (primarily Aymara and Quechua). From a certain perspective, they were, collectively, precisely the kind of rural peasants with whom I had spent the lion's share of my research career in Bolivia; I even noticed several groups who were wearing textiles and vests typical of the province in the part of Potosí Department in which I had conducted my doctoral fieldwork many years before. In short, had I chosen to conduct a form of engaged anthropology, it would have been among and on behalf of exactly these *campesinos*.

Except that *neither* a disengaged *nor* an engaged ethnographic approach was possible at that moment. As I surveyed the assembly, watching for the right moment to approach a group to begin the halting and intrusive type of inquiry that hopefully leads to the exchange of information that later is described as an ethnographic interview, I was suddenly noticed by men in several groups. Then, quite quickly, I was noticed by other men in many other groups so that it seemed like the entire hall had turned its attention to me. This was not a kind of methodological reversal in which the observer is suddenly observed, a moment for clever theoretical reflection from the comfort of the office or seminar room (Stocking 1985). Instead, it was something more ominous, yet ethnographically more important: I was an intruder, a category violation with my pale skin and beard and weathered leather fedora, field notebook in hand and field camera around my neck.

I was soon surrounded by about twenty younger community authorities who demanded to know who I was and what I was doing there. There was a palpable sense of collective anger among my "interlocutors" and a worrying sense of physical threat, something I had experienced on occasion in the *norte de Potosí* in the late 1990s when I had tried to conduct research during violent and unpredictable community rituals called *tinkus*. I explained, as I had done hundreds of times before, that I was an *anthropologist*, which meant that I was there to learn about their organization and their thoughts about the new constitution and, more generally, their thoughts about the process of change brought about by Evo Morales. *Why did I want to know these things?* I was asked. So that your thoughts and voices will be heard by many people outside of Bolivia, I replied. *And how will you do this?* I was asked. I will eventually write a book that will be read by perhaps thousands of people in different countries around the world, I said, at this point not even fully convinced myself. And then one young man, with staff in one hand and whip in the other, stepped right up into my face. His breath was redolent of chewed coca leaves but not a whiff of alcohol. He had a quiet fury in his eyes. *Listen to me, gringu, we will write our own books now. You need to leave and leave right now.*

VOLVERÉ Y SERÉ MILLONES

I got my start politically as a member of the Provincial Agrarian Federation of Communities of Caranavi, which is a very solid organization, a revolutionary organization, combative, one that is at the very center of

the political movement created by our current distinguished president Evo Morales. But really, the place where I come from is much like any other in the country now, part of the great changes taking place. . . . Even though I am now departmental president [of MAS], I'm only a soldier in the process of change and we all hope that what we are collectively working toward will someday benefit the whole country. That is the real difference between what is happening now and what other governments have done: they did nothing for a country in which there are huge differences between rich and poor, between those of different skin color, these are the things that we want to change.

Samuel Guarayo Aruquipa,
president of MAS for La Paz Department

DECEMBER 2008

When I first began to write about Bolivia in the late 1990s, the country occupied a peculiar place in relation to other areas of Latin America in which anthropologists and others conducted research. On the one hand, Bolivia had always fascinated outsiders, although in ways that represented a kind of Orientalist interest in South American alterity: the apocryphal legend of Queen Victoria erasing the young country from the world map in retaliation for the humiliation of a British emissary in La Paz; the double-layered Orientalism that both brought Che Guevara to Bolivia in 1967 and then shaped his later deification as the paradigmatic revolutionary fighting for the benighted Indian Other; and the many forms of topographic Orientalism that have constructed Bolivia's geographies as otherworldly, immeasurably exotic, and pulsing with biomass, from the *Salar de Uyuni* to Potosí's infernal tin mines to the "lost world" that inspired Arthur Conan Doyle.

Yet on the other hand, for a scholar interested in conflict, justice, law, and ideology, Bolivia was an apparent regional outlier, especially in relation to zones of civil strife, economic collapse, and environmental degradation, from Colombia's decades-long internal conflict and Peru's civil war to the economic crisis in Argentina and the tragedy of deforestation in Brazil. Academic interest in Bolivian history, culture, and politics was relatively marginal—though not necessarily marginalized—in relation to many other regions of interest within the problematic Cold War ordering logic known as "Latin American studies." This meant that the points of reference for an anthropologist or historian or political scientist of Bolivia in the late 1990s and early 2000s were fairly well defined; in my case, as a budding ethnographer of the norte de Potosí, these revolved around the writings of a small group of anthropologists, including Tristan Platt, Olivia Harris, and Thomas Abercrombie, and extended out to a group of foundational Bolivian scholars including Xavier Albó, Silvia Rivera Cusicanqui, and Marcelo Fernández Osco.

But within fifteen years, the place of Bolivia as a site of both scholarly and global public interest underwent a profound transformation. During this time, Bolivia became the lodestar for a powerful narrative in which the small land-locked country, which had previously been the "big bang" for neoliberalism in Latin America (Williamson 1992) and then "an unwilling lab for a radical experiment in conservative economic reforms," became instead "synonymous with conflicts over [globalization]" (Draper and Shultz 2008: 2). According to this account, beginning in the early 2000s, Bolivians finally rose up en masse against a "small and wealthy national elite" in movements defined by a dynamic mix of "rage and resistance." "From water rebels and weavers to emigrants and coca growers," Bolivians by the thousands took a stand against the ravages of a global political economic system that commanded the allegiance of world powers from the United States to China and underwrote international relations from the World Trade Organization to the International Monetary Fund (Draper and Shultz 2008: 2–3). If Bolivia had been a coerced central player in the tragedy of what Naomi Klein described as "disaster capitalism" (2007), its citizens had ultimately written a new script, one in which they pushed back against their country's historic condition with "dignity and defiance" in order to fight for a "future very different from the one prescribed for them by others, a future of their own design" (Shultz 2008: 296).

This broader shift in the image of Bolivia, one in which the country became, as South Africa had in the early 1990s, a new global icon for the possibility of radical change in the face of overwhelming economic, geopolitical, and historical odds, unleashed a subsequent academic shift in which Bolivian history, culture, and politics became central themes for researchers and writers. This led to a relative explosion in academic and critical studies of different facets of contemporary Bolivia, including a proliferation of studies produced by Bolivians for Bolivian publishers, newspapers, and policy and development institutions. The result was that, by 2017, the collective (and growing) body of interdisciplinary writing about Bolivia was voluminous. This fact has two direct implications for the current offering, which must take its place among a crowded field. The first is that it relieves me, in a sense, of the burden of having to summarize the state of the art as it relates to studies of contemporary Bolivia. The truth is that there simply isn't a state of the art to be found among the riotous cacophony of analyses, perspectives, and ethnographic accounts that are part of the historic (re)discovery of Bolivia as a modern parable of "people looking at the larger forces shaping their lives and taking a stand, often with great courage, to demand what they believe to be right and to challenge what they believe to be wrong" (Draper and Shultz 2008: 5).

The second is that it is difficult to derive an unobjectionable historical timeline from this profusion of writing on Bolivia in order to provide a general outline against which the ethnographic research of 2006–15 took place. Indeed, the contested question of recent Bolivian history will itself be taken up in different ways and in different chapters throughout the book.[7] Nevertheless, it *is* both possible and vital, in light of these caveats, to establish a chronology that is organic to the book's broader arguments and ethnographic interpretations. What follows, then, is a description of this idiosyncratic chronology; its link with the book's chapters is made partly below and partly in the penultimate section of this introduction.

In order to understand the rise of Evo Morales and the transformations that followed his election in 2005, a good beginning is the election of Víctor Paz Estenssoro in 1985, three years after the restoration of democracy in Bolivia following almost twenty years of military dictatorship, internal repression, and sociopolitical stagnation. Upon taking office, Paz Estenssoro declared that "Bolivia is dying on us," meaning that hyperinflation, the growing influence of narcotraffic networks, and global price instabilities made it difficult for the country to respond to both micro- and macroeconomic challenges. Paz Estenssoro appointed the U.S.-trained businessman Gonzalo Sánchez de Lozada (who came to be known simply as "Goni") as planning minister with a remit to oversee extraordinary measures to reorient Bolivia's economy and society. Goni did this by administering what he described as "bitter medicine" in the form of Decree 21060, an executive order that with the stroke of the pen dramatically devalued the Bolivian peso, raised public-sector prices, froze or slashed public salaries, and eliminated legal rights for public workers so that they could be legally laid off in large numbers.[8]

Although the "New Political Economy" of early 1985 reversed the problem of hyperinflation almost overnight, the crash of world tin prices in October accelerated one of the most consequential sociopolitical events of this period: the firing of 23,000 mine workers from the state mining company, the Corporación Minera de Bolivia, or COMIBOL. This precipitated a massive process of forced internal migration in which thousands of families were uprooted and "relocated": some left the country for Argentina, Spain, or the United States; others moved to work in the coca fields of the Chapare; and still many thousands more moved to the *altiplano* on the rim high above La Paz, a zone called "El Alto," which became one of the fastest-growing urban areas in Latin America. El Alto eventually came to supplant La Paz itself in population as an independent city marked by haphazard construction, pervasive poverty, a lack of public infrastructure, and, critical for my purposes, a culture of radical political activism that could be collectively mobilized during key moments (see Lazar 2008).

Amid these neoliberal dislocations, which continued into the 1990s, Goni himself was elected president of Bolivia between 1994 and 1997, a period that for two reasons was fundamental for the ethnographic research and interpretations that form the basis for this book. First, Goni's government deepened and institutionalized the policies of structural adjustment mandated by the institutions that were promoting a framework that expressed the so-called Washington Consensus. These policies dramatically increased the influence of private transnational corporations in the internal economy of Bolivia, continued the process of privatizing key sectors of the Bolivian economy, and "capitalized" state-owned enterprises so that they could be sold to generate revenue for what was intended to be public goods, including worker pensions. In the end, the hidden hand of the free market did not guide Bolivia to a more just and sustainable future; on the contrary, the displacements of the 1990s created the highest levels of inequality in Latin America.

Yet at the same time, the high point of neoliberalism in Bolivia was a period in which the public articulation of long-standing grievances underwent a profound shift. Beginning in the late 1980s and expanding throughout the 1990s, local activists and movements in Bolivia came increasingly to be shaped by the related discourses of human and indigenous rights. Goni's government enthusiastically embraced the rapidly developing doctrines of multicultural identity and rights-based forms of justice, moves that were signaled by Bolivia's implementation of key international rights instruments such as International Labor Organization Convention 169 and the Convention on the Elimination of All Forms of Discrimination against Women (CEDAW). Two important government initiatives that marked the extent of the Goni government's commitment to the twin pillars of the politics of identity and the principle of (collective) self-governance were the Law of Popular Participation (see Postero 2007) and the Law of Bilingual Education (see Gustafson 2009b). Finally, in 1998 the Bolivian Congress approved Law 1818, which created an institution that would play an important, if contested, role over the following decade: the Defensoría del Pueblo, a national human rights institution with a mandate to promote human rights as the basis for civil society in the country and to hold the government itself to account in cases of official abuse.

Thus, although within ten years the demonization of the neoliberal period would earn it a place next to colonialism and republicanism as abhorrent periods in Bolivian history that the 2009 constitution formally rejected, the fact remained that the discursive shifts that took place during the 1990s laid the ideological groundwork for these future transformations. However, before these transformations—which depended in large part on the juridification of newly valorized categories of identity—could occur, the country had to pass through a period of often violent transition that Mesa Gisbert describes as a "crisis of the state" (Mesa Gisbert 2008: 607). The two most important events during this liminal period were the Water War in Cochabamba in 1999 and 2000 and the Gas War of 2003, which concentrated mobilizations from across the altiplano into the ideological tinderbox of El Alto.

In both cases, the underlying stakes were similar: massive resistance against a loss of control over public resources against a larger backdrop of almost two decades of growing inequality, foreign (particularly U.S. and transnational corporate) intervention, and the tragic failure of the "political system of '85" (Mesa Gisbert 2008: 623). The direct action tactics of protestors in Cochabamba and especially in La Paz and El Alto—which came to a head during Black October of 2003, when Bolivian army and police units fired on crowds, killing almost sixty people and wounding four hundred more—carried an important lesson for understanding developments during the period 2006–15. Even though the language of rights had clearly become a dominant guiding political framework and basic discursive tool for pursuing a collective project of socioeconomic change, its limitations, contradictions, and normative abstraction were recognized in practice every time Bolivians erected a road blockade or engaged in street battles with the police. Indeed, this tension between rights and direct action was codified in the concise and urgent 2000 Cochabamba Manifesto, which grounded ideologically the mobilizations against the transnational consortium Aguas del Tunari. As the Manifesto put it, "Cochabambinos, Cochabambinas—you cannot beg for civil rights. Rights are won in struggle. No one else is going to fight for what is ours. Either we fight together for justice or we let bad rulers humiliate us" (quoted in Olivera 2004).

All of this immediate prehistory led directly to December 2005, in which Evo Morales Ayma, the head of the powerful coca growers union in the Chapare and former member of the Bolivian congress for MAS, was elected president with 54 percent of the national vote, a clear electoral majority of the type that had last been seen in the country during the 1960 election of Víctor Paz Estenssoro (who won with 75 percent).[9] After Morales had been expelled from the Congress in January 2002, he had proclaimed, *"volveré y seré millones,"* or

"I will return and I will be millions." These were the supposed last words of the Indian rebel Túpac Katari before he was drawn and quartered by Spanish colonial troops in the town of Peñas in 1781 (see Thomson 2002), an act of desecration that Burman has called the "root metaphor" for understanding the linkage between history and collective trauma in Bolivia (Burman 2016: 134).[10] In addition to representing himself as the fulfillment of Katari's eighteenth-century prophecy during the campaign leading up to the 2005 election (a typical poster read "Katari, the rebellion, Evo, the revolution"), Morales also promoted the idea that he embodied the spirit of Che Guevara (another poster: "Che Lives! Evo for President!").[11]

On January 21, 2006, Morales was invested with the traditional staff of office in an unofficial ceremony at the ruins of Tiwanaku attended by tens of thousands of Bolivia's indigenous citizens. Reflecting the broader sense of radical change that Morales's election signaled, the official swearing-in ceremony the next day in La Paz was witnessed by an unprecedented number of Latin American heads of state and dignitaries, including the presidents of Venezuela, Chile, Argentina, Colombia, Brazil, Panama, Paraguay, and Peru. The vice president of Cuba's state council, Carlos Lage, was invited to stand at Morales's side during the ceremony, while Eduardo Galeano, who was also present, later gave a speech to thousands of revelers in the Plaza de Los Héroes in which he said that "yesterday was the last day of fear in Bolivia" (quoted in Burman 2016: 171).

After Morales dramatically nationalized the country's hydrocarbon industries in May 2006—during which he personally occupied oil fields owned by the Brazilian energy company Petrobras accompanied by Bolivian soldiers—the Morales government moved to convene a constituent assembly in Sucre in August in order to write a new national constitution, thereby fulfilling a key promise of his campaign to the Pacto de Unidad, a shifting national alliance of social movements and indigenous organizations whose support formed the basis for Morales's victory. This alliance, whose most visible and influential members included the Consejo Nacional de Ayllus y Markas del Qullasuyu (CONAMAQ), the Confederación Sindical Única de Trabajadores Campesinos de Bolivia (CSUTCB), the Confederación Sindical de Colonizadores de Bolivia (CSCB), the Confederación de Pueblos Indígenas del Oriente Boliviano (CIDOB), and the Federación Nacional de Mujeres Campesinas de Bolivia-Bartolina Sisa (FNMCB-BS), had called for a constitutional process that would be animated by the participation of civil society writ large with direct representation by labor unions, the Pacto members themselves, and environmental and gender rights NGOs, among others.

However, the MAS government decided to limit representation in the eventual Asamblea Constituyente to members who were affiliated with political parties, with the ruling MAS party enjoying the largest number. Although some Pacto and social movement members eventually affiliated with MAS in order to participate in the deliberations, the limitation on representation was resented even by some strong Morales supporters. At the same time, the assembly served to catalyze two distinct opposition movements. The first was based in the eastern lowland departments and came to be known as the Media Luna (after their collective resemblance on a map to a crescent moon), an opposition bloc that was driven by a diffuse mix of regional separatism, racial indignation at the unprecedented prospect of the Palacio Quemado in the hands of highland Indians, and economic protectionism.[12] The second opposition movement, concentrated in the historical capital of Sucre, revolved around the quixotic demand for *capitalía*, that is, to restore Sucre as the "full capital" of Bolivia, a status it had lost after the Federal War of 1899 (when the national government was divided between La Paz and Sucre).

The months during which the assembly was active were marked by discord among delegates inside the hall and growing civil unrest outside of it. Even so, despite the withdrawal of opposition parties, violence in the streets of Sucre that left three dead, and the eventual relocation of the assembly to a military academy on the edge of the city for security reasons, a full draft of a new constitution was approved by the assembly and presented to the Bolivian Congress in December 2007.

The following year brought the country to the brink of civil war as the opposition movements of the eastern lowlands and Sucre continued to institutionalize their demands and mobilize their urban, or "civic," populations for what amounted to a permanent state of protest, anti-government action, and, increasingly, racialized violence. Although the idea was to put the new constitution to a national referendum, the instability meant that the Morales government was forced into a series of negotiations with the departmental prefects of the opposition Consejo Nacional Democrático (CONALDE), which was seeking political and economic autonomy for its members modeled on Santa Cruz's unprecedented autonomy statute, which was approved in a department-wide vote in May 2008.

In a bold and risky move, the Morales government decided to give the Bolivian people themselves another opportunity to decide on the country's future just two and a half years after the historic December 2005 elections. The government announced that a national *Referéndum revocatorio*, or vote of no confidence, would be held in August 2008, in which citizens would have the right to retain or oust both Morales and the country's nine departmental prefects. Nevertheless, the underlying question was actually broader than one of a simple political mandate—what was really at stake was whether a majority of citizens approved of Morales's revolutionary program, the most important aspect of which was the approval and implementation of the new constitution.

The year 2008 was thus one of competing national, departmental, and local campaigns both for and against the wider transformations that were heralded by the radical alternative future for the country at the heart of MAS's socioeconomic, legal, and political project. Yet just as the Media Luna and Sucre opposition movements seemed to be gaining in confidence and political capital, two events—one before, the other after, the August national referendum—served collectively as a key turning point in Bolivia's post-2005 history. On May 24, thousands of pro-capitalía activists captured dozens of rural Morales supporters who were arriving in Sucre to participate with the president at a political rally. As the violence spread, Morales quickly canceled the visit, but the peasants were brutally marched into Sucre's historic center, the Plaza 25 de Mayo, beaten and humiliated by the crowds, and forced to strip to their waists, chant obscene anti-Morales and anti-indigenous slogans, and to burn their own *wiphalas*, the flag of Bolivia's indigenous movement.

And on September 11, just one month after the mixed results of the Referéndum revocatorio, in which both Morales and most of the country's opposition prefects were reaffirmed in their mandates, another group of pro-Morales supporters was attacked by armed militants near Porvenir in the Department of Pando. Pando's prefect, Leopoldo Fernández, whose mandate had been reaffirmed in the August referendum, was, along with Santa Cruz's Rubén Costas, one of the most outspoken and racially derisive critics of Morales and the MAS government. As a later international investigation undertaken by the Unión de Naciones Suramericanas (UNASUR) confirmed, *cívicos* under either direct or implied orders from Fernández's office had committed various atrocities against the pro-Morales supporters, including murder, torture, sexual assault, and the desecration of bodies, some of which were thrown into rivers or hidden in the surrounding forest. In the end, UNASUR concluded that at least nineteen people had been killed, although the actual number could very well have been higher.

The immediate consequence of what became known as the Massacre of Porvenir was the arrest of Fernández on various charges, including intent to commit genocide, and his imprisonment in La Paz's notorious San Pedro Prison. But more importantly, the collective national shock over the "Plaza de Rodillas" of May 24 in Sucre and the atrocities of September 11 in Pando led to a widespread loss of support for the opposition cause among key sectors of society in places like Cochabamba and La Paz, including the media and center-left intellectuals who had previously joined with the opposition in criticizing the Morales government. With Morales overwhelmingly confirmed in his office (he had received 67 percent backing in the August referendum, which was also more than any of the departmental prefects except the prefect of Potosí, a strong Morales supporter and member of MAS), with the opposition engaging in tactics that were being described by the government as a "civil coup d'état," and with the armed forces unified behind the popular president, the writing on the wall was clear—the opposition dream, embodied in the Santa Cruz statute of 2008, of dictating the terms of autonomy from the central state, was over; the new constitution would soon be confirmed as the nation's revolutionary "Magna Carta," and the government was now fully prepared to advance the process of change with the complete arsenal of legal, political, economic, and ideological strategies at its disposal.[13]

In January 2009, Bolivia was "refounded" when the new constitution was approved by a wide margin in yet another national referendum. Among its many other radical innovations, the new constitution formally established Bolivia as a postcolonial, postrepublican, postneoliberal, and plurinational state. In addition, the constitution codified two principles that would soon be at the center of the first major crisis of Morales's first term in office under the new constitution (he would be reelected in December 2009 in a landslide, with 64 percent of the vote): the first, that Pachamama, or Mother Earth, was the source of all life, sacred, and thus deserving of both public reverence and the protection of the law; and second, a greatly enlarged version of "free, prior and informed consent," a key facet of international indigenous rights law derived from ILO Convention 169 (1989), in which Bolivia's "native indigenous peasant peoples and nations" were recognized as having ancestral ownership of their territories and the right to manage them according to their traditional cultural practices.

Yet in 2011, as part of a government plan to develop the nation's infrastructure through road-building in formerly isolated areas, a conflict erupted around a proposal to build a major highway through the Isiboro-Sécure National Park and Indigenous Territory (TIPNIS), a protected area of almost 1.5 million hectares that extends from the north of Cochabamba Department into the south of Beni Department. The people living in the TIPNIS, which importantly included the Chapare province of Cochabamba, where Morales rose to political power, organized massive resistance to the planned highway. They argued that they were not consulted or given the ability to reject the plan;

that the highway would cause irreparable damage to the region's rich biodiversity; and finally, that the highway would dramatically increase the presence of coca-growing *colonizadores* in the park, whose farming practices were fundamentally at odds with traditional stewardship of the land.

After two key members of the Pacto de Unidad—CIDOB and CONAMAQ—organized a march from Trinidad, Beni, to La Paz as a public display of interregional indigenous resistance to the government's plan, a march that was met with military and police force, the Morales government soon realized how much damage the conflict was doing to the legitimacy of the broader process of change. Although the conflict ended (at the time) with a nearly complete vindication of the protestors' demands in the form of a national law that declared the TIPNIS forever off-limits to both road construction and land use by people "foreign" to the territory's ancestral owners, it carried several important lessons for understanding the 2006–15 period, including the fact that Morales's base of support in the indigenous movements viewed him more as a strategic ally than as one of their own.

To conclude the chronology that is most relevant for the book's arguments and ethnographic interpretations, something should be said about the critical post-TIPNIS period. Three developments seem to me most pertinent. First, Bolivia's economy experienced significant and steady growth, becoming one of the most stable in the region. Indeed, in an ironic turn, the IMF and World Bank both pronounced the country to be in a state of healthy macroeconomic "equilibrium," despite—or perhaps because of—the fact that its economic growth has come through a national policy of what some critics have described as "extractivism."[14] In 2014, Bolivia surpassed China as the country with the highest ratio of foreign reserves to GDP in the world: almost $14 billion, which was equal to almost half of its GDP.

Second, the period 2011–15 was marked by the pervasive use of the law by the government to consolidate power and institutionalize the process of change. This will be described as "strategic juridification" and developed in greater depth in chapter 5, but the important point here is the fact that through the use of criminal prosecutions, administrative regulations, and national legislation, the government was able to harness the power of the rule of law as a primary mechanism for its revolutionary aspirations.

The final development actually stretches beyond the ethnographic horizon of the book, since it involves moves that the government made in the years after 2015 with important implications for the future. In February 2016, a referendum to amend the constitution to permit Morales to run for a third presidential term was narrowly defeated amid a bizarre scandal involving a young former lover named Gabriela Zapata, their deceased child, and charges that Morales had used his position to secure a job for Zapata in a Chinese company that had conducted hundreds of millions of dollars in business with the Bolivian government. Nevertheless, despite losing the referendum, MAS nominated Morales as its candidate for the 2019 national elections at a December 2016 party congress.

Yet beyond the more concrete question of how the government eventually found a way to use the law creatively to allow this to happen without contravening the results of the February 2016 referendum (see the conclusion), the more far-reaching questions concern the long-term future of Bolivia's "democratic and cultural revolution." Will the Bolivian experiment mature into an important model for postneoliberal state-building, pluralism, and sustainable justice? Can the refounded Bolivian state find a way to reconcile what appears to be a structural tension between the ecological *cosmovisión* that is at the center of its revolutionary ideology and a plan for economic development that depends fundamentally on the exploitation and commodification of nonrenewable natural resources? Is the process of change in Bolivia inextricably bound up with particular charismatic actors (Morales, the powerful vice president, Álvaro García Linera) or a particular political party (MAS), or does its ultimate place in history depend on "the peoples" (plural), as the current government itself argues? Although *A Revolution in Fragments* can serve as a signpost to possible answers to these—and other—broader questions, they must remain, in the end, open and contested.

REVOLUTION FROM THE INSIDE OUT

> *Revolutions are the only political events which confront us directly and inevitably with the problem of beginning.*
>
> —Hannah Arendt, *On Revolution* ([1963] 2006)

To this point, the words *revolution* and *revolutionary* have been used in different ways almost thirty times. Moreover, since the book uses revolution in the title, this is clearly a conceptual anchor. But what, precisely, is meant here by revolution? Without offering a complete answer, since the question of revolution itself is taken up ethnographically in different ways in each chapter, I instead want to come at the question from the side and explain how the book reflects a particular approach to the problem. To do this, I draw a distinction between *normative* and *phenomenological* approaches to the general questions of revolution and the application of these general questions to history. By normative approach I mean the attempt to derive models and typologies through which "revolution" can be distinguished from all other processes of historical transformation; these models and typologies can then be used prescriptively to identify the likely emergence of a revolution given certain social, economic, and political conditions; and, finally, a particular revolution, once properly identified, can be placed alongside other signal moments in history in a broader exercise in comparative social analysis.

Seen in this way, the normative approach to questions of revolution has dominated discussion and debate for centuries, and it is obviously not possible to review this full intellectual history here. So that the reader has an unambiguous sense of what I mean by a normative approach to revolution, a fairly recent example is offered by James DeFronzo (2011).[15] According to DeFronzo, whose model of revolutionary movements draws from the work of other normative revolution scholars such as Foran (2005), Goldstone (1994, 2001), Greene (1990), Gurr (1970), and Skocpol (1979), a revolution is distinguished by the following five phenomena: mass frustration that leads to popular uprisings by urban or rural populations; the emergence of divisions among elites, some of whom turn against the established order; the presence of one or more "unifying motivations" that transcend a society's existing social, economic, and ethnic fault lines; a severe crisis that serves as a catalyzing turning point; and a "permissive or tolerant world context" within which a revolution can emerge without outside interference (DeFronzo 2011: 12–13).[16]

The phenomenological approach, by contrast, sidesteps the prevailing "is it or isn't it a revolution?" problem to focus on revolution as a diffuse, though ultimately bounded, social and historical category that organizes experience in particular kinds of ways. A phenomenological orientation toward revolution finds expression in various genres, through literature (Allende 1982), through long-form reportage (Reed 1919), and through memoir and *testimonio* (Arenas 1993; Burgos-Debray 1984). Somewhat surprisingly, as Bjørn Thomassen (2012) has argued, with certain important exceptions (for example, Donham 1999; see also Greenberg 2014 and Razsa 2015), the ethnographic study of revolution has not been a traditional concern for anthropologists.[17] As he puts it, "though we talk about our own [disciplinary and theoretical] revolutions, we say much less about those that take place around us and continue to shape the world in which we live" (2012: 679–80). As a consequence, the normative approach has dominated debate and shaped the broader understanding of revolution: "Political scientists write volumes about [revolution] without consulting the anthropological literature . . . but these writers can hardly be blamed, for the neglect comes from within anthropology itself" (Thomassen 2012: 680).[18]

The approach to revolution that is developed throughout this book strikes something of an intermediate position between the normative and the phenomenological. This is important because in the case of Bolivia, the normative is not only, or even most critically, a set of ideas about revolution developed by scholars as part of a comparative analysis of historical change. Instead, general theories of revolution derive from specific moments in Bolivian history and are closely connected with a series of hybridizations in which local processes of change, resistance, and state violence have vernacularized the meanings of revolution—both as ideology and as social practice. In this way, the normative and the phenomenological dimensions of revolution have been, if not necessarily mutually constitutive, then closely and dynamically linked as a marker of Bolivia's most important moments of transformation, including the period 2006–15.

This intermediate approach to the question of revolution has both theoretical and methodological implications. Theoretically, it locates the understanding of revolution first and foremost in the interplay between concrete appropriation and what might be thought of as codification. This creates a specifically ethnographic opening to frame revolution as an anthropological problem that can toggle conceptually between idea and action, intention and affect, and "*telos and status*" (Ferguson 2006: 185). Methodologically, the approach developed in this book privileges the hold that revolution has for people, to paraphrase Bronislaw Malinowski, including, critically, no hold at all. Yet if the book adopts an approach to revolution from the inside out in order to explore the consequential ways through which people in contemporary Bolivia find meaning in times of rapid transformation and chronic social instability, it also takes account of how these practices of meaning-making become organized, as we will see, through processes of ideological slotting that are both rooted in doctrine and at the same time open to interpretation, revision, and challenge.

A REVOLUTION IN FRAGMENTS

In January 2009, I asked Antonio Peredo to explain the political, discursive, and ideological extravagance of the new Bolivian constitution, which was soon to be overwhelmingly approved in the national referendum. Peredo was a legendary figure in Bolivian politics: brother to three *guerrilleros* who had fought with Che; Evo Morales's vice presidential candidate in the national elections of 2002, in which the MAS ticket had surprisingly come in second and gained

35 new congressional seats; and an influential senator for MAS who had played an important advisory role during the Constituent Assembly of 2006–7.

Peredo was a famously verbose intellectual of the traditional revolutionary left, and in that sense he was an ethnographer's dream. He could exhaust the space on an SD card with the response to a single question. Yet when I gave Peredo, who died in 2012 at the age of seventy-six, an opening to hold forth on the extraordinary structure and ambitions of the new constitution, he paused. It seemed to me, I remarked, as a way to continue the conversation, that the new constitution incorporated almost every conceivable right, obligation, theory of the state, theory of the economy, and category of identity. Peredo looked at me with a slight smile as he slowly shook his head from side to side: *I know,* he finally said, *we just couldn't say no.*

Peredo's reply, terse as it was, contained the seeds of an insight into how to read across what amounted to, by 2015, a boisterous plenitude of ethnographic data on the process of change in Bolivia. With time, this insight ripened into the central argument of the book: that the process of transformation in Bolivia was constituted through a series of shifting crystallizations, historical, ideological, and institutional fragments that were often in tension with each other. On the one hand, as Peredo acknowledged, Bolivia's "third revolution" (Dunkerley 2007b) was radically different from the one that Peredo and comrades had been fighting for over many decades of Bolivian history. It was deeply hybrid; ideologically ambiguous (if not, at moments, contradictory); delinked from well-defined theories of both historical oppression and historical change; and, above all, shaped by a pervasive mytho-utopian *dispositif* that drew on countervailing concepts of indigenous world-reversal and neoliberal rights-infused cosmopolitanism. The result was a polyvalent vision of transformation that was powerful and compelling despite its diffuseness—or, perhaps, precisely because of it.

On the other hand, this diffuse, ideologically unmoored, and discursively tumultuous process of change was instantiated largely in terms of the instrumentalities of state bureaucracy: legal regulations, administrative orders, the creation of new ministries and the elimination of others, new codes of institutional conduct. Whether or not the constitution of Bolivia's third revolution in terms of these particular kinds of historical, ideological, and institutional fragments must be understood, more generally, as a feature of the era of "revolution through democracy" (DeFronzo 2011) is a question that will be taken up in different ways through the book's various chapters. Yet if there is one key finding of this study, one result that has potential meaning beyond the study's ethnographic boundaries, it is this.[19]

In order to structure the ethnographic interpretation and analysis of Bolivia's fraught process of change, each of the book's chapters examines key themes that emerged through multiscalar research on justice, ideology, and practice over the period 2006–15. Chapter 1 charts the evolution of official state discourse and the diverse efforts to forge a dominant cadre of public and social actors committed to the project of refoundation and postneoliberal institution-building. As the chapter reveals, an enduring dilemma for the MAS government during this period was the inability to maintain an ideological coalition in the absence of a well-defined ruling class.

Chapter 2 analyzes the way law very quickly became a central mechanism through which the government's revolutionary aspirations were expressed. The chapter explores the extent to which so-called revolution by constitution put in motion a series of social and institutional processes that worked at cross purposes to the cause of structural transformation. Moreover, as the chapter shows, the need to make law hegemonic met with various forms of resistance, some of which took the form of alternative practices of justice-making in spaces in which people felt themselves to be "outlawed" (Goldstein 2012). Finally, chapter 2 examines the tensions that emerged from the effort to encode the revolution in law while at the same time reconceptualizing the meaning of law itself within the double layer of plurinationalism and legal pluralism.

Chapter 3 interrogates some of the most important expressions of resistance to the process of change in Bolivia during the period 2006–15. This resistance was ideological, institutional, and embodied. In an allusion to the anthropological thinking of Clifford Geertz, I develop the notion in this chapter that at least until the resolution of the TIPNIS conflict in 2011, the major currents of opposition to the MAS government and the broader process of transformation took the form of a cultural system that was shaped by particular collective memories, a willingness to resort to violence, and the demand to mobilize along ethnic and racial lines.

Chapter 4 unpacks the internal conflicts between competing visions of revolutionary change in Bolivia, conflicts that largely simmered out of view in the rush to construct a patchwork state ideology. In light of the country's long history of syndicalist, Trotskyist, and democratic socialist mobilizations, especially among the formerly influential urban intelligentsia, the MAS government struggled to develop a coherent revolutionary project that was nominally "socialist," while at the same time it was implicitly hostile to Bolivia's various institutions of the traditional revolutionary left. This chapter examines these ideological disjunctures both conceptually and through the experiences of different actors left behind by a revolution without revolutionaries.

The discussion in chapter 5 returns to the problem of justice, focusing on practices that marked the period between 2011 and 2015 in particular. This was a time in which the end of the instability around the government's mandate, the overwhelming electoral support for the new constitution, and the resolution of the TIPNIS conflict ushered in a new phase. This phase was characterized by the increasing use of "strategic juridification"—the selective use of the rule of law to consolidate state power. At the same time, because of the existing framework of Bolivian law, a "prerevolutionary" juridical structure that continued to form the foundation of the plurinational state, the general principles of the Bolivian constitution had to be converted, or "reglemented," into more specific laws that could be acted upon by government ministries and state agencies. As will be seen, the process of breaking down the constitution's sweeping principles of radical change into more limited and technocratic parts introduced fundamental limitations to the MAS government's broader aspirations.

Chapter 6 examines the role that ideologies of collective identity played in Bolivia's "third revolution." Ethnographic research during the period 2006–15 led to a number of surprising findings, including the fact that the status of Morales as Bolivia's "first indigenous president" was contested by some key members of the country's indigenous social movements, including those that made up the Pacto de Unidad. Yet at the same time, some student and peasant intellectuals who defined themselves as "Indianist" or "neo-Indianist" militants viewed Morales, critically, as the very embodiment of a Western-inspired indigenism, as did anti-government intellectuals and activists in the lowland and Sucre opposition movements. And Morales himself? He was more likely than not to self-identify as a *sindicalista*, or trade unionist, one who came of age in the Chapare among his fellow coca growers.[20] The chapter takes up these and other contestations at the heart of what a recent volume describes as the intent to construct an "indigenous state" (Postero 2017).

The book's conclusion both recapitulates the main arguments and points of emphasis and suggests several ways in which the ethnographic interpretation of Bolivia's process of change carries certain lessons when considering the possibilities for, and limitations to, structural transformation more broadly in light of prevailing regional and global political economies.

CONCLUSION: ANTHROPOLOGY IN A WORLD OF MEANING AND CRISIS

In its call for papers for its 2017 annual meeting, the American Anthropological Association (AAA) took stock of the current moment of historical and political uncertainty gripping the world, from the election of Donald Trump in the United States to the withdrawal of the United Kingdom from the European Union, from the reemergence of Russia as a regional power with global ambitions to the campaign by some African countries to undermine the legitimacy of the International Criminal Court. As the AAA rightly argued, the "world of the Anthropocene [is] packed with meaning and crisis" (American Anthropological Association 2016).

As the long-term ethnographic study of Bolivia's contested process of change demonstrates, however, the relationship between meaning and crisis in any one particular case is far from obvious. Nevertheless, what does seem clear is the need to continue to develop collectively an anthropological approach that is capable of elucidating this relationship as an ethnographic problem and, even more, drawing out the broader lessons as a contribution to interdisciplinary social and critical analysis. In this sense, my hope is that *A Revolution in Fragments* responds to this call for what might be thought of as a new anthropology of transformation.

Even more, although it is tempting to modify transformation with "progressive" in this programmatic formulation, I believe that would be a mistake. Not only would it prefigure the meaning—or potential meaning—of progressive in any one context, but it would carry the unwanted methodological implication that only certain kinds of transformative processes were worthy of our ethnographic and ethical attention. That was, I would argue, a key mistake made by the various anthropologies of the post–Cold War that examined the politics of identity. In the end, it was only certain kinds of transgressive or marginalized or cosmopolitan identities that were invested with disciplinary legitimacy; others, particularly those organized around various exclusionary or reprobate categories (nationalism, nativism, apocalyptic religious fundamentalism, racism), were rarely treated or were ignored.

Instead, the kind of anthropology of transformation that is meant to be reflected in this book is one that is both faithful to the phenomenological irreducibilities that partly constitute contemporary transformative processes and open, both methodologically and, one might say, politically, to the coalescence of alternative cosmovisions that can challenge a global neoliberal logic that has only become more pervasive and naturalized since the mid-2000s.

1 HEARING REVOLUTION IN A MINOR KEY

On December 21, 2008, most of the currents of Bolivia's revolutionary moment converged on the Coliseo Cerrado Julio Borelli Viterito, an enclosed arena in the heart of La Paz one block up the hill from the Prado and a long stone's throw from the crumbling adobe walls of San Pedro Prison. The Coliseo Cerrado was named after the Uruguayan architect and athlete who designed it, and it was a well-known venue for national and international tournaments of volleyball, basketball, and *fútbol*

sala, an indoor version of soccer that is popular throughout South America. December 21 is an important day throughout highland Bolivia: it is the Southern Hemisphere's summer solstice and well into the rainy season, a key period in the agro-ritual cycle that promises the nourishment of the Earth, healthy crops, and sustenance of life itself.

Yet this day in 2008 was important for a different reason: it marked the beginning of the MAS government's official "Yes!" campaign, the national mobilization in support of the new constitution, which would be put to a referendum one month later, on January 25. The government had called on trade unions, social movements, and government agencies from throughout La Paz Department to attend the event, which would receive national media coverage and feature speeches by various luminaries in the MAS universe, including Félix Patzi, the former minister of education and culture who was then serving as general secretary for the department's prefecture.

Although the night before had brought one of the worst hail and rain storms in memory, a tempest that left seventeen people dead when a minibus had been swept off the old highway from La Paz to El Alto, the hundreds of people who arrived in large groups to the Coliseo Cerrado did so under sparkling blue skies. They had marched through the streets of La Paz, many all the way from the bus station, behind banners that proclaimed their commitment and devotion to the process of change.

Once inside the stadium, these banners were hung from the walls and balconies, creating a thick blanket of revolutionary slogans and images. The militant Federation of Neighborhood Councils of El Alto declared "El Alto always on its feet, never on its knees" (a reference to the humiliations of the previous May 24 in Sucre, see chapter 3). The government of La Paz Department reminded those gathered that because of the MAS revolution, the country had been declared "free from illiteracy." The City of La Paz announced that "in honor of the martyrs who have defended our natural resources, we will not go backward in the country's process of change." A group of provincial MAS activists from the town of Caranavi in the Yungas said simply "Yes" to the new constitution, the accent mark in the "í" of "Sí" having been replaced by an electoral check mark. The Ministry of Water proclaimed in Aymara "Umax Taqitakiwi," or "Water for All." A banner from La Paz's District 7, which included the wealthy neighborhood of Sopocachi, declared that it was "present in the struggle." One banner brought by a group from the town of Copacabana on the shores of Lake Titicaca featured only a single coca leaf. And a banner from the small Fundación Inti-Coco, which had been founded by Antonio Peredo in honor of his brothers (Guido Álvaro "Inti" Peredo and Roberto

"Coco" Peredo), featured the images of the two comrades of Che under the Bolivian tricolor crossed with the indigenous wiphala.

Each group that arrived was able to march together in one turn around the Coliseo's floor before taking their seats, while a hired drum and panpipe band kept up a lively and festive tune. After all the groups had paraded to their places in the stands, they were followed by the surprising entrance of a man dressed from head to foot in the feathered costume of an Andean condor, who flapped his wings and posed for photographs. At the same time, in order to formally begin the rally, three Aymara yatiris, or ritual specialists, made elaborate preparations for an offering and blessing. They laid all the items out on a blanket: coca leaves, flowers, grain alcohol, bird feathers, and, most important, two dried llama fetuses, a male and a female, which they carefully wrapped with colorful strips of cloth.

When the fetuses were ready, the male was given to Samuel Guarayo Aruquipo, who, as the president of MAS for La Paz Department, would receive the blessing on behalf of all present, while the female was given to a young woman from his office. As Guarayo had told me the week before during an interview, "in order to play the role I have, in order to be an actor in this long fight against those whose only concern is for their own privileges, one must have a never-ending dream, which is to realize the dream of Túpac Katari, the dream to recuperate our cultures and our languages."

Guarayo and his colleague, flanked on one side by the head yatiri and on the other by the yatiri's wife, carried the llama fetuses to two small pyres made of interlacing pieces of wood, where they were placed in the middle upright, their thin dried necks protruding well above the tinder. The yatiris prepared the offering by sprinkling everything with generous amounts of alcohol, after which both were set on fire while the crowd in the stands grew quiet. As the fetuses slowly burned to ashes, a younger yatiri chanted a blessing in Aymara into a microphone while he kneeled, both hands raised above his head, palms facing inward in a gesture of supplication, his eyes lightly closed.

After the yatiris had finished the ritual offering, political figures, including Patzi, who had gathered on a stage, began their short speeches, which were a mix of words of welcome, fiery denunciations of the Media Luna, exhortations to fight for the passage of the new constitution, and encomiums to Evo Morales, whose visage stared down from banners large and small. After one speech, a white sheet was pulled from an object next to the stage to reveal a large bronze bust of the president on a granite pedestal that was destined to be placed later inside the Palacio Quemado. When it was his turn, Patzi gave a lengthy defense of the new constitution, which he argued would become the most important weapon in the struggle to decolonize Bolivia at its very roots, beginning from the institutions of government and extending out to all sectors of society.[1]

In the late afternoon, after the speeches and folk music had finally ended, the MAS activists who had participated in the launch of the official "Yes!" campaign were released into the streets of La Paz to return to their neighborhoods, towns, and provincial villages to devote themselves over the next month to the epochal cause of national refoundation. The large group of militants from the Federation of Neighborhood Councils of El Alto was given the honor of leading the assembly out of the Coliseo Cerrado. As they marched at the head of the crowd, they carried their long white banner, which displayed a hand-drawn image of the sacred mountain Illimani under a slogan that read, "From the highest peak in the world rises the city on which the sun of our race will never set."

REINSCRIBING THE SUBJECT, REFOUNDING THE STATE

On January 25, 2009, the fervent hopes of those who streamed out of the Coliseo Cerrado on December 21 were realized when the constitution was approved by over 61 percent of voters. Support for the new constitution was concentrated in the five highland and valley departments of Potosí (80 percent yes, 20 percent no), La Paz (78 percent yes, 22 percent no), Oruro (74 percent yes, 26 percent no), Cochabamba (65 percent yes, 35 percent no), and Chuquisaca (52 percent yes, 48 percent no), where the rural vote overcame the strident and near universal opposition from the city of Sucre. By narrower margins, the constitution was rejected by the southern department of Tarija (43 percent yes, 57 percent no) and the three eastern lowland departments of Santa Cruz (35 percent yes, 65 percent no), Pando (41 percent yes, 59 percent no), and Beni (33 percent yes, 67 percent no). Yet leaving aside both the sociolegal implications of the new constitution and its later political consequences, problems that will be taken up in subsequent chapters, here I want to pose a more fundamental question: What was actually gained, in ideological terms, with the passage of the new constitution?

Before suggesting several answers to this question, something must be said about the function of ideology itself within Bolivia's process of change. In his study of Marxism and literature, Raymond Williams (1976) distinguishes between three variations on the concept of ideology: (1) ideology as a system of beliefs of the ruling class that form the basis for state action and social engineering; (2) ideology as a system of false ideas that lead people to perceive of, and act in, the world as a form of false consciousness; and (3) ideology as the "general production of meanings and ideas" (1976: 55). All three of these categories are needed in order to understand the function of ideology during the period 2006–15 in Bolivia.

Beginning in earnest with the campaign during the 2005 elections, the chief strategists of MAS worked to forge a ruling class and a set of ruling ideas in a mutually constitutive movement through which dedicated cadres would commit themselves to the cause of ideas that they themselves would be responsible for constructing and promoting. Yet the attempt to forge an ideology in what might be thought of as the conventional Marxist sense remained incomplete. On the one hand, the protagonists and workers in the process of change did not manage to create a distinct ruling class measured either by its control over the means of production or its clear social dominance. And, on the other hand, since the revolutionaries of MAS were not able to form themselves, either at a national or provincial level, into a traditional ruling class, their ideas did not become, particularly by historical standards, the country's ruling ideas.

At the same time, however, the second variation on ideology played an important role during the period of Bolivia's third revolution in specific ways. As we will see at different places throughout the book, charges of false consciousness—that is, claims that particular ethnic groups or political parties or socioeconomic classes had been deluded by false prophets making false promises based on false understandings of history—shaped many of the conflicts of the last decade.

These first two accounts of ideology are what might be thought of as categories of praxis: they both have structured the social and political development of revolution in Bolivia since early 2006. Yet it is Williams's third account of ideology that forms the basis for a more general ethnographic analysis since it encompasses the first two categories and provides a working theoretical model for explaining them. In other words, *both* the effort on the part of MAS to position its institutions and members as a new ruling class responsible for producing a new intellectual architecture for change *and* the wielding of claims of false consciousness as a rhetorical weapon amid conflicts during the Morales era can be described as examples of the "general production of meanings and ideas."

It is this anthropological approach to ideology that I want to deploy here and throughout the book. In her ethnography of ideas and practices of revolution in socialist Cuba, Marina Gold (2015) adopts a similar orientation to the question of ideology. This proved to be especially illuminating in the case of Cuba, since it allowed her to maintain a critical distance from the much more orthodox Marxist claims of the state to be the embodiment of "ideas that transcend the existing order of things, [ideas] which managed to break with the previous existing order [and therefore become] a utopia" (2015: 5). In order to locate these complicated forms of social and historical dissonance ethnographically, Gold develops an analytical approach to ideology inspired by Bruce Kapferer, in which ideology describes a "selective cultural construction whereby certain significances relevant to experience are systemically organized into a relatively coherent scheme" (Kapferer 1988: 80).

With a perspective on ideology, therefore, that is meant to glide between its historically specific meanings and its general analytical value, let us return to the question of what was gained, in ideological terms, with the passage of the new constitution in Bolivia in 2009: Which meanings and ideas were produced through this key turning point in the longer process of change? Which cultural constructions were selected in the constitution and which ones were excluded? How did the constitution create a model for systematically organizing certain kinds of experiences into particular kinds of schemes?

There are two general ideological innovations that I want to emphasize here. (More technical developments around legal and political institutions and jurisprudence will be taken up in subsequent chapters.) First, the new constitution reinscribed not just Bolivian citizenship, but something more fundamental, the Bolivian subject, within what is formally a postneoliberal polity. The preamble is quite explicit: with the adoption of the new constitution, the refounded state "leaves colonialism, republicanism, and neoliberalism" in the past. And what did it mean, ideologically, to be a postneoliberal subject in a plurinational state?

It meant to define oneself in relation to a particular account of pluralism elevated to the status of a metavalue in which diversity did not add up to something greater than the sum of its parts. On the contrary, the lines of ideological difference within which Bolivia's postneoliberal subjects were constituted were understood as the bases for both differential and differentiated forms of individual and collective action. Although the full implications of postneoliberal subject formation in Bolivia were just coming into focus at the time, Nancy Postero's earlier study of Bolivia (2007), which theorized this new and differentiated form of civic pluralism as "postmulticultural," in many ways anticipated what was to come.[2]

Bolivia's postneoliberal subjects were also implored to make timeworking the mode through which historical change took place. The constitution trafficked in creative historicity. Citizens were called forth to both participate in the collective project of altering the country's cultural space-time and then in shaping the diffuse contours of the plurination that emerged. Among other things, this was one clear way in which Bolivia's process of change evoked other, earlier moments of revolutionary timeworking in which refoundation, world-reversal, and diachronic rupture likewise formed an ideological strategy to remake the world.

Finally, to be a postneoliberal subject in revolutionary Bolivia meant to endeavor to live well (*suma qamaña/vivir bien*) rather than live better, a deceptively simple shift that actually implied a wholesale overthrow of a dominant teleological ethics through which moral value was defined by various forms of progress: intellectual, institutional, and, above all, material. Along with the other "ethical-moral principles" codified in the new constitution— including the Quechua *ama qhilla, ama llulla, ama suwa* (don't be lazy, don't lie, don't steal) and *qhapaj ñan* (walk a noble path), and the Guaraní *ñandereko* (live in harmony with others), *teko kavi* (live a good life), and *ivi maraei* (seek to make our world more just, compassionate, and equitable)—living well suggested a radically different social ontology, one in which the state itself was constituted by everyday practices of social, if necessarily plural, coexistence (Vega 2011).[3]

The second general innovation of the new Bolivian constitution was that it encoded an ideology of structural change that rejected particular forms of state violence in favor of democratic legitimacy, self-determination, and the long-term and pervasive decolonization of education, health, national ecology, and political identity. By "particular forms" I mean either those forms of Marxist-Leninist–derived revolutionary violence that are directed toward the physical destruction of the individuals, classes, and ethnic groups that are believed to stand in opposition to the revolutionary state and its vanguard, or forms of armed violence and sabotage that are used as the basis for overthrowing an existing regime that is seen to be a political instrument of capital.[4]

For example, long before he became Morales's powerful vice president and principal revolutionary propagandist, Álvaro García Linera served five years in prison in the early 1990s as a member of the Ejército Guerrillero Túpac Katari (EGTK) for his role in planning bombings and organizing attacks against "Spanish and US embassies during regional celebrations of 500 years of indigenous resistance in 1992" (Ranta 2014: 111).

The ability to conceive of themselves as both revolutionaries and agents of democratic and nonviolent change proved instrumental in drawing a wide range of social activists and provincial peasant leaders into the MAS fold in the years leading up to, and extending beyond, the passage of the new constitution in 2009. This linkage expressed itself in different ways over time, but nevertheless remained a key legacy of the MAS government's ideological program. For example, in 2009, Adolfo Colque Gutiérrez was a mid-level functionary for the Instrumento Político por la Soberanía de los Pueblos (IPSP), the contemporary companion organization to MAS created by Evo Morales during his ascendancy in the cocalero movement in the late 1990s.[5]

Colque had come to La Paz from the far north of Beni Department to participate in IPSP as a member of the Confederación Sindical de Trabajadores Gremiales, Artesanos, Comerciantes Minoristas y Vivanderos de Bolivia, the national union of shopkeepers, artisans, and grocers. His work in La Paz for the IPSP was concentrated in the Political Commission, the branch dedicated to the development and promulgation of the organization's ideology. I asked him to describe the relationship between MAS-IPSP as a ruling political party and MAS-IPSP as a social and political movement, a distinction that the government itself frequently emphasized.

Although we act politically, in order to advance the cause of this new revolution, we are constituted in a different way, through all the social organizations in the country. I'm talking about peasants, miners, artisans, the women from Bartolina Sisa, rural teachers, professionals, youth leaders, domestic workers, and so on. The essence of MAS is social.

But how, I then asked Colque, could MAS direct a revolution in such a diffuse way, without concentrating its governing power or using violence against the opposition if it proved necessary, as some radical critics of the government contended? The intentional provocation of my question was clear: in the country whose soil entombed the unmarked remains of Che Guevara for three decades (they were sent to Cuba in 1997), how could MAS consider itself a real revolutionary movement?

Look, I'm forty years old and ever since I was a schoolboy I've been hearing about liberation and armed revolution. I've even had many chances to participate myself in that call for armed revolution, but I never did. The problem is that the theory of this so-called armed revolution is not convincing, and unfortunately we need to ask ourselves why not. Where is this true revolution [revolución verdadera]? One needs to remember that the government of MAS-IPSP is composed of comrades from many different leftist factions—Maoists, Leninists, Guevarists, Trotskyists, and others who have a progressive vision. But to those who say the only true revolution is an armed revolution, well, especially in the twenty-first century in South America, I just don't believe it. I doubt it because it's been tried various times in Bolivia, but none of the Trotskyists or the Marxists have ever been able to govern. The critics of our movement have only their theories, which don't make any sense in practice, they aren't convincing. And it is here where comrade Evo Morales draws the distinction, when he says, "ours is a democratic and cultural revolution." Because it is easy to speak of armed things, of armed revolution, but in essence, at the base, in practice, I don't believe in it, because I've seen how it just doesn't work.

BURNING ALL THE BOATS AFTER THE BRIDGES ARE BUILT

Sacha Llorenti's office was in a privileged location in Bolivia's Government Palace, a building universally known by its other name, the Palacio Quemado, or Burnt Palace, a moniker that gives some indication of the ominous and violent legacy that surrounded the country's seat of executive power. The Burnt Palace received its name during what José de Mesa (Mesa, Gisbert, and Mesa Gisbert 2008) describes as "the years of confusion." On March 20, 1875, the government of Tomás Frías came under attack by a large mob under the command of the conspiratorial national deputy Casimiro Corral. The mob climbed the walls of the adjacent city cathedral and launched torches and flaming rags onto the roof of the palace. Although the palace was almost completely destroyed in the resulting inferno, troops of the Colorado regiment arrived soon after and opened fire on the crowd, killing almost 130. Their bodies were exhibited the next day in the Plaza Murillo in front of the charred and still smoking ruins as a warning. Nevertheless, only two months later, Frías was overthrown in a coup d'état.

Yet the acts of violence that gave the Palacio Quemado its name were relatively benign—or at least predictable—compared to the most infamous moment in the building's history. On July 21, 1946, another large mob, this one consisting of teachers, university students, and construction workers, converged on the plaza. They had been mobilized by leaders of an unusual left-wing and pro-business right-wing coalition opposed to the policies of the fascist-socialist regime of Gualberto Villarroel, an obscure figure who had been placed in power in a 1943 coup d'état by fellow members of a secret military lodge called Razón de Patria, or RADEPA, which had been created in the Paraguayan prisoner-of-war camps during the disastrous War of the Chaco (1932–35).[6]

Even though Villarroel had announced his resignation at noon on the same day, the mobilized throng assaulted the Palacio Quemado while police officers and soldiers stood aside. The enraged crowd poured into the building and mounted the stairs, passing within steps of what six decades later would become Sacha Llorenti's office. They killed Villarroel along with his aide-de-camp, his private secretary, a transit official, and another politician. The body of Villarroel, age thirty-seven at the time of his death, was thrown from one of the palace's balconies into the plaza below, where all five corpses were "dragged to lampposts and hung together. . . . This all took place in the middle of an inflamed multitude, which proceeded to desecrate and stab the dangling corpses with spikes. . . . It was an image that Bolivia would never forget" (Mesa Gisbert 2008: 482).

In January 2009, however, although the specter of Bolivia's violent history loomed over the recent massacre of Porvenir and the subsequent investigation and report from UNASUR, which had been released to the international public in November, the weeks before the constitutional referendum brought a sense of bureaucratic calm to the Palacio Quemado's cavernous neoclassical vestibule and hallways leading to the third floor, where Llorenti's office had direct access—via an internal passageway—to the president's suite.

I had first met Llorenti in August 2006 when he visited my university's conflict studies institute outside of Washington, DC, at the head of a delegation from Bolivia's Permanent Human Rights Assembly (APDHB), of which he was president at the time. It was the first year of the new MAS government, and Llorenti was building a network of support among foreign academics and human rights activists. As the institute's resident Bolivia and human rights specialist, we met in my own office for a brief and largely superficial conversation about the implications of Bolivia's 2005 elections. Before leaving, Llorenti, who was dressed in a somewhat incongruously conservative dark blue pinstripe suit, presented me with a small box of mate de coca tea bags and the Bolivian coat of arms, fashioned into a small metal lapel pin (Cerro Rico, Potosí's rich mountain, below a condor and above an alpaca, wheat bushel, and palm tree, flanked on both sides by the Bolivian tricolor arrayed as a battle standard, red for the blood of the nation's martyrs, yellow to recognize the importance of the nation's mineral wealth, green to honor the country's abundant natural resources).

Yet it was something else that Llorenti gave me that would prove to be more useful ethnographically—his business card, which listed his private Yahoo email account. By the time I had returned for the 2008–9 fieldwork season, Llorenti had been dramatically elevated from the dilapidated headquarters of the APDHB on the edge of Sopocachi into Evo Morales's inner circle of advisers. In 2009, he was two years into his term as the vice minister for the coordination of social movements and civil society, a completely new government institution that, as Llorenti explained, "was the first such government ministry in the world, as far as we know."

At the time I conducted ethnographic interviews with Llorenti, he had become arguably the fourth most powerful governmental official in Bolivia after Morales himself, Vice President García Linera, and Foreign Minister David Choquehuanca. When I encountered Llorenti again in La Paz three years after our first brief meeting in the United States, he was thirty-seven years old, coincidentally the same age as Villarroel at the time of his postmortem defenestration in 1946 from the same building.

My keen interest in Llorenti was twofold. First, and more strategic, I had ethnographic visions at the time of eventually gaining research access to Evo Morales and had drafted a series of interview questions for such an eventuality around the meaning of revolution, his understanding of the role of law in the process of change, and his response to the opposition's critique that MAS was promoting an ethnically exclusionary project under the guise of autonomy. Given the sometimes uncomfortable informality that can surround even the highest levels of Bolivia's everyday government bureaucracy, I held out some hope that interviews with Llorenti might lead, perhaps without much warning, to a rushed audience with the president himself.

But second, and more important, I had come to view Llorenti as an exemplar of a particular kind of protagonist in the process of change. Like the older García Linera, Llorenti was also a *cochabambino* from a nonindigenous family background. Yet unlike the vice president, Llorenti was neither a well-known public intellectual nor someone with a long and notable personal history with militant and leftist political commitments. Instead, Llorenti was the most highly placed among a large and diffuse category of actors that I would encounter often over the many years of tracking the contested unfolding of the process of change in Bolivia, a category that stretched well beyond the corridors of government to include those working through ethnic social movements, civil society organizations, trade unions, and student associations.

These were people for whom "revolutionary" became a form of identity that combined a sense of historical inevitability and duty to sacrifice with the mundaneness of daily labor—or, rather, it was a process through which the extraordinary nature of the revolutionary commitment became the basis for the quite ordinary practice of everyday life. There was certainly something here that was both transhistorical and trans-ideological: revolution as a vocation. So even though Llorenti and many others like him in Bolivia imagined their social and political roles as the result of a kind of historical compulsion in which you don't get to choose revolution, revolution chooses you, the practice of revolution itself came to assume many of the elements of any other form of public labor: it was institutionalized, broken down into bureaucratic classifications, made the basis for remuneration (either through salary or the distribution of other public goods), and articulated in the language of human resources.

Yet the process through which revolution became a quotidian vocation had to be elicited ethnographically and historically—it was not expressed through the self-understandings of militants nor, obviously, in ideological representations of the process of change, which in Bolivia (as elsewhere) called people to play their given part in a world-historical drama over which they had little control. I asked Llorenti to describe what it meant to participate in the process of change.

In my experience, it's important to underscore the fact that we are trying to make decisions horizontally, something that's never been done in this country before; we are trying to widen the spaces for debate, to include many different voices. But I also must say that this was not really a choice for me. I had worked for many years in human rights but I never had the intention to occupy a public office. Yet because this is a revolutionary process, one must assume one's proper role and build bridges from one side to the other, but then you must burn all the boats because revolution is a journey without return, for good or for bad.

I then asked Llorenti *why* he was on this journey, the journey of revolution for Bolivia, that is, more generally, where was Bolivia flying to?[7]

It's like I said, Bolivia will never be the same again. I traveled with Evo to Coro Coro in the paceño *altiplano last year and there are always large groups of children who rush to meet him. In Coro Coro, the children started to give him presents and I was with him when one of the children gave him a portrait of the president that he had drawn that also had the presidential sash, an image of the medallion of Bolívar the Liberator, etc. This was an Aymara child of around eight or nine years old, and Evo asked him what he wanted to be when he grew up. The boy responded, "I want to be president of Bolivia." That struck me immediately as a symbol of what we are struggling for; it was a qualitative leap. Before, a little boy, a little Aymara boy from the countryside could aspire to be a bricklayer or in the best of cases a police officer or a rural teacher, but for these children, these young people, Evo has changed the world for them. Everything is possible.*

FROM THE OPEN UNIVERSITY TO THE UNIFICATION OF FRAGMENTS

If Sacha Llorenti and other revolutionary functionaries viewed their historical role as one of committed practice on behalf of the cause of changes that were reshaping the face of power in Bolivia,[8] they were not a vanguard in the traditional sense. In "What Is to Be Done?" (1975), his foundational blue-print for building and sustaining a viable revolutionary movement, Lenin was forced to justify the role of intellectuals and other privileged leaders in rela-tion to the working class as a whole. This was partly as a response to an ongo-ing debate with members of the Union of Russian Social-Democrats Abroad, who had argued in their ideological publication *Rabocheye Dyelo* that Marx had insisted on "freedom from criticism," by which he meant—according to them—that revolutionary struggle should be detached from the development of theory.

In reply, Lenin argued that the so-called Economists had misread both Marx and Engels and that what Marx had really intended to condemn (par-ticularly in his "Critique of the Gotha Program") was not theory itself, but "eclecticism in the formulation of principles" (Lenin 1975a: 19), that is, the proliferation of revolutionary strategies without a unifying theoretical logic. Lenin took this to mean that theory—and an intellectual vanguard to develop and propagate it among the proletariat—was both an essential precondition and an ongoing requirement for the success of the workers' struggle. As he put it, "Without revolutionary theory there can be no revolutionary movement. This idea cannot be insisted upon too strongly at a time when the fashionable preaching of opportunism goes hand in hand with an infatuation for the nar-rowest forms of practical activity" (1975a: 19).

Yet it is various forms of practical activity that largely defined MAS's ap-proach to revolutionary change, activities marked by the refashioning of the organs of government, state management of important sectors of the economy, and the redistribution of public resources through targeted social payments and infrastructure projects both symbolic and empirically transformative. With their backgrounds in trade unions and social movements, many MAS operatives, from the seat of government in La Paz to provincial offices, func-tioned, ironically, as the kind of workers who for Lenin were precisely those in need of theoretically flavored ideological guidance.

This is not to say that Bolivia's "democratic and cultural revolution" lacked a vanguard entirely; indeed, specific ideas produced through a collective project played an important role from the early years. But the key distinction is that this vanguard worked through an oblique relationship with the govern-ment, one in which the role of critique was ambiguous at best, and the systematic development of revolutionary theory gave way, more often than not, to a reli-ance on the power of images produced by graphic artists and propagandists in the expanded Communications Ministry.[9]

This oblique vanguard was known as the Grupo Comuna, or more commonly, simply Comuna. Its influence reached into the inner circle of power, since one of its leading members was Álvaro García Linera. Yet Comuna remained independent from the principal ideological organs of the government, and its collective writings did not play a formal role in the articulation of MAS strategy or government policy. Yet as one of its members put it, Comuna must be understood as *una bisagra*, a hinge that formed an intellectual linkage between the diverse aspirations of Bolivia's social movements and the government at key moments in which the exigencies of contemporary conflicts—both pre- and post-2006—had grown beyond the capacity of existing dogmas to explain them. In this sense, Comuna represented a novel form of vanguardist articulation, one in which what Gramsci would have called "assimilated" traditional intellectuals occupied an intentionally equivocal space within the wider revolutionary process.

On the one hand, Comuna supported, in principle, the refoundation of the Bolivian state as a postneoliberal alternative to the neoliberal and capitalist systems that both gave rise to Comuna and continued to dominate regional and hemispheric political economies after 2005. But on the other hand, because of Comuna's commitment to reformulate radical politics in Bolivia around the incorporation of insights from certain continental theorists, it remained skeptical of the translation of critical ideas into state policy, even as one of its main members occupied a position of great power. In this way, I believe it is more accurate to view García Linera's position as a double one. During the regular Monday meetings of Comuna, and through its widely read publications, he acted as a critical thinker engaged partly with Bolivia's actually existing contradictions but also with debates that opened up regionally and internationally around questions of revolutionary mobilization, diversity, economic development, and natural resources, among others.

Yet in his capacity as vice president, García Linera played his role as the president's intellectual bulldog in the process of change, particularly in the years leading up to and extending beyond the TIPNIS conflict of 2011. Here, García Linera acted much more like a one-intellectual member of a traditional revolutionary vanguard, one tasked with both formulating a vision for change and, even more, discrediting those who opposed it. Yet, as will be seen in chapter 5, García Linera sought to impose discipline and marginalize those critical of or actively opposed to the MAS government, not primarily through the police organs of the state, but through the use of legal regulations and criminal prosecutions that gave a juridical form to the fight against what Lenin (1975b) had called "enemies of the people."

Comuna had its remarkable origins in the intertwined experiences of both political and intellectual exile. Political because most of its key founders and continuing members, including García Linera, Raquel Gutiérrez Aguilar, Raúl "Chato" Prada Alcoreza, Oscar "Oki" Vega Camacho, and Luis Tapia, spent considerable amounts of time during the early to mid-1980s in exile from dictatorship and persecution, particularly during the ferocious if short-lived government of Luis García Meza (1980–81), whose regime deployed Argentine-inspired disappearances, extrajudicial killings, and the complete suppression of civil society to further its narcocratic ambitions.

And intellectual because the founders of Comuna came of age during the waning years of the Cold War, when institutions associated with the so-called Washington Consensus imposed a series of economic and social policies on Latin American countries that would soon coalesce into the dislocative political economic order of neoliberalism. Yet this was also a time in which commitments to Marxist and other orthodox leftist critiques were weakening, leaving intellectuals during this period in search of a replacement or hybrid discourse capable of responding to the new forms of what David Harvey (2003) would somewhat later call "capital bondage."

During this period, the young radicals who would later establish Comuna found themselves in Mexico City, in a country that was in the midst of its own socioeconomic crisis. Nevertheless, as Oki Vega put it, when they arrived in Mexico, the country "gave us an opening and extended to us a level of hospitality that was enormous." With the exception of Chato Prada, who enrolled in a master's course in demography in the Colegio de México, most of the others studied in various faculties at the Universidad Nacional Autónoma de México (UNAM), the famous hotbed of Mexican university student activism that was the organizing center for Mexico 68, the movement that paralyzed the capital city during the 1968 Summer Olympics and led to various acts of repression against students by the Mexican state. Although Raquel Gutiérrez was not at UNAM during this time as a Bolivian exile (the Mexican Gutiérrez would meet García Linera, whom she would later marry, as a fellow student in the faculty of mathematics), the Bolivians had gravitated toward UNAM because of its legendary reputation in Latin America as a hemispheric node for radical intellectuals to further their education and ideological training while waiting for conditions in their home countries to allow for their return.

Yet as Vega explained, UNAM was on the decline by the time the group had arrived in the 1980s.

In reality, despite the fact that UNAM *played a fundamental role for South American and Central American exiles during the '60s and '70s, we arrived at the tail end of this period. This was a period not just for* UNAM, *but for Mexico itself, when the post-68 tradition was declining. During the 1980s, both the university and country were in a period of disarticulation, and not just in Mexico, but also throughout Central America. We can't forget that we arrived in a moment that had begun to give off its neoliberal sparks* [sus chispazos neoliberales], *but it was also a period in which the triumph of the Nicaraguan revolution and the beginning of the armed conflict in Guatemala dramatically changed the forms of political debate and political action.*

I asked him whether the distance from Bolivia and the proximity to other conflicts in Central America shaped the experiences of the Bolivian exiles.

Yes, of course, in a very important way. Even though UNAM *was the place that* [in the past] *had sheltered the majority of important figures from Chile, Argentina, Uruguay, and Ecuador, they arrived in Mexico with clear memories of both their academic and political work in their own countries. But when I say that Mexico was in a moment of decline, what I mean is that the traditional modes of political action, especially armed action, were all put into question by both the younger generation and the faculty. I want to emphasize this because today, in retrospect, this period in Mexico taught most of us the importance of developing other modes of political action, especially those that involve collaboration and work with peasant sectors, the peasant unions, and factory workers.*

In fact, the lessons for both revolutionary theory and political action that the future founders of Comuna brought back to Bolivia in the mid- to late 1980s were mixed. Among the group, García Linera and Gutiérrez were the most committed to an orthodox Marxist response to the ravages of neoliberalism that they confronted in a newly democratic Bolivia. This commitment included both the necessity to directly mobilize Bolivia's exploited class, which they understood largely in ethnic, rather than economic, terms, and to engage in armed subversion of the existing state-capitalist order.

Indeed, years before Comuna was established, García Linera and Gutiérrez formed the EGTK along with Raúl García Linera (the vice president's brother) and Raúl's wife Silvia María Renee de Alarcón (a philosophy professor at La Paz's Universidad Mayor de San Andrés, UMSA); the former *katarista* and Aymara nationalist Felipe Quispe Huanca (known as "El Mallku"); and a small cadre of militants made up of peasant dirigentes, miners, school teachers, and students. In describing the particular ideological strategy that García Linera and Gutiérrez promoted, at least until they were imprisoned in the early 1990s, Luis Tapia argued that it was clearly not Guevarist.

Álvaro comes from a different line of analysis than that of Guevarists like Antonio Peredo. What Álvaro wanted to do was to combine Marxism with indianismo or katarismo, that is, to engage in guerrilla war but not in a strict Guevarist sense; he never used a Guevarist discourse.

At the same time, the other main founders of Comuna—Tapia, Prada, and Vega—were much more heavily influenced during their exile in Mexico by post-Marxist and especially poststructuralist philosophy. Instead of offering a blueprint for political action based on a straightforward critique of capitalism, the theories of Jacques Derrida or Michel Foucault, among others, taught them the value of deconstructive critique and the way in which state institutions came to govern citizens through various forms of biopolitical control.

As Prada explained elsewhere, he and other former exiles wanted to use the insights of poststructuralist theory to deconstruct existing institutions, including universities, to make way for "epistemological outcomes . . . [drawn from] paradigms that existed within Aymara cultures, Quechua cultures. . . . We linked these with French social scientists . . . and tried to think of power relations from a Foucauldian perspective as micro-physics of power: as a critique of institutions, as the administration of bodies, of territories; as strong processes and dynamics between [Bolivian] society—social movements—and [state] institutions" (Ranta 2014: 112).

To do this, Prada formed an academic reading and writing circle called Episteme; Tapia, upon his return from Mexico, began teaching at UMSA and established a review for critical theory called *Autodeterminación*, which he would publish until 1996; and Vega began to publish as an independent scholar and consultant.[10] Yet throughout the 1990s, with García Linera and Gutiérrez in prison and the uber-neoliberal government of Sánchez de Lozada firmly in power, the experiments in radical critical synthesis produced by Bolivia's former exiles were dispersed among different institutional and political currents.

This all changed with the release of García Linera from prison in 1997. As Tapia explained, the end of the Goni regime in 1997 unleashed a series of conflicts that revealed, in practice, the basic contradictions of the neoliberal project and the need for a destabilizing alternative. Despite the theoretical and political differences among the younger generation of the Bolivian left, it was time to act.

We formed Comuna in 1999 as a unification of fragments. I came from Autodeterminación, *Raúl came from a group called Epísteme, and the people from the* EGTK, *Álvaro and Raquel.*[11]

For Oki Vega, the unification of the new Bolivian left through Comuna was never meant to have an immediate political objective.

In reality, Comuna was formed because of the necessity to create an open space for political debate that was shaped by the strong presence of theoretical reflection. That is to say, we never believed that we could practice politics as such without an emphasis on theoretical reflection, that is an important point. We need to remember that we are talking about the period of the end of the '90s, a time in which neoliberalism was both hegemonic and discredited. . . . If one wants to identify a common thread among the members of Comuna during this time it is that even though we came with distinct experiences, education, histories, and politics, we wanted to construct a common horizon, which was, we can say, the need to reconsider the place of Marxism as a theory of change.

Comuna constructed this common horizon through an astonishing campaign of collective writing and publishing in which different members collaborated around different themes over more than a decade, beginning with the group's first publication, *El fantasma insomne* (Gutiérrez Aguilar et al. 1999), a "rereading" of Marx's *Communist Manifesto*, as Oki Vega put it.

This was our first book, which seems like we were beginning our reflections among the dinosaurs. But we believed that in that moment it was very important to reestablish the bases for struggle and emancipation. It was for that reason that we began with the Communist Manifesto *as our first effort, to return to and reread the work in order to understand which things were still valid and which elements were not.*

Most of Comuna's books were published through their own publishing house, Muela del Diablo, and over time its publications reached a wide regional and international audience, which brought Comuna members into contact with global intellectuals such as the Portuguese sociologist Boaventura de Sousa Santos and the Argentine semiotician and literary theorist Walter Mignolo, among many others.[12]

Up through 2010, Comuna's publications represented a notably expansive critical response to Bolivia's process of change, one that evolved collectively through the struggles over the new constitution, the reelections of Evo Morales, the rise and fall of the lowland opposition, and the first stirrings of resistance to the government's development plans among MAS's peasant and indigenous strongholds.[13] This response was structured by four transversal themes, four principles that formed boundaries around what was otherwise a diverse and often centrifugal theoretical intervention.

First, Comuna sought to give epistemological depth to at least some of the various ideas that were circulating among the government's ideological programs, most notably the idea of "living well." The group agreed that this alternative ethic had sufficient conceptual potential to serve as the basis for a radical post-Marxist critique of capitalism.

Second, the writings of Comuna provided the theoretical framework for the government's position that the locus of transformation was not at the level of class, ethnic group, or political party, but at the level of social movements. This move reflected a deep skepticism among the group about the role and potential of political organizations, but it also expressed the desire to theorize the social in a way that invested it with the kind of directive power that had previously been associated with formal political structures.

Third, the members of Comuna attempted to expand the government's ideological commitment to pluralism beyond the question of plural collectivities. In this sense, the group was influenced by the writings of Hardt and Negri (2000), who argued that radical, global change would eventually be propelled by radiating and pluralist alliances that they described with the ambiguous category of the "multitude." For Comuna, pluralism in Bolivia had a similar resonance. It was not simply, or even most importantly, a way to understand cultural diversity; rather, it captured something essential about the catalyzing potential of decentralized and diffuse social action.

And finally, the writings of Comuna sought to reorient the relationship between state and society. As Oki Vega explained in 2009, "state-society relations [in Bolivia] . . . have always been such that the object of change is the society and the state is the subject that allows this transformation. . . . What we are experiencing in the [current] Bolivian process is that the object of change and transformation is not society but the state, and the subject of change is society" (quoted in Ranta 2014: 113).

Thus, although the membership of Comuna ultimately fractured around the time of the TIPNIS conflict in 2011, for over a decade it developed, obliquely to the government, central theoretical threads that could, in certain cases, be woven together to create a coherent ideology of postneoliberal and post-Marxist revolutionary change that was nevertheless deeply embedded in Bolivia's fraught existing conditions.

How often do I lull my seething blood to rest, for you have never seen anything so unsteady, so uncertain, as this heart.

—Goethe, *The Sorrows of Young Werther*

Somos indias, putas y lesbianas juntas, revueltas y hermanadas.
[We are Indian women, whores and lesbians together, in rebellion and joined as sisters.]

—Graffiti on the wall outside UMSA's School of Law

In 2011, several months before the effects of the TIPNIS conflict had begun to shift the national debate in measurable ways, I asked Sandra, an activist in the

Department of Social Work at UMSA, to describe the mood among her fellow students in one of the departments with a reputation for being the most militant in the university.

Well, what I can say is that for me, for us really, what we want is for there to be major changes, structural changes [in the country]. *Now in order for there to be changes like this, there needs to be a revolution, complete change, not just a change from here to there* [indicates a short distance], *and this is what is being done with the new constitution. But we need to take care because we have had constitutions in the past that were principally developed by the large landowners* [latifundistas] *while the participation by indigenous people was excluded. In fact, the indigenous people were excluded on principle for a very long time, but now everything is changing, there is much greater inclusion, even though there are some deficiencies that we must recognize. We in the Department of Social Work will not hesitate to protest even against this revolutionary government of* MAS *if we think enough is not being done.*

During this same period, student organizations in UMSA's School of Law were challenging the university's departments of social work and sociology in an unofficial intra-university struggle to develop the most radical university presence as both foot soldiers and critics in the process of change. This struggle was taking place partly along ideological lines and partly for reasons of institutional space. The departments of social work and sociology were located in UMSA's main building on the Prado, where they formed the militant core of the Juventud Socialista (JS), a Trotskyist student organization with close ties to its parent faculty organization, the Unión Revolucionaria de Universitarios Socialistas (URUS), which was founded around the time of the April 1970 "university revolution" during the leftist and relatively open regime of General Juan José Torres.

The April 1970 university uprising in La Paz was led by faculty and students inspired by the "May 68" student occupations in Paris (Mesa Gisbert 2008: 541). They took control of the university buildings and purged faculty members who did not support their calls for Marxist revolution and the restructuring of Bolivian society. The university revolution came to a head when the building was retaken by "Phalangist groups and juvenile delinquents (the 'marqueses')," after which political reforms were put in place that profoundly altered university governance through power-sharing and regular elections (Mesa Gisbert 2008: 541).

The School of Law, however, was located in a large open building on Calles Potosí and Loayza, among the precipitous streets three blocks down from the Palacio Quemado. Its students did not organize under the banner of the Prado-based JS but rather within three separate organizations: the first, a student branch of MAS, whose members collaborated on projects with MAS's national and departmental agencies; the second, a much smaller Maoist organization called the Convención Progresista Universitaria (CPU), which took its inspiration from Peru's Shining Path; and the third, which was the most active and visible among law students, the Resistencia Universitaria de Trabajo Autónomo (RUTA), an organization that distinguished itself from the other two—and from the JS—through its adherence to orthodox Marxism-Leninism.

In 2011, RUTA was led by Soledad, a law student in her final year. But behind the scenes, RUTA received its organizational and tactical instructions from Julio César, a thirty-one-year-old Peruvian political refugee who had been a member of the Movimiento Revolucionario Túpac Amaru (MRTA) in his late teens. Soledad and Julio César were a magnetic collective presence in the law faculty's large open courtyard. During the day, between classes, when the area filled with students, the two militants were in a constant state of revolutionary movement, which implied action, organizing, agitation, and, more than anything, a kind of earnest projection: of permanent concern, of indignation, of the need for self-sacrifice in the cause of structural transformation. They moved quickly from small group to small group, arranging meetings, making phone calls with their cell phones, shaking hands with comrades.

When they finally did agree to discuss RUTA's revolutionary objectives, and the role of Bolivian students more generally in the process of change, they took me by the arms and led me briskly out of the building, down several streets, and into a run-down café, where (still leading me by the arms) we walked through the main dining room, up the back stairs, and then to a set of tables at the far end of the deserted second floor. This was their regular meeting spot—it was isolated from prying eyes and ears and therefore an ideal redoubt from which they could direct revolutionary strategizing.

I asked Julio César to describe the meaning of revolution to him and the place of the young, of students, in the process of change.

Well, students are fundamental to the revolution, now, here in Bolivia, as always. Why? Because students combine two essential elements—passion and knowledge, both of which are necessary to the revolutionary struggle. But I want to distinguish between two kinds of revolution, something I always try and emphasize to my comrades [in RUTA, and perhaps among students more generally]. *The first is the practical revolution, that is, the strategies of mobilization and social action, which for us means a Marxist-Leninist line* [una tendencia marxista-leninista]. *But there is a second kind of revolution, which you can say is even more important than the first. This is the internal revolution. What I mean is the lifetime commitment to radical transformation, something that I did when I was younger.*

What was so notable about the outward expression of Julio César's particular internal revolution was that he didn't seem to be angry, or on the verge of resorting to some form of violent action, something I observed among other student militants during these years. Instead, his laser-focused revolutionary energy had a certain hopefulness to it, something enabled also by the fact that there was no shortage of nonviolent "projects"—a revolutionary term of art, I later learned—through which to channel his commitment to justice for Bolivia's exploited working classes and rural peasantry. Indeed, on the day I first met Julio César, he had just returned to La Paz from a week of what he described as "revolutionary service" with a rural farming cooperative.

Yet it was Soledad whose sense of commitment most clearly reflected the idea that youth—in Bolivia and elsewhere—were drawn to the cause of revolution less because of particular goals derived from well-defined ideological histories, but because the idea of revolution itself crystallized youthful passion; it condensed it into a single word.

I first asked her when she knew she wanted to be a revolutionary, when she was sure she wanted to make that kind of commitment.

Look, it was in high school, when I was sixteen years old, it was just an instinct that pulls you, one of rebellion, a kind of stubbornness, but it's true that I became a revolutionary earlier than many of the others.

Were you influenced by your teachers in high school? I asked her.

No, I tell you that I was probably the most radical, but it was still a time for me of much reflection since I was still trying to decide who I was.

I then asked Soledad to describe what it meant to be a student revolutionary in Bolivia, to be committed to structural change.

Well, here is how I would explain it. Some people say that it's hard to be a revolutionary, that you need to be a cold person, very tough, to be someone who only has deep feelings [sentimientos más profundos]. *But for me it's not like that, it's a different kind of feeling, a kind of love. Are you going to love your people as such, your neighbor who lives from here to who knows how far? You want equality for all, justice for all, and this is your love, right? To ask for better education, to ask for health, for better access to health for all, that is a noble sentiment, something worth respecting.*

Did the women revolutionaries among her fellow students share a common vision, one that was, perhaps, different from the men?

I think that women have their own feelings as women that allow us to love the revolution as if it were our children, as if it were a part of us that we have to carry forward despite what it weighs. I think that this is what is most notable among us [female revolutionaries], *this sublime devotion to the revolution as such, no? This is why women play a fundamental part in every revolutionary process. It is the woman who organizes, the woman who guides, the woman who has the capacity to lead, no?*

Finally, I asked Soledad (who was twenty-two years old) if she thought she would be able to sustain her commitment to revolutionary mobilization for a long time, whether she could imagine herself changing her life's commitments by the time she was, say, forty years old.

No, I don't think I would ever change my commitment to revolution, that would be like committing treason against myself and also treason against my people. But it's true, some students think like that, to become professionals later in life, with a family, a house, a job, but I think that there is always another life apart from these things and that is what I'll be struggling for even after I receive my degree. I'm just going to continue the struggle elsewhere.

FROM THE PERMANENT STRUGGLE TO THE BALANCE SHEETS OF GOVERNMENT

By 2015, the process of change in Bolivia had evolved yet again. Indeed, a notable discursive shift took place in which the language of revolution itself, which was so prevalent at least until the TIPNIS conflict of 2011, had slowly given way to the softer *proceso de cambio* among MAS officials and party activists as the primary ideological category used to describe the government's historical aspirations. This is not to say that the ideology of revolution had disappeared—quite the contrary. As will be seen in chapter 4, the claim to support a true, or real, revolution became a line of division and a rhetorical weapon among Bolivia's fractured and marginalized traditional left as critiques of the government grew stronger in the early post-TIPNIS years (although their collective volume had diminished by 2015). But the increasing bureaucratization of MAS's revolutionary project, as well as the challenges posed by the normatively unwieldy, if radical, new constitution, created pressures on the government that were reflected in key ideological permutations.

Yet from an ethnographic perspective, the subtle transformations in MAS's ideological orientation, especially after TIPNIS, should not be read as a form of we-knew-it-all-along disingenuousness, in which the crisis over the Villa Tunari–San Ignacio de Moxos Highway and government acquiescence to the economic demands of the country's large foreign-owned mines, among other examples, is taken to mean that Evo Morales and other key protagonists were simply ethnic-extractivist-neoliberals in revolutionist clothing all along.

A psychosocial analyst might argue that this increasingly common response is more a reflection of a kind of projection engendered by disenchantment among various groups of intellectuals, including anthropologists, for whom the utopian promises of revolution will always hold a certain allure (and rightly so). Nevertheless, I think it is more ethnographically accurate to understand the evolution of MAS's governing logics as the result of the government's desire to promote a state ideology that was in clear and sometimes tragic tension with underlying political economic and historical imperatives.

For example, in late July during the 2015 fieldwork season, La Paz experienced a massive protest by hundreds of miners, civic leaders, and students from Potosí, who had arrived in the capital along with a smaller group of sixteen that had made the journey on foot over nearly two weeks from Potosí itself, a route of about eight hundred kilometers that passes through an especially forbidding stretch of the central altiplano. The mobilization had been organized by the Comité Cívico Potosinista (Comcipo), led by Johnny Llally and Marco Antonio Pumari. Comcipo had made a wide range of public demands as part of a general campaign to advance the interests of both the city and the department, including the construction of a new airport, the building of new cement and glass factories, and a number of other development projects for the department's rural provinces. They also demanded the resignation of the department's governor, Juan Carlos Cejas, and Potosí's mayor, Willian Cervantes, both members of MAS, on charges that they had failed in their obligation to secure local resources from the national government.

During its brief time in La Paz, the Comcipo mobilization had a dramatic impact on the city. For one, the movement was symbolized by a photogenic dog named Petardo ("Firecracker"), who appeared with the organizers during interviews and at the head of the group's marches around the Plaza Murillo and down the Prado. Petardo was often seen wearing a miner's helmet and a collar made of *pasankalla*, the ubiquitous popped corn that is often sweetened. But for another, the July 2015 Comcipo mobilization was represented by a large contingent of *potosino* miners, who served as its foot soldiers, with the responsibility for protecting other marchers and handling the highly dangerous sticks of dynamite, which the marchers exploded as they moved through the streets of La Paz.

Among Bolivia's many street marching traditions,[14] the sight of hundreds of hardened miners—their helmets plastered with images of the iconic red Central Obrera Boliviana logo, with its crossed hammer and *pututu*, pushing ahead with the sound of dynamite blasts echoing between the downtown office buildings of La Paz—was something exceptional, historically dense, and fearsome (see also Thomson 2009).[15]

The violent manifestation of potosinos in the seat of government was extraordinary for another reason: Since 2005, both the city and the department of Potosí had been key pillars of MAS's national electoral base. In the 2009 constitutional referendum, the department's support was 80 percent, and in the December 2009 national elections, 78 percent of the department had voted to reelect Morales. Yet by the time of the 2014 national elections, only 55 percent had voted for Morales, with stark lines of difference emerging between rural provinces and the city of Potosí.[16] Yet although leading MAS officials like García Linera would have been expected to find common ideological cause with the activists from Comcipo, whose shouts of *"por la lucha permanente,"* or "for the permanent struggle," were drawn from a common discursive vocabulary, in fact, the response was strategically confrontational.

At an event carefully chosen for its symbolic value, an anniversary celebration at the Autonomous University Siglo XX, located in the important Potosí mining town of Llallagua, García Linera rejected Comcipo's demands on behalf of the government with a simple reference to its yearly balance sheets. Comcipo was wrong to demand more from the government since Potosí Department received 3.9 billion Bs (about US$560 million) yet only produced 800 million Bs (about US$116 million) in revenue, which wasn't enough, on its own, "to pave the department's highways" (*Página Siete*, August 2, 2015).

As he elaborated, "If they had said, 'Vice President, Potosí lacks investment,' I would say to them, 'Yes, you are right,' because Potosí, Llallagua, Siglo XX, Cerro Rico, Colquechaca, Central Sud have given so much to Bolivia that has helped Bolivia develop, this is correct. But to say that nothing has been done [for Potosí], that we have forgotten, is a lie, an injustice, and a fallacy" (*Página Siete*, August 2, 2015). And then García Linera drew the ultimate economic contrast as a rhetorical weapon against Comcipo's claims: "In reality, Potosí gives very little these days. It used to produce much but now there is much more money to be made through [natural] gas and Potosí doesn't produce gas. This is the problem with the brothers from [Comcipo], at times they speak of things without knowing what they are speaking about" (*Página Siete*, August 2, 2015).

García Linera was pilloried for his role as the spokesperson for the government's ideological shifts that took place in the post-TIPNIS years, particularly with regard to the development and implementation of the Ley de Otorgación de Personalidades Jurídicas (Law on Legal Entities, or Law 351), a 2013 law that was passed to give the government more freedom to regulate, or, as critics claimed, undermine, the work of NGOs—both foreign and Bolivian—in the country.

But in viewing ethnographically the ideological landscape over the entire 2006–15 period, an alternative narrative emerges. Instead of understanding the ideological shifts of the post-TIPNIS years as the reflection of increasingly Machiavellian state governance at the service of an unsustainable and hypocritical development policy, I would argue that something else was at work: a shift, which was in part unique to Bolivia (in its specific expressions), through which a politics of revolutionary idealism gave way, as it must, to a prevailing politics of revolutionary pragmatism.

In *The Anatomy of Revolution*, Crane Brinton recounts the story of a Danish man in Copenhagen who had gathered his sons together to tell them, with tears in his eyes, that the Bastille had fallen, "that a new era had begun, that if they were failures in life they must blame themselves, for henceforth 'poverty would vanish, [and] the lowliest would begin the struggles of life on equal terms with the mightiest'" (Brinton 1965: 90–91). This is what Brinton calls the onset of the "fever of revolution" (1965: 205), a period of months or years in which people and their new leaders rejoice in the very idea of limitless possibility and the potential for long-desired structural change.

Yet without necessarily adopting Crane's general classificatory schema, there is something of value in thinking of the process of change in Bolivia as one with its own revolutionary logic through which an initial idealism was forced to confront the exigencies of governance and economic policy-making within broader regional and global capitalist political economies; an opposition whose principles of resistance often masked an underlying racial animus; and the ultimate limits of law as a mechanism for social transformation.

Brinton would call the later period of revolutionary pragmatism in Bolivia its Thermidor, in which society's return to "quieter, less heroic times" is seen as a kind of "convalescence" from the dislocations and upheavals that accompany the early years of often violent transition. Yet by shifting from a rhetoric of idealism to an ideology and, even more, a practice, of hard-edged pragmatism, one must consider how this evolution—whether or not it is associated with the nature of revolutionary politics as such—will eventually come to be understood by revolutionary youth like Soledad, or by more senior protagonists like Sacha Llorenti, who later agreed to be scapegoated for the TIPNIS conflict in exchange for an honorable sinecure as Bolivia's permanent representative to the United Nations in New York City.

Will they themselves come to understand it as a form of betrayal, as critics of the MAS government—both in Bolivia and internationally—have argued? Or will they rather understand it as the beginning of a longer period in which those in power eventually came to find common ground even with erstwhile opponents for the greater good, a period in which the "politically proscribed are amnestied, and come back[,] sometimes to be caught up again in the scramble of competitive politics" (Brinton 1965: 209)?

CONCLUSION: HEARING REVOLUTION IN A MINOR KEY

On August 10, 2008, I conducted ethnographic research in various districts of La Paz and El Alto on the day of the Referéndum revocatorio. With certain exceptions, national elections in Bolivia took place on Sundays and voting was compulsory. The state provided a range of services for people to facilitate widespread compliance with this mandate, including providing detailed informational guides on candidates and policies, staffing polling stations throughout the city, and offering vouchers for people with reduced mobility or of the so-called third age (*la tercera edad*) to allow them to take taxis to and from their assigned polling place.[17] The day was a festive one, something like a national holiday, and although all businesses and government offices were closed, a flourishing nine-to-five fiesta economy existed, often centered around the polling stations themselves, in which people could buy meals and snacks and toys and generally spend several hours with friends and family after voting.

After moving among polling places in La Paz, including in Zona Sur, Miraflores, and Chasquipampa, I arrived in La Ceja, the pulsing commercial, political, and artistic center of El Alto. It was late in the afternoon and most people had voted many hours before. The streets were packed; children played games of street soccer; and groups of young men swayed among the crowds, clearly intoxicated. A larger than normal police presence kept watch from numerous street corners.

I found a voting station at a neighborhood *colegio*, but it was almost empty except for the officials from the Corte Electoral Departamental, who were required to keep the urns open until they were promptly sealed at 4 PM. However, I noticed a man observing the courtyard of the school from a first-floor balcony that overlooked it from across the street. I stood underneath him and asked if we could talk. A minute later, he appeared through the ground floor door. He was middle-aged, about fifty-five years old, and could have been the owner of the convenience store below the apartment, which was locked with the ubiquitous metal pull-door for election day. I asked him how he voted. He said, "obviously, I voted for the president." I asked him why, was it because he supported the revolution, the process of change?

Well, let me tell you something, although I voted for Brother Evo, I don't agree with the idea of what's called a democratic revolution. What Bolivia really needs is a little revolution [una revolución pequeña].

Puzzled, I responded—isn't this what Evo and MAS are doing?

No, what I mean is that Bolivia needs something stronger, a stronger revolution, one in which blood is shed. It doesn't matter what anyone thinks, the right wing in Santa Cruz and Sucre is never going to participate in a democratic revolution, that's a fantasy.

I asked him how this little revolution was going to take place if the government had already rejected violence and was instead promoting pride in indigenous cultures.

Well, let me tell you something. We hear that there are some small groups [in El Alto] *who have been acquiring weapons; they say they have connections with movements in Peru and Colombia.*

I asked if this meant there would be some kind of insurrection in El Alto, one that began a more violent revolution.

Well, that's what they talk about, but so far it is only talk and not action.

Somewhat shaken by the thought of armed movements forming in the buildings around me, I prepared to hail a taxi to return to La Paz, when

I noticed another man leaving the colegio with his *certificado de sufragio* in his hand. He was clearly younger and was wearing rubber sandals rather than closed shoes, which often marked someone as a recent arrival from the countryside. I asked him if I could speak with him for just a few minutes and he reluctantly paused.

I told him I was talking to people about voting and the process of change more generally. Could he tell me a little about himself? He said that he was thirty-five and that he came from Santiago de Machaca, an Aymara town in the far west of La Paz Department on the high altiplano near the Peruvian border. But he lived now in El Alto with his family and tried to find work in construction, if possible in Sopocachi or Zona Sur, the wealthier districts of La Paz. I asked how he voted in the referendum. He looked around before answering and lowered his voice, almost to a whisper.

I supported Evo like all the neighbors; we support the president absolutely.

I asked him why he supported the president, was it because of the political changes or the possibility that the government would write a new constitution?

He stepped even closer as a look that seemed to combine both pain and insistence came over his face.

No, let me tell you something. There is a lot of racism here, a lot of discrimination, a lot of intolerance. When I'm working [in La Paz's wealthy districts]*, I see it every day. That's why we support Evo, we share the same face* [tenemos el mismo rostro].

This struck me as significant—the idea that Bolivia's revolution was being understood by people in many different ways, at different levels of ideological pitch and structure. Although it was easier, at least until the turning point of the TIPNIS conflict, to see and hear the signs of revolution expressed in what might be thought of as a major key, it was much more difficult, ethnographically, to see and hear the signs of revolution expressed in a minor key, softly, discordantly, perhaps a bit sadly, in a social whisper. I thought, then, of how challenging it was, methodologically and epistemologically, to capture the polyvalent experience of transformation with the tools at my disposal: the culturally sensitive interview; the encompassing observation; the historically nuanced critical reflection.

As the years passed with each fieldwork season, and "revolution" gave way to "the process of change," it became even more important to hone this attention to quiet phenomenologies and subtle shifts. In many ways, this capacity, or at least willingness, to hear below the normal ethnographic registers is something that the writers and poets have more mastery over. The Romanian American poet Romana Iorga (2000) has described what I'm thinking of here as "auz simplu," or "simple hearing," the ability to encounter and appreciate changes in life in front of, or aside from, our social categories. And of course there is the lovely image from Arundhati Roy, who also gives shape to what it means to hear, and to live, a revolution in a minor key: "Another world is not only possible, she's on her way. Maybe many of us won't be here to greet her, but on a quiet day, if I listen very carefully, I can hear her breathing" (2003: 75).

2 LEGAL COSMOVISIONS

The aging peach-colored building on the Prado was unmistakable: it housed Bolivia's Ministry of Justice. Unlike many of the other major government ministries, which were located in buildings away from public view on the steeply inclined and densely built side streets of La Paz, the Ministry of Justice was one of the most strikingly visible buildings in the heart of the city. It was built in an early republican architectural style, a stark contrast with its bland modern neighbors. Its façade, which faced southwest onto arguably the most public of spheres in Bolivia, was adorned with sharp white trim, its first floor above street level framed by an impressive marble balustrade. The entrance to the ministry passed through an arched doorway underneath an elaborate set of friezes that had been painted on either side to give the illusion that the door sat between two tall columns, which were topped by their own friezes and cornices.

The republican-liberal materiality of Bolivia's Ministry of Justice, in other words, had proved much more difficult to transform than the shifting set of vice ministries that the building had housed in the years after the election of Evo Morales in 2005. In many ways, the architectural incongruence of the Ministry of Justice was a metaphor for the tensions and points of disjuncture that marked the legal as a fundamental category within which the MAS government's transformative projects were crafted, legitimated, and put into practice. In this sense, the period 2006–15 in Bolivia served as one of the most important historical examples, at least since the end of the Cold War, of a sustained national effort to reimagine law as both a conceptual foundation and an institutional mechanism for radical structural and ideological change. Indeed, although Evo Morales's whirlwind preinaugural world tour of January 2006 was in part a campaign to promote himself for the Nobel Peace Prize,[1] it stopped in South Africa for another reason: Morales's advisers wanted to know what lessons could be learned from the experience of that country's own revolution by constitution, which was set in motion during the liminal years of the early 1990s.[2]

The lessons they took with them, to be applied over the coming years during the battle over Bolivia's own constitution and beyond, were twofold: first, to concentrate the process of change around cultural, democratic, and institutional norms, rather than around more direct instruments of rapid transformation, including state violence; and second, to make the constitution an uncompromising framework for the plurinational state's cosmovisión.[3] As Antonio Peredo explained it to me in 2009, the African National Congress lawyers who had played an important role in drafting the South African constitution believed, in retrospect, that too many concessions had been made during the process of negotiation, particularly to entrenched business and agricultural elites who controlled much of the country's socioeconomic power. Thus, the message delivered to the MAS counselors in the shadows of Morales's public meetings with leading figures from the government and trade unions, including President Thabo Mbeki, was clear: if the process of change was to be instantiated through law, as it must, it should be done expansively, with deep ideological commitment, and without regard for rigid preconceptions concerning jurisprudence, the role of legal experts, and the relationship between the judicial and political branches of government. Yet as the ethnography of the struggle to harness the logics of law to the cause of transformation in Bolivia revealed, juridification and the revolutionary imaginary made for an uneasy partnership.

Inside of its peach outer walls, therefore, the Ministry of Justice was the site where many of these dilemmas, misalignments, and normative aporia were expressed, contested, and eventually institutionalized. The challenges of reconciling the state's revolutionary vision with the law were perhaps most clearly reflected within the vice ministry whose mandate was at the very leading edge of the state's early sociolegal aspirations: the Vice Ministry of Community Justice. In 2009, its director-general—the second-in-command to the vice minister—was a twenty-nine-year-old lawyer named Petronilo Flores Condori. Flores, who was the vice ministry's founding director-general at the request of the government, had moved to La Paz from a small law practice in the city of Potosí. Although he had graduated from the law faculty of the Universidad Autónoma Tomás Frías in Potosí in 2002, he had grown up in a small rural settlement in the far southwest of Chuquisaca Department in Nor Cinti Province. Flores had come to the attention of MAS officials through his recent work as an adviser to CONAMAQ and his earlier consulting practice in the historic mining town of Llallagua, although he was quick to point out that he was never a "functionary" in the indigenous movement, but rather "someone who was simply part of the same large process of change."

In contrast with the way high-ranking indigenous legal officials often dressed later during the 2006–15 period, for example, in brightly woven vests with distinctive patterns, Flores wore the quasi-official uniform of the successful sindicalista: polyester slacks, synthetic wool sweater over a checkered collared shirt, and a black leather jacket, which he wore at his desk. Flores had a distinct sense both of his own role in the process of change and of the fundamental importance of law as its framework, although he was also keenly aware of the fact that the contours of "community justice" were still highly contested. Indeed, he was openly critical of the ways in which, in his view, anthropologists had contributed to a distorted perspective on indigenous sociolegal structures on the one hand, and, on the other, to the problematic concept of "community justice" itself, which Flores—despite being the first director-general of the Vice Ministry of Community Justice—questioned at its foundations.

I asked Flores how the project to develop government institutions committed to supporting community justice would contribute to the wider process of change, especially in light of the fact that the vote on the new constitution would take place soon and the result was a foregone conclusion. His response was surprising.

Well, the first thing to say is that there really isn't a reason at this point to talk about community justice, because when I was a rural peasant union leader [dirigente] in my community, we never spoke about community justice. For us, it was always something different, native indigenous justice [justicia indígena originaria]. What I want to say is that the idea of community justice didn't come from us, it was Mr. Ramiro Molina and other researchers, anthropologists, who wanted to introduce these terms, along with NGOs.

If there is no such thing, in fact, as community justice, then what should we be talking about? I asked.

We should be talking about native and indigenous justice.

Well then, I responded, in order to agitate the ethnographic encounter to a certain extent, in speaking of native indigenous justice, what do you think about what took place in Achacachi? (A few days before, a young man had been lynched in the center of Achacachi in Omasuyos Province on the southeastern shores of Lake Titicaca, a town known to most Bolivians as the home of the radical Aymara leader Felipe Quispe, El Mallku.)

That was not indigenous justice! That was just a lynching. The problem is structural, the institutionalization of state justice [justicia ordinaria] is weak, it's marked by corruption, it doesn't have any credibility, there is no access to the legal system, it's too expensive, too many delays, there is a general sense of legal insecurity [inseguridad jurídica]. The dilemma is that in many small towns indigenous people must try and resolve problems in the state legal system, despite all these problems, and even though state law knows nothing of indigenous justice, which leads to judgments that are a kind of double abuse. But what happened in Achacachi was the result of delinquent acts against the town's population. Still, we shouldn't stigmatize Achacachi even if the Achacachi of today is not the same as the Achacachi of before. What happened was that these delinquents were caught, they were taken away, but there is no way in which what happened was indigenous justice, it can't be thought of like that. The death penalty doesn't exist in indigenous justice and it never has.

I responded to Flores that I was confused. How can we say that what happened in Achacachi, a lynching, something that was supported by most of the people in the town who are also indigenous, was not, at some level, an expression of indigenous justice?

Look, here is how I would explain it to you. During the history of indigenous people, colonialism, there was a general weakening, a loss, and many indigenous people, for example, those close to cities, like in the mining centers in

the north of Potosí, they adopted new ways of life, created new kinds of authori-
ties, and these new and shocking styles led to many problems like the use of the
death penalty. But this is not justice; the death penalty is not indigenous justice
and it should never be confused as such. It was the Spanish who applied the
death penalty, whippings, public lashings, punishments, blood, they applied these
things as we know from the archives in Potosí, in Sucre, in La Paz. These archives
tell us things like "whichever Indian shall not go to Church or to pray shall be
whipped in the town center with thirty lashes." They did these things, but now we
are the ones who use whips.

In many ways, Flores's subtle and historically thick understanding of
justice practices in Bolivia crystallized the challenges the government would
face in the coming years as it sought to reconcile the various competing conceptions of law, indigenous rights, human rights, and security. At the same
time, Flores's skepticism about even the most culturally expansive interpretations formulated in national seminars and through the innumerable capacity-
building workshops signaled another critical tension that was emerging: that
between accounts of legal pluralism embedded in international covenants and
national academic discourse and the much more dissonant actually existing
legal pluralism that constituted the normative lived reality of many Bolivians,
particularly in rural areas. Yet, as will be seen in this chapter, there was no
way—politically, ideologically, or culturally—to avoid these frictions.

CONSTITUTIONAL REVOLUTION AND THE LOGICS OF LAW

Let me explain why our new constitution is unique. Look at what happened
in the United States. They founded the country with thirteen colonies and then
committed themselves to exterminating the indigenous people because they
weren't part of the constitution. The difference is that in countries like Bolivia
there was already a civilization, there was already a state, so it wasn't possible
to just eliminate the indigenous people. Look at the case of Chile and Argentina
where the new republics also committed themselves fundamentally to extermi-
nating the indigenous people. In Bolivia, it wasn't possible to do this so they kept
the indigenous people in a condition of feudal bondage, one established by the
colonial regime. For this reason, the republic was a lie, it was actually a republic for
nobles, for the whites, but for the people it continued being a form of colonialism. . . .
Concretely, our new constitution discovered this fact. That is to say, the new consti-
tution is not just a recognition of certain historical conditions, but a discovery
that the country itself was based on lies.

Antonio Peredo, 2009

By the time Evo Morales was inaugurated at the end of January 2006, the mechanism through which MAS's revolutionary project would be launched had long been predetermined. Throughout the 2005 campaign, leaders from the indigenous and labor movements that made up the Pact of Unity had made the promise to convene a constituent assembly in order to write a new national constitution as the basis for their collective support of MAS. In the case of social movements like the Federación Nacional de Mujeres Campesinas de Bolivia-Bartolina Sisa, the call for a new constitution dedicated to indigenous rights and the juridification of ethnic, gender, and linguistic identities was closely connected to its organizational ethos. In the case of other Pact members, especially the Confederación Sindical Única de Trabajadores Campesinos de Bolivia (CSUTCB), the push for a new constitution as the foundation for change was a political move that was historically revealing precisely because it was so ideologically awkward.

The CSUTCB had been established in 1979 under the leadership of Genaro Flores in opposition to government-supported peasant unions that had historically formed part of a conservative–peasant alliance known as the Military-Peasant Pact. The CSUTCB went on to reinvigorate the decimated Central Obrera Boliviana (COB) during the reestablishment of democracy in the early 1980s, thereby linking indigenous-peasant politics even more closely to a program of change centered on socialist economic planning, workers' control over the means of production, and the restoration of communal land tenure. As with other social movements with roots in Bolivia's various leftist traditions, the CSUTCB had never—before the 2005 elections—focused its ideological attention on rights-based constitution-making, since it adhered to the classic Marxist antipathy to state law in general, and claims for (bourgeois) rights in particular. Yet by the mid-2000s, shifts on the broader regional and global landscape had profoundly impacted Bolivian politics in ways that narrowed the grounds on which the plurinational state's democratic and cultural revolution could be articulated.

As the legal scholar Ran Hirschl has argued (2004), the decline of support for leftist, grassroots political action gave way during the years leading up to the end of the Cold War to a replacement model that channeled demands for change into the instruments and logics of law. This, according to Hirschl, represented a profound historical shift, since the development and contestation of what he calls "mega-politics" had traditionally been reserved for the various, and uncertain, mechanisms of popular organization. But because grassroots political action is by its nature unpredictable and often associated with violence, Hirschl argues, elites in various countries, supported by international institutions, began to push for the "judicialization of mega-politics" as a way to preserve order amid widespread social and political uncertainty. This basic reorientation of sociopolitical change under the rubric of law gave rise, eventually, to what Hirschl calls "juristocracy": the emergence of a new logic of governance in which rights-based law becomes the only legitimate framework within which political claims can be articulated and, even more consequentially, new structures of political rule justified.

By the time of Morales's election victory in 2005, however, the era of revolution by constitution had lost much of the novelty that characterized, for example, the constitutionalization of democratic transition and postconflict reconciliation in South Africa (one of Hirschl's country studies). Instead, the MAS government took power in early 2006 at a time when rights-based constitution-making had itself become a kind of hegemonic model for new or refounded states, a model that was being aggressively promoted by a wide range of actors, including international organizations, engaged academics, regional organizations, national development agencies, and transnational good governance NGOs.

For example, a little-known unit called the Constitution-Building Processes Programme of the Swedish intergovernmental organization International IDEA (Institute for Democracy and Electoral Assistance) worked behind the scenes under the guise of technical assistance to shape the form and content of what became the 2009 Bolivian constitution. From its small office in La Paz's Calacoto neighborhood, IDEA's Bolivia team introduced constitutional models that it had developed for other countries during earlier periods in the post–Cold War. Since the importance of constitution-making for managing sociopolitical transition had already been well established, International IDEA focused its attention on developing constitutional tool kits and normative primers that could be readily adapted to each new constitutional process.

Throughout the contested 2006–7 Constituent Assembly in Bolivia until well into the process of implementation in the years after 2009, IDEA-Bolivia representatives worked closely with MAS government officials and members of the Plurinational Legislative Assembly to ensure that the 411-article constitution that was eventually adopted closely followed, at least structurally, a blueprint guided by the principles of inclusivity, human and collective rights, and power-sharing between different branches of government and different sectors of society.

Yet if it is true, as Ricardo Tito Atahuichi Salvatierra (2007: i) has argued, that Bolivia's new constitution was "an organ of democratic power constituted, at its base, by the power of the people, who possess absolute sovereignty," what does it mean that this sovereign power was translated into the categories of law and confined within the four corners of a new social contract whose normative footprints bore the marks of the global push to make constitutionalization itself the basis for socioeconomic transformation? In general, there were three major consequences that were key to understanding the role of law throughout the trajectory of Bolivia's process of change.

First, at the level of everyday practices of governance, juridification imposed a set of expectations about the relationship between state policy and state action that had the effect of transposing the public sphere from the street and plaza to nondescript meeting rooms and judicial offices and, at the same time, reducing what took place in these para-public spheres to a series of legal technocratic processes that relied problematically on a set of assumptions about institutional legitimacy and the integrity of legal interpretation. For example, much of the juridification of Bolivia's process of change was entrusted to two small units in the Vice Ministry of Justice and Fundamental Rights within the Ministry of Justice. There, a handful of young lawyers were tasked with legalizing the process of change at the normative microlevel through a law-by-law and article-by-article process of legal harmonization: How did the entire corpus of existing Bolivian law conform, or not, to the fundamental ideological principles codified in the new constitution? As Annelise Riles's (2000) study of the documentary legalization of human rights principles in Fiji demonstrated, the quotidian mechanisms of juridification create their own context for what Sally Engle Merry (2006b) has called "vernacularization" by translating broader ideological and ethical values, including those committed to revolutionary change, into forms of practice that are concerned with quite different problems of statutory construction, conflict of laws, and the need to "solidify" (Riles 2000: 86) legal texts through the careful consideration of specific words, phrasings, and jurisprudential references.

Second, the constitutionalization of sovereign power in Bolivia revealed an ongoing tension between the image of constitutional law in the post–Cold War and its more divergent realities. Throughout the 2005 general elections, during the violence surrounding the drafting of the new constitution in 2006–7, and in the years leading up to and after its adoption in 2009, the constitution—first as idea, then as draft, then as the new social contract in force—was invested by its proponents with many meanings, including a kind of enlightened utopianism. The constitution was believed to be at the same time the practical mechanism par excellence—potential or actual—through which the process of structural change in Bolivia should take place and a normative-ideological mirror in which a long list of historical injustices was reflected, including the oppression of the vulnerable, the theft of land, cultural genocide, and the spoliation of Mother Earth.

As Samuel Guarayo Aruquipo, MAS president for La Paz Department, put it in mid-January 2009, on the eve of the national constitutional referendum,

With the new constitution, thousands of people will become literate, [Bolivia] will be the third country in Latin America to be free of illiteracy. . . . But look at what the former governments were like—they were shameful, they had blood on the face [sangre en la cara] because of what they did to this country. So how can they [the opposition] question this government? How can they attack our president when the constitution demonstrates at an international level that everything we are doing is correct now in this country? This fact dignifies our comrade Evo Morales, it dignifies our country. . . . On January 25 [the day of the referendum], for the first time in the republican life of Bolivia, Bolivians, each one of us, will get to decide on this new constitution that was demanded by native and indigenous peoples, by the workers, because they were always excluded from the protection of the law. This new constitution is a great responsibility, and on January 25 the majority of Bolivians are going to vote for it with much love for their country and with much courage because we will never return to the past.

Yet as the utopian euphoria of 2009 around the constitution gave way to the 2011 TIPNIS conflict, in which the government's ideological principles confronted both political economic realities and a kind of localization of power that reflected small-scale interests rather than sweeping sentiments of love of country, a certain disenchantment took root, the kind that always follows from the realization that a utopia can never be a guide to policy-making. Indeed, something similar accompanied the disenchantment that followed closely on the heels of an earlier constitutional revolution in the hemisphere. As Gordon Wood explains:

The republican revolution was the greatest utopian movement in American history. The revolutionaries aimed at nothing less than a reconstitution of American society. . . . They sought to construct a society and governments based on virtue and disinterested public leadership and to set in motion a moral movement that would eventually be felt around the globe. . . . But the ink . . . was scarcely dry before many of the revolutionary leaders began expressing doubts about the possibility of realizing these high hopes. The American people seemed incapable of the degree of virtue needed for republicanism. Too many were unwilling to respect the authority of their new elected leaders and were too deeply involved in trade and moneymaking to think beyond their narrow interests or their neighborhoods and to concern themselves with the welfare of their states or their country. (Wood 1993: 229)

At the same time, the association of constitutionalism as such with positive structural change, an association that was, as we have seen, fostered as much at the level of global activism as it was in debates in Bolivia's Constituent Assembly, began to weaken in the years after the 2011 TIPNIS conflict. This was not because of the simple instrumentalization of law by the government, either in order to pursue a hypocritical policy of resource extractivism or in order to consolidate its political power in the face of presidential term limits (themselves codified in the constitution). Rather, it was because the idea that constitutionalism was a necessary condition for a particular kind of emancipatory politics, one based in equality, respect for difference, and the full palette of rights, turned out to be flawed both conceptually and historically. Indeed, as a result of his important ethnographic studies of the first post–Cold War constitutions, those of the new states created from the former Yugoslavia, Robert Hayden showed that in certain cases, "constitutionalism itself can be anti-democratic" (1992: 673).

And finally, the constitutionalization of sovereign power in Bolivia during the period 2006–15 reaffirmed a set of subtle points about the working and limitations of law made most forcefully by the British Marxist historian E. P. Thompson at the end of his classic study of the English Black Act of 1723. After demonstrating in close historical detail how a new landed Whig elite in Walpolean England used the law as a sharp-edged instrument to protect and advance its class interests, Thompson is forced, against both his historical and Marxist instincts, to acknowledge something surprising: that the landed gentry was, on occasion, prevented from using the law to benefit its political economic interests because of what Thompson (1977: 262) calls the "logic" of law. As he puts it, "class relations were expressed, not in any way one likes, but *through the forms of law*; and the law, like other institutions which from time to time can be seen as mediating (and masking) existent class relations . . , has its own characteristics, its own independent history and logic of evolution" (1977: 262; emphasis in original).

Thompson uses this insight to reflect more generally on the limitations of what he calls a "highly schematic" (1977: 259) Marxist approach to understanding law. Even if the law is often used as an instrument of class power, it also, on occasion, constrains the interests of the powerful, an important difference that critically distinguishes the rule of law from "the exercise of direct unmediated force (arbitrary imprisonment, the employment of troops against the crowd, torture, and those other conveniences of power with which we are all conversant)" (1977: 265). Yet, as will be seen in different places throughout this book, the ethnography of Bolivia's constitutional revolution revealed something like an opposite dynamic at work—yet one shaped by precisely the same kind of "complex and contradictory" (1977: 264) logics that Thompson encountered in his history of the Black Act.

If the law can constrain the exercise of power by ruling elites, it can also constrain the exercise of power in the interests of revolutionary transformation. As Thompson knew all too well, the "exercise of direct unmediated force" had been an important dimension of twentieth-century revolutionary change at least since Lenin and later the Soviet state had made the "dictatorship of the proletariat" the result of "class struggle [taken] to its logical conclusion" (Lenin 1975c: 489). But as we have seen, the end of the Cold War also brought an end to the period in which certain forms of "direct unmediated force" could be ideologically legitimated as the primary mechanism of social change; what remained, instead, was the transformative promise of law in general, and of rights-based constitutional law in particular. Yet as the ethnography of Bolivia's juridified process of change suggests, the reinscription of law as the foundation for structural transformation exposes and reinforces a double limitation: that of law, whose logics are often ill-suited to the task, and that of revolution itself, since its constitutionalization denudes it of what the French Montagnard Louis Antoine de Saint-Just (2004) described as *l'esprit de la révolution*, its vital essence, its creative and unpredictable collective passions.

THE HAU OF LAW: THE CONSTITUTION AS TALISMAN

The working of this double limitation at the center of Bolivia's process of change did not, however, alter an important fact: that the country's 2009 constitution proposed a remarkable, beguiling, and radically new social contract. In the rush to unpack and problematize Bolivia's "third revolution" at the level of practices of governance, political economic compromises, and ethnic tensions, among others, the landmark nature of the 2009 constitution has often been obscured. And beyond its many innovations as a legal and political charter, the constitution should be understood in yet another way: as an artifact that was invested with a range of fluid and shifting social and ideological meanings. In this way, the constitution itself—as object, as talisman, in certain instances, as fetish—acquired its own power; it became, ontologically, agentive. Thus, in this alternative register, Bolivia's 2009 constitution functioned not as law at all but as a materialization that interwove a particular narrative about Bolivia's past into a particular vision of its unfolding future.

In December 2008, I participated in an event at the Alianza Francesa in La Paz to commemorate the sixtieth anniversary of the Universal Declaration of Human Rights. In his remarks, the president of the Permanent Assembly of Human Rights of Bolivia (APDHB), the potosino Methodist bishop Rolando Villena Villegas, who would later become the country's Defensor del Pueblo (see chapter 5), gave an expansive account of the constitution's novelties.

As human rights activists, we want to deeply honor the final text of the constitution, which will be put to a national referendum early next year, because beginning in its first part, the first chapter, the first section, we are shown the model for a new state that we are going to build; we are talking without any question about the complete refoundation of the state. It is in this spirit, something that seems to us very important, that the first, second, and third articles say that Bolivia is composed of all Bolivian men and women, isn't that right? This means all the urban areas, with their different social classes, the native indigenous and peasant nations and peoples, the intercultural and Afro-Bolivian communities. The theme of gender, without any question beginning right from the first article, is very important, especially for a society like ours that is used to practicing a macho culture that has violated the human rights and dignity of women. We believe that the content of the constitution systematically addresses the rights of all the sectors of Bolivian society that have suffered violations, that have been ignored. . . . It's true that there is a large public debate right now about the constitution, but most of the opposition is based on a lack of knowledge about what it contains, its humanistic content, its political content, also its anthropological content, all of which mean that the country's new Magna Carta will be approved next year. What this will mean, concretely, is that the content of the new constitution will allow us, despite our country's limitations, to build a different Bolivia, an inclusive Bolivia, a Bolivia that is respectful of all human rights, all liberties, all identities.

Bolivia's constitution was radical in ways that were both deeply specific to Bolivian legal, political, and social history and of a kind with post–Cold War constitutionalism more generally, which by 2006 had become, as we have seen, an institutionalized and professionalized global movement shaped by the experiences of the early 1990s, particularly South Africa's "globalizing constitutionalism" (Klug 2000), conceptualized and legitimated through the writings of internationalist legal scholars and social theorists, and promoted by a range of influential institutions, including the World Bank, IMF, and the United Nations Development Programme (UNDP).

The uniqueness of Bolivia's new Magna Carta was dramatically announced even before the first article—that is, in the preamble, which, even by the standards of post–Cold War rights-based constitutions, was historically striking. The overall sentiment of the preamble to Bolivia's 2009 constitution was one of liminal excess; it was a poetic ode to the spirit of normative promiscuity invoked by Antonio Peredo (see the introduction)—*we just couldn't say no.*

It drew a sweeping arc across the centuries, linking the late eighteenth-century "indigenous anticolonial uprising" led by Túpac Katari and Bartolina Sisa with the "water and October wars" (meaning the conflicts of 1999–2000 and 2003; see the introduction). What followed was a veritable cornucopia of values on which the new state was being founded: "respect and equality among all . . . sovereignty, dignity, complementarity, solidarity, harmony, and equity in the distribution and redistribution of social goods, in which the search for living well predominates; respect for the economic, social, legal, political, and cultural pluralism of all our land's inhabitants; [and] collective coexistence with access to water, work, education, health, and lodging for all."

The preamble then asserted that the "new [Bolivian] state" represented an alternative epoch, a different stage in history, in a way that subverts the ethical implications of Johannes Fabian's (1983) critique of cultural timeworking. Instead of pushing back against the denial of coevalness, that is, the process through which hegemonic societies construct a multi-temporal world in which only they can inhabit a privileged and advanced present, the Bolivian constitution fully embraced it as a normative value. In "leaving in the past" colonialism, republicanism, and neoliberalism to become something sui generis in the world, a "Unitary Social State of Plurinational Communitarian Law," the constitution carved out its own juridical space-time in which, as the conclusion to the preamble put it, a "new history" had begun.

Yet Bolivia's new history did not begin and end with the preamble to the constitution—its contours were fleshed out across the vastness of its articles, chapters, rights, and obligations. Indeed, although India's postindependence (1949) constitution was by far the longest in the world measured by number of words (146,385), according to the Comparative Constitutions Project (CCP), it only managed to guarantee forty-four fundamental rights throughout its 444 articles, while Bolivia's constitution guaranteed eighty-eight fundamental rights across 411 articles (Comparative Constitutions Project 2017). Despite the fact that the outcome was never in doubt, in the months leading up to the late January 2009 national referendum, different articles of the new constitution were the focus of intense and revealing public debate.

One of the most heated exchanges concerned Article 398, which was formulated in the alternative in order to be the subject of its own vote in the referendum. This article was an attack on the large latifundia of Santa Cruz Department, where vast holdings of agricultural land and cattle ranches formed the basis for the department's enormous wealth and regional power. The two alternatives to Article 398 both imposed a series of social tests on the validity of large landholdings: they were to be given legal protection only if they served the "collective interest," contributed to the "development of the country," and fulfilled a "socioeconomic function." Bolivians were asked to choose between option A, which set of a limit of 10,000 hectares for ownership, and option B, which set a limit of 5,000 hectares (in the referendum, option B received over 80 percent of the votes). In promoting the importance of Article 398, Evo Morales explained:

> Let's say that we have a *camba*, comrade Isaac . . . who has 100,000 hectares . . . and lives in Santa Cruz. If the Bolivian people vote yes on 5,000 hectares, Isaac will have to return 95,000 to the Bolivian state for the people who don't have any land. . . . The agricultural revolution must deal with nonproductive latifundia. If we don't deal with the latifundia, how can we speak of a revolution? This is why we all have an enormous responsibility to approve the new constitution. (*La Razón*, December 19, 2008)[4]

Another round of debate involved Articles 277, 278, and 279, which established the basis on which departments would relate to the state and each other within a system of autonomy. The various positions on the question of autonomy also reflected the wider ongoing conflict between the MAS government in La Paz and the opposition centered in Sucre and Santa Cruz. Carlos Dabdoub Arrien, the leading intellectual of Santa Cruz's anti-government movement and one of the authors of the department's own 2008 autonomy statute, argued that the proposed structure for autonomy in the new constitution, "a spurious document with no legality," was defective and contradictory because it gave the central government a basic role in its realization. As he dramatically put it, he would vote against the autonomy provisions and the constitution itself in order to preserve his "liberty, [his] religious faith, and the future of [his] country" (*La Razón*, January 9, 2009).[5]

Despite the fact that, relative to other South American countries, the topic of religion and religious leaders did not generally shape public debate in Bolivia, the prominent place of the Pachamama in the constitution did generate considerable controversy among the country's nonindigenous, particularly urban, populations. As the paceño Jaime Macías put it, the point of contention was threefold: first, that the constitution "announces the Mother Earth as 'sacred' and describes her in capital letters, in the first person, treating her like a god/person"; second, the constitution "gives the place of honor to the Pachamama by placing her name before that of God. . . . Moreover, the constitution refers to 'our Pachamama,' treating it like a settled fact that all Bolivians accept Pachamama as our little female god!"; and third, "indirectly, [the constitution] makes a comparison between God and the Pachamama by mentioning them together, which treats them as two equivalent 'spiritual beings'" (*La Razón*, January 11, 2009, A6).

Finally, there was considerable discussion during this period around the concept of *jurisdicción indígena originaria campesina*, a radical move to create a separate and independent legal system within Bolivia, in part by giving full legal recognition to existing nonstate systems of law and dispute resolution in all their historical and cultural heterogeneity. Article 179, an extraordinary provision, made the state and indigenous legal systems structurally equal, while Articles 190 and 192 gave the indigenous legal system(s) almost complete jurisprudential independence and required all public officials to respect decisions made by indigenous legal authorities. (The constitution also recognized a third distinct legal system in Articles 186–89, an "agro-environmental" system, with its own jurisdictional hierarchy, supreme court, and competence over disputes related to landownership, natural resources, and issues that "threaten the ecological system and the conservation of species or animals." However, the agro-environmental legal system did not have the same coequal status as that of the state and indigenous systems.)

Valentín Ticona Colque, a former high-ranking ayllu authority from the north of Potosí Department, who was the vice minister of community justice, made the government's extended case for jurisdicción indígena originaria campesina:

It is a system of norms and procedures that regulates the social life of the indigenous people based on principles that are not known to the state legal system, and because of this lack of knowledge and understanding, the state legal system has always denied the rights of [Bolivia's] indigenous populations. Indigenous law is oral, free, preventive, restorative, and public; its authorities serve their communities and they are not paid. It is a form of justice that does not judge but only guides, or directs the process of justice. By recognizing indigenous law like this, we will eliminate lynchings and killings because there will be many more active indigenous legal authorities. From time immemorial, this type of justice has existed in the communities even if it was always necessary to coordinate with the local state prosecutors and judges, some of whom understood the reality of indigenous justice, others not. In reality, [the constitution] is only recognizing practices that have always existed within the ayllus. (*La Razón*, January 11, 2009)

By contrast, one of the leading opponents of Bolivia's radical legal reorientation was Jorge Lazarte, a prolific writer and public intellectual who was at the time a professor of political science at La Paz's elite private university, the Universidad Católica Boliviana, and the former vice president of the Constituent Assembly (2006–7). Echoing the sentiments of many legal scholars and urban intellectuals, even those who supported, in general, the idea of a plural society that promoted the rights of Bolivia's historically marginalized indigenous populations, Lazarte's critique raised a number of conceptual, practical, and political questions:

There are various problems with what the constitution calls community justice, because it assumes a symmetrical relation to the state legal system, something that weakens the idea of law. It's always been true that the decisions of state law must be obeyed by every person and every authority in the country. But [with the new constitution] we will end up with a system that favors so-called community justice even if it's not valid for the whole population. For a country to be properly organized, you can't speak of two parallel systems of justice, there has to be only one system that covers all the others, they all can't be on the same level. At the same time, no one knows what this so-called community justice consists of exactly simply because there's not a single norm that says *this is what it is*, that defines it and its principles and its procedures. It's a form of law based only on customary practices [*usos y costumbres*], a spoken law. It's not codified anywhere. (*La Razón*, January 11, 2009; emphasis in original)

Yet beyond these and many other debates around specific articles, debates that revealed the contested significance of juridical content that would soon form the architecture of the country's ongoing process of change, Bolivia's new constitution was at the same time undergoing a different kind of transformation. It had begun during the battles of 2006–7 in Sucre, when the very idea of a new social contract provoked various forms of what Daniel Goldstein (2004) has described as collective "spectacular" performance. Some fought for the possibility of a new constitution as the embodiment of a future they had both longed for in a less structured way and had been taught (with the rise of indigenous rights mobilization) to long for as members of vulnerable populations protected under international law.

Others fought against the possibility, indeed the likelihood, of a new constitution as the embodiment of a future they had long feared, one that would bring an end to decades, if not centuries, of ethnic privilege, the monopolization of wealth and political power, and the comfort that came from a sense of historical continuity.

And still others—many others, perhaps the majority of Bolivians—did not fight either for or against the new constitution. From the vantage point of places like the north of Potosí Department—that is, for most of Bolivia's rural provinces, remote and crumbling *reducciones*, and scattered aggregated settlements—news that university students in Sucre were battling with police as part of a quixotic campaign to restore the city as the country's "full capital" was greeted, when it was greeted at all, with varying degrees of bewilderment.

Nevertheless, the differentiated experiences that accompanied the drafting, ratification, and promulgation of Bolivia's new constitution revealed that with each passing month, and with each turning point in its social "fabrication" (Pottage 2004), the constitution was being transformed into a cultural-juridical artifact that was infused with something that transcended its contested normative content, something like the spirit, or *hau*, that Marcel Mauss famously invoked in his 1925 study of gift exchange economies.

As Mauss argued, human societies had traditionally been structured through social relations that were represented in objects that were exchanged according to various logics of reciprocity, mutual trust, and ongoing obligations. Yet beyond the members of society, even beyond the Geertzian webs of meaning that were created through—or as—interconnected social relations, it was the spirit of the things exchanged that endured in "minds, as much as in . . . actions, either on occasions of qualitative leaps of sweeping crises in . . . life trajectories, or in the dull routine of eventless everyday life" (Santos 1995: 473). Mauss himself interpreted this insight as one that prevented law from being reduced either to its procedural instrumentalities or to its function as the safeguard of modern capitalist economies, since the law was essentially, as he put it, moral. That is, in regulating society through the spirit of things in a kind of never-ending circulation, the law ensured a "happy medium [prevailed] between the ideal and the real" and thus that the "heart of normal social life" continued to beat through "sentiments that are in action all the time" (Mauss 1967: 67–68).

The new Bolivian constitution likewise emerged as an object whose spirit circulated among different social networks in ways that expressed sentiments in action—even if these sentiments, and the visions for society that they articulated, were diffuse, in conflict, and far from the kind of unifying organizing force that Mauss had imagined. But simply as object, in the first instance, the Bolivian constitution took on a particular, and remarkable, materiality. For the different constituencies at the heart of Bolivia's contested process of change, the constitution-as-object very much spoke for itself—*res ipsa loquitur*.

Beginning in October 2008, the MAS government began mass producing copies of the constitution after it had been approved by the Bolivian Congress in preparation for the January 2009 national referendum. It was a 10.5 cm × 15 cm booklet printed with minimal design on recycled paper. On the front cover, the "Republic of Bolivia" and the "Constituent Assembly" were the collective authors of the "new political constitution of the state." The front cover also displayed, as was tradition, the republican coat of arms; on the back cover, the word *yes* appeared over the waving Bolivian tricolor, the accent above the "í" a square box that had been checked to reinforce the point that the government fully intended the "free distribution" of the booklet to encourage people to vote for its adoption some months later.

This artifact from the historic period of liminal transition—that is, the period of passing between Bolivia's republican and plurinational incarnations— was published as an object whose intended agency was embodied in its very form. Its size was carefully chosen to be pocket-sized, and therefore capable of being easily and readily carried in everyday life, but not too small, for fear that its significance would be reduced. Many Bolivian laws, or collections of laws, were published and sold on street corners in true pocket-sized editions, measuring 8 cm × 10 cm, but this possibility was likely rejected in favor of a version whose size would best lend itself to a process of objectification and distribution that would "motivate inferences, responses, [and] interpretations" (Küchler 2004: 240–41).

By 2015, six years into its contested life, the Bolivian constitution had become a ubiquitous talisman—an artifact to be kept close, displayed at ritually significant moments, wielded as a prop to support various arguments, and, on occasion, actually opened, so that its normative contents could be reverently, mockingly, or indifferently consulted. As object, it was no longer produced and distributed like a cheap legal penny dreadful, its rough covers hiding prurient tales of refoundation and devotion to the Pachamama. Instead, the talisman had undergone subtle but important material modifications.

While the government maintained the harmonious balance in size of 10.5 cm × 15 cm, the most common version was now printed with more substantial semi-glossy white covers. And the much greater expense to produce the constitution-as-cultural-juridical-artifact was reflected not only in the quality of the paper. It was also apparent in the 2015 edition's design, publication values, and weight, since its 411 articles were printed with double spaces between individual articles and between sections of articles, which required 203 pages, whereas the 2008 official version crammed what was then 410 articles into 132 pages using both narrower margins—the text came almost to both edges of the page—and single spacing throughout.

The text on the front and back covers of the 2015 edition of the constitution also showed key transformations. While the traditional (that is, republican) coat of arms was retained, its symbolic status having been reaffirmed in Article 6(1), its size was greatly diminished and it had been moved from the center to the top of the front cover. However, it was no longer the coat of arms of the Republic of Bolivia, which did not exist, but of the Plurinational State of Bolivia. Most important, however, is the fact that the 2015 materialization of the constitution incorporated key design elements of the government's robust propaganda program, which saw the Ministry of Communication develop into a world-class producer of ideological objects including posters, documentaries, public billboards, television programs, and branded apparel.

Here, the front and back covers of the 2015 edition featured what is certainly an unintentionally ironic high modernist composition that seemed to owe something to both geometric abstractionism and Op art, since it took the by-then iconic seven colors of the wiphala and broke them up into pixilated squares, which seemed to be spilling off the bottom of the cover. On both the first page after the copyright page and the back cover, a new symbol appeared: a design that looked vaguely like a Sanskrit swastika, created in this case not with squares but with brush strokes of wiphala color that gave the impression of rightward rotation. Finally, reflecting yet another major shift from 2008 to 2015, the fully articulated version of the constitution invited its citizen-votaries to "follow us" on both Facebook and Twitter, since the hau of the constitution respected the same logics of circulation as other spirits of things in the digital age.

Yet if Bolivia's new constitution became an object with a spirit that traveled among the currents of conflict and hope that flowed through Bolivia's process of change, it was a form of circulation by "continual displacement" in which the constitution-as-object successively took on and shed points of reference through differential "chain[s] of inscription" that marked key moments in the struggle over which "involuted fictions" would take precedence and which ones would be suppressed (Pottage 2004: 18–19). For example, by 2015, the government's constitutional technocrats were at work on a ten-year project to reconcile the nation's residual republican jurisprudence with the new provisions of the constitution. Laws that were believed to be consistent with the new norms would be retained; those that could be harmonized through statutory modification would be reformed; and those that clearly violated the fundamental values of the new plurinational state would be stricken from the "chain of inscription." This was a project that relied on an evolving sense of fabrication at the core of the MAS government in which the constitution was no longer the same kind of talisman that it was in 2009—that is, an object whose spirit expressed millenarian upheaval. Instead, it was in the process of becoming a revolutionary artifact that embodied the fiction of long-term, even bureaucratic, production. As Cecilia Urquieta, the thirty-five-year-old head of the Office of Constitutional Development, explained to me:

> It is important to make a distinction between that which is constituted [by the constitution] and the constitution itself as the legitimate source of new norms. Regarding the first, we inherited over 85 percent of the existing, pre-revolutionary norms, primarily in codes. But regarding the second, which is for us now much more important, the constitution will be the source of many new codes or those that replace existing ones. Some of the existing codes are going to be easier to replace than others.

Yet at different moments and in different places in the process of "continual displacement," the hau of the constitution was inscribed in terms of radically opposing "notion[s] of value" (Mauss 1967: 69). For the militants at the head of Sucre's dual struggle for the recognition of its historical suffering and the restoration of its rightful status as Bolivia's most important, indeed capital, city, the constitution was an object that materialized historical injustice, political charlatanism, and La Paz's duplicity toward the country's other regions. As Aydée Nava Andrade, the mayor of Sucre, explained in early January 2009:

> The government says the constitution will construct a new state. But for who? Just for La Paz? What about Sucre? This city lives on tourism, but we have an airport that uses solar power, which means that when it rains or is cloudy, tourists can't arrive on planes. Do we have adequate roads? What will the constitution do about that? The constitution is actually only for La Paz, like it has always been for us here in Chuquisaca. For me, the new

FIGURE 2.1 Anti-MAS poster in Santa Cruz's historic Plaza 24 de Septiembre imagines a descent into political tyranny, social chaos, and cultural savagery if the new constitution is approved, January 2009.

constitution is yet another imposition. What they are doing is not demo-cratic, the constitution is not really legal, it doesn't have legal legitimacy for every region. For us, the new constitution is yet another form of pressure [from La Paz], *in this case one that also involves pressure from the social movements* [based in the La Paz highlands]. *The new constitution will mean that we are practically in a form of authoritarianism. Here in Sucre, the people will vote against the constitution because they want something the constitution cannot give them: a Bolivia in which power is truly diffused, decentralized, and built upon an autonomous solidarity* [autonomía soli-daria], *not an autonomy that is built by destroying the other side.*

FIGURE 2.2 A militant from the Unión Juvenil Cruceñista (UJC) defiles a draft copy of the new constitution during anti-government mobilizations in Santa Cruz, February 2008.

Finally, the process of continual displacement that objectified and reobjectified the Bolivian constitution took its most charged forms in Santa Cruz, especially in the months leading up to the January 2009 referendum, when the range of involuted fictions that made up its notion of values was at its widest and most volatile. Here, the spirit of the constitution was a malevolent and terrifying one, a specter that loomed over a country on the brink of civil war, threatening to unleash across the land the full spectrum of apocalyptic pestilences, including communism, oppression, narcotrafficking, sadism, tyranny, powerlessness, terrorism, usurpation, cynicism, illegality, hate, and the denial of liberty, democracy, and human rights (see figure 2.1).

For the foot soldiers of Santa Cruz's separatist Camba movement, the young militants of the Unión Juvenil Cruceñista (UJC), the fight against this great evil involved destroying its talismanic materialization with fire, or, on occasion, by desecrating it (see figure 2.2).

In March 2004, during the relatively calm months of Carlos Mesa's care-taker presidency following the cataclysmic rupture of Black October 2003, an important seminar was held in the heart of late-republican Sucre at the Instituto de la Judicatura de Bolivia (IJB), an institution that served multiple functions in Bolivia's former legal order, including training judges, organizing judicial capacity-building, and promoting debate on sociolegal questions through public events and publications. It was located in a modest building within several blocks of the Bolivian Supreme Court (which became the Supreme Justice Tribunal); the Department of Chuquisaca's Justice Tribunal, the department's court of last resort; the office of Derechos Reales, which regulated the system of property rights and managed the cumbersome process of land titling and mortgage registration; and hundreds of nearly identical one- and two-room offices, in which lawyers engaged in a desperate, often futile, wait for clients in the daily struggle to earn a living from their profession.

The March 2004 event, which was co-organized with the National Agrarian Tribunal (which became the Agro-Environmental Tribunal) and the Programa de Investigación Estratégica en Bolivia (PIEB), an influential research institution and policy NGO based in La Paz, brought together leading Bolivian researchers and government ministers to consider the question of "community justice," with the objective of producing a draft law that would form the basis for future policy-making and legal reform. The participants included René Orellana Halkyer, a future high-ranking government official and ambassador who had recently defended a PhD in legal anthropology at the University of Amsterdam based on a study of interlegality and semi-autonomous social fields among Quechua communities (Orellana 2004); Juan Antonio Chahín Lupo, former vice minister of justice; Elba Flores Gonzáles, a researcher with the Centro de Estudios Jurídicos e Investigación Social (CEJIS), a Santa Cruz institution with a particular focus on sociolegal questions concerning lowland indigenous communities; Ramiro Molina Rivero, an anthropologist and prolific public intellectual; and Xavier Albó, the Jesuit linguist, anthropologist, and historian who had cofounded the La Paz–based Centro de Investigación y Promoción del Campesinado (CIPCA) in 1970 in order to "search for the most effective means so that Bolivia's peasants will find the proper channels for their structural development and integration in the country" (CIPCA 2017).

The 2004 seminar on community justice took place against the backdrop of four important historical and legal considerations. First, Bolivia's early (1991) ratification of International Labor Organization (ILO) Convention 169, the "Indigenous and Tribal Peoples Convention," had focused national attention on the problem of community justice or customary law (*derecho consuetudinario*) at least since the early 1990s, since the convention made (in Articles 8 and 9) the recognition and protection of indigenous legal systems a principal means through which the state should "protect the rights of [indigenous peoples] and . . . guarantee respect for their integrity."

Second, these discussions around community justice in the early 1990s led fairly quickly to significant institutional action when Bolivia's last republican constitution, the 1967 constitution, was amended to reconfigure in both form and content Article 171. In its original formulation, Article 171 declared that the "state recognizes and guarantees the existence of the peasant union organizations" (*organizaciones sindicales campesinas*). However, soon after Bolivia ratified ILO 169 during the presidency of Jaime Paz Zamora, Article 171 became the basis for debate since it was the one place in the existing constitution in which the state seemed to recognize the existence of important nonstate institutions within what was otherwise a "unitary Republic."

Thus, in the waning years of the Paz Zamora regime, the first reform to the 1967 constitution was proposed (Law 1473, April 1, 1993), in which Article 171 was completely transformed. In a sense, the new Article 171 represented an attempt to encapsulate most of the central normative provisions of ILO 169 into a single constitutional article. The new article took legal force two years later during the first Goni government with the strong support of Víctor Hugo Cárdenas, the indigenous Aymara vice president and former katarista leader. With the elaboration of the complete text of the reformed 1967 constitution (through Law 1615, February 6, 1995), the new Article 171 (in section III) articulated what had become the internationally standardized language of ILO 169–derived legal pluralism: "the natural authorities of the indigenous and peasant communities will be able to exercise the functions of administration and application of their own norms as an alternative solution to conflicts, in conformity with their customs and procedures, *as long as these are not contrary to this Constitution and the nation's laws*" (emphasis added).

Third, because it was necessary to put the principles of the new Article 171 into practice through subsequent legislation, the Code of Criminal Procedure was later amended in March of 1999, during the government of Hugo Banzer Suárez. Its new Article 28 recognized in Bolivian law, for the first time, the concepts of both "community justice" (*justicia comunitaria*) and "indigenous customary law" (*derecho consuetudinario indígena*). More precisely, Article 28 drew a distinction between "community justice" as a new jurisdictional category and "indigenous customary law" as the set of norms and practices that were given formal recognition, as long as several procedural requirements were met: (1) that the particular crime or misdeed (*el delito o la falta*) had been committed within an indigenous or peasant community; (2) that the crime involved a violation only between members of the same community; (3) that the process of conflict resolution was overseen by the community's recognized authorities; and (4) that the terms of such resolution did not violate the "fundamental rights and guarantees" of the national constitution. The use of the category of "indigenous customary law" in Article 28 reflected the influence among Bolivian legal scholars and social scientists of scholarship within wider Latin American debates, particularly the writings of the Mexican sociologist Rodolfo Stavenhagen, who had written extensively on the concept in a series of widely cited publications (e.g., Stavenhagen 1988, 1990).[6]

Finally, the 2004 gathering in Sucre took place in the aftermath of the 2002 general elections, in which Evo Morales's surprising second-place showing had forced the question of indigenous rights onto the national agenda, less as a strategy for resistance and more as a framework for future governance. Although the years between the resignation of Goni in October 2003 and the elections of 2005 were consumed by political questions of transition as the sun slowly set on republican Bolivia, the writing was on the wall—an epochal shift was coming and it would be one in which the liberal conception of a "unitary Republic" governed by *the* law would have to give way to an ambiguous vision of plural legal orders, multiple legal systems, and unequal autonomies, since concepts like "community justice" and "indigenous customary law" were meant to exclude as much as to include.

Thus, the national seminar on community justice in March 2004 was more a culmination than a beginning. It was the culmination of more than ten years of discussion, local political activism, international and transnational "capacity-building"; debate in the country's op-ed pages; domestic and outside empirical (especially anthropological) research; and voluminous publishing— by Bolivian academics, social movements, indigenous communities, and others—on the status of law as the foundation for cultural revalorization.[7] Yet the seminar was also a culmination in another important sense: it marked the end of a particular way of conceptualizing and promoting legal pluralism in Bolivia, an ILO 169–centric approach in its terminology, its understanding of history, its indebtedness to wider Latin American indigenous rights discourses, and, perhaps most significantly, its conception of the role of the state as the central legal node around which "indigenous customary law" must ultimately revolve.[8]

The draft law that emerged from the 2004 event itself implicitly recognized that it was being written at the end of a distinct sociolegal history, beyond which nothing was at all clear. Although it pushed the normative and institutional capabilities of indigenous customary law as far as they could go, they were still structurally confined within an existing model in which the very terms of diversity were tightly regulated, defined, and subsumed to the interests of the state. For example, the draft law's Article 2 asserted that the basis of legitimacy for indigenous customary law was the fact that Bolivia was a "multiethnic" and "multicultural" society.[9] However, this way of framing diversity within a "unitary Republic" did not fully grasp the approach to pluralism that was being developed outside of elite circles within the social movements that were propelling Bolivia to its 2005 historical rupture.[10]

This alternative, and much more radical, approach to pluralism took the form of "plurinationalism" during the 2006–7 Constituent Assembly, a form that was eventually codified in the new constitution in its very first article. As both concept and logic of governance, plurinationalism would evolve over time. Yet from the first years of the new Morales regime, it was clear that plurinationalism represented a profoundly different vision of both the importance of pluralism as an ideological value and the role that pluralism should play in the construction of the refounded state.

There were two especially striking aspects to plurinationalism. First, the concept imagined the "nation" as the basic unit of diversity. Instead of a mosaic of different cultures or ethnic groups coexisting within a single national identity, plurinationalism anticipated hardened cultural and institutional boundaries that were meant to create both ideological and territorial spaces in which Bolivia's separate nations could preserve their distinct cosmovisions and develop their own autonomous forms of law and governance.[11]

In the context of legal pluralism, plurinationalism was a dramatic departure from the frameworks developed by scholars such as Stavenhagen, Santos, and Moore, since it envisioned the proliferation in Bolivia of fully (not semi) autonomous legal systems (not orders), each with its own independent jurisdictional limits. The idea was to reduce, not promote, "the conception of different legal spaces superimposed, interpenetrated and mixed in our minds, as much as in our actions" (Santos 1995: 473). Plurinationalism formed the basis for a model that went far beyond the "legal pluralism of traditional legal anthropology, in which the different legal orders are conceived as separate entities coexisting in the same political spaces" (Santos 1995: 473). Rather, plurinationalism was a framework in which different legal *systems* in Bolivia would be conceived as separate entities within *different* political spaces.

And second, plurinationalism was based on what might be thought of as a retributive theory of the nation in which the category of "nation" applied only to those populations that had been the subject of marginalization and structural violence across the long arc of Bolivia's colonial and republican histories. These thirty-six "nations and peoples" were specified in Article 5 of the 2009 constitution.[12] As with the other most far-reaching and controversial articles of the constitution (see above), the implications of Article 5 were hotly debated in the weeks before the late January referendum.

Among its critics, the former Movimiento de Izquierda Revolucionaria (MIR) Senator Erika Brockmann argued that it "denationalizes and de-Bolivianizes [*desbolivianiza*] many who were born in our country, it rejects the principle of equality, and it makes the existence of two types of Bolivians official state policy. It reneges on the idea of the Bolivian Nation. The recognition of thirty-six nations will take the country far from the principle of unity in diversity and will instead lead us into fragmentation."

Savina Cuéllar, the self-identifying indigenous prefect of Chuquisaca Department, said she would vote "no" on the new constitution because Article 5 "divides the country into thirty-six nations when what we want is a single homeland [*una sola patria*]."

Víctor Hugo Cárdenas called the new constitution illegal because Article 5 "created a [system of] differentiated citizenship in which indigenous people have greater rights than people who don't have an indigenous origin."

And the alteño sociologist Carlos Hugo Laruta argued that he would vote against the new constitution precisely because "it defines Bolivia as plurinational, that is to say, comprised of many nations, which runs the risk that Bolivia itself will be considered the thirty-seventh nation. Bolivia ought to be indigenous, mestizo, and white to the same degree, and this isn't guaranteed in the new constitution."[13]

Nevertheless, the conceptual shift from the ILO 169–centric approach to a plurinational legal pluralism based on multiple, separate, and independent legal systems was undermined in at least one important respect: the imagined legal systems of Bolivia's thirty-six nations were believed to share similar rules, procedures, and institutional values, a uniformity that was described as "native indigenous peasant justice" (*justicia indígena originaria campesina*). That is, at the same time that the constitution established the basis for a plurinational state with thirty-eight separate and distinct legal systems (including the "ordinary" state system and the "agro-environmental" system), it also introduced a fundamentally monolithic conception of the juridical nature of the thirty-six separate indigenous legal systems. Although the new category of "native indigenous peasant" was the product of a compromise reached in the 2006–7 Constituent Assembly between MAS's indigenous, rural syndicalist, and "intercultural" wings, its extension to law resulted in a framework for legal pluralism that was structurally unprecedented but normatively impoverished, even Orientalist.

By 2015, this basic tension was being keenly felt by the magistrates on the new Plurinational Constitutional Tribunal (TCP) in Sucre, which was tasked with giving jurisprudential form to the constitution's vision for legal pluralism. Among the most vocal proponents of a critical approach to the development of native indigenous peasant justice on the tribunal was Efrén Choque Capuma. Choque was fifty-nine years old and came from Escara, an Aymara town about 200 km southwest of Oruro in the far west of the department off the main highway to the Chilean border. Choque had been sensitized to the gaps between simplistic conceptions of difference and actually existing ethnic diversity from an early age. His mother was a native Chipaya speaker, while his father spoke Aymara as a first language like most people in Escara. Choque said that he was regularly bullied as a youth: *It was terrible, they never let me alone if Chipaya words came out by mistake when I was in school.*

His office featured an extraordinary collection of textiles, political posters, traditional instruments, pottery, and other markers of material culture that expressed his pride in the journey that had brought him—like the president— from the desolate altiplano of Oruro to a position at the highest levels of state power. Choque had received his law degree from one of the oldest law faculties in Latin America—that of Sucre's Universidad Mayor, Real y Pontificia de San Francisco Xavier de Chuquisaca, founded in 1624—and had taken advanced courses in legal pluralism and interculturalism in La Paz at CIDES, UMSA's renowned graduate center for development studies. In Choque's analysis, the challenge of building a system of post–ILO 169 legal pluralism in revolutionary Bolivia was twofold.

There are two main problems with the so-called legal revolution in the country. The first is ideological and the second is epistemological. Ideologically, we remain dominated by the positive law. We see this all the time here [on the tribunal]. Law means rules, rules mean codes, and codes are largely as they've always been. I can go even further and say that justice in Bolivia is dominated by a hyper-positivism. There's been very little opportunity for imagination, for critique, even though that is precisely what's needed at the moment.

But what about the new constitution? I asked him. Isn't it a radical departure from this account of Bolivia's legal history?

Well, look at the constitution. The language is radical. It calls for interculturalism within a plurinational state. But how to do this? How to build a fully realized system of legal pluralism? More specifically, how to articulate and define the epistemology of interculturalism within law? There's no doubt that what is needed from the outset is an interdisciplinary approach to law. But what do we have instead? The various vice ministries—we have them for everything, but especially within [the Ministry of] *Justice—are filled with lawyers. Filled! Until sociologists, anthropologists, and others who can bring a cultural and critical perspective to* [the question of] *legal pluralism participate, we are screwed* [estamos jodidos]. *Until we are able to build in practice what the constitution specifies in grand words, the revolution will remain a phantom.*

I told him that the Office of Constitutional Development in La Paz, though staffed entirely by lawyers, seemed to be sensitive to the problematic legacy of positivist jurisprudence. In fact, I had been told that the government had no plans to try and produce any substantive codes of native indigenous peasant law.

I agree, that's not the goal. To make indigenous justice just like the positive law would be a disaster! No, what I'm saying is that we need to question the whole process of law in Bolivia, which has its roots in colonialism and the positive law. There are in fact many systems of law, many forms of justice [in Bolivia].

I asked Choque if he could suggest a better approach to the problem of legal pluralism.

What we need is to build law from the bottom to the top, not from the top to the bottom, as it's always been. But there is no sign that our legal revolution is being built from the bottom to the top and that is why I spoke out [in an August 2015 *Correo del Sur* article]. *I see it every day here on the tribunal. Even though there are other magistrates who think as I do, we spend all our time fighting over technical matters, with our heads down. When I've protested about this to my colleagues, it goes in one ear and out the other. The constitution needs to be socialized among the people before they can play an important role* [in building law from below]. *But it's not being done like that, not at all.*

Finally, I asked him what the ideal system of legal pluralism in Bolivia would look like, if Choque had his way.

What is most important is to develop models of legal pluralism that are based on real understanding—as I said, understanding from various fields and points of view. How does indigenous justice actually function? That's the real question, and we don't yet have an answer to it on the tribunal.

CONCLUSION: LIVING LAW AT THE LIMITS OF CONSTITUTIONALISM

In his 1913 *Fundamental Principles of the Sociology of Law*, the Austrian legal scholar Eugen Ehrlich drew what was at the time a startling analytical distinction: between the law created through judicial decisions on the one hand,

and, on the other, what he called the "living law"—norms that crystallized within the give-and-take of everyday social life and that were directed not so much toward the resolution of conflicts, but toward the structuring of specific relationships in specific communities. Moreover, given this fact of essential legal pluralism, according to Ehrlich, the grounding of legal legitimacy would likewise always be plural, shifting, and contested.

But as the struggles of legal functionaries like Cecilia Urquieta, indigenous jurists like Efrén Choque, and the seminar participants at the Instituto de la Judicatura de Bolivia demonstrated, there were limits to the extent to which the living law could be condensed into a category of governance and, even more, social transformation, no matter how expansive or radical the underlying ideology. Up through 2015, those responsible for elaborating the concept of legal pluralism as the basis for revolutionary change in Bolivia could not escape several fundamental problems: the realization that pluralism itself was a relatively thin bulwark in the face of a historic bias in favor of normative certainty and legal positivism; the fact that there was "very little opportunity for imagination, for critique," even for those most dedicated to the country's constitutional revolution; and an unwillingness to take the vision of plurinationalism to its logical conclusions because of an enduring, if unacknowledged, commitment to a unitary conception of the state.

As we have seen, the specific challenges of forging an entirely new model of the state based on the devolutionary principle of plurinational legal pluralism were subtended by a more basic tension: that between the imperatives of revolutionary change and the form of governance through which such change was institutionalized—constitutionalism. To return to the critical analysis of Ran Hirschl (2004), the constitutionalization of what he calls "mega-politics" imposed a number of limiting factors on the possibilities for true transformation from below, in addition to establishing the means through which those in power could preserve existing hegemonies in the name of the rule of law.

Although some Bolivian critics of the post-TIPNIS MAS government complained to me that an "Aymara oligarchy" based in La Paz was emerging, it would be difficult to view the relatively fluid circle of leading government officials during these years as an elite in the traditional sense, particularly since their hold on power was only indirectly associated with the country's political economy. Nevertheless, there is no question that categories of law, reinforced by the ideological principles of the 2009 constitution, were used strategically by MAS officials—especially those in the president's inner circle—to consolidate power and suppress opposition (see chapter 5).

Despite these structural constraints, organic intellectuals like Efrén Choque continued to explore the possibilities of law as a foundation for transformative change animated by an alternative cosmovisión for society, social relations, and history. These efforts, though occupied with technical and bureaucratic questions, as Choque lamented, demanded considerable creativity, since they took up "concepts and categories" (Berlin 1979) at the same time; that is, the content of categories like plurinational legal pluralism was inseparable from the need to reformulate the concept of law itself. At least by the end of 2015, this ambitious project to forge a radically new account of law in Bolivia, one detached from the centralizing power of the state and responsive to the everyday contingences of the "living law," remained incomplete, fragmentary, emergent.

3   OPPOSITION AS A CULTURAL SYSTEM

Myth, Embodiment, Violence

To get a sense of how the long history of division between the Bolivian highlands and lowlands expressed itself in stark, often violently materialized ways, one only needed take the short flight between El Alto and Viru Viru, the international airport of Santa Cruz de la Sierra. After takeoff from the terracotta-hued and windswept altiplano, the plane climbed precipitously in order to gain the altitude necessary to cross the high, snow-capped peaks where the southern end of the Cordillera Real gave way to the Cordillera Quimsa Cruz. On its southeastern heading, the plane seemed to pass dangerously close to the 5,000-meter Cerro Tunari, with the departmental capital of Cochabamba lying deep in the valley below. But very soon, the rocky crags of the Andes gave way to a lush and verdant expanse, as the earth flattened quickly into the Parque Nacional Carrasco and then the Parque Nacional Amboró. With the mountains close behind, the plane made its approach to the city of Santa Cruz, with its vast urban and periurban sprawl and nested *anillos*, or highway rings; even combining La Paz and the rapidly growing El Alto, Santa Cruz was still Bolivia's largest and fastest-growing city. Although not the Amazon basin proper, the contrast between the dizzyingly high and dry plains of the Titicaca basin and the low and humid tropical savannas of Santa Cruz was striking.

When I made the trip in the first days of 2009, I had just spent over a month conducting ethnographic research amid the fervor of revolutionary optimism, with the epochal national vote on the new constitution set for the end of January. Indeed, it had been only two weeks before that I had participated in the government's launch of its official Yes! campaign, a day of great joy for the MAS activists whose celebratory confidence and sense of historical purpose cast a glowing arc over the city of La Paz (see chapter 1). Thus it was that a sense of topographic shock was met with a shock of a more ideological kind when I happened to glance out of the taxi window on the road from the airport to the city center, and the first graffiti I saw scrawled on a low barrier wall proclaimed in large, unmistakable, black letters—*Evo chupa la verga de Chávez*, Evo sucks Chávez's dick. This rude welcome to the center of the antigovernment opposition marked an important turning point in my research, the beginning of a new phase in which I would have to try to understand the process of change in terms of quite different cultural, historical, and ideological logics.

This shift was accompanied, admittedly, by various kinds of ethical, ethnographic, and personal apprehensions, since Santa Cruz was then a hotbed of racially inflected violence, far-right propaganda, and what appeared to be an ethnically separatist politics that had brought the country to the brink of a civil war. Yet what I learned over the following weeks, months, and years was that the conflict was never as dichotomous as I had come to believe. I had even naïvely framed my research in its early phases as the study of revolution and counterrevolution, the ethnography of radical social change on the one side and of the conservative ethnic, economic, and regional forces that opposed it on the other.

It all seemed so clear, so historically predetermined: the MAS Bolsheviks versus the *cruceño* White Army—the former fighting for emancipation after centuries of socioeconomic servitude, hopelessness, and racism, the latter fighting for the preservation of the ancien régime under the banner of anti-communism, liberty, and regional self-determination. And in light of this imaginary construction of the conflict, I had styled myself a kind of anthropological John Reed, bravely heading to the front at a crucial historical moment, fully aware of the fact that it was now Bolivia's turn to shake the world.

In the event, the ethnography of opposition in Bolivia during the period 2006–15 revealed a much more muddled and much less ideologically prefigured narrative. This is not to say that many elements of the imagined dialectic were not present and important factors in what was, in retrospect, a nonlinear process that was deeply embedded in and shaped by Bolivia's distinct regional mytho-histories.[1] As will be seen in this chapter, the resistance to the government's far-reaching projects *was* often expressed in the language of anti-Indian and anti-highland rhetoric; the leaders of both the Santa Cruz and Sucre opposition movements *were*, in fact, typically themselves, or representatives of, the moneyed, industrialist, and landed classes that feared the possibility of massive appropriations of property and the eventual collectivist transformation of the country's economy; and the street soldiers of the opposition in both cities *were* more than willing, especially during the fraught period between 2007 and late January 2009, to use escalating and sometimes brutal violence to try to destroy society rather than see it refounded on a model they despised at a visceral as much as at an ideological level.

Yet at the same time, the ethnography of resistance to the MAS ascendency in La Paz, the writing and promulgation of a new Magna Carta, and the forging of what Nancy Postero (2017) has described as an "indigenous state," uncovered surprising points of convergence and moments of ideological adaptation; the coalescence not of a single and unified "counterrevolution," but the proliferation of what were envisioned as multiple, and competing, alternative revolutions, each with its own claim on what was best for the country; and, perhaps most surprising of all, not a conflict that culminated in a final clash of opposing powers, each bent on the destruction of the other, but a kind of anticlimactic involution in which the twin forces of economic self-interest and legal and political bureaucratization conspired to denude the conflict of its primal dangers as months turned into years and years into a decade. Ultimately, the ethnography of right-wing mobilization in Bolivia during the period 2006–15 yielded broader theoretical and historical lessons that were ambiguous at best.[2]

From a methodological perspective, the study of these divergent currents of opposition created any number of dilemmas, especially for an anthropologist sensitized to the imperative to engage with interlocutors in a common project of what Terence Turner (1997) had called an "emancipatory cultural politics." Within this vision of anthropological research, the production of knowledge was seen to go hand in hand with the participatory commitment to social change. But how was it possible to make this epistemological move in the midst of ethnographic research with key figures in Sucre and Santa Cruz who, in more unguarded moments, referred to the president as an *indio de mierda*, or shitty Indian? Would a true "engaged anthropology" (see Low and Merry 2010) have been one in which I actively sought to undermine the opposition by providing intelligence on its activities, since over time my research uncovered a unique base of ethnographic knowledge about the antigovernment movements in Sucre and Santa Cruz?[3]

And then there was the question of my own subject-position as a white, male, North American academic. In order to conduct deep ethnography among those who opposed the government's process of change, both during the highly charged period of 2008 and 2009 and over the longue durée as the opposition was eventually transformed, co-opted, and (in certain cases) suppressed, it was necessary to develop relationships of trust with people whose viewpoints I often found repugnant. This I did without any real ultimate objective, save for vague claims of social understanding, but there is no question that much of this research would have been impossible, even dangerous, without approaching it with a kind of carefully crafted ideological agnosticism.

For example, on January 2 and 3, 2009, I conducted ethnographic interviews with Héctor "Chiqui" Renato Laguna Paniagua and Luis Baldomar Salgueiro, the general director and general counsel of the Cámara Agropecuaria del Oriente (CAO), the powerful trade organization that represented the interests of Santa Cruz's largest agribusiness and cattle ranching concerns. I had heard from contacts in La Paz that the CAO was the real center of power in the department, a shadow force that held the actual reins of influence behind the more public officials associated with the departmental prefecture or the Comité pro Santa Cruz.

At the time, apart from daily manifestations against the new constitution, Santa Cruz was also the national center of public support for Leopoldo Fernández, the most notorious figure in Bolivia, the former prefect of Pando Department who was then being held in preventive detention in La Paz's San Pedro Prison, accused of crimes against the state and intent to commit genocide during the September 2008 massacre at Porvenir (see introduction).

In the course of our interviews, I happened to mention to Laguna and Baldomar that I wanted to learn more about what had happened in Porvenir, that is, the "real story." Again, I was not saying anything outright; I obviously did not mean to signal that I too was skeptical of the government's account of what had taken place. But it was just enough to change the tone of what had been up to that point a very difficult interview, one filled with clipped answers, as many questions to me as responses, and barely veiled hostility on the part of two powerful men who clearly preferred to exercise influence in private.

Laguna suddenly interrupted my attempts to learn more about CAO's position in the anti-government opposition:

Do you want to talk to Don Leopoldo? We know his youngest daughter, Pamela. She's here, in Santa Cruz, right now.

With visions of snowball sampling dancing in my head, I said yes, of course, I would be most appreciative. So Laguna picked up his cell phone and dialed.

Pamela, hello, this is Chiqui. How are you? I'm at Fridolin [a café on Av. Monseñor Rivero between the first and second anillos] *with Luis Baldomar and Marcos, an American anthropologist who would like to talk with your father. Can you meet us here? Very well, we'll see you soon.*

In the fifteen or so minutes it took Pamela Fernández, the youngest of Leopoldo's five daughters, to arrive, the three of us engaged in small talk about Blooming, one of Santa Cruz's two professional football teams, and the mysteries and pleasures of Florida, since Laguna's son was studying journalism at the University of Florida in Gainesville. The mood had become light, friendly; the invisible line between methodological awkwardness and anthropological rapport had been crossed.

Pamela, then twenty-four years old, arrived and slid into an empty chair. I explained to her, as I did to many interlocutors, that I was in Bolivia to "learn more about the conflict"—an intentionally vague description of the research that I used in order to sound interested enough to be taken seriously but elusive enough that I could not be ideologically pigeonholed at a time of intense polarization. And anyway, there I was, having a casual coffee with members of the Santa Cruz elite, hardly something to be expected from the kind of pro-government, left-leaning academic *norteamericano* who had helped make of Morales a global celebrity, particularly in the years before TIPNIS unleashed a backlash of disenchantment.

Although young, Pamela studied me closely. She was at the very beginning of what turned out to be a nearly decade-long public relations campaign to convince the world that her father was innocent of all charges, that he was a political prisoner, that he was the most high-profile victim of the government's efforts to equate principled opposition to its policies with sedition, treason, fascism. She must have decided in an instant that I could be of some use to the family cause. She picked up her phone.

Daddy? How are you? Did you get the package we sent last week? I'm with Chiqui Laguna and Luis Baldomar and an American anthropologist who wants to talk with you. . . . About what's going on. Here.

And then she handed me her cell phone.

I had not actually prepared any interview questions for Leopoldo Fernández and stumbled as I heard a man say, in a very clear voice, "How can I help you?" I repeated again that I was in Bolivia to learn more about the conflict and that I very much wanted to interview him. He asked me when I was going to be in La Paz. I told him in about three weeks. He asked, "At the end of January?" and I said, yes, about the end of January.

Fernández then told me that I should come to San Pedro Prison when I returned but that I must call him the day before so that he could put my name on a prison visitor list. I thanked the most infamous prisoner in Bolivia, a man accused of ordering departmental paramilitaries to torture and kill progovernment peasant activists, with a warmth that later, in retrospect, made me queasy. He was a virulently anti-government and anti-Indian lowland elite who was likely responsible for one of the worst massacres in recent Bolivian history, and yet he was also a condemned man, a husband, a father.

Although research on the opposition in Bolivia would evolve and be transformed as the opposition itself was transformed over the next six years, these first, problematic encounters would form the basis for everything that would follow. As Ruth Benedict once put it, the goal of anthropology should be to contribute to "a world made safe for differences." Of course, even in the case of Benedict, the study and elaboration of difference was not for its own sake, since her "dual use" (Price 2016) research on the Japanese was a strategic response to the fact that they "were the most alien enemy the United States had ever fought in an all-out struggle. In no other war with a major foe had it been necessary to take into account such exceedingly different habits of acting and thinking" (Benedict 2005: 1). But there is no question that Benedict's study was not just a war manual; she clearly intended to use her knowledge of these "habits of acting and thinking" in order to interpret them to a hostile U.S. readership so that peaceful postwar relations might be based on mutual understanding, even respect.

But what happens when the habits of acting and thinking include racial animus, ethnic nationalism, and the formation of cults of embodied historical injustice that demand violent action and patriotic sacrifice? These were the kinds of differences that the ethnography of opposition in Sucre and Santa Cruz revealed, particularly in the years surrounding the great constitutional rupture.

As will be seen in this chapter, I never managed to completely escape from these ethnographic and ethical binds.[4] Yet because the raw intensity of conflict in Bolivia around the process of change diminished over time—to be replaced by forms of "strategic juridification," economic self-interest, and a kind of historical weariness on all sides (see chapter 5)—I never had to fully confront the troubling implications of conducting long-term ethnography among separatists, youth paramilitaries, and anti-Indian demagogues. In retrospect, what remained was a reluctant, even resentful, ethnography, even if, as for Benedict, it was also necessary.

DARKNESS IN THE CITY OF WHITE

In January 1899, Bolivia was riven by an earlier period of strife, the civil conflict known as the "Federal War." The conflict took place during a time of profound national transition—the fin de siècle was also the end of decades of rule by oligarch families who had made their wealth in the silver mining industries of the south. Their estates and economic interests were centered in the historic mining city of Potosí and the "constitutional" capital of Sucre, where the "first shout of liberty" in the Spanish Americas was heard in 1809 and where the independent Bolivian republic was itself proclaimed in 1825.

At the same time that world silver prices declined, those of tin rose dramatically and with them the fortunes of the new tin mining elites based in La Paz and Oruro. These economic and regional differences in Bolivia were expressed politically: the southern elites of the old order were affiliated with the ruling Conservative party, and those from the north, who sought greater control over national institutions, with the ascendant Liberal party. Although the resulting civil war was formally fought over the concept of "federalism" that had been developed earlier in the century by intellectuals such as Lucas Mendoza de la Tapia (Mesa 2008), this was merely a "flag" under which "regional sentiments calling for the transfer of power [from Sucre to La Paz] could justify a rebellion" (Mesa 2008: 407) that was, at its base, a struggle between different regional socioeconomic power bases.

However, beyond the eventual realignment of national political dominance, the Federal War was important for yet another reason. Entirely for strategic reasons, the leader of the Liberals, José Manuel Pando, entered into a military alliance with the Indian militant Pablo Zárate Willka, who later came to be known in the national press as *El Temible*, the Fearsome One. From the side of Zárate Willka and his indigenous, mostly Aymara, soldiers, the opportunity to join with the Liberals was also strategic, since Aymaras from the La Paz region had been involved in at least eight uprisings against the legal and economic abuses of the hacienda social order of the Conservatives between 1880 and 1899 (see Albó and Barnadas 1990: 156; Condarco Morales 1983).

In late January 1899, on the altiplano about 150 km south of La Paz, near the settlement of Cosmini, Liberal and Aymara soldiers attacked a convoy from the Conservative Sucre Battalion, which consisted mostly of young men from prominent Sucre families, many of them students at the august Universidad Mayor, Real y Pontificia de San Francisco Xavier de Chuquisaca ("Universidad San Francisco Xavier"). During the so-called Battle of the First Cross (named for nearby intersecting roads), a Conservative munitions caravan exploded, causing many injuries and the rout of the young troops from Sucre (Mesa 2008: 408).

During the general retreat south, some of the most grievously wounded *sucrenses* were forced to take refuge in the church of the municipality of Ayo Ayo. The forces of Zárate Willka surrounded the town and laid siege to the church. Exactly what happened in the church on the night of January 24 is not known for certain. What is known is that at some point Zárate Willka's soldiers stormed the church and killed all twenty-seven of the wounded members of the Sucre Battalion, two locals from Ayo Ayo, and the church's chaplain, Fernández de Córdoba (Mesa 2008: 408).

Yet early reports of what became known as the Massacre of Ayo Ayo depicted acts of terrible cruelty, torture, and desecration that night in the church. Subsequent accounts of the events became increasingly macabre, as the deaths of the young Sucre soldiers in January 1899 became over the decades the central episode in a civic myth in which the city of Sucre suffered endlessly at the hands of greedy La Paz elites and the savage Aymara *ponchos rojos* who did their bidding. The stories of the tragedy of Ayo Ayo, when the flower of Sucre's youth was destroyed in acts beyond words, became widespread over the years.

For example, in his memoir of traveling in Bolivia in the first decade after the Federal War, the young British mining engineer Anselm Verener Lee Guise recounted the tale he heard on his travels through the region about what happened "in the church at Ayo-Ayo, a village of the plain, through which I passed on my way up to the mine":

The bloodthirstiness and cruelty of the Indian were given full scope during these massacres, the details of which are revolting. The last soldier to be killed in the church of Ayo-Ayo was the commanding officer, who thought to save himself by standing behind the big crucifix over the altar, in the belief that the Indians would respect the emblem of Christianity. He was seen, however, seized, and mutilated, and, whilst still alive, his heart was cut out and eaten on the spot. When all was over, the walls of the church were blood-bespattered to the height of a man, the stains being visible to this day wherever the whitewash has worn thin (Guise [1922] 1997: 30).

Other accounts of the killings in Ayo Ayo were equally ghoulish: cannibalism; the dismemberment of bodies; the crucifying of corpses to the walls of the church; and the drinking of blood mixed with the traditional alcohol *chicha* from human skulls.[5]

Thus it was with these gory mytho-poetic narratives shaping the civic imaginary—of Sucre's university students being literarily consumed "[i]n the midst of a Dante-esque scene of mutilated bodies . . . [in which] the saints themselves were crying blood" (Kuenzli 2013: 147)—that the city mobilized against what it saw as the latest in a long line of historical usurpations against its sacred claim as the birthplace of the Bolivian republic. Violent, daily protests in 2007 against the Constituent Assembly unfolded at two levels. At one level, they were driven by the demand for *capitalidad plena*, that is, that Sucre be recognized in the new constitution as the country's only seat of national power, which would have required all of the branches of government to be consolidated in La Ciudad Blanca. But at another level, the sucrenses who filled the streets around the university and the city's historic Plaza 25 de Mayo were infused with a collective sense of heroic vengeance-seeking against those they imagined as the descendants of the altiplano Indians who had massacred the *universitarios* in Ayo Ayo long ago.

To Sucre's most ardent civic militants, the MAS *asambleístas* who arrived in Sucre to debate the constitution were the historic enemy, an invading campesino army that had to be driven from the city limits. Any local, whether sucrense or *provinciano*, who chose to support the constitutional revolution was a traitor to be hounded, ostracized, and, in certain cases, threatened with death (see figure 3.1).

And when the violence in the streets of Sucre culminated in the deaths of two university students and a local lawyer over three days in late

FIGURE 3.1 Large banner in Sucre's Plaza 25 de Mayo targeting "traitors" to the anti-MAS and pro-Sucre cause, including David Sánchez, Chuquisaca Department's prefect, who was forced into exile in Peru in November 2007.

November 2007, civic leaders were quick to memorialize their deaths by building a monument in Sucre's cemetery and adding their names to the list of martyrs from 1899, who also had a monument in the same municipal burial grounds (see figure 3.2).[6]

The public face of the opposition movement in Sucre was the Comité Interinstitucional por la Capitalidad (CIC), an umbrella organization that operated independently of both the city and departmental governments, although in close collaboration with both, since some leading members of the CIC were also elected officials. The purpose of the CIC at the time was to unify opposition to the constitutional process under way in the city by bringing together influential figures from business, civic associations, and politics in a way that would reinforce a permanent state of unrest at the street level through regular public declarations of grievances and the promotion of capitalidad as the ideological foundation for resistance.

FIGURE 3.2 Monument to the martyrs of Ayo Ayo, General Cemetery, Sucre, August 2015.

The most important members of the CIC were Jhon Cava, president of the Comité Cívico de Intereses de Chuquisaca (CODEINCA), the main civic organization of Sucre; Fidel Herrera, president of the municipal council; Aydée Nava, mayor of Sucre; Jaime Barrón, rector of the Universidad San Francisco Xavier; and Savina Cuéllar, a *mujer de pollera*[7] and former MAS assembly member who had turned her back on the Morales government to become the first woman and first indigenous person elected prefect of Chuquisaca.

However, although the lines of influence were difficult to trace with the same ethnographic precision, what might be thought of as the *private* face of the opposition in Sucre was composed of representatives of what people described, usually guardedly, as the *sangres azules*, or "blue bloods," the small group of old "noble" families that had shaped regional and, at times, national, political and economic life since the last decades of the nineteenth century, when most of them had earned their fortunes as Potosí silver mining oligarchs. The most well known of these Sucre blue blood clans claimed descent from the families Argandoña and Urioste, who had built the Castle of La Glorieta on the outskirts of the city after having been granted a principality by Pope León VIII in 1898, thereby making Francisco Argandoña Bolivia's only prince and his wife Clotilde Urioste de Argandoña Bolivia's only princess.[8]

Other Sucre families who by the early twenty-first century still controlled most of the city's real estate and business wealth included the families Arce, Herrera, Pacheco, Arana, Calvo, and Rodríguez.[9] Some of these families had actually gone through the process of acquiring titles of nobility in Europe at the end of the nineteenth century, which included the purchase of family *escudos*, or coats of arms. For example, the family Herrera became the Marquises of Herrera, and their noble coat of arms could still be seen adorning the family's weathered mausoleum (see figure 3.3).

Among the most powerful of these behind-the-scenes actors in Sucre was Luis Pedro Rodríguez Calvo. A distinguished man in his mid-sixties, Rodríguez was the head of Sucre's influential hotel owners association; a former high-ranking official with the Central Bank of Bolivia; honorary consul of Spain in Sucre; and the owner and executive director of Sucre's Parador Santa María La Real Hotel, one of the most distinctive colonial buildings in Latin America since it had been the former palace of the Audiencia de Charcas, the Spanish colonial jurisdiction created in 1559 that included the silver mines of Potosí.

When I first met Rodríguez in late December 2008, the city was still reeling from months of violence, which had severely impacted Sucre's lucrative tourism trade. Nevertheless, it was clear both where his political sympathies lay and who was actually responsible for directing the policies of the city's civic movement. His use of the amorphous, and slightly ominous, first-person plural was particularly revealing.

We are very disappointed in the way the government organized the constituent assembly. Did you see what happened? It was completely disorganized, right here in our streets. We thought the demands for capitalidad were reasonable; we made those demands in a peaceful way. There is no question that our demands were just. But what happened? As always, the forces from La Paz were violent, brutal, they used the forces of order against university students! We don't understand how they [the national government] *can refuse our claims. Of course, this is part of a longer history, as you might know.*

I asked Rodríguez about the role of the CIC, which had given almost daily press conferences in which it denounced the constituent assembly, the

FIGURE 3.3 Coat of arms of the Marquises of Herrera above the family's aging mausoleum, General Cemetery, Sucre, August 2015. The two tiles on the left are being held together by a piece of transparent adhesive tape.

upcoming national constitutional referendum, and the refusal by the state to launch an investigation over the deaths of the three sucrenses in November 2007 (see figure 3.4).[10]

Look, it is important for us to have a unified front, an institutional face, and that is what the Comité is for us. We think it still makes sense to resist, in certain ways, the government's so-called democratic revolution, which is neither democratic nor a revolution. But it is also true that we have suffered because of this resistance. Look around. For example, our business [at the Parador Santa María] *is down 40 percent.*

I then asked him to explain the extraordinary fact that Savina Cuéllar, an indigenous woman from rural Chuquisaca, had been elected prefect. Did

FIGURE 3.4 Press conference in Sucre with the main leaders of the Comité Interinstitucional por la Capitalidad (CIC), including Jaime Barrón (second from left), Aydée Nava (middle), and Jhon Cava (second from right), New Year's Eve, 2008.

this mean Sucre was changing, becoming more open to the kind of radical pluralism that was at the center of the process of change? A very slight smile appeared as Rodríguez answered.

Yes, it's extraordinary, isn't it? A mujer de pollera in the palace! We thought that Savina would change the discussion. We think she has done very well under the circumstances. Of course, as she herself would admit, we don't think she has permanent political ambitions.

Although her election as prefect of Chuquisaca might have been engineered by Sucre's elites as part of a broader campaign to counter the national government's claims that the opposition to the process of change was motivated by anti-Indian, right-wing racism, Cuéllar's background and self-understanding painted a more ambiguous picture. In early 2009, Cuéllar was forty-five years old and on her way to becoming a national icon to many on the right: the former Morales supporter and indigenous MAS asembleísta who had renounced the president for his hypocrisy and delivered Chuquisaca Department to the opposition. She had been elected the previous June with 55 percent of the departmental vote—most of it coming from Sucre itself—in a special election that had been called after the former prefect, David Sánchez of MAS, was forced into exile in Peru after he and his family received death threats from unknown figures in the civic movement.

Cuéllar was born in the community of Chupampa in Chuquisaca's Yamparáez province. Yamparáez, which borders Sucre's Oropeza Province to the southeast, was well known throughout Bolivia for the town of Tarabuco and its Sunday market and March Pujllay festival. Cuéllar came from a ranching family; her father was fairly prosperous and was active in municipal politics and regional trade and came regularly to Sucre to sell beef. Cuéllar's life had been marked by tragedy, and her entry into politics was a response to these experiences. In 1981, during the military dictatorship of García Meza, Cuéllar's father, who had been active at the local level as a supporter of Hernán Siles Zuazo and the Unidad Democrática y Popular (UDP), was detained and tortured for more than two weeks before finally being released to his family.

But it was in 2001, when Cuéllar was thirty-seven years old and married with seven children, when the greatest calamity of her life unfolded. As she told the story:

As I've said, I come from a family of cattle ranchers. We've always worked with cattle—my father, my husband, my brothers. Well, in 2001, my father wanted to take his cattle for the winter to Monteagudo and then later sell some of them there. So he said, "we need to go through the mountains, it's a long way to Monteagudo."[11] He took with him my husband and my brother-in-law Máximo, who was my sister's husband. But I tell you, the three of them were murdered in the mountains near Monteagudo; they were killed by cattle rustlers who took their money and cattle. They were killed . . . my daddy . . . they didn't show up, they didn't show up for two weeks, so we looked and looked, there were many people and families looking for them. So we kept looking, returning to Monteagudo; we even went to La Paz. Also, we are Christians, evangelicals, so my brother starting working with the missionaries in Yamparáez and the church starting helping in the search, even from the United States. Finally, we found the three of them buried in the ground in the mountains near Monteagudo and then we carried their bodies back here, where they were buried near our house.

After a pause, in which I allowed myself to take in the unprecedented image of Cuéllar sitting at her desk in the cavernous and historic office of the departmental prefect, dressed in her pollera and her trademark black broadbrimmed sombrero, I asked her why this tragedy led her into politics.

I'll tell you, at some point, it would have been in 2003, they found some men from Potosí who had committed the murders and robbery. So we filed a complaint and we waited for six months for the public prosecutor in Monteagudo to investigate. We wanted the judge to find them guilty and pass a sentence. We wanted justice. But in the end, the judge let them go, they dismissed the case against them. We were furious! I was furious! There was no justice, no justice at all for what happened to my daddy, my husband, and my brother-in-law. That was when I decided to go into politics, because Evo Morales was talking about big changes, about bringing justice for people like us, so I began campaigning for him, and then later I was elected to the Constituent Assembly here in Sucre.

Given this history, I then asked Cuéllar, why did she turn against Morales and MAS? Why did she join the opposition to the constitution and the broader process of change?

Because nothing has changed, nothing has been done for us here in Chuquisaca. There haven't been any social changes, not to mention a revolution! What has happened instead? Fighting, confrontations on all sides, all the time, lots of name calling—"they are Media Luna, they are for big business, they are the oligarchs"—that is all, just names. With this approach [from the side of MAS] nothing is going to change, nothing. If a person is born in the countryside, a native peasant [campesino originario] . . . what a life! What suffering! You can't imagine! They don't have the intention to become rich, you can't even think about being rich if you come from the countryside. But if you are clever in work, you can become a business owner, you can become a worker, a farmer, a producer, but it's through hard work. Still, no one should say, "you are for big business, you are the oligarchy," no one can say that like they do now. I was born in the countryside, poor, but through hard work I was able to go into business, we became business owners, we were able to buy things here in Sucre, houses, any manner of things, through our earnings.

But if Savina Cuéllar played a complicated role in Sucre's opposition movement, one in which she forged a unique path while being manipulated by the city's powerful interests at the same time, the same cannot be said of Comité Cívico President Jhon Cava, who was, along with his Santa Cruz counterpart Branko Marinkovic, the bête noire of Bolivia's "third revolution," the round-faced *derechista* who haunted the dreams of MAS supporters throughout the altiplano.

At the beginning of 2009, Cava was thirty-five years old, married, with a nine-year-old daughter and a seven-year-old son. His wife was from Monteagudo, the same town that figured in the killings of Savina Cuéllar's father, husband, and brother-in-law. Cava himself was from the town of Azurduy, also located in the far south of the department, near the border with Tarija Department. Like most of the leading members of the *public face* of the Sucre opposition movement, Cava was not from Sucre and had no family or business connections with any of the city's blue blood elites.[12] Indeed, it was clearly an important fact that the most ardent advocates for capitalidad and the use of violent resistance against the usurpations of La Paz—Jhon Cava, Jaime Barrón, Aydée Nava, and, of course, Savina Cuéllar—were what old family sucrenses described as provincianos, people from outside Sucre who aspired to greater public visibility, better economic opportunities, and the chance to play a role in the governance of the department.

In Cava's case, he had come to Sucre from the south to study agricultural engineering at the university. After only a year of working in agricultural development, Cava decided that his fortunes would be better served elsewhere and he joined the civic movement. His commitment to the cause was striking from the beginning of his new career and he rose quickly through the hierarchy. He was a delegate from Azurduy Province; then a member of the executive board of the departmental association of provincial civic committees, of which there were twenty-seven; and then, finally, the association's president. In December 2005, his dedication and zeal were rewarded when he was elected president of CODEINCA, the highest-profile position in the civic movement, with responsibility over the entire department, but above all for Sucre.

This meant that he had assumed this position of power at the exact historical moment when the conflict with the central government was about to explode. Cava's entire tenure as president of CODEINCA had been marked by strife, and his visibility as the leading ideologue of the Sucre opposition movement was the reason he was both lionized by his brothers-in-arms in Santa Cruz and demonized by the majority of Bolivians who supported the president and the country's revolution by constitution.

Although it wasn't clear at the time, when I first met Cava, on New Year's Day 2009, he was already a marked man. In retrospect, with the overwhelming pro-government results in the August 2008 Referéndum revocatorio behind and polls pointing toward an even greater pro-government victory in the upcoming January vote on the constitution, the opposition had by that point already begun its decline. Cava himself seemed to realize that his own personal trajectory, which was so intimately tied to Sucre's anti-government civic movement, was heading to an uncertain future. Much had changed since his triumph of November 2007, when his fiery denunciations of governmental tyranny had played an important role in the civic beatification of Durán,

Serrudo, and Cardozo, the three locals killed at the height of the violence against the Constituent Assembly.

Yet even at this moment of dawning awareness that the world he had struggled and sacrificed for over sixteen long years was collapsing, Cava could still channel a frightening amount of collective grievance; he could still embody better than anyone the mythic narrative of Sucre's imagined history of civic victimhood—despite, or perhaps precisely because of, the fact that he was a provinciano from the far south, that he would never be a real sucrense, a reality of which he was keenly aware. In discussing the violence of November 2007, Cava came alive, his eyes flashing with righteous indignation.

Why was there violence in the streets? Why were the streets of Sucre filled with tear gas? You wouldn't believe it, it was like a war, mothers and children couldn't walk safely in the streets. But we were not going to allow the treason of Mrs. Silvia Lazarte to pass without a fight.[13] *Even though she had signed an agreement to consider our demands* [for capitalidad], *she later said, "well, there will be no more discussion of it here* [in the Constituent Assembly]." *Then she went to La Paz, on the twenty-first, to receive new orders* [from MAS officials]. *When she returned, she said, "comrades, we are going to move the assembly to a military academy, we are done compromising." So we organized a meeting in the plaza and we decided to completely renounce everything that was happening at the military academy. From that moment on it was clear: the government's actions were antidemocratic, illegal, they discriminated against us, they didn't listen to us, everything had been trampled on, all the rules of the game. Then they sent out a call to arms and they brought them in from El Alto, they brought in the cocaleros from the Chapare, and they came here and said, "we're going to beat the shit out of the* chuquisaqueños, *we are going to plant the wiphala right in the center of the Plaza 25 de Mayo."*

I asked Cava what the leaders of the civic movement did in the days and weeks after the violence, after the deaths of the three locals.

No matter what they say, it wasn't an equal fight, it was stones and sticks against bullets. But you ask what we did. We lodged a complaint on behalf of the families [of the dead men]. *But there was no response, even until today—nothing from the Ministry* [of Justice], *nothing from the chief of police, nothing from the government. On the contrary, they have begun a process against us for the same events, and we are cooperating, we have given statements, because we are not guilty for what happened. If anything, we tried to avoid what happened.*

Yet when I tried to shift the conversation to the other historic day of rage in Sucre, May 24, 2008, Cava's mood suddenly darkened. He squirmed in his seat and grew uncharacteristically silent. Can we talk about what happened in May, I asked him?

Look, I will only comment quickly on what happened on May 24, but what they all say is not true, it's a lie. Everyone says, "Sucre is racist, the cívicos hate the peasants," but how can an entire city be racist? It's not possible. But that is the story they are selling to the whole world. Yet what I can say is that we have condemned those in our movement who did participate, who were there in the plaza on that day. It was a conflict of the moment, a political conflict, sure, but still . . . there are the photos and the videos, you can see the peasants being attacked, being beaten, there was a huge crowd, the crowd was enraged, but yes, there were some who were obscene, brutal, there were hundreds of people, but in the end, what they did escapes our responsibility.

So why did Cava refuse to say any more about the events of May 24, while those of November 2007 sent him into a long and indignant narration? Because for Sucre's opposition movement, November 2007 was its apotheosis, the purest distillation of the civic myth that began with the Massacre of Ayo Ayo. The dark day of May 24, 2008, however, was the inversion of that myth, it was the day on which all the racial animus that had infused the opposition's substrata suddenly erupted to the surface for all the world to see. It was a shocking day, a day of infamy.

When the draft of the new constitution was approved by the Constituent Assembly in December 2007 from its final location in Oruro, where it had been moved following the violence in Sucre in November, the Morales government returned to campaign mode in preparation for the August 2008 Referéndum revocatorio. The idea for the referendum was to gauge support for political leadership at the departmental and national levels after the turbulence that accompanied the drafting of the new constitution but before it would be put to a national vote. The move was also, in retrospect, a shrewd gambit on the part of the MAS government, since it was a dramatic way to demonstrate the extent to which the majority of Bolivians supported the process of change despite the strength of the opposition.

Being in campaign mode meant that the Morales government devoted considerable time and resources to launching new public projects and then spending what seemed like an equal amount of time and resources celebrating and promoting such initiatives. So it was that in May 2008, the national MAS government organized an event in Sucre that had two main purposes. The first was to launch a series of major development initiatives for Chuquisaca, including the donation of ambulances to rural communities. The second was to participate in the annual May 25 events, the most important day in Sucre, the day that honored the 1809 "shout of liberty" during the beginning of the independence wars. However, the CIC made it clear that Morales and MAS officials would be met with resistance if the May 25 events were held in the Plaza 25 de Mayo itself, the traditional site for the multi-day civic festival.

Despite these warnings, the MAS government made the decision to continue with the planned events, while moving them to the city's main sports arena, the Estadio Olímpico Patria. It was a clear provocation, since it was read by Sucre's civic leaders as a refusal to address the raw bitterness of November 2007 over the deaths of the three sucrenses. Nevertheless, supporters from the pro-MAS peasant unions and community associations from the surrounding provinces began arriving on the morning of May 24; many took the typical open-bed *camión* and were dropped off in the upper barrios of Sucre, where they would be able to make their way on foot to the rally. The hundreds of peasants included women, children, and the elderly, who anticipated a joyous celebration with their president. Morales had planned to arrive by helicopter directly from La Paz in midafternoon.

However, MAS officials, including Sacha Llorenti, who had arrived as part of an advance team, decided to cancel the event in the late morning on May 24. As Llorenti explained to me, it was clear that the CIC was planning to bring thousands of people into the streets to oppose the arrival of Morales and violent confrontations were highly likely. The problem was that the rally was canceled too late for the hundreds of pro-MAS supporters, who were already streaming into Sucre and making their way to the Estadio Olímpico, which was less than 2 km to the north of the Plaza 25 de Mayo.[14]

The MAS supporters were met by various mobs of sucrenses, who were armed with clubs, stones, powerful slingshots, and sticks of dynamite. The warlike assault on the pro-MAS peasants on May 24 was partly organized and partly spontaneous. Businesses, schools, and the university were already closed for the May 25 celebrations, which meant the city's workers and students were available to be mobilized en masse. The CIC called for the city to turn out in force as a general show of defiance. Smaller organizations, especially the university's Federación Universitaria Local (FUL) and the far-right cadres of the Falange Socialista Boliviana (FSB), whose national chairman, Horacio Poppe-Inch, was the son of a prominent Sucre family, were given more specific orders to set up roadblocks, attack the pro-MAS peasants, and drive them from the city. Many of the most violent students and far-rightists were masked during the May 24 attacks; they had come to commit atrocities and wanted to hide their identities from the inevitable cell phones and video cameras that would record their actions, a lesson learned during the November confrontations.

It was a tragic and toxic encounter. On the one side were the peasant families, hearts filled with pride and hope, whose wiphalas and *sindicato* banners expressed their confidence in the government's revolutionary aspirations. On the other side were thousands of enraged sucrenses, still seething over the martyrdom of their three compatriots. The violent implosion of the glorious cause of capitalidad had rendered the city's civic warriors desperate and unpredictable. The turning point on May 24, the shift that unleashed the chaos of mob violence, was the fact that neither the army nor the police had been mobilized to maintain order. At the departmental level, the institutions of governance were in turmoil. David Sánchez, the MAS prefect, had gone into exile in Peru in early December, after his family home was burned and ransacked, and the department would have to wait for a special election in June to find a new prefect.

At the same time, national MAS officials were reluctant to call out soldiers from Sucre's Second Infantry Regiment to protect the pro-MAS peasants. On the one hand, images of soldiers and riot police firing on large crowds of protestors in November 2007 had been used by civic leaders to justify the claim that they were living under the yoke of an authoritarian regime. On the other hand, the government's aversion to using the military against the opposition— whether in Sucre or Santa Cruz—went much deeper, since the violence of Black October 2003, when soldiers fired on protestors in El Alto, killing at least sixty people, was a central thread in MAS's revolutionary narrative.

Thus, as they descended into Sucre, the pro-MAS campesinos, men, women, and children, were confronted by a sea of sucrenses, unmediated by the rule of law or the power of the state. The peasants were hounded; they were beaten; they were struck with rocks and clubs; women's long plaited braids were pulled and they were dragged to the ground; dynamite was thrown at them as they tried to escape back into the upper barrios. Many men and women suffered serious injuries, including head wounds. Some peasant children were also struck by stones and suffered trauma from the attack. Fleeing pro-MAS peasants who fell to the ground on the steep streets in flight from the mob were kicked until they were pulled away.

Amid this mob violence, in the early afternoon of May 24, a group of around forty men were captured—there is no other word for it; they appeared to have been singled out because they were dirigentes, or leaders, of their respective community organizations and rural peasant unions. Ironically, given the importance of the foundational myth of Ayo Ayo to Sucre's civic opposition, the men were not Aymaras from La Paz; instead, they were Quechua speakers from nearby provinces, some of whose ancestors could very well have been heroes of the 1816 Battle of Jumbate, when local Yamparas drove out Spanish troops during the War of Independence.

In a scene that evoked earlier historical round-ups likewise driven by an ideology of racial hatred, the forty men were frog-marched from the outer districts, especially from El Abra, down through the streets into the historic center, where they were led into the Plaza 25 de Mayo as the crowds continued to swell. Each man among the forty was surrounded by his own personal group of two or three captors, who shouted abuse and pushed their captive forward. As the procession made its way through the city, the men were punched or abused by those from the crowd on either side, whose numbers condensed into a tunnel of raging cívicos as they came closer to the plaza. The parade of ignominy was led by several men, both masked and unmasked, including one very tall and serious man in his mid-thirties. He didn't shout or gesture, but he was a full head taller than the others and his calmness and sense of purpose made him all the more menacing. He kept a vise-like grip on the back of the neck of the peasant dirigente at the head of the line, over whom he towered.

When the line of captives finally reached the plaza, they were herded together in a tight line, stomachs pressing against backs. The looks on their faces were those of simple terror—there was not a police officer to be seen and the sucrense mob was swelling as the afternoon grew longer. The crowd milled around in what became an oddly and grotesquely festive scene. The leading political and social members of Sucre could be seen among the maddened university students and the inflamed shopkeepers. In its languorous and unhurried violence, the afternoon of May 24 evoked images of whole towns turning the extrajudicial lynchings of African American men in the early twentieth-century U.S. South into community picnics.

The campesinos were first forced to strip to their waists, a highly shameful act of physical exposure with deep cultural resonance. They were then pushed to their knees in front of their captors in a brutal moment of collective submission. Then the various shouts began—"take their pants," "kiss the flag," "say that Evo is the son of a whore," and, most ominously, "kill them!" The peasants were forcibly draped in the white and red flags of Sucre; their wiphalas were ripped from their hands and put into a large pile in front of them. Several of the peasant community leaders were led in front of the others, where they were forced to burn their own wiphalas, the symbol of the indigenous movement in Bolivia and the cultural icon that embodied the country's

FIGURES 3.5 May 24, 2008. Supporters of President Morales are captured by an enraged mob of pro-Sucre militants, forcibly marched into Sucre's Plaza 25 de Mayo, and beaten and humiliated on a day of infamy that came to be known as the Plaza de Rodillas.

process of change more than any other. There was no resistance from the peasant leaders; they were surrounded by hundreds of cívicos, their apparent meekness more likely a form of resignation of the kind that comes to people being led to the gallows (see figure 3.5).

As the shadows lengthened, a dangerous moment of uncertainty hung over the plaza. What would happen next? There were some in the crowd who wanted the proceedings to move from the symbolic violence of charred wiphalas to violence of a more direct, murderous kind. But for reasons that perhaps will never be understood, at that critical point in the trajectory of unmediated mob atrocity voices were heard calling for an end—for the masked men who were acting as ringleaders to release the dirigentes. Again, for unknown reasons, those sudden voices of restraint were not, in that moment, met with more powerful or persuasive ones demanding the deadly opposite. So it was that the humiliated and bloodied peasant leaders were yanked to their feet and herded out of the plaza. Despite the reprieve, the last thing they heard was the cacophonous shouts of racist epithets, and the last thing they smelled was the burning of their wiphalas, which must have seemed, on that day of catastrophe, like the burning of their dreams of a new Bolivia.[15]

THE THIN GREEN LINE BETWEEN AUTONOMY AND SEPARATISM

Three weeks before images of the Plaza de Rodillas in Sucre shocked the conscience of many Bolivians, especially urban mestizos who up to that point had remained ambivalent about both the election of Morales and the most strident anti-government rhetoric, the opposition movement in Santa Cruz was celebrating its proudest moment: the referendum on the department's "Autonomy Statute," a regional socio-juridical charter that was drafted in parallel to the new national constitution. As a direct rebuff to the new constitution that had been presented to the Bolivian Congress on December 14, 2007, Santa Cruz's autonomy statute was promulgated the very next day, December 15. While negotiations over the national constitution dragged on into early 2008, leaders of the Santa Cruz opposition sought to preempt the process by holding a departmental referendum on their own covenant for regional refoundation. On May 4, 2008, the statute was approved by popular vote with the overwhelming support of 86 percent of cruceños.

The popular approval of Santa Cruz's own, opposing, Magna Carta in May 2008 was the culmination of a longer process of departmental mobilization against the rise of the MAS government in La Paz that had attempted to straddle an ambiguous line between "autonomy"—an emergent term of juridical and ideological art—and a much more hardened form of separatism, which was often expressed by its advocates in ethnic or racial terms. And although the national and international media typically conflated the most important centers of opposition in Sucre and Santa Cruz under the banner of the Media Luna, in fact, the two were profoundly different along a number of important axes: regional identification, oppositional ideology, and organizing mytho-history.[16]

Even within Santa Cruz, opposition to the process of change developed along three principal tracks in the critical period surrounding the turning point of 2009, when the new national constitution was approved in January and the mandate of Evo Morales was then unambiguously reaffirmed eleven months later in the national elections. The first was the intentional bureaucratization of resistance centered on the governmental offices of the department, specifically the Secretariat of Autonomy, Decentralization, and Development.

The second was the behind-the-scenes actions taken by Santa Cruz's agribusiness, cattle ranching, and commercial elite, represented by the CAO (see above), the Federación de Empresarios Privados de Santa Cruz (FEPSC), and the Cámara de Industria, Comercio, Servicios y Turismo de Santa Cruz (CAINCO), which included significant financial assistance to the department's political and pro–Santa Cruz civic organizations.

And the third was the waves of militant street mobilizations ordered by the civic elders from the Comité pro Santa Cruz and carried out by the paramilitary foot soldiers of the Unión Juvenil Cruceñista (UJC), those cadres of green-and-white-bedecked young cruceños and cruceñas whose seething visages filled the nation's evening television broadcasts.

Yet regardless of these important nuances, all three currents of the Santa Cruz opposition were grounded in the ideology of Camba nationalism.[17] Although the origins of the regional-ethnic term *Camba* were unclear, by the early 2000s Camba had developed into an imagined community that claimed to encompass both the diverse populations of the Bolivian lowlands and the collective resistance to centuries-long domination and betrayal by the ethnic groups and political regimes of the highlands. Among Camba nationalists, a modified map of Bolivia was widely circulated at the time, which expressed the simplified Camba worldview in stark geographical terms.

The heart of the Camba nation consisted of the peoples of Pando, Beni, and Santa Cruz Departments. The people of Chuquisaca and Tarija departments, while not members of the Camba nation, were nevertheless "related" to it by both shared political interests and—in the case of Sucre—a common history of subordination to the powers of La Paz. The Yungas region of Cochabamba Department was identified as an iniquitous border region of mercenary cocaleros, or coca farmers. Finally, the second large nation of Bolivia within the Camba nationalist ideology, that which was the ultimate source of all the Camba nation's historical traumas, was the Aymara Quechua nation (see figure 3.6).

Many of the ideological contours of Camba nationalism were articulated by the prolific propagandist and luxury home builder Sergio Antelo Gutiérrez, whose 2003 treatise became a foundational reference for Santa Cruz's political, economic, and ethnic anti-MAS activists. In it, Antelo argued that the Camba people should be understood—conceptually, politically, and legally— as a historically subordinated nation with the right to self-determination. He compared the plight of the Camba nation with that of other stateless nations, including East Timor, Canada's Québécois, and the Kurds. In Antelo's analysis, the Camba people were forced to "become Upper Peruvians at gunpoint" through a series of historical betrayals that took different forms in different epochs.

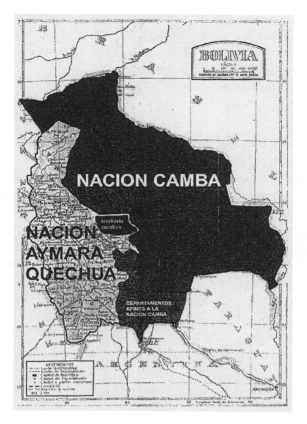

FIGURE 3.6

It is important to note that Antelo's blueprint for the Camba nation was published after the 2002 national elections, in which Morales's strong showing pointed to the coming realignments, but before the seismic election of 2005 would reveal to lowland elites just how much the ideological landscape had shifted. By 2017, what had been for Antelo in 2003 a more diffuse problem of "Andean radicalism" and "internal colonialism" had become something more specific: it was what he described as the "coca-centric ideology of the Upper Peruvian state" that posed the greatest threat to Camba identity (Antelo Gutiérrez 2017: 121).[18]

In January 2009, however, it was Antelo's proposal for a new structure of political federalism that proved to be most influential for members of the department's political elite, including its secretary for autonomy, decentralization, and development, Carlos Dabdoub Arrien, who was, at least up to the

TIPNIS conflict of 2011, the intellectual anchor of the lowland opposition. Although the department's prefect (later governor), Rubén Costas, was the public face of Santa Cruz's political resistance, it was Dabdoub who shaped internal discussion and whose political vision for autonomous regions formed the basis not only for Santa Cruz's oppositional policies, but for those of the entire Consejo Nacional Democrático (Conalde), the bloc of Media Luna prefects that initially included (in addition to Costas) Ernesto Suárez (Beni), Leopoldo Fernández (Pando), and Mario Cossio (Tarija).[19]

Dabdoub, the sixty-three-year-old principal author of Santa Cruz's 2007 autonomy statute, was a retiring, bookish ideologue who weighed his words carefully. Like many leading cruceños, he had been formed politically in the city's civic movement, serving as president of the Comité pro Santa Cruz in the mid-1980s before accepting positions at the national level, including national deputy, minister of health during the government of Jaime Paz Zamora, and finally candidate for vice president in 2005 on the Unidad Nacional (UD) ticket of Samuel Doria Medina. Dabdoub was a well-regarded neurosurgeon by profession who had completed medical residencies and training programs in Brazil, various European countries, and Japan.

For Dabdoub, the origins of Camba nationalism were to be found in the region's centuries-long isolation from the political and economic power centers of the highlands. It was simply unjust, according to Dabdoub, for the central government to promote a vision of national political unity under the banner of change while ignoring the legacy of conflict around development in the lowlands. The promulgation of Santa Cruz's own Magna Carta, in Dabdoub's perspective, was the only way to formally recognize and permanently legitimate the region's historical de facto autonomy. Dabdoub underscored the fact that this autonomy had very much worked against Santa Cruz until the late 1930s, when the national government under the military regime of David Toro had nationalized the oil fields of Standard Oil in the Chaco, thereby making the department a key element in the national economy. Yet even into the 1960s, according to Dabdoub, Santa Cruz was "backward":

Throughout most of the first half of the twentieth century, Santa Cruz was still a small village. There wasn't any asphalt on the streets, there wasn't any potable water, no electricity, no telephones, the roads were just dirt, sand; meanwhile, in Cochabamba, La Paz, Oruro, Potosí, they already had asphalt, public services. That is why in the 1950s we started to form institutions to oversee our own development, without the central government, to look after our own interests.

Even if Dabdoub's rhetoric could at times slip into a more racialized language of opposition, his main concern was to articulate a full-blown theory of autonomy that would be consistent with historical precedent and international law.[20] As he explained, with the didactic use of an elaborate diagram on a whiteboard behind his desk,

Bolivia was a unitarian state, and a unitarian state has three forms. One, which is centralist. A second, which is decentralist. And a third, which is unitarian but with autonomy. Our autonomy statute recognizes Santa Cruz's status within the third category of unitarian state.

I asked Dabdoub if the model of autonomy "within a unitarian state" was the same thing as federalism.

No, no, not at all. There is a big difference between the federal and the unitarian state. In the federal state, you have a congress in each state, you have a judicial branch in each state, you have the executive power in each state. In our case, the judicial branch doesn't exist, there is only one judicial power [in Sucre]. We have something like a congress here, but it has fewer powers, fewer rights, so these are the main differences between the federal systems and what we are struggling for here.

I then asked Dabdoub *why* Santa Cruz was not struggling for a federal system, why they were willing to concede the fact that the department would necessarily have less power than the central government even if it respected the terms of their autonomy statute.

Because Bolivia is not ready to be a federal state. If you have a department called Pando that has only 30,000 people, you don't have the economic or administrative capacity to form a federal state. Now this is not to say that I would not like, at some point, for the country to become a federal state, but the reality is that it's not possible to think of a department becoming a state within a proper federal system, at least not yet, that's why we struggle for autonomy, but who knows what will happen with time?

In terms of historical models, Dabdoub was quite clear that the exemplar in Santa Cruz's struggle for autonomy was Spain, which had refounded itself, he explained, in its 1978 constitution as a unitarian state with autonomy by granting Catalonia, the Basque region, and Galicia extensive powers of self-governance. But how, I asked him, could this vision of liberal self-determination be reconciled with the international image of Santa Cruz's anti-government activists as racists motivated by anti-Indian sentiments?

Look, it's difficult to understand our movement in terms of the traditional politics of the left and the right. We are not counterrevolutionaries, as some claim. It's not true that Morales wants change and we don't. No, that is false, although that is precisely what the government wants people to believe. No, it is a question of different kinds of revolution, different kinds of change. Their revolution is one that

seeks to concentrate power, to destroy institutions. But ours is also a revolution,
one that seeks to redistribute power and to deepen democracy. It's more accurate to
speak of two revolutions in Bolivia right now because we are also revolutionaries.

Nevertheless, Dabdoub's apparent commitment to democratic revolution for Santa Cruz was tempered by a certain cynicism that one often encountered among lowland elites with extensive personal and business connections with the United States, Europe, and the wealthier countries of Latin America. When I asked him if Norway could serve as a possible model for economic development in Bolivia, given its similar population size and historical reliance on the exploitation of fossil fuels, Dabdoub responded with a knowing smile:

I'll tell you what. I would accept this as a perfectly acceptable model for Bolivia on one condition.

What condition?

That we are allowed to exchange 8 million Bolivians for 8 million Norwegians.

Yet while Dabdoub and the Secretariat of Autonomy, Decentralization, and Development rushed to ensure that a preexisting legal and political framework was in place before the adoption of the new national constitution in January 2009 would, to a large extent, both co-opt and paradoxically centralize the movement for autonomy, Santa Cruz's business elites were vigorously promoting economic growth in the department. They did this by underwriting a massive regional credit regime through the Banco Ganadero; bypassing the central government to invite foreign direct investment by private agribusiness, petroleum, and construction concerns; and, increasingly, negotiating directly with countries like China to support regional development, especially at a time in which competing aide from Chávez's Venezuela was playing a key role in the transformation of La Paz's infrastructure.

By the time of the 2009 referendum on the new constitution, Santa Cruz had become the economic powerhouse of Bolivia through a diversified approach to economic development that was a far cry from the impoverished period that Dabdoub described, and even far removed from the cocaine capitalism boom years of the 1970s and 1980s. Indeed, Santa Cruz business leaders had become so confident in the department's economic independence and future prospects that they agreed to the inclusion of a provision in the department's autonomy statute (Article 104) that would outlaw the existence of latifundia, "large tracts of unproductive land . . . that are contrary to the collective interest and which fulfill no social or socioeconomic function." This apparently anticapitalist article tracked almost identically the language from the controversial section of the new national constitution that would likewise prohibit latifundia.[21]

Although major regional trade organizations like the FEPSC and CAINCO, which served as parallel structures of governance and power in Santa Cruz, were located near the central Plaza 24 de Septiembre, the organizing base for the Cámara Agropecuaria del Oriente (CAO) was housed on the sprawling grounds of the Feria Exposición de Santa Cruz, or Fexpocruz. Far more than a mere fair and exhibition center, Fexpocruz functioned as a key alternative civic, moral, and commercial space. Fexpocruz featured its own well-defined geographical boundaries (between the third and fourth anillos, due west of the city center), security force, and internal neighborhoods, where hundreds of private companies, social and civic organizations, and national and international institutions maintained offices that were lightly staffed for most of the year in the lead-up to Expocruz. This was an annual ten-day event in September that brought tens of thousands of people to the site, where hundreds of millions of dollars in deals were struck over commercial distribution rights, cattle futures, bilateral trade agreements, and agricultural investment, among many other deals.

For the rest of the year, Fexpocruz was a city within a city, where beauty pageants where held; children would attend customized live performances based on international movies such as Harry Potter and Lord of the Rings; local universities would organize information days; and dozens of more specialized *ferias*, or festivals, would take place, such as the three-day "Complete Woman's Festival" (Feria Integral de la Mujer), in which a particular vision of the "complete woman" was promoted through health regimes such as yoga and aromatherapy and with insights from the Chilean high-end New Age–inspired lifestyle magazine *La Tercera*, whose articles examined topics such as "Aruba: Wellness Destination" and "Goodbye to These Eight Myths about Diets."

But for the power brokers of the CAO, Fexpocruz was the gated and protected citadel from which they could consider the consequences of the constitutional revolution and new policies announced in La Paz and engage in an extensive process of risk management that had as its primary objective the continued economic expansion of the department. In a sense, the economic elites of Santa Cruz during the period 2006–15 wanted nothing less than to make the department itself a larger-scale Fexpocruz—walled off from the rest of Bolivia and embedded first and foremost in regional and international economic networks, a place where a cosmopolitan self-image of Santa Cruz's "productive mentality" could be cultivated far removed from the frightening "MAS hordes" of the frigid highlands.

For Chiqui Laguna, the CAO general director in 2009 and 2010, the struggle for Santa Cruz's economic autonomy and growth was a historic one, rooted in the clashes of the 1950s over a national law that eventually granted Santa

Cruz department 11 percent of the royalties earned by Yacimientos Petrolíferos Fiscales Bolivianos (YPFB), the state-owned oil and gas company. But in the fifty years since the Movimiento Nacionalista Revolucionario (MNR) government of Hernán Siles Zuazo had codified the principle of 11 percent in favor of Santa Cruz and other oil-producing departments (through a 1959 interpretation of an earlier 1938 law), Santa Cruz had moved well beyond dependence on scraps from the national coffers.

Laguna shared the general profile of many of Santa Cruz's economic leaders. He had received his political and ideological formation in the UJC as a young man (he had served as the UJC's education liaison between 1986 and 1988) and was descended from a prosperous family of *hacendados* from the region of Portachuelo, the traditional breadbasket of the department 70 km north of the capital that was noted for its rice cultivation and extensive cattle herds. Laguna, who had received his undergraduate degree in environmental engineering from the University of Miami, owned over 600 hectares of prime agricultural land—mostly soybeans—and was a wealthy man with homes in Miami, Brazil, and Santa Cruz. I asked Laguna about the position of CAO toward the national process of change, especially the provision in the constitution that would restrict the size of landholdings.

This might be surprising, given how we are shown [in the national media], *but we* [the members of CAO] *are also the enemies of the latifundio. Why? Because we are the enemies of any land that is unproductive and we support the idea of redistributing land among those who will make it work, this is our philosophy. But this doesn't mean we support the way the government is doing it, that is just an abuse of power, they don't understand anything about agriculture here in the lowlands.*

Why not?

Well, just because we can say that we also believe in the theme of the social function of land does not mean that this principle can be enforced with a single law like this government wants to do; that is too simple. And some land that the government would call unproductive is actually part of a complicated system, an agricultural system. To maintain a sustainable agricultural economy it is sometimes necessary to leave some land fallow or uncultivated, at least for a period. You can't compare the Chaco with the north of Santa Cruz, you can't compare cattle ranching with soybean farming, you can't compare soybean cultivation with potato farming. Here in the lowlands, in the interior, it's very different, but these people [from the national government] *want to use these laws to measure everything with the same ruler. This is the reason why we can't support the government even though we too don't approve of latifundia.*

I then raised the highly charged point made by MAS activists in La Paz that Santa Cruz's large landowners opposed the process of change because they continued to rely on forms of servitude on their lands that included the enslavement of indigenous Guaraní.

How much more time can you spend in Santa Cruz? . . . because that is a lie. This is not to say that something like that doesn't take place in isolated cases, but it's very atypical. What's more, I would dare say something else, that servitude, as you call it, is a much greater problem in La Paz than here in Santa Cruz.

Do you mean in the mines?

No, in the houses of the city. That's a totally different kind of servitude; the house servants in La Paz have a terrible life compared with people who work in agriculture here in Santa Cruz. I can't even understand the system there [in La Paz] because in my house the maid always ate with us, she always ate our food, but there the maids eat with the dogs. So that's a big lie, the idea that there is slavery here in Santa Cruz and not in La Paz, right at the heart of the government.

But what, I finally asked Laguna, are we to make of the images of ferocious opposition here in Santa Cruz? Wouldn't it make more sense for cruceños to cooperate with the government in La Paz, especially since the regional economy was booming?

Look, I'll be honest with you. There are differences here, different ideas about how to carry on the struggle. But despite the fact that it is true that many here hate the government, I would say that 70 percent or more of the people in the department don't think at all about autonomy or Morales. You know what they are thinking about? Where the food for the next day's meals is going to come from. That's what they are thinking about.

What about the new constitution?

To them, it's just paper. You can't eat paper.

Yet if Laguna was indeed right, and the extraordinary scenes of destruction of public property, the beating of random people with apparent origins in the highlands, and the descent of central Santa Cruz into an orgy of chaotic violence (see figures 3.7, 3.8, and 3.9), masked a prevailing apathy in the face of the country's epochal transformations, this undercurrent of indifference was certainly not shared among those in the department's civic movement.

On the contrary, for the legions of civic militants, the crisis years of 2007–9 were the moment when the decades-long struggle for regional autonomy would accelerate into open rebellion against the central government, whose revolutionary proposals in the wake of Morales's election were seen to create an unbridgeable chasm, a final rupture in relations with what Dabdoub had called the "Colla bourgeoisie."

FIGURES 3.7 AND 3.8

FIGURE 3.9

Although the Comité pro Santa Cruz endeavored to maintain an air of institutional dignity, even during the height of the violence under the leadership of its lightning-rod President Branko Marinkovic, its youth paramilitary wing, the Unión Juvenil Cruceñista (UJC), was mobilized around a set of quite different logics. Along with the much less visible Comité Cívico Femenino (formerly the Unión Femenina Cruceñista), the UJC had been founded in October 1957, at the height of an earlier conflict over the region's development.

With the opening of the landmark asphalt highway connecting Santa Cruz with Cochabamba in August 1954, the department's political and social aspirations grew along with its rapidly expanding economic base (Mesa 2008: 522). Although the conflict came to a head nominally over the "fight for the 11 percent," the regional struggle was articulated in the more diffuse terms of racial difference, historical injustice, and an ideology of martyrdom. In this context, while the Comité pro Santa Cruz (founded in 1950) normally presented a more staid institutional front for cruceño interests, the UJC was created as a force that would "conquer, or die with glory," its official motto.

Much like the Sucre cívicos, the members of the UJC were inspired to fight against the usurpations and imagined savagery of the highlands through their own organizing myths, one of which—like the Massacre of Ayo Ayo—

was also described as a "massacre," or, even worse, a "Holocaust." In December 1957, just two months after its founding, armed cadres of the UJC clashed with government troops and "moronista" irregulars in the so-called Battle of the Mangroves, which took place across Avenida Cañoto near Santa Cruz's Club de Tenis. During the exchange of gunfire, a *unionista* named Gumercindo "Cachete" Coronado was killed and soon after was transformed into a martyr by his UJC comrades.

In May 1958, as the civic violence increased, the national MNR government declared the largely Falange Socialista Boliviana (FSB)-led revolt a coup d'état in order to suppress the uprising with a more decisive military intervention. As FSB and UJC militants were quickly rounded up, a small group of mostly university students attempted to escape along the new Santa Cruz–Cochabamba highway. At kilometer 12, near the town of Terebinto, they were met by an overwhelming force of armed peasants from communities around the Cochabamba town of Ucureña.

The peasant militia had marched the 465 kilometers on their way to Santa Cruz under their leader José Rojas on the orders of the national government as part of something like a "pact of reciprocity" (Platt 1982), since the MNR had supported the radical anti-hacienda movement of Ucureña in the early years after the 1952 National Revolution (in August 1953, Víctor Paz Estenssoro had signed the agrarian reform law in Ucureña; see Albó 1987).[22]

In order to understand the symbolic importance of what happened during and after this encounter, one must turn to the civic legend of the "Holocaust of Terebinto," as told by none other than Carlos Dabdoub. After killing the students on the highway, the peasant army continued into the city of the Santa Cruz.

> Before arriving in Santa Cruz, they had killed the fugitives in a cruel and bloody manner after having tortured and mutilated them. . . . At the same time, in the capital [another group of armed peasants] committed various "outrages, pillaging, arson, the rape of women, and the sacking of offices (the Comité pro Santa Cruz, the Club 24 de Septiembre, etc.) and the homes of distinguished families" (quoting Ardaya Paz 1981). "The number of our brothers who were savagely burned alive will forever be preserved in the memory of all good cruceños as the victims of an ancestral loathing that has always opposed the development and progress of Santa Cruz" (also quoting Ardaya Paz 1981). Others testified that the invaders persecuted, imprisoned, banished, humiliated, tortured, and murdered young people, children, and the elderly with a ferocity that was only comparable

to the atrocities committed in Europe by the armies of Attila, "King of the Huns," between the years AD 450 and 453 (Dabdoub 2009).[23]

With this mytho-history as their ensanguined lodestar, generations of unionistas had trained over the decades precisely for the kind of confrontations that had paralyzed Santa Cruz during the conflicts of the first Morales presidency. According to the UJC's statute, a young man was eligible to join the "hereditary organization that is the guardian of the ideals and the memory of the civic struggles and of the founders of *cruceñidad* and the mysticism of its heroes, intellectuals, and martyrs," as long as he was younger than thirty-five years old, a cruceño "by birth," a member of the "Camba Culture," and committed to the cruceñista struggle. In January 2009, there were about two thousand active members of the UJC, and its president was Víctor Hugo Rojas Vaca, an engineering student at the Universidad Autónoma Gabriel René Moreno, who had just entered office.

The UJC headquarters was tucked into the back corner of the large cívico compound on the oddly named Calle Cañada Strongest,[24] along with the headquarters, library, and administrative offices of the Comité pro Santa Cruz and the small office of the relatively idle Comité Cívico Femenino. I had been invited to meet UJC members and sit in on a strategy meeting as part of their anti-constitution mobilizations. The UJC conference room was unremarkable: a large central table with room for around twenty people, smaller side tables on which they had placed various stacks of propaganda pamphlets for members to distribute, and a small bookshelf with pro-Camba treatises and regional histories.

On a large whiteboard, Rojas had drawn two triangles side by side. Inside of each, in black letters, he had written, simply, "UJC." But on the three points of one triangle, in red letters, Rojas had written "discipline, professionalism, organizational planning," and on the points of the other, "service, honor, cruceño pride." Before we began our conversation, Rojas gave me a copy of the "Nación Camba/Nación Aymara Quechua" map and a copy of the UJC governing statute, which had been substantially revised during a UJC general congress held in the far southeastern border city of Puerto Suárez in 2002 and approved by a special UJC general assembly held in 2004 in Minero, a town about 85 km north of Santa Cruz in a rich agricultural region.

I asked Rojas how he would describe the UJC.

Well, I would say we are an expression of the cruceño sentiment [el sentimiento cruceño].

What is the cruceño sentiment?

Actually, for example, the cruceño sentiment is based in an ideological struggle, so this is part of it. The other parts are, well, about progress, about work, about peace, about unity, and about many other things that make up the cruceño sentiment. Also, there is the youth struggle, the struggle for the interests of the department.

I asked Rojas why he wanted to lead the UJC during a time of such conflict and even violence.

I think there were various factors, no? One is . . . look, we have always had our differences in Bolivia, huge differences, and always over the ethnic question, the question of heritage. Now, more than ever, these types of differences have deepened and so it is necessary to defend ourselves.

Defend yourselves against what or whom? Rojas paused, as if struggling over how to respond.

Against . . . for us it is a struggle between East [Oriente] and West [Occidente], no? a struggle against the Andeans, those from the altiplano, no? between Collas and Cambas, if I can be very direct about it.

I asked Rojas to explain these great differences between Colla and Camba.

I think that, well, we must start with behavior, with personality, that is very important. For me, all you need to know about the differences between the Collas and the Cambas is found in the whole problem of personality. If we look at the Nación Camba or the Camba culture or if we look at a Camba or a Colla, the behavior, the whole aspect, is completely different. I want to make a very important point, and that is that what they always fall back on is five hundred years of slavery, they talk with a lot of resentment, a lot of hate, about the fact of five hundred years of Spanish colonialism. But we don't have any problem with this.

Cambas don't have a problem with Spanish colonialism?

No, for us, colonialism doesn't mean something terrible, no, for us colonialism is understood only as a process of change.

Wasn't it also a period of slavery, or servitude, something that was also bad for people?

Not at all, not for us. This is one of the great differences, no? They [Collas] always protest, always with resentment, always with hate, and it's always focused on us, as if we were the colonizers.

Then why does the media claim that the struggle between Cambas and Collas is about racism? Is there racism here in Santa Cruz, in your movement?

Look, as I said, our struggle is not racial, it is a struggle for Camba interests. But I want to return to what I said, the differences are in the behavior, the personality, between Cambas and Collas. In the highlands, people are very shy, very withdrawn, very . . . they are very afraid, they live in fear. Here in the East, in Nación Camba, people are very charismatic, very sociable, they look after anyone no matter where he comes from. That is why one of our symbols is the hammock, because the traveler could always sleep in the countryside no matter which property or town.

But I pressed Rojas—if racism was not part of the Camba struggle against the highlands, how could he explain the racist slogans I had heard at UJC rallies, such as "indio de mierda" and "llama de mierda"?

It's true, some of that is the result of our own anger. Even though ours is a peaceful struggle at the base, we must remember that the struggle has various levels.

Including those that demanded the use of violence?

For us, it depends on the situation, no? I want to return again to the question of difference, of different personalities. These people, these indigenous peasants, according to history, they have invaded Santa Cruz several times, in '57, in '71, in the '60s, they have always wanted to take power from the East . . . uh, and they have committed many atrocities against our people, no? So there is always a fear here that these people will return again and again to commit the same kinds of crimes, the same violations. That's why we must prepare ourselves; we are facing the hate of all the peasants, the militants, the masistas.

But how are you going to defend yourselves if they have the support of the government?

We know how, I can say that, and we are right now building up our equipment so that we can confront the government from a position of equality, no? Here in the East, people are very used to hunting, every weekend, everyone has his shotgun, his hunting lodge in the forest, many have two shotguns, three, it depends, no?

And is the UJC prepared to use these weapons if it becomes necessary, depending, as you say, on the situation?

Yes, we are ready, the people are ready to use them, to speak plainly. Isn't this why we organize, why we train? But the official answer is no, armed resistance is not part of our plans.

CONCLUSION: "WHEN INDIANS WERE JUST INDIANS"

Santa Cruz de la Sierra dolorosa,
mi sangre está hecha de tu sangre y tu martirio es mi martirio.
En tu rostro se va el beso como una huella de traición,

en tus lágrimas se va el musgo de aguaceros perseguidos.
Ay Terebinto, Terebinto.

—Pedro Shimose, from "Terebinto" in *Poemas para un pueblo* (1968)

The ethnography of ideologies and practices of opposition in Bolivia was an ethnography of mirages. The racist, right-wing, anti-Indian counterrevolutionary who stalked the nightmares of indigenous activists and the cosmopolitan international media alike seemed to disappear just at that moment when I felt as if I had found him (or *her*, see figure 3.7). Perhaps this was a function of the broader ideological moment, the second decade of the post–Cold War, in which the politics of identity had replaced the politics of the traditional revolutionary left. In a time and place in which only *certain* identities were the basis for both moral positioning and political power, no one was willing to embrace *sentimientos* that clashed so obviously with the prevailing currents. These lines of inclusion and exclusion were transparent even to the decolonizing pluralists of MAS. As one government official told me in a discussion of the differences between Morales and García Linera, "Álvaro will never lead this country. He doesn't have the right face."

Yet despite the internal contradictions that seemed to plague Bolivia's anti-government movements, a less masked, more primordial, oppositional cosmovisión was never far from the surface. In January 2009, I spent several hours discussing the fine-grained details of Santa Cruz's political economy with Luis Baldomar Salgueiro, CAO's general counsel. It was a conversation that was frankly wearying. Baldomar seemed to want to drown me in economic statistics and lose me in arcane digressions about import–export relations and the price of soybean futures in order to throw me off the topic I was really interested in—the role of Santa Cruz's economic elites in the regional opposition movement. But then a slip occurred and his mask fell, at least for a moment. I asked him whether or not the MAS government's economic program would be good for the department.

Look, let me tell you honestly, we don't need revolutionary change in Santa Cruz. Everything that's happened here, our progress, whether you are talking about two hundred years or even five hundred years, has depended on the whites [los blancos].

But what about the history of servitude in the region? Wasn't there a time in which indigenous people couldn't even walk through the plaza?

Baldomar, perhaps tired himself, smiled ever so slightly.

Yes, there was even a law. But still, that was when Indians were just Indians.

4

A REVOLUTION WITHOUT REVOLUTIONARIES

El proceso de cambio in a Trotskyized Country

Tu amor revolucionario
te conduce a nueva empresa
donde esperan la firmeza
de tu brazo libertario.

—FROM THE SONG "Hasta Siempre,
Comandante" BY Carlos Puebla (1965)

In an unforgettable chapter entitled "Mines as Cemeteries" from his elegiac *Requiem for a Republic* (1969), Sergio Almaraz Paz gave one of the most searing portraits of the life of a Bolivian miner ever written, the (textual) encounter with which must come prior to any attempt to understand the contradictions, compromises, and sense of betrayal that characterized the place of Bolivia's traditional revolutionary left within the wider post-2005 process of change. Even more, Almaraz's description of the conditions in Bolivia's mines serves as an important reminder that the social category of "worker" was always intended to generate allegiances that were historical and programmatic rather than affective, since the actual lived realities of those who were forced by broader structural circumstances to sell their labor spanned a wide and often tragic range, despite being fictive kin members of the same political economic class.

First, there was the sheer inhumanity of a Bolivian miner's life, one in which the mines he was forced to navigate were deep and dangerous fissures on a remote and unforgiving landscape that seemed to reject the presence of the miners with its utter toxicity.

> At four or five thousand meters above sea level, where not even the *stipa ichu* grows, lies the mining settlement. The mountain, angered by man, wishes to expel him. Poisoned water wells from that metal-filled belly. In the mineshafts, the constant dripping of a yellowish and evil-smelling liquid called *copagira* burns the miners' clothing. Hundreds of kilometers away where there are rivers with fish, death arrives in the form of the liquid poison proceeding from the waste heaps of the ore-processing mills.[1]

Amid this miasma, the Bolivian miner and his family attended to the exigencies of the everyday, despite knowing that inside of every miner, inside of every provider, inside of every worker, that the breath of life was steadily and inevitably being stolen.

> And there, in that cold, seeking protection in the lap of the mountain, where not even weeds dare to live, are the miners. Settlements lined up with the symmetry of prisons, low-roofed shacks, walls of mud and stone lined with old newspapers, corrugated iron roofs, earth floors; the wind from the high plains creeps through the cracks, and the family huddled in improvised beds—usually a few sheepskins are enough—which doesn't catch cold runs the risk of suffocating. Hidden behind those walls are the people of hunger and diseased lungs, those of the three shifts of the working day, the round of twenty-four hours. Without past or future,

this misery has swallowed everything. . . . In this sordid eternity, its inhabitants recall the penal servitude of a Czarist village because one feels that they are equally isolated and a sentence hangs over their lives.

With a lifespan of around thirty-five years, the end came quickly for a Bolivian mine worker. Bolivia's mining settlements were filled with 30-year-old widows and their young children.

The particles of dust produced by the drills driving into the rock remain stuck in the lungs, hardening them gradually until they produce, clearly and slowly, death. The shift has come to an end: shriveled, with a deathly complexion, inflamed eyes, overcome by huge fatigue, those who have taken their daily dose of annihilation return from the mineshaft. The disease for which there is neither a cure nor drugs is hidden as long as can be, but the burning eyes, the skin stuck like dry leather to the cheekbones, and the constant tiredness cannot be concealed for long. He and his comrades know what is going on; so do the women: when the first symptoms—vomiting blood—appear, they keep silent. There are no desperate gestures. The women understand and resign themselves to it.

When the 31 or 33 or 35-year-old mine worker could not descend into the *socavón* any longer, he was obliged to die politically before his actual death, otherwise the family he left behind would have been even more destitute than it already was.

The end will be brought on by a brief visit to the doctor; the certificate will say: "permanent and total incapacity." This will be followed by a bizarre bureaucratic funeral in the social security offices in La Paz where the dying man will struggle to achieve the qualification for a "pension" for incapacity, which will never be more than half his salary and often one third or a quarter. It is the way in which Bolivian society worries about the destiny of those who have been annihilated. . . .

In the end, within a broader political economy in which the exploitation of the Bolivian miner reached to the very substance of life itself, in which the body became a means of production to be exhausted and then discarded, the miner's own labor was of very little value within the larger extractive system. He didn't even exercise control over the circumstances of his own life.

These condemned men are not the owners of the mineral. In truth they never were. If anything really belongs to them, it is death. They are not possessed by the "cursed thirst for gold" which Virgil speaks of; outsiders to their own fate, they have been nailed there by the mechanism of the world economy. . . .

And was anything of lasting value left behind? As Almaraz puts it, mining in Bolivia was a Faustian bargain that left only emptiness in its wake.

There is a monstrous reality: whoever has tin will have the country, but that possession signifies the destruction of those who produce it. Mining is the sinkhole through which the vitality of the country drains away. Over more than three centuries it left nothing, nothing at all.[2]

Yet despite the bitter truth in Almaraz's account, something critically important did emerge from a legacy of exploitation so iconic in its extremes that it formed the foundation for Eduardo Galeano's (1971) metaphor—the "open veins of Latin America"—used to describe the five hundred years of embodied pillage of an entire continent. When a traditional revolutionary left finally crystallized in Bolivia between the late 1920s and the mid-1940s, the Bolivian miner was at the very center of its ideological articulation, political mobilization, and, perhaps most importantly, its moral imagination.

As Mesa has explained, this was largely the result of Bolivia's peculiar internal economy, which was dominated by what he describes as "a system of pre-capitalist production" (2008: 431). In comparison with neighboring Chile and Argentina, Bolivia did not have a significant national proletarian base in which an emerging global and regional ideology of workers revolution could take root. Although "socialist and anarchist ideas from Chile and Argentina" played a role in the formation of early Bolivian labor associations such as the Unión Gráfica Nacional (1905), the Sociedad Mutualista Ferroviaria (1913), and even the Federación Obrera del Trabajo (1926, the most important forerunner of the Central Obrera Boliviana, or COB), these movements were essentially confined to "a small group of intellectuals with minimal labor support" (Klein 1982: 173).

However, the organic development of a revolutionary left in Bolivia was eventually accelerated by the catastrophe of the Chaco War (1932–35), which fractured Bolivia's ancien régime and made possible the creation of a distinct ideological tradition whose influence would remain an important current up to and throughout the post-2005 period. This tradition was marked by three key events. The first was the role of Tristán Marof (the nom de guerre of Gustavo Navaro) in the foundation of the Partido Obrero Revolucionario (POR) in 1935. Marof, a sucrense born in 1889, was originally a supporter of the last of the national oligarchs, the Republican Bautista Saavedra. But during the 1920s, Marof traveled to Europe, where he underwent something like a conversion to Marxism, after which he penned the radical treatise *La justicia del Inca* (1926), in which he argued for "land to the people, mines to the State."

As Mesa puts it, Marof was "violently anti-fascist and *antimovimientista*" (2008: 468) and was one of the most high-profile intellectuals to be openly and publicly opposed to the Chaco War, for which he was forced into exile (POR was founded in Córdoba, Argentina). Even though Marof broke with the co-founder of POR, José Aguirre Gainsbourg, in 1938 to form a new political party, the Partido Socialista Obrero Boliviano, it would be POR that would endure over the decades as a force of waxing and waning degrees of importance in Bolivian economic, political, and social life.

The second key development in the emergence of an organic revolutionary left in Bolivia was the adoption and later ideological elaboration of the principles of the Fourth International by POR after 1938.[3] At a general level, the Fourth International was a way to describe the explicit challenge that the exiled Leon Trotsky made to the hegemony and perceived ideological heresies of Stalin. In casting the Fourth International as the representative of the true road to socialism, in opposition to the Third International or Comintern, which were dominated by Stalin and the Soviet Union, Trotsky sought to claim the ideological high ground, in part as an explanation for his tragic fall from grace and expulsion from the center of Soviet power.[4]

But more specifically, the Fourth International promoted the concept of "permanent revolution," which emphasized the international dimensions of socialist mobilization against the global capitalist system, and argued that the proletariat in "backward countries" like Bolivia should not wait for a series of "separate historical epochs" to create the conditions for revolution. Instead, as Trotsky urged, the workers in the so-called backward countries should struggle for the capacity to "carry[ ] on independent politics" in order to "liquidat[e] . . . feudal heritages" and "overthrow . . . the imperialist yoke," which was, crucially, in all cases a global yoke whose national effects were "determined by the peculiarities and specific conditions of each backward country and to a considerable extent by the degree of its backwardness" (Trotsky 1938).[5]

The third important development, one whose effects remained relevant into the Morales period decades later, was the ideological and political alliance forged between POR and the Bolivian miners' union, the Federación Sindical de Trabajadores Mineros de Bolivia (FSTMB). If it was true that Bolivia lacked a real proletarian class because the economy was still largely agrarian and "pre-capitalist," the exception was the thousands of miners, who labored—as we have seen—under atrocious conditions within a national industry that epitomized capitalist exploitation. What remained was for Bolivia's miners to coalesce into a vanguard in Bolivia's struggle in the wider permanent revolution. To provide the doctrinal blueprint for this turning point, the new leader of POR, Guillermo Lora, offered a set of ideological principles to the FSTMB at its First Special Congress held at the Hochschild-owned Pulacayo mine in 1946, just two years after the founding of the FSTMB.

Lora's "Thesis of Pulacayo" argued that the Bolivian miners' movement should occupy a unique and privileged position in the broader workers' struggle. This was because the "class struggle [had] taken on an extremely war-like character" in the country, a development that demanded the militancy of hardened men whose working lives were defined by "extreme boldness" and "incomparable vigor" and yet were "practically virgin in politics," without the kinds of allegiances that tarnished "the 'leftists' who had sold out to Yankee imperialism."

At the same time, Lora's thesis sought to lay the ideological groundwork for the inclusion of other potential allies in the struggle, even if Bolivia's miners would form the central core: "the proletarian revolution in Bolivia does not imply the exclusion of other exploited layers of the nation; on the contrary, it means the revolutionary alliance of the proletariat with the peasants, the artisans, and other sectors of the urban petite bourgeoisie."

Although an ideological alliance with the peasantry would take on more obvious importance, particularly during the National Revolution and subsequent agrarian reform, it was the gesture to the other "exploited layers" that would have a more subtle and arguably longer lasting influence into the post-2005 period. As will be seen below, Lora's inclusionary rhetoric would form the foundation for the enduring influence of Trotskyist ideology among radical factions in Bolivia's urban workers' movements, especially the teachers' unions. The principles from the 1946 "Thesis of Pulacayo" explained and justified the role of *all* Bolivian workers in the global "fight [against] Yankee imperialist plunder" at the same time that it recognized the vanguard position of the miners, whose place at the "economic axis of national life" made them the "political axis of the future revolution."[6]

Although in later years Lora was known to make the extravagant claim that "*Bolivia es un país trotskizado*" (Bolivia is a Trotskyized country) (quoted in John 2009: 5), there is no question that the influence of these early ideological traditions would continue to shape the trajectory of Bolivia's revolutionary left even in the course of the rise and fall (or at least the transformation) of other more politically effective parties such as the Movimiento Nacionalista Revolucionario (MNR).

Even more, as will be seen in this chapter, the enduring influence of Trotskyism throughout Bolivia's workers' movements created clear tensions with the hybrid and identitarian ideology of MAS, tensions that were completely obscured in the general rush to situate Bolivia's process of change within putative regional categories like the "Latin American New Left" or, even more unilluminating, the "pink tide in Latin America" (Chodor 2015).

Indeed, the ethnography of clashing ideologies in Bolivia in the period 2006–15 pointed to three critical ways in which the "democratic and cultural revolution" of MAS represented a radically new form of social and political mobilization, one that was neither merely a new phase in a longer history of revolutionary left politics nor a movement to socialism in the traditional sense. First, the Trotskyist legacy of key workers' organizations like POR, the FSTMB, and even the more diverse COB, whose symbol was the iconic hammer and pututu, brought them into what might be thought of as ontological tension with the political orientation of MAS.

The Trotskyist doctrine of permanent revolution was based in a very different vision of historical change, the origins of social suffering, and, most importantly, the end point toward which the revolutionary struggle was directed. Moreover, given Trotsky's own exile from the mechanisms of political power, it is not surprising that the ideological currents of the Fourth International were structurally hostile to the state. Like all such movements, the Trotskyist revolutionary left in Bolivia imagined a future in which the dictatorship of the proletariat would bring a workers' state into being on the road to communism. From the perspective of Bolivia's traditional revolutionary left, however, the Bolivian state—from the military dictatorships to MAS—remained a willing or unwilling agent of the global capitalist system. This meant that even into the post-2005 period of "democratic and cultural revolution," the state endured as the historic antagonist of the workers' struggle.

Second, despite Guillermo Lora's efforts to develop a revolutionary doctrine that was both faithful to the Fourth International and grounded in the "peculiarities and specific conditions" of Bolivia's ethnic and agrarian reality, the ideological alliance between the Trotskyist revolutionary left and the peasantry remained fraught with contradictions in the decades after a brief period of solidarity during the National Revolution. For example, it was during the regimes of General René Barrientos (1964–65, 1966–69), a fluent Quechua speaker from Tarata (Cochabamba) and a "man of incredible personal charisma" (Mesa 2008: 534), when the Bolivian state first maneuvered to form a "military-peasant pact." Barrientos's overtures to the country's sindicatos campesinos, or peasant unions, exploited a basic incompatibility between the ideology of global communist revolution and the cultural and economic values of (mostly highland) peasant life.

Later, during the military dictatorship of Hugo Banzer, the terms of the military–peasant pact were expanded: "under the pact, the state would guarantee peasant control over the land, or distribute new plots, in return for peasant loyalty" (Thomson et al. 2018). In a 1974 speech in the Palacio Quemado to a group of peasant union dirigentes, Banzer described the supposed hostility between Bolivia's peasants and the country's Trotskyist revolutionary left in stark, brutal terms:

> The country needs order, it requires that people work in peace. That is what Bolivians want. We are going to kick the agitators out of the country. If it is necessary, punish them with the death penalty. What I want is for our peasant brothers to work in peace. Peasant brothers, I will give you instruction as your leader: the first communist agitator who goes to the countryside . . . I authorize you . . . I take responsibility. . . . You can kill him. If not, bring him to me, so that he deals personally with me. I will give you a reward. They are interested in disorder and poverty which are their breeding ground. The peasants should know that communism will take away their lands and return them to the state, but we will defend the lands of peasants. In what communist country in the world does the land belong to peasants? Everything belongs to the state. Whereas we are going to help you to maintain your lands, and if the lands you have are not enough, I offer to give you larger plots in Alto Beni. (quoted in Thomson et al. 2018: 437–38)

During the period 2006–15, the underlying ideological differences between Bolivia's traditional revolutionary left and the peasant movements and the more specific legacy of political manipulation under the military–peasant pact formed the background to yet another explanation for the marginalization of Bolivia's workers' movement from MAS's democratic and cultural revolution. Although Morales emerged from within the cocalero workers' association, the importance of the transformation of 2006 and later was articulated in the language of indigenous empowerment, through the ontology of the Pachakuti ("world renewal" or "world reversal"), and (for some) as the reestablishment of Qollasuyu, the neo-Indianist polity that marked the definitive overthrow of the European colonial order (see chapter 6; see also Postero 2010).

In other words, although the category of "peasant" was at least recognizable within the doctrine of the Fourth International as articulated and vernacularized in the development of Bolivian Trotskyism, the category of "Indian" was not, even less "indigenous," which took on a very different meaning in the post–ILO 169 (1989) and then post-2005 periods from the one it had during the brief florescence in Bolivia of the wider Latin American movement known as *indigenismo*. It is no surprise, therefore, that the heart of support for Evo Morales throughout the 2006–15 period was composed of social movements that were organized around the politics of identity—indigenous, intercultural, indigenous women—rather than the politics of class.[7]

Finally, the process of change represented a historic break with the legacy of Trotskyist ideology and political mobilization for yet another reason. As we have seen, Bolivia's "third revolution" (Dunkerley 2007b) was not just driven by the juridification of the politics of identity writ small (see especially chapter 2). Rather, it was based in the constitutional development of plurinationalism, which projected a new model of the state organized around the devolution of powers by *nation*—ethnic collectivities that would have autonomy over legal, political, and economic matters within their recognized boundaries. Despite the fact that the subsequent articulation of plurinationalism remained very much incomplete and contested in practice, it nevertheless represented a logic of both change and governance that was profoundly different from the vision of the Trotskyist permanent revolution, which was internationalist, anti-ethnic, and driven by the vigor of a radicalized proletariat.

As will be seen below, the deep alienation of Bolivia's traditional revolutionary left from the process of change during the period 2006–15 had important consequences for the development of transformative politics more generally, and not only within Bolivia (see Webber 2017b). These consequences were often experienced in quite visceral ways, as the ethnography of these ideological fractures and moments of disenchantment revealed. From the side of Bolivia's Trotskyist left, the appropriation of the legacy of revolution by the MAS government was nothing less than an unforgivable act of ideological treason. In the "political declaration" that emerged from its 2013 national conference, POR had concluded that MAS was in fact a "pro-imperialist" wolf in revolutionary clothing.

In the tract, POR engaged in a direct attack on Álvaro García Linera, who was held in particular loathing by the PORistas because of his background as a former katarista radical. POR claimed that García Linera was in "open conflict with Trotskyism" in order to "justify the bourgeois appeasement of his government." They decried the fact that it was García Linera who made the government's public argument in support of a recently signed contract with the massive Anglo-Swiss mining company Glencore, which owned Mina Bolívar.

As quoted in the POR declaration, García Linera said during a speech at the mine, "This small group of Trotskyists. . . . Even today they continue mobilizing the miners against us, criticizing us, saying, 'how is it possible that a revolutionary government signed a contract with a private company?'" Then, later in the speech, according to the POR account, García Linera "grabbed a volume from the complete works of Lenin and read a paragraph in which Lenin justifies the agreements that the new Soviet state made with private companies as part of the New Economic Policy." Yet, in a terse phrase that captured just how gaping the chasm was between the ideologues of MAS and Bolivia's Trotskyist old guard, whose sheer marginalization lent it a certain moral authority (if wrapped in pathos), POR showed that it wanted nothing to do with the vice president's invocation of Lenin. As they put it, García Linera, and by extension the entire MAS regime, was nothing more than a "sophist defender of capitalism" (Partido Obrero Revolucionario 2013).

LA EMANCIPACIÓN DE LOS TRABAJADORES SERÁ OBRA DE ELLOS MISMOS

For an up-and-coming unionist with long-term national aspirations, Felipe Machaca Quispe had an unusual background. In 2008, Machaca was the second general secretary of COB, which meant that he was the third most powerful dirigente in the organization. By both COB statute and the traditions of the confederation's hierarchical praxis, the executive secretary of COB was always a miner, someone who had begun his career with mining settlement activism at places like Huanuni or Pailaviri to eventually work his way up through regional *cargos* to culminate in the leadership of the FSTMB and then COB.

The first general secretary of COB, meaning the organization's second leader, was by tradition drawn from the leadership of the country's manufacturing union "matrix," the Confederación General de Trabajadores Fabriles de Bolivia (CGTFB, founded in October 1951), someone who had likewise arrived near the pinnacle of Bolivia's national sindicato leadership after years of establishing bona fides first as a laborer, then as a local shop leader, and finally as a man (it was always a man) who was seen to possess the ideal mix of capacity and charisma to take on responsibilities for the welfare of the sector itself.

COB's second general secretary—the third member of its executive leadership—was by tradition a representative of the peasant union structure, which did not mean the more radical indigenista or indianista (or even neo-indianista; see chapter 6) organizations affiliated with the Consejo Nacional de Ayllus y Markas del Qullasuyu (CONAMAQ), but rather those under the banner of the Confederación Sindical Única de Trabajadores Campesinos de Bolivia (CSUTCB).

Yet Machaca was not a typical CSUTCB leader. He had not emerged from one of the immediately recognizable highland regions that produced most of the CSUTCB power brokers, such as the provinces around Lake Titicaca or the norte de Potosí. Machaca had instead come up through the local peasant union organizations representing communities in what he called the "tropical arc" formed by the southern boundary of the Parque Nacional Madidi in the north of La Paz Department, a remote and culturally interstitial region. It is no surprise, therefore, that Machaca viewed what he called his "union career" as a stepping-stone to a wider and more interconnected world.

Machaca, who was thirty-seven years old in late 2008, had begun to play a role within CSUTCB's leadership in 1996, during the first government of Sánchez de Lozada. Later, in the course of regional protests during the 1999–2000 Water War, he developed a reputation within CSUTCB and COB as a young but distinctly radical ideologue, one who could articulate a preternaturally sophisticated vision of revolutionary change that was consistent with Trotskyist dogma yet practical enough to form the basis for direct mobilization. During the highly charged years of his tenure within COB's leadership, Machaca was seen as a "far more combative" (Webber 2011: 224) spokesperson for the traditional revolutionary left than COB's maximal authority himself, the forty-eight-year-old ex-miner from Catavi, Pedro Montes González. Machaca was a shrewd tactician of permanent revolution. His understanding of strategy was anchored in a historical perspective.

The most important thing to emphasize is that COB is a revolutionary workers' movement that is committed to structural transformation and the establishment of a workers' state. In order to accomplish this goal, we utilize three methods in our struggle: the blockade, the mobilization in the streets of the masses, and the hunger strike. It really depends on the moment in history. During times of military dictatorship, we used the hunger strike as our main form of direct action. It can be done in offices or buildings and there is little threat of repression [by the government]. Street mobilization and blockades are not techniques to be used against a dictatorship because they will be violently stopped. But during the time of democracy, as now, the main methods [of direct action] are the march and the blockade. These allow us to confront the state directly with many comrades.

But why, I asked Machaca, would COB and the broader workers' movement want to confront the government of Evo Morales if it were true that it was at the head of a movement to socialism and committed to the revolutionary transformation of Bolivian society?

Look, the question of Comrade Evo is very complicated for us, I'm not going to deny that it isn't. You can say that he used to be a revolutionary. Let's remember that Comrade Evo was a dirigente and fought against the state while he was a cocalero in the Chapare. But now he's forgotten his worker comrades in COB, in the CSUTCB, in CONAMAQ, in Bartolina Sisa. The main problem is that Comrade Evo has surrounded himself with q'aras, including many who served in the neoliberal governments of the right.[8]

Did Machaca believe that this group of "q'aras" was responsible for the fact that the government had placed so much emphasis on the new constitution as the instrument of change?

We in COB don't care about the new constitution, or the so-called Constituent Assembly. Our statute doesn't speak of such things. We believe, as I said, in self-government [auto-gobierno] and we realize self-government through our institutional congress.

He went on.

However, speaking of the Constituent Assembly, we workers had no voice because we are not a political party. We are a workers' party committed to real, structural revolution. Comrade Evo has forgotten not only the workers of Bolivia, but himself. He has forgotten where he came from, his status.

It sounded to me, I remarked to Machaca, as if the conflict between the workers and the government was more complicated than simply a struggle over doctrine, over which vision of revolution was most legitimate or consistent with Bolivia's current circumstances. What did he mean by "status"?

Well, look what happened during the different blockades that we [in COB] supported from the national level. We are very obedient and disciplined when it comes to knowing how to elevate a struggle to the national level—it starts at the base. When our local comrades are calling for support and we decide to take direct action at the national level to support them, we do it with discipline. And I personally go to the blockades to reinforce my comrades, no? because they want to see their national leaders with them when they struggle. They think like that, that a local blockade should also be a national blockade, that the union leaders should be out in front and not hiding in an office in La Paz. That's why I was elected in the national congress [of COB], because I will always be out in front with my comrades. That is what bothers him [Evo], the fact that we are willing to take direct action to support our worker comrades. For example, when we had the last meeting with him, the last dialogue as they called it, he was extremely upset and he tried to insult me. Can you believe it? Me, an Aymara, and he, an orureño, me a paceño, as I said, I'm from La Paz, the provinces, and he's a quirquincho [someone from Oruro]. . . . But it didn't matter, during this so-called dialogue he kept trying to insult me, using nasty words, I had to defend myself. That's just not right, a dirigente, a president of the republic, can't offend COB *like that.*

So was it true to say that the dispute between the workers and the government was really about personal differences rather than ideology?

That's not quite true. The ideological conflict, as you call it, is very real, as we discussed. But the president can't just offend COB *like that in front of all of the comrades. All I said was, "Comrade, or Mr. President, you have promised to give a political response to the workers but yet you haven't." That made him angry again, because he said, "if my advisers, if my ministers don't respond, then I am going to respond to these demands myself, like a president." But then in just a few minutes he forgot about the promise and all I did was remind him of it. Yet even though I was under great danger, they could have destroyed me, I still came to the meeting [with the president]. I sat in that seat, in the president's office, and I tried to represent the workers. But I was ignored, I was insulted. I just can't believe that a president of the republic would say those things to his brother, to his brother Aymara who is a* paceño *from the provinces.*

Yet if Felipe Machaca's own complicated relationship with Morales and the MAS government was an apt symbol for the ambivalent position of COB more generally as an overarching, multilayered national workers' organization that struggled to represent both its radical and oppositional and its more pragmatic constituents, the same could not be said of the FSTMB, which occupied a unique, even sacred, position within Bolivia's traditional revolutionary left. As we have seen, although the FSTMB predated COB, it played a central role in the national workers' confederation from the beginning, and its longtime executive secretary, Juan Lechín Oquendo, was also a long-serving executive secretary of COB (FSTMB, 1946–87; COB, 1952–87). But as the representative of the nation's miners, the FSTMB was distinguished in several key ways.

First, as Almaraz's account at the beginning of this chapter suggests, the life of the Bolivian miner was one with its own ineluctable history, mytho-practices, and even eschatology, in which:

> Miners cross themselves as they enter the mine and pray to the saint in the chapel at level zero, but once they enter the lift to go down to their work levels, they are in the domain of the Devil, or Tío, the Spanish term

for the pre-conquest Supay or Huari. They cannot utter the names of the Christian saints or deities, nor can they bear any Christian symbols such as a cross, and they are even wary of working close to the veins of metal with a pick, which looks like a cross and might cause the Tío to withdraw the riches he has revealed. (Nash 1993: 7; see also Taussig 1980)

Yet the daily descent into the mines was also the daily encounter with the miner's own death, one in which the symbols and gestures from multiple eschatological traditions were brought together in an "embrace [of] apparently contradictory systems" (Nash 1993: 7).

The effort to construct an elaborate Geertzian web of meaning within which the ravages of mining could be endured, the wasting away of the miner's body, the slow suffocation, the retreat of the life force in front of family and comrades, and the intimate relationship with the spirits of the underworld, all marked the miner as a worker whose life was tragic, heroic, and roughly poetic in completely distinct ways. In this sense, the FSTMB did not merely represent a body of workers who were, like all members of the proletariat, structurally exploited by the global capitalist system. Rather, it was the political and social voice of a class of workers and their families whose singular embodied suffering and resilience paradoxically expressed something essential about the Bolivian reality itself.

Second, as the representative of the nation's miners, the FSTMB promoted an ideology of emancipation that was partly derived from Marxist doctrine but was also influenced by the peculiar forms of worker solidarity that miners developed in the face of constant danger. The motto of the FSTMB, taken from the *Communist Manifesto*, which was emblazoned on the bronze plaque that adorned its ramshackle offices that had become over the years squeezed into a commercial zone in the heart of the Prado in La Paz, was, "the emancipation of the workers will be the job of the workers themselves." This was an ideology for transformation that was both political and profoundly anti-political at the same time.

It was political in that it called on Bolivia's miners to always consider how their class position was part of a wider political economy whose contradictions and modes of violence demanded its eventual destruction. Yet it was anti-political in that it implied a strategy of collective self-reliance that was rooted in the miners' experiences of solidarity against a long line of institutions and actors—the mine owner, the military regime, the democratic state—that exploited, repressed, or ignored them. This is what Bolivian miners meant when they insisted that theirs was a workers', rather than a political, movement. As

Guido Mitma, the FSTMB executive secretary in 2008, explained to me, "we are not committed to any national government. We are committed to the principle of democratic self-governance uncontaminated by the interests of *any* government and its desire to control us."[9]

And third, the FSTMB occupied a unique position within Bolivia's traditional revolutionary left in the way that it conceived of itself as a vanguard whose forms of mobilization were what might be thought as "para-ideological"—that is, they took shape in relation to the Trotskyist principles of the "Thesis of Pulacayo," but at a certain sideways remove. In this way, the FSTMB served as a vanguard of permanent revolution that worked in parallel with the vanguard practices of the intellectualist POR. If POR was often content to express the imperatives of revolutionary change in the abstract, as a matter of doctrine, the miners of the FSTMB expressed these imperatives viscerally, bodily, with a simmering rage that threatened explosive violence.

It was no surprise, therefore, that POR was always much more influential among Bolivia's urban teachers' unions (as will be seen below) than it was in the mining camps. Rather than stacks of Lora's monumental five-volume *Historia del movimiento obrero boliviano*, the miners of the FSTMB were known (and feared) for their use of dynamite during protests, which brought the sound and fury of a miner's life to the streets of La Paz; their mining helmets, which were covered in stickers (an ominous favorite was one of a death's head, itself wearing a mining helmet); and their sheer physical presence, in which the sight of hundreds of determined and reputedly fearless miners marching shoulder to shoulder was one that troubled the soldier, the police officer, and the politician in equal measure.

KNOWLEDGE BREAKS THE CHAINS OF ENSLAVEMENT

In the first years after the Russian Revolution of 1917, one of the most influential artists to emerge during the golden age of Soviet propaganda posters was Alexei Radokov, a satirical caricaturist from St. Petersburg. He was particularly well known for a series of posters created for the revolutionary news agency (ROSTA) that were designed on the model of the traditional Russian *lubki*, which were popular prints created to educate a largely illiterate population about moral, nationalist, or religious themes. Radokov's work focused on an innovation of the early Soviet government, which was to make universal education a key pillar of revolutionary change.[10] In a striking 1920 poster, Radokov depicted a Russian peasant against a bright blue and red background walking over a cliff, blindfolded, arms outstretched. The caption reads: "The uneducated is like a blind man. Misfortune and failure await him everywhere." And in another celebrated 1920 poster, also on the theme of revolution and education, Radokov drew a heavy chain between two dark factories against a mustard-colored sky. A black cloud hovers over the top of the scene. From within the cloud, evoking Michelangelo's Sistine Chapel, an omnipotent hand emerges to push down on the chain with a large stack of weighty tomes topped by a feather writing quill. Under the picture, Radokov writes: "Knowledge breaks the chains of enslavement."

An uncannily similar image was used as the official symbol of the Federación Departamental de Trabajadores de Educación Urbana de La Paz (FDTEULP), traditionally the most radical teachers' union within the nationwide Confederación de Trabajadores de la Educación Urbana de Bolivia (CTEUB). The FDTEULP was located in a historic building on the corner of Calle Ingavi and Calle Genaro Sanjinés, about three blocks from Plaza Murillo in the very center of the city. The La Paz union was by far the largest among the twenty-eight national urban teachers' federations, with more than 30,000 members. During the period 2006–15, its headquarters in central La Paz, which had been the locus of mobilization and ideological training for decades, was an oppositional Trotskyist redoubt surrounded by the hostile MAS forces of the central government just blocks away.

Hanging over the FDTEULP's large meeting hall was the union's wooden *escudo*, which, given how far the union had fallen out with MAS leaders, was appropriately shaped in the form of a shield, ready to be wielded in battle. Over a painting of La Paz Department and a sash in the colors of the Bolivian flag, the FDTEULP crest depicted the majestic Illimani with a blazing sun rising behind it. In front of and larger than both the mountain and sun were two hands, one of which held an open book upright. The other hand was a clenched fist, the symbol first used in 1917 by the Industrial Workers of the World, which went on to become a popular symbol of revolutionary resistance and solidarity. The two hands on the wooden escudo were bound by shackles and a chain, which had broken in the middle—knowledge breaks the chains of enslavement.

The walls of the FDTEULP were covered with lithographs, posters, paintings, and photographs that spanned the full range of the union's traditional revolutionary heritage. The contrast that these visual symbols of Bolivia's Trotskyist labor movement made with the government's constitutional and identitarian revolution was stark. A 1989 watercolor by Mangel Machicado depicted a throng of teachers marching in support of three hunger strikers during the nationwide mobilizations against the "pro-imperialist and *fondomonetarista*" (Mesa

2008: 578) policies of the Siles Zuazo government (1982–85). Another 1989 watercolor by Machicado was even more dramatic: a tight line of workers—teachers, miners, peasant laborers—surges forward with clenched fists outstretched like battering rams. They push violently against a small group of men that includes Paz Estenssoro (with an MNR arm band), a Spanish conquistador, a Bolivian Central Bank official, Uncle Sam (in red, white, and blue top hat), and, somewhat incongruously, Batman. At Paz Estenssoro's well-shod feet lies a crumpled brochure for a Bolivian mine with the words, in English, "For Sale." The marchers, men and women, carry a large banner against their adversaries that says "Bolivia Will Not Be a Hacienda for the Gringos."

A lithograph by "MAMD" from 1995, during the height of the Sánchez de Lozado government, featured Uncle Sam again, this time sitting at a table in front of the Palacio Quemado with various government officials moving toward him in a gesture of fawning accommodation. The embodiment of North American power plays with various toys on which are written the acronyms of the five major national enterprises that Goni was then in the process of "capitalizing," including the Empresa Nacional de Electricidad (ENDE), Yacimientos Petrolíferos Fiscales Bolivianos (YPFB), the Empresa Nacional de Telecomunicaciones (ENTEL), the Empresa Nacional de Ferrocarriles (ENFE), and Lloyd Aéreo Boliviano (LAB), the national airline. On the table, Uncle Sam has written "Bolivia: The New Colony—capitalization, educational reform, popular participation."[11] There is a look of worry on Uncle Sam's face, and the Bolivian toys he is playing with have begun to topple over because a group of workers is about to launch stones into his face with slingshots and *huaracas* (Andean slings) from point-blank range.

Another lithograph on the walls of the FDTEULP, a tableau, was simply entitled *Communism*. Nine separate images within the panorama depicted revolutionary history: the bushy bearded Marx and Engels; Lenin, "Father of the Russian Revolution"; "repression of the Russian people by the Tsar's armies"; Trotsky, "the force behind the permanent revolution"; "Lenin inciting the people to rebel against the Tsar"; an image of a strangely stereotypical European or North American family standing in front of a factory, the wife holding a bouquet of flowers in one hand and a sickle in the other, the man raising a hammer above his head, the son with a soccer ball, the blonde daughter dressed in what appears to be an aerobics outfit, underneath all of whom the caption proclaims solemnly, "in communism, the means of production will be for all"; Mao Tse-tung, "creator of the Chinese revolution"; Ho Chi Minh, "Vietnamese leader"; and, finally, a photograph of Guillermo Lora in his ever-present newsboy cap.

A final piece of revolutionary propaganda on the walls, from the years of the second Morales government, was a poster just outside the office of the FDTEULP's executive secretary. Under "Federación Departamental de Trabajadores de Educación Urbana de La Paz" in simple black block writing was a drawing of an arm and hand reaching toward the sky against a red background. On the arm, an image portrayed a shadowy line of workers marching in a single file line; the hand clenched a loaded Bergmann MP35 submachine gun, the weapon that was used by the Nazi SS but later confiscated by the Soviet Union only to be exported as foreign aid to places like Cuba, Angola, and Vietnam. In a direct warning to the Morales government, the slogan underneath the raised arm read, "Neither Elections, nor a Constituent Assembly. Long live the popular insurrection!"

This sense of behind-closed-doors yet robust militancy was palpable during the years after the national elections of 2009 but before the turning point of the 2011 TIPNIS conflict. As time passed, however, it became clear to those in the traditional Trotskyist left that their revolutionary vision was being excluded from MAS's process of change. As a consequence, the cadres of unionists eventually returned to their historic posture of antagonism toward the Bolivian state, which returned the favor by moving against the Trotskyist workers' organizations legally, politically, and ideologically. Yet at least until the end of 2010, the militants in the FDTEULP remained openly and publicly critical of the Morales government and MAS more generally, which they viewed as false prophets of revolution. FDTEULP's executive secretary during these years was José Luis Álvarez, a highly visible ideologue who was rumored to rule over the large teachers' union with an iron fist.

Although he considered his own biographical history an irrelevant distraction from the important questions of revolution and class struggle, Álvarez received his early and formative ideological education in the militant mining settlements of southern Potosí. He was born in the COMIBOL-owned mining town of Telamayu, which was connected by a short bridge to the "civil town" of Atocha in Sud Chichas Province in the far south of the department, about 100 km from the Argentine border. Álvarez became an orphan at age three when both of his parents died, first his mother, in childbirth, then his father, who was a miner. He was raised by a sister of his father in Telamayu, where he attended the COMIBOL school until he was seventeen. As he explained:

It was after my oldest brother returned to Telamayu that I got my first real taste of politics. It would have been around 1979 or early 1980. My brother became a dirigente, he had been persecuted [during the Banzer dictatorship]. *He gave me a book, a little book by Lora, called* La Cartilla del Obrero, *in which everything about historical materialism is clearly explained. After reading that book, that was it, I was committed to* POR *and the revolutionary line. It would have been in 1980, because I remember that there was a large miners' congress [in Telamayu]. The mining congresses were very politicized, they had a good level of political understanding. Now [2010], the workers' movement, in general, has a very low level of politics, much has been lost. . . . Anyway, during the congress [in 1980] there were many spirited debates, a lot of planning for the future. I was getting ready to graduate and a group of us went to the congress to sell soft drinks and coffee to the miners and the people who were in town for the graduation. That was when I definitely became a militant for* POR *and dedicated my life to the struggle. Right after, I served in the army, then I entered the teachers' training college, where I helped organize the Unión Revolucionaria de Estudiantes Normalistas, which was definitely on the Trotskyist line. Later, I came to La Paz for university and I was a leader in the* URUS, *the Unión Revolucionaria de Universitarios Socialistas, also a Trotskyist movement.*

In Álvarez's political and ideological analysis, the workers' movement had become too closely intertwined with the Morales government. He was particularly critical of the close relationship between COB leaders and MAS.

We believe that capitalism is a global system and therefore we reject the theory of revolution in one country. That's what was developed in Russia, but the decay of Marxism there showed that the theory was not viable. So we have always promoted and struggled for the alternative, permanent revolution, and because of this we [Trotskyists] *have contributed enormously to the capacity of the Bolivian workers' movement to remain independent as much politically as organizationally. We must remember that* COB *was born from this same idea. . . . Unfortunately, what happened after the revolution of '52 is happening now. The majority of union leaders are always pulled along by the party in fashion—then it was the* MNR, *now it's* MAS. *Remember that* COB *took as its banner the "Thesis of Pulacayo" during its first congress, which meant that it was officially committed to revolution as a necessary condition for the development of the country. But beginning with the second congress [of* COB], COB *was already co-opted by its leaders, who had quickly become tied to the interests of the state. We must remember that Lechín was an MNRista, and it was not surprising that he managed to become the vice president in the government of Víctor Paz. So we have always believed, from this period on, that the workers' movement should be in opposition to the government as a true channel for revolutionary ideas, even if other elements of the workers' movement, especially its leaders, have become, as now, a channel for the politics of the bourgeoisie. In this sense, the leaders of the*

*workers' movement have developed both revolutionary and counterrevolution-
ary currents from the inside of the unions. That's what is happening now—the
leadership of* COB *has again become a counterrevolutionary force that is openly
masista* [followers of MAS].

But how, I asked Álvarez, could he argue that COB was "counterrevolutionary" because of its close support of MAS, since the MAS government was
committed to a cultural and democratic revolution that embraced many socialist principles?

*Those are just words. In fact, the government of Evo Morales is neither
socialist nor revolutionary.*

If not, what it is?

*From our perspective, it is clear that this government is bourgeois reform-
ist. He* [Morales] *will say to you, openly, "we are not going to destroy large-scale
capitalist private property." In fact, this government is protecting the large estates.
This is the opposite of a real revolutionary politics. Why? Because we know that the
cause of our suffering, of our misery, is the existence of bourgeois private property.
But Evo Morales has a lot of respect for these property owners. He says, "I'm not
going to fight with the transnational corporations because I want to be partners
with them." For this reason, in our analysis, the policies of this government change
absolutely nothing structural from what had been done under Sánchez de Lozada.
In reality, Evo Morales is for us an obstacle in the struggle for a workers' revolution.*

But didn't Evo Morales take part in the fight against the neoliberal governments and their policies, including the privatization of natural resources?

*Yes, he did play a role, that is what is so disappointing for us. You need to
remember that in 2003, 2004, and 2005 the workers were marching for something
specific—the destruction of the capitalist system and everything that supports it,
including the parliament, the state's laws, the state's authorities. Yes, Morales was
part of these mobilizations. But for what purpose? Only to preserve this capitalist
system? The problem is that after he was elected, Morales put all of the government's resources into what was, in effect, the cause of bourgeois democracy. He
made the people who supported him believe that all of their structural problems
could be overcome through things like elections, the Constituent Assembly, and
so on. But in fact, this is never going to happen. All those peasants who were
marching in the streets, who were mobilizing, believed that they were going to be
able to recover their lands that had been taken. But in the constitution that was
just approved* [in January 2009], *it reaffirms the protection for the large estates,
they are not going to be confiscated, everything stays the same even with this new
category called the social function.*[12]

What, I then asked Álvarez, is the alternative to the constitutional revolution of MAS? What is the end toward which he and his comrades continued to struggle?

Well, for us, the real question, the immediate question, is always, "What is the true path to revolutionary transformation?" We say that it is impossible to speak of revolution at the same time you preserve the protections and system that support the owners of private property. He [Morales] is going to continue to use the culture, the educational system, the laws, and the army to maintain his privileges because society, including the current one, has been created in his own image. No, we say that the only way to be able to ensure real transformation is through the revolution, by which we mean armed insurrection.

And is there no relationship between their vision of revolution and the one being promoted by MAS?

Absolutely not. Evo Morales tells us, "we are in the midst of a peaceful process of change, we shouldn't speak of structural revolution but rather a cultural revolution."

But the government says that it wants to "refound" Bolivia. Isn't this simply another way of describing the kind of structural revolution that is at the center of POR's ideological vision?

No, not at all, it has no relation to our vision of revolution. Why not? Because this so-called constitutional revolution doesn't touch the base of the capitalist system. Which is? Large private property. How does one know if a government is revolutionary or not? In relation to the position it assumes toward private property. If it respects and preserves private property, it is a government of and for the bourgeoisie. Now a government might want to implement some reforms, some modifications, it might want to make the capitalist system more humane, and so on, fix some things, but all of this takes place within a bourgeois orientation. For us, it's really quite simple: the only real revolutionary government is one that intends to eliminate, completely, private property, and replace it with social property.

Did Álvarez believe that there was a basic contradiction between constitutional change and revolution?

Yes, you can say that. The kind of revolution that transforms the base of the capitalist system must use certain methods, direct action against property, and armed insurrection. But not with the armed forces and not even through guerrilla mobilization. Guerrilla warfare becomes a method for terrorists. We reject that. The problem with guerrilla mobilization is that it creates groups that are specialized, armed, and who eventually replace the masses as the locus of revolution and then force the masses, in the end, to submit to them. This was the approach of Che, an approach that has failed. It was also the theory of the Sandinistas in Nicaragua, but it also failed because in that case the guerrilla movement was always controlled by elements from the middle class and petite bourgeoisie. The limitation is that this approach always fights for democratic liberties, for democratic governments, this is why sandinismo *didn't end up creating a socialist country in Nicaragua, but only a more democratic one.*

Finally, I asked Álvarez to reflect on the future of permanent revolution in Bolivia with the traditional left under constant threat from the government and peasant support for Morales at historically high levels. For example, were Bolivia's Trotskyists arming themselves for the kind of insurrection that they believed was necessary?

Well, I can't speak for all segments of the workers' movement, but no, the teachers are not armed, at least not any more. The method that we use in the most serious cases is the hunger strike. We learned how effective the hunger strike could be in 1989, at the beginning of Jaime Paz Zamora's government. Everyone was still suffering under the neoliberal politics of 21060 [the 1985 decree of "shock therapy" against hyperinflation]. *When we* [the teachers] *decided to call for a mass hunger strike, the method had become widely discredited, it was like a joke, people would say, "it's more like a vacation for them, the hunger strikers emerge from the strike fatter than when they started." So we knew this but decided to call for a real hunger strike, a hard one, one that would last for at least twenty-four days or until Paz Zamora lowered prices and raised the salaries of workers. The problem at the beginning was that it was the end of the school year and teachers were only thinking about the summer break after a long year of teaching. But there was real camaraderie* [compañerismo]. *We decided, collectively, to do a severe hunger strike, only with water, no food at all.*

Was it effective as a method?

Well, they didn't believe that we were serious in the beginning. But as the days passed, it became clear that we were involved in something different, a different kind of hunger strike. They started to analyze our blood every three days in order to prove to everyone that we were not actually eating, that we were truly in the midst of a real hunger strike. By the tenth day, and definitely by the fifteenth day, we were starting to become really sick; several of us fell into a coma. At that point, many of our comrade teachers who supported our decision to go on a hunger strike pleaded with us to stop, for our own health. But we all said no, if we were going to use the method of the hunger strike we were going to have to see it through, to the end, even if it put some of us in the ground. That hunger strike shook the entire country. Here in La Paz there were around 3,000 hunger strikers. We managed to create a state of siege, the first during a democratic government.

In the end, the government began forcibly feeding the strikers with injections and they also put around 1,500 into confinement. But we succeeded. The government created two new social benefits: one that included more funding for schools and the other that provided funding for books and teaching supplies for teachers. After that, the more radical branch of our movement gained more and more power, until the catastrophe of 2006.

The election of Evo Morales?

Yes, that was a disaster for our movement. Beginning in 2006, our group within the teachers' union, the group from 1989 and before, began to lose support, lose elections; our comrade teachers started to move their support to MAS. Although I was elected in 2008 [as head of the FDTEULP], our support was already collapsing, it was less than 40 percent for the first time in decades.

Had Álvarez and his revolutionary comrades in the teachers' union lost hope?

No, truthfully, I don't believe we have. We have a different understanding of transformation, one that requires a long perspective. The workers' struggle is a struggle for ideals, no? You can hope not to pay the price for everything we have achieved over the years, the benefits, the better conditions for teachers, but there is always a price to pay, and not only during the times of dictatorship. No, we understand that our struggle is marked by a certain paradox, that we must suffer, we must be miserable, as a price for our ideals.

OUR STRENGTH IS IN OUR IDEOLOGICAL FORCE AND CONSISTENCY

If Bolivia's Trotskyist left continued to exercise its historic—if diminishing—influence within the country's workers' movement, especially within the teachers' unions and in the regional and national branches of the FSTMB, throughout the first and second Morales governments, by 2015, much had changed. After managing to weather the storm of the 2011 TIPNIS crisis, the MAS government moved to consolidate its power through the use of political patronage and the strategic use of law to circumscribe various currents of opposition, from the anti-government civic movements in Sucre and Santa Cruz to nongovernmental organizations with close ties to international research and development networks (see chapter 5). The October 2014 general election, in which Morales and García Linera crushed the fractured opposition yet again—despite losing several percentage points in a worrying sign that would continue in the 2015 regional elections—seemed to confirm the government's decision to move forward with its ambitious plans for economic development and social restructuring by further tightening its control over the conditions of public dissent.

With MAS leaders actively working to restore control over the indigenous organizations that had abandoned the Pacto de Unidad after TIPNIS, the COB leadership effectively taking its orders from the national government, and with traditional revolutionary dirigentes like Álvarez under mounting legal and political pressure, it fell to a dwindling group of increasingly isolated PORistas to carry forward the torch of permanent revolution from well outside the structures of either political or syndicalist governance. Bolivia's Trotskyists continued to publish *Masas*, POR's historic ideological organ, once a week in a print edition that was available for 1 boliviano. Because of the sense that POR's propagandists had yet again become targets for government repression, *Masas* was published strictly anonymously so that its broadsides against the government could not be linked to any one militant.

For example, in *Masas* #2411 (August 7, 2015), one political cartoon depicted a MAS official exclaiming, "Bolivia changes, my boss [i.e., Morales] keeps his word," while pointing to a map of Bolivia covered with a white sheet on which was written "sovereignty," "progress," "wealth," "industrialization," "investment," and "economic bonanza." Another man stands to the other side of the map with a scowl on his face wearing a cap that says "Comcipo," which referred to the Comité Cívico Potosinista, the civic organization of Potosí that had been in a series of conflicts with the national government since 2010 over the problem of regional development (see chapter 1). The Potosí cívico pulls the white sheet aside to reveal the real map of Bolivia while the MAS functionary strikes a pose that mimics Edvard Munch's *The Scream*. The uncovered—that is, according to the POR cartoonist, the real—Bolivia is labeled "imperialist pillage," "extractivism," "backwardness," "capitalist crisis," "poverty," and "abandonment."

Articles in the same 2015 *Masas* accused the "ridiculous and arrogant" Morales of using Bolivia's claims against Chile over access to the sea to divert the country's attention from its domestic failures (see chapter 5); of using a "heavy hand to suppress all forms of protest by the exploited and oppressed"; of conducting a "million dollar demagogic campaign that brutally clashes with a reality that it can't hide"; of "dividing and buying off the indigenous leaders who oppose oil exploration in the national parks"; and of leading a "bought-and-sold, exploitative, bourgeois dictatorship of the transnationals" that was the mortal enemy of the idea that "socialism is the road to communism." It's no wonder that POR's ideological struggle against what it perceived as the pretenders in the Palacio Quemado was waged, especially in the post-2014 period, through increasingly clandestine forms. Indeed, through the use of social media and the internet, Bolivia's loyal Trotskyist opposition became more and more virtual.

POR maintained two parallel websites: the more established www.partidoob
rerorevolucionario.org and the newer www.masas.nu, which used the country code top-level domain assigned to the remote Polynesian island nation of
Niue. (Domains with .nu were promoted by Niue especially to organizations
that wanted to maintain anonymity for various reasons.) In addition, POR established a Facebook page (3,144 likes and 3,164 followers as of October 2017),
which was updated regularly with videos, photos, and links to articles critical
of the government. POR also maintained a YouTube channel ("PORmasas"),
where viewers could watch a video recording of the "Song to Leon Trotsky";
Trotsky's famous 1938 speech from Mexico on Stalin's show trials in Moscow; and
a dramatic reading of the *Communist Manifesto* set against a background of
discordant images that ended with the American animation Looney Tunes
closing sequence, except that instead of Porky Pig, the manic music plays
while a stern image of Karl Marx announces, "That's *Not* All, Folks!"

On its websites, POR made available archived copies of *Masas*; provided
links to a vast electronic library that included most of the historical books by
Lora and key documents such as the "Thesis of Pulacayo"; included access to
a photographic library of images from Trotsky's life and political campaigns;
and gave browsers the ability to link to the websites of POR's national representatives in Brazil, Chile, and Argentina.

One especially harsh series of attacks on the MAS government was reached
through a photo link that depicted Morales and García Linera wearing red,
white, and blue Uncle Sam top hats while sitting on a vast pile of U.S. dollars. A
sign on the photo flashed in multiple colors, "The Corruption of MAS: Ama Sua,
Ama Llulla, Ama Llunk'u, Ama Ke'lla."[13] Clicking on the image, readers were
directed to a page entitled "The Corrupt and Corrupting MAS," which featured
dozens of articles that portrayed the government as a hotbed of scandal,
financial wrongdoing, manipulation, organized crime, and even transnational
sex trafficking. Throughout POR's virtual universe, all content was anonymous, no organizational contact information was available, and readers were
simply referred back to POR's main web pages in an endless loop of protective
recursivity.

However, despite this general withdrawal, a small cadre of POR militants continued to maintain an openly anti-government profile, even if they
carried on their political work with a distinct sense of themselves as the last
of a dying ideological class. One of the most intrepid of this dwindling group
of aging Trotskyists was Vilma Plata Arnez. Professionally, Plata Arnez was a
long-serving teacher at Ismael Montes Primary School in La Paz's barrio San
Sebastián. But politically, she had been for more than thirty years one of the

most high-profile and admired POR militants in the country, a comrade-in-arms of fellow leading PORistas like José Luis Álvarez, and a fierce critic of MAS's process of change.

In 2015, Plata Arnez was sixty-one years old. She had lived for the first twenty-five years of her life in Buenos Aires, where she had received her formative early training in revolutionary ideology. She returned to Bolivia in the fraught year of 1979 and became a POR militant at the same time she began her teaching and syndicalist careers. Over the decades, she had earned her Trotskyist bona fides in the course of numerous hunger strikes, street mobilizations, ideological recruitment among her fellow teachers, and, most significantly, a sentence of six months in Obrajes Prison on the orders of the "fascist former Minister of Education Tito Hoz de Vila during the neoliberal period," as she put it.[14]

Plata Arnez had a nuanced understanding of what made the MAS "democratic and cultural revolution" so problematic for Bolivia's traditional revolutionary left. She said she realized that the cause of permanent revolution would confront a totally new kind of crisis as early as the presidential campaign of 2005.

I'll tell you a story. In 2005, I was arriving from abroad the day after the elections. I hadn't heard the results yet, so I asked the taxi driver, "Who won?" He said that Evo Morales had won and then he began crying. He said, "We can't believe it, it's like a dream. He has our skin, our faces." As a Trotskyist, I still tried to discuss this with him. I said, "Just because the new president looks like you doesn't guarantee any real changes."

(Here, she paused in her story to make a link between this point and the case of Barack Obama in the United States. *What has he done for the blacks? Nothing! He's still an imperialist!*)

She continued.

I tried to discuss the political situation with him [the taxi driver], *but it was no use. He cried almost the whole way to my house. After I paid him, I got out of the taxi and he looked at me through the open window, still with tears in his eyes, and said again, "I can't believe it."*

I asked her whether the government's promotion of ethnic pride and new sociopolitical categories like "indígena originario campesino" had caused POR to reconsider its resistance to the cultural dimensions of oppression.

No, we still believe that our ideology represents the best method to fight capitalism. In fact, we are not even convinced that MAS wants to fight capitalism! For example, MAS supports peasants in their development as petite bourgeoisie. This is an error and a betrayal of the historical struggle. Even more, we [in POR] *totally reject the possibility that MAS's ideology or its politics is developing a real road to socialism because it doesn't touch the base of capitalist production. At the* same time, MAS's so-called revolution is focused only on the indigenous population, which makes culture more important than relations of production.

But what about the taxi driver, I asked? How can POR deny that indigenous people are experiencing a different kind of revolution under MAS?

This doesn't mean that we don't support the development of the indigenous nations as part of a real revolution. In fact, we supported the law of consultation and the principle of autonomy. We also denounced the government's actions during TIPNIS.

If MAS was so committed to the status quo, as POR maintained, why did so many people, peasants in particular, support what she called the "indigenous-bourgeois pro-transnational" government of Morales?

I think it is not just related to the question of indigenous identity. It's also related to the decline of the workers' movement in general in Bolivia. This is not very well known, perhaps, but I think the most critical tactic has been the way MAS has divided the different workers' confederations from the federations. Almost always, MAS controls the confederations at the national level even if a particular federation is critical of the government. Eventually, the confederation exerts pressure on the federations and [in this way] can suppress dissent.

But what about the decline of support for POR specifically and the Trotskyist tradition more generally?

Without a doubt, the most important reason has been the disappearance of the miners from the vanguard of the workers' movement.

Why, I then asked Plata Arnez, does POR continue to struggle for permanent revolution in the face of these historical shifts? Wouldn't it be more effective to build bridges with MAS?

Not at all. That would be a betrayal. We are struggling against the panorama of penury that will eventually arrive. We already see this in the recent reductions in spending and the fall in prices [for natural gas]. When austerity comes, and it will, we will be ready with an explanation. In fact, we want the economic bonanza to end because then it will allow for a real confrontation with the MAS government that is the only way for the workers to defend themselves and animate the revolution. The government knows that this confrontation is coming and they are preparing by arming themselves and by bringing in agents from Cuba and Venezuela. In many ways, you can say that we are in a prerevolutionary phase that is waiting for the workers to become actually revolutionary.

Yet isn't it difficult to wait like this, hoping for economic crisis? The country's economy had been growing steadily for almost a decade, even with the recent fall in prices.

Yes, it is difficult. But our strength in the face of these pressures is in our ideological force and consistency.

Finally, I told Plata Arnez that it sounded to me as if POR was becoming a utopian movement, one based on an ideology whose linkage with current political and economic realities was becoming increasingly abstract, remote, idealist. Plata Arnez looked at me with a certain weariness and she seemed to lose herself momentarily, as if distracted by something. But then she quickly recovered and rejected such a heretical proposition.

Socialism, which is the end of bourgeois private property, is not a utopia. It is a historical necessity. The only historical alternative to real socialism is barbarism.

CONCLUSION: THIS IS OUR REVOLUTION, PLEASE NEVER FORGET THAT

Just off the northeastern edge of El Alto International Airport, adjacent to Bolivia's largest air force installation, was an extraordinary facility: the Sistema de Archivo Histórico de COMIBOL (SIAH). Built in 2004, during the short-lived government of the ill-fated historian Carlos Mesa, the SIAH housed what it claimed was the world's most extensive collection of archival materials related to mining. Among its documentary riches, the SIAH contained the full artifactual spectrum of Bolivia's postcolonial mining history, including the business and political records of the Rosca tin barons (Patiño, Hochschild, and Aramayo); the original copy of the "Thesis of Pulacayo" ("paradoxically typed on the letterhead of the mining company of Patiño, the King of Tin"; Gumucio Dagron 2017); and tens of thousands of *expedientes* in which Bolivia's dying miners made their claims for legal protection and a sliver of financial support for their survivors.

The SIAH was a sprawling and impressive structure with high walls topped with barbed wire and a level of security that paralleled the procedures used in the embassies of Sopocachi. Visitors first had to pass through an entrance building staffed by national police officers who verified the reason for the visit by making an internal phone call to the reception office in the main building. After being cleared, visitors were required to leave a form of identification in exchange for a badge, to be worn at all times around the neck.

However, in order to reach the main SIAH building, one had to cross a large internal courtyard that featured a statue of two miners, including a *perforista* wielding a pneumatic jackhammer like a battle lance, and the rusting hulks of several of Patiño's armored luxury sedans. More ominously, the otherwise empty grounds of the SIAH were patrolled by two menacing German shepherds. When I first visited the facility in August 2015, I asked to be escorted from the guard station to the main building.

Perhaps through an act of architectural justice, the interior spaces that contained the archival histories of men and women who spent their short lives laboring in dark, sulfurous, and cramped mining galleries were voluminous and filled with light. The foyer of the SIAH main building was cavernous, like the entrance to a Gothic cathedral. The walls of the SIAH were lined with massive social realist murals and the full series of oversized photographs of Bolivian mining families, mining camps, and miners at work, taken by the Swiss former professional soccer player (FC Moutier and FC Chiasso) and documentary filmmaker Jean-Claude Wicky between 1984 and 2001. From its inception, one person had exercised an outsized role in the promotion of the SIAH as a resource of universal value: Edgar Ramírez Santiesteban.[15]

Edgar Ramírez was a legendary figure in the history of the Bolivian miners' movement. Born in Potosí in 1947, Ramírez got his start as a miner in Potosí's Empresa Unificada del Cerro de Potosí in 1969 after returning to Bolivia from a two-year exile in the United Kingdom during the Barrientos dictatorship. But because of his radical politics and distinct sense of the dangers of mining, Ramírez began looking for a way out of the mines almost as soon as he began working. As he told me in 2015, "there are only three ways out of the mines. First, you can become a chief of gallery, which makes you a supervisor responsible for others. Second, you can enter the sindicato system. When you become a leader, you no longer have to work [as a miner]. And finally, you leave the mines when you die." Ramírez chose the second path.

He left the mine at Potosí in 1971 after only two years of work and quickly ascended the ranks of the local, regional, and, eventually, national mining sindicato hierarchy, even though much of his early reputation was made during a second period of exile in the Netherlands and Chile during the Banzer dictatorship. It was during these early years that he earned the nickname of "Hurricane" Ramírez for his skills as a powerful orator and the force with which he advocated for the interests of Bolivia's miners.

With the exception of a period during the García Meza dictatorship, when he was forced to go into hiding to avoid being detained and likely killed, Ramírez continued his ascent in syndicalist politics, finally becoming general secretary of the FSTMB in 1988, a position he held until he retired from the miners' union in 1994. Although he had only worked in the mines for two years, he retired after twenty-three years of syndicalist leadership with silicosis in 43 percent of his lung tissue. In 2015, at age sixty-eight, Ramírez told me,

I feel just OK, but much better than when I was younger. My friends tell me I actually look better now, mostly because I have lost a lot of weight. You should have seen me when I was working [in the mines]. I looked very much like a miner [más minero]. But I'm much luckier than most of my friends from Potosí because I got out with only 43 percent; 60 percent is bad, 75 percent or 80 percent, you would have been dead a long time ago.

This was also part of the reason Ramírez was, as he explained, the longest serving employee of COMIBOL—everyone else he had come up with through the system had died. Like the Trotskyist teachers of POR, Ramírez also had an acute sense of himself as one of the last of a generation that was almost gone.

In order to continue his struggle for Bolivia's miners even as the syndicalist movement declined, Ramírez developed an early interest in archival techniques and documentary history; for many years, he was the chief archivist for the FSTMB, work that led him eventually to COMIBOL. In 2015, he had presided over the SIAH for eleven years as its director. He had a reputation in these later years as a fiercely protective advocate for Bolivia's mining history. As the essayist and journalist Alfonso Gumucio Dagron has put it, Ramírez "was like one of those dragons that guards the entrance to a mythical cave" (Gumucio Dagron 2017).

Like the rest of the SIAH, Ramírez's director's office was immense, with high ceilings, windows tightly shut against the altiplano winds, and walls covered with various certificates, memorabilia from a life well lived, and prize photos of Comrade Che, who remained one of Ramírez's heroes. Despite its size, his office was kept stiflingly hot through the use of several space heaters. As he explained, "with my lungs, I can't tolerate the cold air."

I wanted to know how, as perhaps the definitive living voice of Bolivia's traditional revolutionary left, Ramírez perceived the Morales era: the constitutional revolution of 2009, Bolivia's supposed movement to socialism, its historic process of change. He first insisted on making short work of the wider critique—one that was partly being made within Bolivia, but mostly by international academics (including many anthropologists)—that the MAS government was somehow politically cynical or ideologically Janus-faced because of its readiness to allow private transnational companies to continue working in the country, especially within the mining and construction sectors, a critique that was usually described as "extractivism."[16]

I have no tolerance for this [critique], *despite the different problems I have with how things have been going over the last years. Our country has always depended on mining and exploration and it always will, no matter the government in power. This is not a question of socialism, or capitalism, or neoliberalism, it's a question of who has the power to decide* [these agreements] *and what is done with the resources that are produced. It is only right that the current government would want to negotiate* [with international companies] *in order to expand the resource base. For example, if I wanted to be a taxi driver, would I learn how to build my own taxi? No! I'd buy a Toyota and get on with my business!*

Nevertheless, despite the fact that Ramírez found the "extractivist" critique wanting, this did not mean that he fully supported the way in which the MAS government had struck the balance between resource development, technology transfer, and the historic needs of Bolivia's workers. In the mining sector, as he explained, over 54 percent of the mineral resources were under the control of only four large transnational conglomerates. In Ramírez's view, this would be the most important task in the coming years—not the abandonment of the country's plans for resource development and exploration, but the diffusion of control over these projects among a range of worker-controlled institutions, including the kinds of local cooperatives that had been on the decline.

Finally, like so many of Bolivia's aging revolutionaries during the period 2006–15, Ramírez had a difficult time fully condemning the Morales government, despite its manifold ideological weaknesses and inconsistencies. As he explained, although the MAS government had its problems, and although some critics described it as neoliberal, its failings were nothing compared to what he called the "dark years" of Bolivian history, years marked by disappearances, exile, torture, and the state-directed murder of opponents. And as always, the personal dimension played a role in how Ramírez viewed the process of change.

I know Evo, I've known him since he was a boy. We both come from the sindicatos. Even though we have never been given a place in the government, you have to remember that we [on the traditional revolutionary left] *have always struggled for the workers rather than simply to gain political power. But I've been around for a long time, I've seen many things, many governments. One time, just after he was elected, I saw Evo, I think it was at a ceremony at the Palacio* [Quemado]. *When I had the chance, I told Evo, "Look, this is our revolution, please never forget that."*

5

THE UNSTABLE ASSEMBLAGE OF LAW

In late December 2008, Petronilo Flores Condori was troubled by the emerging contradictions that characterized the role of law at the heart of Bolivia's process of change. With less than a month remaining before the national vote on the new constitution, Flores Condori understood quite well what it would mean for the government's revolutionary aspirations to be reinscribed in terms of legal forms, logics, and institutions. Although the new constitution articulated a vision of a plurinational state structured by decentralizing and decolonizing processes of autonomía, it was a vision that was nevertheless dependent on the Bolivian state and its instrumentalities of governance, which were, to be sure, themselves very much still emergent. Indeed, Flores

Condori's own position reflected this destabilizing, if perhaps necessary, ambiguity: as we saw in chapter 2, he was at the time the second-in-command in the Vice Ministry of Community Justice and the spokesperson who was charged with defending its position in the first Morales administration, even though the new constitution would soon render the concept of "community justice" obsolete and destined to take its place in the historical dustbin with the other normative misadventures from the neoliberal era.

As a government official who had gotten his start as a "natural authority" from (minor) Ayllu Collana in Chuquisaca's Nor Cinti province and later as a well-regarded legal adviser to the militant indigenous organization CONAMAQ, Flores Condori viewed the prospect of a "refounded" Bolivia as one infused with categorical tensions. To begin with, there was the problem of discordant politics in which the concept of national state-building—whether grounded in republican, neoliberal, or plurinational ideology—was at odds with the traditional ways in which Flores Condori's family members and fellow social movement activists conceived of and enacted collective belonging. As he put it,

In our entire history, the so-called indigenous movement has been one of self-identification in which our identity is something we claim for ourselves, in our own terms. There is actually nothing radical about this. However, something you need to understand is that for many people the country of "Bolivia" doesn't exist. Bolivia exists only in the cities, for professional people, through urban institutions. But outside of this, most people don't know what "Bolivia" really is.

Yet the effort to replace a colonial and then republican model of the state with one shaped by a "postliberal" (Escobar 2010) logic was problematic, according to Flores Condori, but for a different reason. In defining the plurinational terms of a refounded Bolivia, it had been necessary to codify the country's diversity through law, most importantly within Article 5 of the new constitution. This provision named what it described as the "nations and native indigenous peasant peoples" that were meant to form the basis for the decentralized structures of governance anticipated by the concept of "autonomies." In asserting these thirty-six distinct "nations and peoples," key MAS activists within the Constituent Assembly had relied on research and policy papers produced by sympathetic legal scholars and social scientists, including anthropologists. But in Flores Condori's view, the codification of research on Bolivia's different ethnic groups depended on a series of misunderstandings that were merely well-meaning versions of longer-standing category errors that were the result of external definition, which led to inevitable inclusions and exclusions.

The entire approach [of Article 5] is mistaken. . . . One can't speak of thirty-six indigenous peoples, these [categories] are based on ethno-linguistic and anthropological criteria. But anthropologists have always misunderstood us. . . . The correct approach is one that combines self-identification with information from a longer history. In the lowlands, there are thirty-four indigenous peoples, that is, collectivities that identify as indigenous peoples. In addition, there are twenty-two suyus in the highlands, a number that finds support in the Memorial of Charcas from 1500, something we know about from archives in Potosí, in Tucumán, in Buenos Aires, in Lima. These archives have allowed us to investigate much more about who we are, our diversity. Many of us have very old historical documents with us in the countryside, but for now, we are not going to show these documents to anyone. We are like that, it's very difficult to convince us to share what we know [about our history]. But we are talking about fifty-six actual nations and indigenous peoples despite what the new constitution says.

But if the new constitution was so badly mistaken about the empirical reality of Bolivia's indigenous populations, was this entirely the fault of researchers and legal activists?

No, it's true, we have fought among ourselves for many years, we have allowed ourselves to be defined and divided ever since Christopher Columbus mistakenly called us Indians. But what has always existed has been our internal organizations, long before the [category of the] peasant, long before we were given the nickname of "MNR," all those peasant things. The problem is that this long history of division and infighting has led to many contradictions, contradictions that can't be made to disappear through these [legal] categories. The constitution won't solve all of these problems, despite what everyone has been saying. These experts, these professionals, pretend that this new legal category "native indigenous peasant" will resolve everything, but it's really like an anticucho [a cheap meat dish sold on the street]. *In fact, we have our own internal concepts, our own structures, that are at times very difficult for people to understand. We know this but we are not worried, we are calm because we are becoming professionals, we are becoming anthropologists, sociologists. . . . The most important thing is to think from the ayllu, not in the sense of discrimination but in the sense of making our own theories [of identity].*

And did Flores Condori think that these indigenous theories would eventually make their way into legal categories, with sufficient participation by lawyers who know how to "think from the ayllu"?

Possibly. But for now, the new constitution does not reflect this kind of thinking. In many ways, even more than the anthropologists, the lawyers have been our worst enemies. In general, they have very small heads [tienen una cabeza bien chiquitita], *they don't know how to think, the only thing they know is "this is what the law says." Compared to all the others, it is the lawyers who are the bearers of a rigid colonial mentality.*

If the last chapter examined the ambivalent and marginalized status of Bolivia's traditional revolutionary left within the process of change during the period 2006–15, this chapter returns the focus to the center of the process of change itself, one constituted within legal technologies—legislative codes, executive decrees, autonomy statutes, administrative rulings, state prosecutions, international court filings—by legal functionaries, state officials, and indigenous rights activists, many of whom struggled with a self-awareness of the historical contradictions and misalignments described by Flores Condori. At stake was a basic tension between an ideology of indigenous history, ethics, and the promotion of "our own structures," and the role of the contested juridical as the cornerstone of the MAS regime.

As Flores Condori put it, the problem was that having "turned their backs on both the Marxists and the indigenistas," that is, "all those who treated the problems of Bolivia's indigenous peoples as a kind of game, an amusement," the task of giving pervasive and transformative "social form" to the state's ideology of change fell to institutions least able to fulfill it. Indeed, it was a historical irony that the institutions of social control and regulation that were most clearly freighted with the legacies of a "rigid colonial mentality" were those charged with bringing Bolivia's experiment with *refundación* into the world, sheltering it in its infancy, and then protecting it as it suffered setbacks on its path to maturity. If it is true, as the Spanish legal historian Javier Malagón Barceló once put it, that "[Latin] America was born beneath the juridical sign" (1961: 4), then something similar could be said about the "historical challenge to construct collectively the Unitary Social State of Plurinational Communitarian Law."

FASHIONING PLURINATIONALISM THROUGH AUTONOMY AND DECOLONIZATION

In the early 1870s, a curious political and social movement took root in Santa Cruz, led by Andrés Ibáñez. Ibáñez was a lawyer from a wealthy hacendado family with lands in the fertile agricultural and cattle region on the left bank of the Río Grande (or Río Guapay), about 55 km east of the city of Santa Cruz de la Sierra. Although Ibáñez had received the kind of education expected of young men from his social class, having graduated from the law faculty of Sucre's Universidad San Francisco Xavier in 1868, he underwent a surprising political metamorphosis soon after. Although the precise circumstances of his awakening are a matter of some dispute (see Molina Saucedo 2012; Schelchkov 2011), there is evidence that he was influenced by reports arriving from Europe of the Paris Commune of 1871, the short-lived and ultimately tragic revolutionary uprising that had paralyzed Paris for two months after the collapse of the Second Empire.

After being elected to the national Congress in 1871, Ibáñez began to agitate against Santa Cruz's political and economic elites on behalf of the city's small shopkeepers, domestic workers, artisans, and recent migrants from the countryside. He founded a social movement called the "Equality Club" in 1872 as well as a political organ entitled *The Echo of Equality*. In 1874, during a subsequent political campaign, Ibáñez "confronted his rival in the central plaza of Santa Cruz, taking off and throwing to the ground his frock coat and shoes in a profoundly symbolic gesture to identify himself with the common people who were called 'those without jackets'" (quoted in Thomson et al. 2018: 232). Ibáñez's emerging political vision was based on the principle of "autonomy" at a time when the power of the central government in Sucre was carefully protected in law and, if necessary, through the use of military force.

In October 1876, Ibáñez and his fellow cruceño autonomists broke decisively from the government of Hilarión Daza Groselle, even though Ibáñez had supported Daza in the early 1876 presidential elections, in which Daza had lost to Tomás Frías Ametller but then had overthrown the Frías government in a coup d'état. On October 2, Ibáñez, Urbano Franco, and Simón Álvarez promulgated the Acta del Pueblo, which declared Santa Cruz autonomous from the central government. According to the Acta, autonomy was justified by the doctrines of egalitarianism, political federalism, and the abolition of servitude throughout the region. As the Acta's stirring yet ambiguous revolutionary rhetoric put it:

> The hour of regeneration is about to strike on the clock of your destinies. . . . An epoch of peace, equality and brotherhood will open up no matter how many obstacles are placed in its way by the centralizing and tyrannical form of unitary government. . . . The blood which may be shed will be our baptism. And the sacrifices which you may make will serve to smooth the road which you intend to take. The Federation, the new Messiah of the oppressed peoples, already looms in the heart of the Nation. . . . A dawn of beneficence and fortune will shine forth for the peoples! The people are hungry and thirsty for justice and for freedom. . . . Freedom watered with the blood of so many martyrs— brotherhood, the sacred link which joins all the Peoples—and equality,

the holiest of creeds flowing from the martyr of Golgotha, will overtake you. They will restore your well-being, they will wipe the blood from your scars with their caresses, and you will crush beneath your powerful steps the tyrants who enslave you with such vehemence and cruelty. (quoted in Thomson et al. 2018: 232–33)

Nevertheless, in order to put down what was viewed from Sucre as an act of insurrection against the state, Daza sent the army against Ibáñez and his followers. In early 1877, the historically fleeting egalitarian movement was violently and conclusively routed through a series of military sweeps, confiscations, and executions in the city of Santa Cruz. Ibáñez himself, along with a small band of hardcore autonomists, fled the city with the intention of escaping over the border into Brazil. But he was captured by the army before he could escape, dragged before a kangaroo military court, sentenced to death, and executed by firing squad the same day (Mesa 2008).

Although the memory of Andrés Ibáñez and the autonomist doctrines of the egalitarian movement was preserved locally in Santa Cruz by historians and political writers, the legacy of this period proved to be problematic during moments of intense pro–Santa Cruz mobilization in subsequent decades, particularly during the 1950s in the aftermath of the National Revolution and, most importantly, within the institutionalized departmental resistance in the early years of the first Morales government. The reason for this ambivalence is revealing. As an anti-elite militant with revolutionary socialist leanings who was also a radical advocate for social leveling based on class and, to a lesser extent, ethnicity, Ibáñez and his movement represented a threat to all existing structures of entrenched power and privilege.

Yet, as we have seen (in chapter 3), the anti-government autonomy movements of Sucre and Santa Cruz were largely driven and supported by economic and social elites who viewed the central government's "movement to socialism" as an existential peril that threatened their carefully forged, exclusionary ways of life. This is why pro-autonomy leaders during the late 2000s were more likely to identify their cause with either the earlier heroes of the anticolonial wars, who fought for "liberty" rather than equality, or the martyrs of the anti-MNR cívico movement, whose regionalist sentiments were grounded in a mystical conception of sacrifice tempered by anti-Indian racism.

Thus it was that Santa Cruz's 2008 departmental autonomy statute, drafted in large part by the cruceño ideologue Carlos Dabdoub Arrien, who later became the department's inaugural secretary of autonomy, decentralization, and democratic development (see chapter 3), made no mention of Andrés Ibáñez or the principles of egalitarianism. Instead, Santa Cruz's regionalist constitution was meant to be the expression of other values—tolerance, humility, reverence for God, the belief in historical identity, and a commitment to democracy and autonomy as the "vocation . . . of the cruceño people" (Article 1). Nevertheless, Santa Cruz's 2008 statute and the department's broader autonomy movement did share something important with the region's forgotten communards of 1876: they represented a direct threat to both the integrity and the legitimacy of the central government.

In light of the ambiguous status of the idea of autonomy within Bolivian political history, it was the height of Machiavellian shrewdness when the MAS government chose to call one of the most critical juridical pillars of the process of change the "Andrés Ibáñez Law of Autonomies and Decentralization" (Law No. 31 [2010] as amended by Law No. 195 [2011] and Law No. 705 [2015]). In so doing, the government co-opted the category of "autonomy" at precisely the moment in which the anti-government opposition had suffered a series of catastrophic setbacks (see chapter 3) while at the same time reinterpreting the meaning of autonomy in a way that reinvested it with some of its late nineteenth-century emancipatory urgency. The preamble to the Andrés Ibáñez Law of Autonomies and Decentralization ("Law of Autonomies") revealed this act of appropriation with undeniable clarity:

> Among all the actions, rebellions, and processes, we must highlight the egalitarian revolution of 1877 led by Andrés Ibáñez, who with a shout of "We are all equal!"—which he uttered in the middle of the parade ground in the midst of the representatives of the patriarchal feudal order in Santa Cruz—managed to call into question the very basis of the hierarchical order that prevailed throughout the country. . . . This was the source of their egalitarian revolution: the taking of a public stand in favor of the dispossessed. This fundamental conviction led the egalitarian movement to demand a reform that would overcome the stifling concentration of power in the republican Bolivian state. Thus, the struggle for equality and justice is inseparable from a scenario in the process of change that ensures the inclusion and participation of all of the diversity that defines our country. In this way, Andrés Ibáñez is a vanguard example of the autonomist process that is founded in the struggle for social justice.

The Law of Autonomies established a set of procedures through which four different types of entities could seek to be declared legally autonomous: departments, municipalities, regions, and native indigenous peasant "autonomies."

The sections on departmental autonomy did not significantly alter existing—that is, pre-2010—departmental structures. In many ways, the most important reform in the status of Bolivia's nine departments came in the first months of 2005, when the Mesa government was pressured by the emerging opposition in Santa Cruz to abolish the long-standing process through which departmental prefects were directly appointed by the particular central government in power. Beginning with the 2005 elections, prefects (who later became governors) were chosen through departmental elections. The 2010 Law of Autonomies reaffirmed this independence of departmental executives and specified certain conditions through which department "assemblies" would serve the legislative function, including being composed of members chosen according to demographic, territorial, and gender equity criteria.

In addition, all departmental assemblies were required to have representatives from the department's native indigenous peasant peoples and nations, who were to be selected "according to their own norms and procedures" (Article 31[1]). Although the section on departmental autonomy did not point to major shifts in comparison with other parts of the law, it did have one important immediate effect: it rendered Santa Cruz's 2008 autonomy statute invalid, since this departmental constitution was promulgated before both the 2009 national constitution and the follow-on 2010 autonomy law. With the implementation of the 2010 Law of Autonomies, the legal erasure of Santa Cruz's aspirations for autonomy on its own terms was completed.

The second type of autonomy under the 2010 law was even more specifically regulated by the jurisdictional status quo. As Article 33 put it, "all the existing municipalities in the country . . . have the status of autonomous municipalities without the need to submit to any additional requirements or to comply with any additional procedures." The reason for this oddly conservative approach to municipalities in an otherwise sweeping legal instrument is related to an administrative transformation that took place in 1994, ironically at the high point of neoliberal reformism.

The 1994 Law of Popular Participation had extended the status of municipalities throughout the entire country as the administrative unit below the department and province but above the cantons. Although later critics read the decentralizing policies of the Law of Popular Participation as a cynical neoliberal strategy to "civilize the popular" (e.g., Medeiros 2001), in an earlier work (Goodale 2008a) I explored the ways in which the ideological devolution of power to the municipalities came with real material consequences, especially for isolated provincial capitals that suddenly found themselves awash in resources.

More often than not, these resources—which often doubled or tripled local budgets—were put to use in the construction of paved roads, the restoration of local cemeteries, the expansion of municipal and rural schools, and the establishment of health clinics in strategically located hamlets outside the provincial capitals (see also Postero 2007). By identifying Bolivia's existing three hundred–plus municipalities as "autonomous" within the meaning of MAS's ideology of state refoundation, the 2010 Law of Autonomies was—at least in part—an unexpected homage to the signature social achievement of Gonzalo Sánchez de Lozada, the embodiment of neoliberal debasement who was at that very moment living in exile in the United States with a standing Bolivian indictment against him for crimes against humanity for the events of Black October 2003 (see the introduction).[1]

The third type of autonomy under the Law of Autonomies was a nebulous category—"regional autonomy." At the time the 2010 law was announced, I read the inclusion of this new administrative level as yet another effort to use the law to dilute the territorial basis for anti-government opposition through the creation of a jurisdictional alternative that would compete with, and perhaps come to supplant, the troublesome departments. However, during a public debate on the 2010 law held in Geneva in November 2015 that included the new Bolivian Minister of Autonomies, Hugo Siles Núñez del Prado, a Latin American specialist from the Swiss Federal Department of Foreign Affairs, and a Swiss professor of development studies, I learned that the concept of "regional autonomy" was a much more elliptical response to the conflicts of the first Morales government (see figure 5.1).

Among the four types, "regional autonomy" was understood less as a new political-administrative category and more as an organizational logic through which something called the "Fiscal Pact" would be put into action. During the presentation in Geneva, the Fiscal Pact was described by Siles as the "process of concentrating and implementing agreements between the central government and the various autonomous entities . . . regarding the best use of public resources." This vague account was nevertheless one of the first public admissions by a member of the Morales government of the existence of an explicit strategy of foreclosing the possibility of a return to the kind of crises that marked the period 2006–9 by extending considerable economic autonomy to Bolivia's "regions." The implication was that the relatively wealthy agricultural and industrial urban districts, particularly in the eastern lowlands, should conceive of themselves as both economically autonomous and, at the same time, closely bound to the state by a "pact of reciprocity" (Platt 1982).

FIGURE 5.1 Public conference entitled "The Transformation of Bolivia's Plurinational State and the Autonomy Process," which took place at the Graduate Institute of International and Development Studies, Geneva, on November 13, 2015. Minister of Autonomies Hugo José Siles Núñez del Prado (far right) takes notes while the author (second from right) gives a summary of his research findings.

In exchange for acknowledging that the country's economic interests should take precedence over all those older ethnic, historical, and political grievances that had proven so destabilizing, the state would agree to let the country's regional economic elites pursue their livelihoods without interference.[2] With the country's economic power base safely brought into the fold, the government would then be free to use other laws to silence or juridically disappear those who either continued to resist the process of change, or who had done so in the past based (usually implicitly) on ethnic or racial animus rather than economic arguments (see below).

Yet despite this, it was the fourth type of autonomy that was clearly the most significant since it was the autonomy that most closely reflected the ideological ideals of the plurinational state. Article 5 of the 2010 Law of Autonomies defined the principles that underlay the concept of autonomy. The seventh principle formed the foundation for this last, and most far-reaching, category—"The Preexistence of the Native Indigenous Peasant Peoples and Nations." As it explained: "Given the precolonial existence of the native indigenous peasant peoples and nations, their free determination is guaranteed within the framework of state unity, a freedom that is expressed through their right to autonomy, to self-determination, to their culture, and to the recognition of their institutions and the consolidation of their territorial entities."

Article 43 of the Law of Autonomies then specified in detail what it described as the "character" of the "native indigenous peasant" who was entitled to claim membership in a native indigenous peasant autonomy.

> The idea of the native indigenous peasant is an indivisible concept identified with the peoples and nations of Bolivia whose existence is prior to that of the colonial empire, whose populations share a defined territory, culture, history, language, and organization, or their own distinct legal, political, economic, and social institutions; at the same time, they self-identify only as indigenous people, or native peoples, or as peasants, and by so doing, they are entitled to have their autonomy recognized under the conditions . . . established in the Political Constitution of the State, based on the territories they currently inhabit. . . . The Afro-Bolivian people are included within the scope of this definition in accordance with Article 32 of the Political Constitution of the State.

With this exclusionary principle of indigenous self-identification as a key limiting device, the Law of Autonomies specified what appeared to be a fairly straightforward three-step procedure through which native indigenous peasant autonomies could be created. However, in practice, the mandated process proved to be extremely laborious, subject to political manipulation, and under-supported by the Ministry of Autonomies, whose regional offices were lightly staffed by personnel whose sense of mission was indefinite at best.

The three-step process for native indigenous peasant autonomy required the following: first, approval by popular referendum to begin the process according to unspecified "proper norms and procedures" overseen by "territorial authorities"; second, the design of a course of action, also according to local "norms and procedures," through which an autonomy statute would be drafted with the assistance of the ministry's Intercultural Service for the Strengthening of Democracy; and, finally, after the statute had been finalized, its collective approval by both "proper norms and procedures" and "later, by referendum."

By August 2015, only four native indigenous peasant autonomies had made significant advances through this process. In the case of the first autonomy set in motion, that of the Guaraní Nation of Charagua Iyambae (Guaraní Nation), this meant a period of more than five years simply to produce a draft statute. The other three statutes were those of Mojocoya, a Quechua-speaking "culture" located in Zudáñez Province in the north of Chuquisaca Department; Totora Marka, an Aymara municipality in Oruro Department that sought to be converted into a native indigenous peasant autonomy; and Uru Chipaya, a "native nation" located on the altiplano north of the Salar de Coipasa, also in Oruro Department.

The statutes themselves were printed in colorful booklets that also featured images of members of the communities (especially children) and political mobilizations that were linked to the autonomy movement. The frontispiece of Totora Marka's printed statute also included a drawing of a *pututu* (a cow horn used to summon or warn community members), a *vara* (staff of office), and a *tarka*, the wind instrument played during the *tarqueada*, an indigenous highland dance that was the basis of a 2009 Bolivian application to UNESCO to be included on its "intangible cultural heritage" registry.

The significant costs of printing and distributing hundreds of copies of these four autonomy booklets were covered by a curious assortment of actors including the Ministry of Autonomies; the United Nations Development Programme; the Rosa Luxemburg Foundation (the policy and development wing of the German far-left political party Die Linke); and the ALICE Project (motto "Strange Mirrors, Unsuspected Lessons"), a five-year (2011–16) European Research Council initiative led by the Portuguese sociologist Boaventura de Sousa Santos that was committed to "re-thinking and renovating socio-scientific knowledge in light of the epistemologies of the South" (ALICE Project 2016).[3]

In August 2015, Alfredo Carry Albornos was overwhelmed with preparations for the most important moment for the country's autonomist project: the October referendum on the Guaraní Nation's statute. Carry, a thirty-eight-year-old *licenciado* in communications originally from Chuiquisaca Department, was the head of the native indigenous peasant autonomies (AIOC) unit in the Ministry of Autonomies. In the months before the momentous October vote, he was based in the ministry's Santa Cruz office, one of the few buildings in the city to display the wiphala in addition to the traditional national flag. The office's spare conference room contained various books and language pamphlets for the use by ministry staff in their meetings with Guaraní activists. On the whiteboard, someone had written "Eguahé porá" followed by the Spanish translation "Bienvenidos" ("Welcome").

Although Carry emphasized that his community "partners" had been fully committed since 2009 to the process of autonomy in order to "reconstitute the great Guaraní Nation," his work had become mired over the years in a political and legal quagmire that threatened to engulf what the government desperately hoped would be the first and most important step toward realizing its plurinational aspirations. The Guaraní autonomy process had been beset on all sides by infighting, regional anti-government opposition, and the circumstances created by the 2011 TIPNIS conflict. As he explained:

There have been three main problems for the Charagua autonomy process. First, you need to understand that there are rivalries among the Guaranís themselves that are based around different communities and especially different families. Some of these struggles are also over very technical legal and political questions—the Guaraní técnicos have been occupied for years with very specific details of the process, more than you might imagine. The second problem is that the Charagua autonomy was opposed from the very beginning by all the government officials in Santa Cruz, starting with Costas [Rubén Costas, the department's governor]. What people don't realize is that the provincial civic committees work very closely with the Comité pro Santa Cruz and in this way the process [in Charagua] faced strong opposition and division in the municipality. Finally, and probably most importantly, is that the process was slowed after 2011 because of TIPNIS. What happened is that TIPNIS created alliances between the cívicos and the Guaraní political movements. There was a lack of trust and the whole TIPNIS conflict drove the Guaranís away from the process of autonomy. It was almost impossible to do our work with them during those years.

Nevertheless, despite the sense of frustration and fatigue that Carry felt as the government's leading proponent for native indigenous peasant autonomy, he remained a true believer in the broader cause. Like many MAS activists during the later years of the period 2006–15, Carry attributed most of the difficulties in the course of the process of change to the fact that nine years was still a brief moment in relation to Bolivia's wider history. As he put it,

The constitution is still very young. The revolution it is establishing [implantando] is still in a process of construction.

In the October 2015 referendum, the Charagua statute was approved, although a strong bloc of opposition remained, consisting of municipal civic leaders, cattle ranchers, and some "mixed" communities that were outliers to the mainstream of the Guaraní autonomy movement. Yet it wasn't until January 2017 that the first Gobierno Autónomo Indígena Guaraní Charagua Iyambae was sworn into office during a historic ceremony attended by Vice President

García Linera, Minister of Autonomies Siles, leaders of the Asamblea del Pueblo Guaraní (APG), and several UN officials.

By contrast, in a development that sent shock waves through the MAS government and the autonomy movement more generally, the Totora Marka statute was soundly rejected in a September 2015 referendum that likewise was the culmination of a long-drawn-out local process. The defeat was attributed to a generational conflict between older ayllu authorities and younger aspirants to political position, who feared that the creation of a native indigenous peasant autonomy would codify and deepen a fiesta cargo system of authority that privileged older men.[4]

Yet if the devolutionary framework for building plurinationalism through autonomies was one central pillar of Bolivia's process of change during the period 2006–15, another was its policy of legal decolonization. Although the importance of decolonization more generally as an ideological centerpiece was formally represented by the Vice Ministry of Decolonization (see Postero 2017), which was somewhat awkwardly attached to the Ministry of Culture and Tourism, the more focused approach to this principle took place in Sucre, within the Tribunal Constitucional Plurinacional (TCP). There, within the institution that had the primary responsibility for building the legal architecture for Bolivia's refoundation, a special unit was created to direct the process through which Bolivian law would first be cleansed of its colonial legacies and then reconstituted as the juridical embodiment of the state's transformative ambitions.

In July 2016, the TCP's Office of Technical Assistance and Decolonization was headed by Rudy Nelson Huayllas.[5] Nelson was a thirty-seven-year-old from Santuario de Quillacas, south of Lago Poopó near the border with Potosí Department. After studying anthropology at the Universidad Técnica de Oruro, Nelson had returned to Santuario de Quillacas to begin a steep climb within the regional ayllu power structure, eventually becoming a Mallku of Suyu Jatun Quillacas. He was proud of his triple identity: as an anthropologist, as a former high-ranking ayllu authority, and as a judicial official charged with purging Bolivian law of its stubborn "logic of coloniality" (Mignolo 2007).

Nelson led a team of sixteen specialists in legal decolonization who were brought together from different academic disciplines, with expertise in different languages and with knowledge of Bolivia's different cultural and regional traditions. As Nelson explained, the TCP team was staffed primarily by those who—like Nelson himself—had significant experience in the country's various indigenous legal and political authority systems. This was critical, Nelson emphasized, because the team members worked closely with indigenous authorities at the local level throughout the country.

The TCP team's legal decolonization work involved both consultative and educational dimensions. Nelson and the other staff members provided technical assistance to indigenous authorities who sought advice about the resolution of "concrete cases." The team's role was to ensure that the highly diverse development of native indigenous peasant justice was taking place in a way that was both true to its plural realties and consistent with the norms of the 2009 constitution. This was a difficult and ambiguous task. As Nelson explained, the main problem was that the socio-juridical concept of "native indigenous peasant justice" embodied practices that were partly derived from processes put into place after the 1952 National Revolution during the wave of rural peasant union mobilization. As he put it:

This new category [native indigenous peasant justice], *which is so important to the process of change and for us* [in the TCP], *is really a difficult combination. For example, the statutes and structures in many rural areas, which guide the resolution of conflicts, come from that time* [of the National Revolution] *and therefore reflect colonial elements. At the same time, ayllu justice is not written and doesn't have its own statutes in the same sense. So our challenge is to promote the development of native indigenous peasant justice in a way that preserves what is real, what reflects our values, while eliminating what doesn't belong. But we understand this job as one of promoting legal pluralism through decolonization even if there will never be a single code of native indigenous peasant justice. It's impossible to create a single system without transforming it negatively.*

At the same time, the TCP team traveled throughout Bolivia to promote capacity-building in the principles of legal decolonization. They sought to instill in traditional authorities the importance of following legal procedures that were faithful to their local cultural norms. However, as Nelson explained, the ideology of legal decolonization often encountered resistance for quite pragmatic reasons: local legal authorities, from the eastern lowlands to the altiplano, had always performed their duties through a nuanced form of forum-shopping in which local, regional, and national legal strategies were variously mobilized depending on community expectations, likelihood of outcome, and the possibility of gaining often quite self-interested advantage. It had never been important before *how* these various strategies were justified at a normative level, let alone whether or not they reflected authentically "indigenous" or compromising "colonial" histories. Nevertheless, despite these difficulties, Nelson remained committed to the process of legal decolonization as the foundation for the broader process of transformation, a process that he emphasized had to be distinguished from the political fortunes of the Morales government itself.

Yet in reflecting more generally on the ways in which both autonomy and legal decolonization were invested with foundational importance as mechanisms of change during the period 2006–15 (and beyond), it is clear that these two logics existed in a state of tension that was ultimately destabilizing. Much like the principle of legal pluralism envisioned in Article 190 et seq. of the 2009 constitution and later through the Ministry of Justice's framework for legal pluralism entitled "Building Confidence, 2013–2025" (the legal sector's contribution to the country's "Patriotic Agenda 2025"), the autonomist road to plurinationalism was one that was supposed to lead to the proliferation of semi-independent entities: autonomous municipalities, autonomous departments, autonomous regions, and, most important, para-sovereign native indigenous peasant configurations that would eventually take a form of internal nation-statehood.

Thus, if the autonomist project formed the basis for a wider "struggle for social justice," as the preamble to the Law of Autonomies put it, it was a response grounded in category difference, hostility to the dangers of centralized power, and an exclusionary account of historical suffering. At a fundamental level, the centrality of autonomies was meant to undermine the prevailing model of the state itself, a "colonial, republican, and neoliberal" model that was discursively "left in the past" by the 2009 constitution.

The project of legal decolonization, however, was shaped by quite different visions of both transformation and governance. Legal decolonization—like decolonization more generally—was at its core a state-building project, one that sought to salvage the instrumentalities of state power through a process of public reckoning and historical atonement that nevertheless remained largely ideological. Yet in seeking to decolonize the law in order to purge it of its associations with Bolivia's prerevolutionary past, the new institutions of the refounded state—like the TCP—reinforced the state's political and legal hegemony, its monopoly over the use of force, and its significance as both the fount and guardian of society's "ethico-moral principles."

What resulted was a wider process of change marked by a structural friction in which the state purported to devolve itself while at the same time it articulated an ideology in which the state—a very centralist, if decolonizing, state—was paramount. As will be seen in the following sections, this friction could not endure for long. Even as the pluralizing aspirations of the Morales government remained ideological, even symbolic, the centralizing forces of law became increasingly instrumental, strategic, and disciplinary.

When I first met Jaime Barrón, on New Year's Eve 2008, he was at the height of his powers as a public intellectual, a leading citizen of Sucre, and a man whose anti-MAS militancy was leavened by the moral authority he exercised as rector of the city's venerable (if aging) Universidad San Francisco Xavier. He was much at ease in the grandeur of the rector's chambers—which encompassed an entire wing of the university, including a waiting room, secretary's office, and several offices of his own—despite the fact that an air of trauma, collective violence, and uncertainty hung over Sucre like a thick fog (see chapter 3).

Even though, in retrospect, the waning months of 2008 marked the beginning of the end of Bolivia's defiant anti-government opposition movements, this reality was not understood at the time by Barrón or any of the other key members of Sucre's Comité Interinstitucional por la Capitalidad (CIC), of which he was at that moment serving as president. Instead, Barrón projected an image of world-weary historical patience: as a distinguished academic, as a sucrense, and as a civic leader at the head of a movement grounded in an ideology of righteousness, he was careful to take the long view from the high ground.

Despite the warning signs that were beginning to encircle him, he was quick to point out that he had been a strong local supporter of Evo Morales in the period before the conflict over the Constituent Assembly had plunged the city into chaos.

Yes, we helped a lot during those first months. In fact, the [central] *government provided substantial resources so that we could remodel the city's infrastructure, including the town center, the university, the* alcaldía, *and Colegio Junín* [a historic local high school founded in 1826]. *All of this support was part of the constitutional process that was going to take place here, and we were very grateful to collaborate with the government in the planning. So we supported the process, we weren't against the* constituyente. *On the contrary, I'd say that there was much sympathy in Chuquisaca for the government of Don Evo Morales. I should mention to you that during the first months of this government, I played soccer with Don Evo Morales as a sympathizer of a government that was beginning with ideas of change, of revolution. I thought then, and still believe now, that everything that is revolutionary in a positive sense is very good for the country.*[6]

At the time, Barrón was forty-nine years old, an economist who had spent his entire career at the Universidad San Francisco Xavier as professor of economics, chair of the department of economics, dean of the faculty of economic and business sciences, vice rector, and, finally, as rector. Although he was not a member of one of Sucre's elite "blue blood" families (see chapter 3), which formed the foundation of a small socioeconomic cabal that exercised wide-ranging influence away from television cameras and political appointments, Barrón nevertheless commanded tremendous respect across the entire range of the city's business, political, and social sectors. He was particularly beloved by the students of his university, who looked to him for guidance during a turbulent historical moment in which the mere pursuit of academic knowledge or professional training seemed beside the point.

Barrón viewed the current moment through a studied equanimity and with an unshakable belief that the CIC's demands for both "full" civic recognition for Sucre and justice for the "martyrs of La Calancha" would inevitably be met if only his fellow sucrenses would not give up hope.[7] But in fact, as the year 2009 dawned, Barrón stood at the very edge of an unseen precipice that marked his legal erasure, the annulment of his political life, and his rendering into *Homo sacer* as one of the most prominent among many who were destined to be "outlawed" (Goldstein 2012) by the Morales government.

In April 2010, Barrón was elected mayor of Sucre from the local Pacto de Integración Social (PAIS) party. In a television interview he gave on the night of the election, Barrón was still full of confidence: "We are very happy with the election results from the city of Sucre, which encourage us to work as hard as we can for our people. . . . We thank our fellow citizens for the confidence that they bestowed on us and we will ensure that our time in office is marked by transparency. I will not take advantage of the support that my people have given to me and I will defend the dignity of Sucre" (Barrón 2010).

But Barrón was only allowed to serve two weeks in office. In May 2010, the Morales government invoked a controversial article of the Law of Autonomies, Article 144, which had been drafted specifically for this purpose. This provision called for the suspension of political authorities who had been accused of crimes by a public prosecutor. Since Barrón had recently been indicted for his leading role during the May 24, 2008, violence and humiliations against pro-MAS peasant activists in Sucre (see chapter 3), he was removed from office.

From there, the full power of the law was turned against Barrón, and his juridical reconfiguration by the state quickly picked up pace. In mid-November 2010, he was taken into custody and remanded to Sucre's San Roque Prison after Chuquisaca's Superior Court had found that he was a potential risk to flee the country while the case against him moved forward. After almost a month in prison, Barrón was transferred to house arrest (*detención domiciliaria*) and forced to pay a fine of 30,000 Bs (about US$4,350, fifteen times the average monthly income in Bolivia). His passport was confiscated, his movements were restricted, and his house in an upscale barrio of Sucre was put under police surveillance.

Over the next six years, Barrón's life was carefully controlled by the mechanisms of the legal process brought against him and the other defendants for the events of May 24, 2008, including Jhon Cava, Savina Cuéllar, Fidel Herrera, and Aydée Nava. Because Sucre's public prosecutor argued that the city's local tribunal was poisoned by pro-capitalía and anti-government sentiments, an extraordinary change of venue was ordered that moved the location of the trials to the distant town of Padilla in Chuquisaca's Tomina Province. This meant that Barrón—and the other defendants and their lawyers and supporters—were forced to travel over three hours by car in each direction for the regular court hearings, some of which lasted less than an hour.

When he wasn't traveling to and from Padilla or participating in court proceedings, Barrón spent the remainder of these years in his house, where he gave the occasional television interview and continued to try and maintain something of a political presence, although Sucre's alcaldía and municipal council would themselves eventually come to be controlled by MAS politicians. As the years passed, Barrón and the other high-profile Sucre cívicos increasingly faded from public consciousness, even with the occasional reporting from Sucre's *Correo del Sur* on technical or procedural developments during the never-ending trial in Padilla.

When I interviewed Barrón again in August 2015, he was a completely transformed man. In the course of over five years of legal and political erasure, the commanding rector, CIC president, guru to youth militants, and moral leader was gone. In his place was a humbled and broken defendant in what seemed like a perpetual legal process, a man accused of instigating racial violence against peasants, the one whose slow juridical transfiguration represented the farthest fall from grace, the purest embodiment of a profound shift in the way the MAS government understood the relationship between law and structural change. Despite his position by 2015, Barrón remained quietly reflective.

The ironic thing is that I'm actually not opposed to the government and never have been. I'm an academic and was the rector for many years. I have spent most of my life on the left in the same way as Aydée [Nava] *and Fidel* [Herrera]. *But this government needed for me to be part of the opposition because of who I was. . . . The point I want to emphasize to you is that ours was always a struggle for, not against, something. Ours was always a regional struggle, just as it was during the Federal War* [see chapter 3].

I asked Barrón what went wrong with this regional struggle, why did it turn out the way that it had?

Well, one must begin with Savina [Cuéllar], *that's when things began to change. Savina showed a new face to the country, a peasant face, and that's why we chose her to run* [in 2008] *and not me. But after Savina was elected, she committed an error—as we now know—by working too closely with the right in Santa Cruz. When she did this* [as prefect], *it completely changed the nature of our struggle. Both before and after La Calancha, our struggle was always civic, always institutional. But after Savina allowed certain forces in Santa Cruz to appropriate our struggle, it became much more ideological.*

What did Barrón think of the unprecedented recent MAS takeover of the city's government?

Over the last five years, they have exerted almost complete control over the provinces. In the city, there is more opposition, but MAS has worked to consolidate control in the outer districts and then work toward the center. . . . But more generally, there is no question that the economic bonanza has benefited the MAS project.

Did Barrón feel he was simply on the wrong side of what the MAS government described as a democratic and cultural revolution?

I don't agree, I mean with the point about a revolution. I agree, clearly, my situation is bad, but not that I was on the losing side of a true revolution. To them [the MAS government], *revolution can only mean one thing: permanent power.*

García Linera perhaps best represents the saying, "those who were once oppressed will now be the oppressors." But this so-called revolution is only symbolic, only ideological. Where have the changes been in education? The productive activity is not apparent. The government has terribly managed the resources from this bonanza. The growth has only been on paper, through prices, not in the real economy, not financially.

Finally, I asked Barrón, given the fact that he faced an inevitable guilty verdict in the May 24 proceedings, whether or not he had any regrets about his role in the anti-government mobilizations. His response began with the personal and ended with the ideological.

Well, I do have a few regrets actually. I think the first is that I trusted too many sectors during our struggle and many of them turned out to be acting in bad faith, as we saw later. Another is that I wished we had been more willing to compromise with the [central] government. The atmosphere was just too polarized, without a doubt. But if you are asking if I regret struggling [luchando] for Sucre, the answer is no.

In March 2016, Barrón, Jhon Cava, Savina Cuéllar, Fidel Herrera, Aydée Nava, and five other civic leaders were sentenced to six years in prison, to be served in San Roque. This was nevertheless considered something of a defeat for the MAS government, since the prosecutor had asked the court in Padilla to give the defendants sentences between fifteen and thirty years for the violence of May 24. As for Barrón, he was scheduled to be released from San Roque in 2022, when he will be sixty-three years old.

———

The intentionally drawn-out legal effacement of the former leading anti-government Sucre cívicos was not the only such process during the key years of Morales's second term in office (2010–15), during which law was mobilized as part of a wider transition from the projection of power through electoral politics to the consolidation of power through a politics of legal subjugation. For example, in the case of the Porvenir Massacre, in which up to twenty pro-MAS peasants and rural teachers were killed by civic functionaries and anti-government militants in the Amazonian department of Pando in September 2008, the legal processes that followed against the departmental prefect, Leopoldo Fernández, and three other regional political leaders were even more protracted.

As we have seen (in chapter 3), Fernández was taken into custody in late 2008 and was in preventive detention in La Paz's San Pedro Prison, a judicial measure that was not only the symbolic exercise of legal force by the state: of the nearly thirty people who were charged with various crimes for the violence of September 2008 in Pando, almost all had fled the country before they could be arrested.[8] While the prosecutor slowly built a case against the defendants, Fernández was moved between San Pedro and La Paz's other notorious prison, Chonchocoro, a windswept and brutal outpost that housed, among others, the former dictator Luis García Meza. Fernández was released from preventive detention in 2013 for medical reasons to allow him to seek treatment for cancer, although his movements were carefully controlled and he was subject to house arrest.

In 2015, after more than seven years, the trial against Fernández and the three other remaining defendants finally began. In March 2017, Fernández was found guilty and sentenced to fifteen years in prison, to be served in San Pedro Prison. Although Fernández had been charged by the government for the entire spectrum of the most serious crimes, including mass murder, terrorism, criminal conspiracy, and great bodily harm, he was convicted on a lesser single count of criminal homicide as a responsible authority (*homicidio en grado de autoría mediata*).

But the strategic use of law by the Morales government was not limited to criminal prosecutions. In March 2013, the Plurinational Legislative Assembly passed a law that was drafted under the close supervision of the vice president's office, a law that at the time received very little public notice. Law 351 appeared to be just another form of *reglamentación*, the process through which fundamental norms—for example, in the 2009 constitution—were implemented through subsequent legislation that was intended to give concrete juridical effect to broad normative principles.

And the title of the law—"Law of Granting of Legal Statuses" (Ley de Otorgación de Personalidades Jurídicas)—hardly drew attention to its true purposes. However, by mid-2015, this innocuously framed law had become a powerful tool for the Morales government, one that represented—along with the concurrent prosecutions of opposition leaders—a maturing understanding within the administration that the law offered a unique logic through which its ambitious plans for governance could be both projected and legitimated.

The rationale for Law 351 must be understood in relation to the government's response to the TIPNIS conflict of 2011. The resolution of the conflict was seen as both a victory of sorts and a defeat. It was seen as a victory in the sense that the first serious crisis of the post-2009 period, one that took leaders by surprise and threatened to undermine several of the MAS government's central ideological pillars, did not, in the end, become the kind of national rupture that could bring the government down.

It was seen as a defeat, however, particularly by García Linera, because the hastily drafted law that formally resolved the conflict—Law 180, the TIPNIS Protection Law—appeared in retrospect to be an unforgivable concession, not to the lowland communities that had opposed the highway project, but to an amorphous global conspiracy that wanted to deny to Bolivia its right to exploit its natural resources. As García Linera and other MAS ideologues framed it, the transnational critique of the TIPNIS project was in fact a subtle form of neocolonialism masquerading as environmentalism.

On this reading, one that demonstrated yet again that García Linera's ideological commitments pulled much harder toward the historical materialist than the indianista elements in his katarista background, the critical reaction to the TIPNIS project was a coordinated effort to prevent the Morales government from developing the country's economy without the historic dependence on foreign interests. Yet in this case, in an ironic inversion, instead of a dependence that was based on opening the veins of Bolivia to nourish the Global North, it was a dependence that demanded that Bolivia keep its veins tightly closed. And instead of transnational mining companies or foreign currency speculators, the outside interests that wanted to manipulate domestic affairs through the TIPNIS conflict were transnational NGOs working in close collaboration with Bolivian nonprofit foundations.

In this subtle discursive extension of the more traditional Marxist concept of exploitation, the preservationist approach to Bolivia's rich biodiversity was seen as yet another form of Western oppression. The wealthy northern countries, those responsible for the global climate change crisis, demanded that Bolivia perform its role as the lungs of the planet even if this meant forgoing or limiting national economic development. As the Morales government interpreted the conflict, the resistance to the TIPNIS highway project by local communities was either a form of false consciousness, in which their environmental interests were being determined by a neo-imperialist global agenda, or based on simple communal avarice, since many of the communities had received transnational development assistance funneled through national foundations that were often critical of the Morales government.

Law 351, although promulgated as a straightforward regulatory process, was in fact something much more: within the government's ideological vision, it was a legal weapon in the fight against what it later took to describing as "green colonialism" (see Tellería 2015). The law required all NGOs in the country to have their legal statutes recertified based on a set of criteria that included having an organizational statute that outlined how the NGO worked for the social good of the country; forbidding NGOs from expanding or modifying their activities without again going through the process of recertification; and, most onerously, requiring all NGOs to demonstrate how their activities were aligned with the state's development plans.

By 2015, the existence of Law 351 had become something of a scandal for the Morales government, with condemnations coming from a diverse set of actors, including the UN Human Rights Council, Human Rights Watch, Bolivia's Defensoría del Pueblo (see below), and prominent international and national scholars and public intellectuals. With echoes of the TIPNIS conflict sounding in the distance, the government mounted a spirited rhetorical counterattack against these critical interventions. In August 2015, García Linera gave a lengthy defense of Law 351 during a public event in the town of Cotoca in Santa Cruz Department. He singled out two well-established NGOs in order to explain the necessity for the government's legal strategy: Fundación Tierra, a La Paz–based foundation known for its studies of agrarian issues; and the Centro de Información y Documentación Bolivia (CEDIB), a Cochabamba organization that focused on documentation, archival research, and public policy.

As he put it, "we must watch out for these two NGOs because they lie on behalf of foreigners." He then argued that "Fundación Tierra is owned by an ex-minister of Sánchez de Lozada and CEDIB is owned by a bunch of Trotskyists who act like environmentalists depending on the day in a clear demonstration of their political opportunism." He continued, "They are committed to lying. They lie in order to defend the interests of the big foreign companies, they lie in order to benefit other countries." Regarding the financial support that Bolivia's environmental NGOs received in assistance agreements, the government saw this as nothing more than an attempt to convert Bolivians into "park rangers" (*guardabosques*). García Linera went on:

> They don't want us to plant corn, chia, rice. Since all the foreign countries have been left without forests, now they want us to take care of ours. They don't want us to cut down any trees, but then, we ask: What are we going to eat? How are we going to live if we don't open up lands so that we can plant what we need to survive? They want us to live like it was 500 years ago, they want us to live like animals. So what is our response [to all of the criticism of Law 351]? We are going to care for our forests, but we also have the right to produce our own food. We have the right to combine both things and no foreigner is going to tell us how to do it. (*Correo del Sur*, August 9, 2015)

Finally, as part of its expanding efforts to mobilize law as a mechanism for both transformation and social, ideological, and political control, the Morales government turned to international law. In April 2013, a year that became its *annus mirabilis juridicus*, the Bolivian government filed a claim against Chile in the International Court of Justice (ICJ) in the Hague. The claim was based on a long-running dispute over the resolution to the War of the Pacific (1879–84), in which Bolivia lost more than 400 km of ocean coastline (around 120,000 sq km of territory) to Chile in the first of what would be several disastrous military defeats for the country.

The humiliating and euphemistically named Treaty of Peace and Friendship, which finally fixed the postwar boundaries between Bolivia and Chile in 1904, also set in motion a process in which successive Bolivian governments called upon Chile over the decades to renegotiate the terms of the 1904 treaty so that Bolivia could regain at least part of its former coastal territory. This enduring demand was based on a deeply embedded national narrative in which "Bolivia's sovereignty over the coasts of the Pacific Ocean" had not been legally ceded by the 1904 treaty and, even worse, its "economic and social development [had] suffered for more than a century as a result of its confinement," as the ICJ filing put it.

Indeed, during my first research trip to Bolivia, in June 1996, I was confused by the headlines in the Cochabamba newspaper *Los Tiempos*. On my first day in the city, the newspaper's front page announced, in a font size normally associated with events of global importance, that the president of Chile had agreed to discuss the "sea question." The details of this apparently historic development, however, were curiously vague—the Chilean president had only offered to add the "sea question" to a list of other issues to be discussed during a regional summit.

As I came to learn, this had been the form through which the sea question in Bolivia had been constructed for almost a hundred years: governments routinely, even ritualistically, exaggerated the importance of any communication with Chile over access to the sea, no matter how minor; Chile, for its part, simply played along throughout the decades, in some years in more good faith than in others, yet with no intention of ever returning territory to its much poorer northeastern neighbor.

Yet despite the continuities, the filing of a legal dispute against Chile under international law in the ICJ (*Bolivia v. Chile*, April 24, 2013) represented a significant reconfiguration of what had largely been a one-sided political conflict, one that had shaped the public imaginary in Bolivia in ways unknown in Chile. For example, in the common propaganda image that could be found on public buses, posters, and in widely distributed calendars (among others), the demand "Mar Para Bolivia!" was accompanied by a large cruise ship, the *Costa Romantica*, sailing on an unnaturally calm ocean, while an abnormally massive Bolivian flag towered over the cruise liner amidships—the flag's scale in relation to the size of the ship and its placement indicating that the designer's understanding of things nautical was forged in carefully cultivated fantasy.

Nevertheless, despite the fact that the case itself entered the kind of slow procedural death spiral long associated with the country versus country proceedings in the Hague,[9] the Morales government used the legal maneuver as a way to argue that it was fully committed to law itself at all levels—legal pluralism at the local level, a new social contract for the state, and now international law among the community of nations.[10] In addition, in a profoundly political gesture of public depoliticization, the Morales government appointed a negotiating team to guide the ICJ legal process that consisted of an impressive cross section of leading public figures drawn from well outside the MAS orbit, including former presidents Jaime Paz Zamora, Jorge Quiroga, and Carlos Mesa.[11] The legal team was headed by a newly appointed ambassador to the ICJ, Eduardo Rodríguez Veltzé, who had served as the country's caretaker president from the resignation of Mesa in June 2005 until the inauguration of Morales in January 2006.

Thus, in considering the ways in which the Morales government refined its appropriations of law, particularly in the years after—and in relation to—the 2011 TIPNIS conflict, these sociolegal projections can be located, theoretically, somewhere between the juridification or judicialization of politics (see, e.g., Couso, Huneeus, and Sieder 2010) and what John and Jean Comaroff (2006) have described as "lawfare." For the first, political values are transformed into legal categories and practices as part of what Pilar Domingo (2010) has called "novel appropriations of the law in the pursuit of political and social change." In this sense, the political is rendered legal; it is juridified; what was once political becomes legal.

But for the second, lawfare, something like the opposite logic is in play: legal categories and practices are wielded as instruments of political power, the legal is rendered political, what was once—at least formally—legal becomes political. As the Comaroffs explain this disciplinary politicization of law, the state turns to "its own rules . . . its duly enacted penal codes, its administrative law, its states of emergency, its charters and mandates and warrants, its norms of engagement—to impose a sense of order upon its subordinates by means of violence rendered legible, legal, and legitimate by its own sovereign word" (2006: 30).

Yet from the drawn-out prosecutions of former opposition leaders to Law 351 to the case against Chile at the ICJ, what was at work in Bolivia, especially in the years after the 2011 TIPNIS conflict, was something that was at the same time less pervasively violent and more carefully targeted. Through a logic of "strategic juridification," the Morales government harnessed forms of law instrumentally, selectively. This was done partly in order to legitimate its moves symbolically "beneath the juridical sign." But strategic juridification also emerged as a response to a more ideological imperative, one in which the turn to law was seen to represent an important shift in revolutionary tactics in which power, legibility, and the law were conditionally and problematically fused.

THE TRAGIC DISSONANCE OF HUMAN RIGHTS

In November 2008, a small group of survivors of the Porvenir Massacre moved from their homes in Pando to take up a position outside the walls of San Pedro Prison. For over two months, several men and their young sons lived under tarps in a hastily constructed encampment under a banner that read "Pando Presente," or "Pando Is Here." Nearby, another banner read "No to Impunity! Prison for the Murderers!" over large photos of Leopoldo Fernández and seven other prominent anti-government militants and members of Pando's prefecture. An eighth image on the banner was of two shadows next to a question mark that was labeled "and many others." The small group had been encouraged to move to La Paz by their lawyer, Mary Carrasco Condarco, a prominent human rights advocate and legal scholar who had become famous in Bolivia during the early 1990s as the lawyer who represented Álvaro García Linera during the katarista trials.

The men and their children had come to La Paz for several reasons: to be present as Carrasco pursued justice for them in tandem with the state's public prosecution of Fernández and the other Pando defendants; to seek medical and psychological treatment for their injuries; and to serve as a striking and embodied reminder of the events of September 11, 2008, simply by being ever-present outside the walls that held the indicted ex-prefect of Pando. Two of the men, Roberto and Félix, were encamped with their two sons, both eight years old. They said that they had to rely on passersby for most of their food and water as they did not have any money. Their greatest fear, they said, was that the powerful Fernández, who was known for many years in Pando as "El Cacique," the most feared person in the region, would be rescued from San Pedro in the dead of night by well-connected friends who would bribe prison officials to look the other way as the wealthy Fernández slipped through the gates.

Ironically, although San Pedro was also known colloquially as "El Panóptico," the Panopticon, its carceral logic was precisely the opposite of Bentham's design. Instead of an all-seeing system of control that managed prisoners through surveillance and moral discipline, San Pedro, like many other large urban Latin American prisons, was marked by the near absence of internal surveillance and regulation by state officials. In their place, San Pedro's inmate population governed itself through spectacular forms of punishment (including killings, beatings, and targeted maiming), material inequalities, and spatial hierarchies.

Despite having endured weeks of miserable and increasingly rainy conditions on the sidewalk at the congested intersection of Calles Cañada Strongest and Nicolás Acosta, Roberto and Félix were eager to talk about their experiences when I met them in late December 2008. They were very lucky to have survived.

ROBERTO: They came for us in trucks and they had guns, rifles, pistols, and some automatic weapons. I knew some of them, I recognized a few of them from the alcaldía [in Cobija] and from the prefect's office. But there were many of them in the trucks, most I didn't recognize. They came to take us. They came to kill us. You could see it in their eyes.

FÉLIX: There was shooting and screaming. I heard a woman scream and I heard a bad sound and I think she was shot dead. It's true that some of us [MAS supporters] had sticks, to try and defend ourselves, because we are used to the attacks whenever we try and mobilize or hold a [pro-government] political event. But this time was different. They did not come to fight or to stop us. They came to kill us. . . . When I heard the shooting, I tried to hide. Something whizzed above me and a branch fell and hit me on the head here [he showed me a wound underneath his hair]. I had my little boy with me [the one living with him in the city encampment] and I tried to protect him and hide even though I was losing consciousness.

I asked them how they felt about that day. Did they feel fortunate to be alive?

ROBERTO: Yes, we feel lucky, of course we do. They had come to kill us and they did kill many of us, even more than have been reported. There are bodies in the forest, in shallow graves. They threw bodies in the river and who knows where they are now? The report [from UNASUR] calls what happened in Porvenir a massacre. It was a massacre. They wanted to kill all of us, even women and children.

You said before that you are living out here in order to demand justice, to make sure justice is done. But what exactly does justice mean for you, what can it mean?

FÉLIX: Well, many of our friends and family are dead now. Their bodies are rotting right now in the forest. There will be no justice for them. They are dead and their souls are in heaven. The prefect [Fernández] has many powerful friends, senators, business owners, people in the media. We are only two people here, plus our sons. People pass by and they sometimes show kindness, sometimes they don't do anything. Sometimes they give us some food, especially for the boys. But all we can do is be present. I don't even think we can prevent them from freeing him [Fernández] if they want to. We are just here.

Despite the understandable confusion and profound trauma experienced by the victims of the Porvenir Massacre, the broader context was clear enough: gross human rights violations had been committed against pro-MAS activists by anti-government militants in Pando on September 11, 2008. Indeed, in the final section of the November 2008 UNASUR report, the international body recommended that the Bolivian government take legal action against any public officials or institutions in the country that committed similar "criminal acts that violate human rights" (UNASUR 2008). Nevertheless, as the months and then years dragged on, even as the legal case against Fernández continued to grind forward, a curious transformation took place in the way in which the Porvenir Massacre was invoked and deployed by the government.

What made the events of September 11, 2008, so terrible, so extraordinary, was not the fact that they represented the kind of violence—torture, the desecration of remains, the killing of political opponents—that Bolivia had largely avoided after the restoration of democracy in the mid-1980s, even as its neighbors to the north and south were wracked by civil and dirty wars. Rather, it was that the events of Porvenir, much like the May 2008 humiliations and violence in Sucre, represented a new form of political escalation in the resistance to the wider process of change. That is, as the Morales government constructed it, the Porvenir Massacre deserved opprobrium not because it was an unprecedented violation of human rights, but because it showed what the "fascist right" was capable of in its efforts to undermine the country's historic refoundation.

The absence of human rights from the rhetoric of the Morales government was something of a puzzle, particularly since rights discourse had played such an important role in both the political and ideological development of MAS during the transitional period of the early to mid-2000s (see Goodale 2008a). Yet in considering the perplexing question of human rights within the wider historical and discursive trajectory of the period 2006–15 in more depth, it became increasingly apparent that the logics of human rights activism clashed in key ways with the Morales government's vision(s) of sociopolitical change. The discursive tonality of human rights—its transcendent claims, its universalizing language, its normative horizontality—sounded more and more dissonant, tragically dissonant, especially in relation to the government's post-TIPNIS legal strategies.

The kind of discursive hollowness that eventually came to undermine human rights as a potential framing category for the Morales government marked a different problem than the one described by Goldstein (2012), in which despite certain earnest gestures, the weakness of the Bolivian state created "outlaw" zones where the law protected neither rights nor citizen security. Instead, as the Bolivian government consolidated its national position by harnessing law's regulatory, symbolic, and transcriptive powers, the place of human rights became increasingly untenable, even marginalized.

The tragic dissonance of human rights amid the normative clamor of Bolivia's process of change, although expressed in ways both glaring and subtle, was most clearly reflected through the rise and fall of an important governmental institution: the Defensoría del Pueblo. The Defensoría was established in 1998 during the early years of Hugo Banzer's democratic presidency, although the initiative for its creation had begun as part of the suite of neoliberal human rights projects during the first Sánchez de Lozada government.

The Defensoría was a National Human Rights Institution (NHRI), an innovative development promoted by the Office of the United Nations High Commissioner for Human Rights that encouraged countries to establish independent institutions to monitor state compliance with human rights standards within their own borders (see Mertus 2009). Bolivia's NHRI was among the first in Latin America to have been granted "A" status, which meant that it met a series of rigid criteria known as the "Paris Principles," including independence from the government, the capacity to issue critical public opinions regarding human rights compliance without fear of reprisal, and a broad mandate to educate the public about human rights.

Bolivia's Defensoría had played a key public role in all of the major conflicts since its foundation, including the Water and Gas Wars, the violence during the Constituent Assembly of 2007, the mobilizations of the pro-autonomy and capitalía movements, and, finally, the 2011 TIPNIS conflict. In each instance, the Defensoría, represented by the *Defensora* or *Defensor del Pueblo*, attempted to fulfill its institutional mandate by reframing the conflict through the lens of human rights, assigning blame for human rights violations among competing narratives, and issuing stern judgments when the state failed in its obligations to protect human rights.[12]

Yet in retrospect, although the Morales government tolerated the interventions of the Defensor Waldo Albarracín, who served for six years between 2004 and 2010, this was only because the Defensoría found itself aligned with the new MAS regime against anti-government and separatist mobilizations that represented clear and present threats to human rights. Critically, however, the nature of the threats was understood quite differently by the Morales government and the Defensoría. To the government, the violence of 2007–9 was only the most serious among several barriers to its transformational policies; to the Defensoría, the racialized violence reflected a rapid deterioration of human rights standards in the country, a decline that was particularly worrying because it showed many of the hallmarks of dehumanizing conflict in the "predictable but not inexorable" (Stanton 2013) spiral into genocide.

It was during and after the 2011 TIPNIS conflict, not surprisingly, that the actual chasm between the Morales government and the Defensoría was revealed in all its starkness. When it was the government, and not the opposition, that was being accused by the Defensoría of rights violations, including ethnic discrimination, arbitrary detention, and, perhaps most devastating of all, denial of the right to free, prior, and informed consent for indigenous peoples, the response was both swift and telling. In its attacks on the Defensoría, the Morales government accused it of seeking to undermine the process of change, of putting the demands of international institutions before the interests of national development, and of advancing a neocolonial agenda. Indeed, as a result of the government's confrontations with the Defensoría, "human rights" became a semiotic category through which the Defensoría could be associated with the anti-government opposition and the shadowy "fascist right."

The ill-fated Defensor del Pueblo during these years was Rolando Villena Villegas, the person who represented the Defensoría during its precipitous fall from grace. Because of the underlying fault lines between the Defensoría and the Morales government, its decline on Villena's watch was not the result of a failure to fulfill his duties; indeed, quite the opposite. In many ways, it was appropriate that Bolivia's Defensoría should face an existential crisis under Villena, a remarkable and visionary man who rose from humble beginnings in a rural hamlet in Potosí's Nor Chichas Province to become a Methodist bishop, Bolivia's leading human rights defender, and one of the most influential critics of the post-TIPNIS Morales governments.

By August 2015, the curtain had almost come down on Bolivia's Defensoría, at least in the institutional form it had known since 1998. Villena was weary from the many battles with the MAS government and realized that, in the specific struggle between the lofty human rights mission of the Defensoría and the gritty, zero-sum politics of the government, the Defensoría had become dangerously isolated. His tenure as Defensor had been marked by discord from the beginning, even before the historic rupture of TIPNIS.

Let me tell you. I took office in May 2010. Two, three months later we suddenly had Caranavi [a conflict in the Yungas]. Of course we intervened, demanding an inquiry into the circumstances around the deaths. Within one day of our public statement, that room out there [gestures to the waiting room outside his office] was filled with a group of high-ranking politicians [from MAS] and their legal advisers. They asked me, "Brother Rolando, can you let us know what you are going to do, what kind of report you are considering?" I told them that we were just going to investigate any human rights abuses as we are obligated to do according to the mandate. They stared right at me and one of them said, "Brother Rolando, you know who you are talking to, right?" I replied, "Yes, I know. I also know who I am."

I then asked him whether or not that was the only time he was visited by MAS officials in what was clearly an effort to put pressure on the Defensoría.

No, that was just the beginning of many such visits. I've also been called to the Palace many times. Each time, I tried to explain that human rights are not something that can be made up along the way, they are not subjective. When there are violations, there are always facts, objective facts that cannot be denied. . . . Like other institutions, like others who have been critical from time to time of the government, even I have been accused of being an agent of the right, can you believe it? I have been fighting for human rights my whole life, since the time of the dictators. But every time we get a warning visit from oficialismo, it reminds me exactly of how it was during the time of the dictators. One time, Evo himself came here [after the TIPNIS conflict]. I told him that our mandate was clear. He put his finger up to stop me and said, "I am the only one who can command in this country. I am unique" [Yo soy único].[13]

CONCLUSION: THE UNSTABLE ASSEMBLAGE OF LAW

As we have seen, the place of law within the process of change in Bolivia during the period 2006–15 defied easy characterization. The ethnography of Bolivia's experiments with autonomy, legal decolonization, criminal prosecutions, and human rights also reinforced the critical importance of historicizing the frame of analysis, because the contested modes of law underwent key transformations that were often a response to background political and ideological conflicts. In addition, it is necessary to peel apart the concept of law itself, since key actors and institutions themselves developed the capacity to view law as a plural, unstable assemblage of procedural, institutional, and normative logics that could be harnessed for different purposes with different potential outcomes based on different strategies of justification.

For example, although the Morales government found the regime of criminal law—which was largely left in place by the 2009 constitution—ideally suited to its evolving strategy of adapting the rule of law as a mechanism of change, it found international human rights law to be a burdensome imposition, threatening, the hidden hand of the Global North seeking to dominate Bolivia's domestic affairs by other means. Yet on balance, it is true that the ways and means of law became increasingly important, even foundational, to the MAS government as its vision for change narrowed and became more exclusionary, especially in the post-TIPNIS period, which, as we have seen, proved to be a significant turning point.

Finally, another problem that remained throughout this period was a basic tension between the increasingly centripetal approach to power adopted by the MAS government and the ongoing ideological commitment to radical pluralism that suffused government ministries and allied social movements. The various structures of law not only proved incapable of resolving this tension; in many instances they deepened it and made it a more problematic marker of the process of change, especially after 2011. This tension between existing frames of law and the pluralizing imperative could also be tinged with problems of ethnic identity. As the TCP magistrate Efrén Choque Capuma put it in August 2015, in discussing the status of human rights within the process of change:

The fact is that human rights is the law of the elites, like the positive law more generally, as I've been saying. The problem with human rights is that they don't open spaces for generating intercultural justice [or law]. The other problem with human rights and positive law is that they treat indigenous people like objects, not subjects. But we are our own subjects of law and jurisprudence.

6 AND THE PUTUTU SHALL SOUND

I am not a writer nor a literate mestizo. I am an Indian. An Indian who thinks, who makes ideas, who creates ideas. My ambition is to forge an Indian ideology, an ideology of my race. Once I was alone, now I will be millions. Alive or dead, completely conscious and lucid or made of dust, I will be millions. I will make rubble out of the infamous walls of "organized silence" in which the Bolivia of Indian submission has enclosed me.

—Fausto Reinaga, *La Revolución India* (2007a)

In December 2008, at the height of the racial polarization in Bolivia during the period 2006–15, I was traveling in a taxi after conducting ethnographic interviews with upper-class university students at La Paz's private Universidad Católica Boliviana (UCB). UCB was located in a transitional zone called Obrajes between La Paz proper and the Zona Sur, the southern, and, most importantly lower, district that included the neighborhoods of Calacoto, Alto Florida, and Cota Cota—an intentionally isolated area of gated and guarded mansions, upscale restaurants and shops, foreign embassies, and private schools for the children of diplomats and Global North expatriates.

The narrow two-lane road that connected the Zona Sur with central La Paz was often clogged with taxis, private cars, buses, *trufis*, motorcycles, and sometimes carts being pushed by itinerant merchants selling all manner of goods. In the early afternoon, the traffic on the road was crawling at best and drivers were becoming agitated. Some drivers attempted to pass those in front, even around blind curves on the winding road. I was in the taxi with one of my PhD students, an Ecuadorian researcher who had joined me during the 2008 field season in order to get firsthand experience with ethnographic field methods. Because it was the middle of the Bolivian summer, the weather was seasonably warm and we and the taxi driver had our windows rolled down.

Our taxi driver was in his early twenties and was an Aymara from the small town of Jesús de Machaca near the southern end of Lake Titicaca. The region of Jesús de Machaca was well known in Bolivian history as the site of a massacre in 1921, during which the regime of Bautista Saavedra sent about 1,500 Bolivian infantry and cavalry troops to quell a rebellion by indigenous peasants against the town's abusive local leaders (see Choque 1986; Choque and Ticona 1996). In the ensuing actions against the area's ayllus and rural hamlets, the government troops engaged in a scorched-earth campaign in which an unknown number—but probably hundreds—of men, women, and children were killed in retribution; hundreds of houses were burned; and livestock was seized or destroyed (Mesa 2008). On the window just above the rearview mirror, our taxi driver had affixed two stickers, facing inward: one was an image of Jesus Christ in all his bearded, robed, celestial glory; the other was a small photo of Evo Morales over the slogan "Evo Se Queda, Mi Revolución Avanza" (Evo Remains, My Revolution Advances).

As we inched along the road on our way to Plaza Murillo, where I had an interview scheduled with Gustavo Guzmán, the former Bolivian ambassador to the United States who had been declared persona non grata by the United States in September as a response to the expulsion by the Morales government of U.S. Ambassador Philip Goldberg, I mentioned to the taxi driver that we had an appointment in the city center. Perhaps hoping both to show his driving skills and to increase the size of his tip, the taxi driver suddenly swerved to the left to pass the cars in front. Yet just at that moment, a car coming down the road appeared around the corner and both cars screeched to a halt in a jumble of blaring horns and jostled bodies.

No one was injured, but as I lifted my head to look at the other car, I saw that it was a late-model luxury sedan being driven by an older man who was likely on his way from his office in central La Paz to his gated Zona Sur home for the midday meal. As our taxi driver remained frozen out of both shock and gratitude that a serious accident had been narrowly averted, the other driver started again slowly but stopped right against our driver's door. He almost scraped us. He rose up in his seat and leaned across so that his head was almost inside our taxi driver's window. His face was red with rage and inches from that of our driver. Like a cannon shot, he yelled "¡indio!" and then quickly pulled his head into his own car and sped off.

Without saying a word, our taxi driver turned back into traffic and we continued the trip to Plaza Murillo. The three of us sat in pained silence; I kept a close eye on the taxi driver in the rearview mirror from our spot in the back seat. The look on his face was not one of anger and neither was it one of defiance; rather, it was a look of fear tempered by sadness. It seemed, for a time, as if he was on the verge of tears. Yet he had recovered by the time we reached the Ministry of External Relations. Standing outside the open passenger-side window, I gave him a 20 Bs note for a 12 Bs fare. As he reached for change, I said to him, "No, don't worry about it, keep the change." And then I leaned into the window and said, in a much-lowered voice, "I'm sorry you had to suffer that act of racism. It must be common these days." He didn't look at me while he replied, but at the radio, which coincidently at that very moment was broadcasting a press conference with the government minister Sacha Llorenti on the anniversary of the signing of the UDHR (December 10). *Yes*, the taxi driver finally said, still looking at the radio, *it is very common*.

Amid the ideological hybridity, normative violence, and contentious politics that marked Bolivia's "democratic and cultural revolution," its process of change, its refoundation, there was, as the December 2008 moment of everyday racism revealed (a moment to which, I must add, I was an accidental witness), an element that was always in the background, and often in the foreground: a complex series of struggles over collective identity. By constructing and then harnessing the full symbolic power of his status as the first indigenous president of Bolivia, Evo Morales and the government's expert propagandists, particularly those in the Ministry of Communication, clearly understood the ways in which a politics of recognition could be interwoven with law, history, and a "sense of justice" (Brunnegger and Faulk 2016) to produce a potent strategy both for governance and for the projection of a kind of moral power. Indeed, the centrality of what might be understood as a prismatic conception of collective identity was announced in the very first paragraph of the preamble to the 2009 constitution:

> We inhabit this sacred Mother Earth with different faces [*rostros diferentes*] and it is from this starting point that we must understand the living pluralism of all things, our diversity as beings and cultures. It is in this way that our peoples must be understood [as part of a system of living pluralism], and never through the racism that we have suffered beginning with the disastrous time of colonialism.

Yet despite the foundational importance of collective identity within MAS's governing project, it could never be fully reduced to specific legal or political categories or rendered into a limited number of historical narratives. Rather, the problem of collective identity ranged much wider; its contours were much more opaque; its layers were much deeper. In fact, as will be seen in this chapter, the ethnography of identity politics against the background of change, violent reaction, and revolutionary ennui suggested an analytical approach shaped by three factors—*intersectionality*, *relationality*, and *contention*. First, although categories of cultural and ethnic identity dominated much of the conflict and public debate during the period 2006–15, there were other categories that played an important role in shaping practices and meanings. Yet rather than understanding the interplay of these multiple categories through an account of intersectionality that is limited to an explanation of the nuances of category discrimination, here the descriptive claims to intersectionality go further.[1] As will be seen below, the interactivity between identity categories in Bolivia—cultural (for example, indigenous), gendered, social (for example, class), and regional—was more basic, more constitutive.[2]

Second, the place of collective identity within the process of change in Bolivia was marked by a thoroughgoing relationality. What this means is that collective identities were constructed, performed, and refashioned through shades of relations that reflected various degrees of agency and ascription, including constraints on agency and ascription. Even if collective identities were never fixed—either in ideology or in practice—the extent to which people had control over these identity assemblages, the extent to which particular individuals or communities had control over how they were defined in contexts that mattered, varied considerably.

In addition, the relationality of collective identity in Bolivia was marked by various inside/outside narratives, including those framed at the level of the state itself. For example, at the same time that Evo Morales was emerging as a regional, hemispheric, and even global symbol of empowerment as the first "self-identifying"—thus embodying both agency and the power of (self-) ascription—indigenous president of Bolivia, his own status as an indigenous leader was being questioned even by his own supporters within the indigenous social movements in the Pacto de Unidad. Moreover, reflecting both intersectional and relational currents, the question of Morales's ethnic identity was also refracted through gender norms, especially those linked to the ontologically significant act of marriage.

Finally, the social and discursive domains in which the problem of collective identity shaped the trajectory of transformation in Bolivia during the period 2006–15 were characterized by a particular kind of contention, a push-and-pull movement between institutions of governance—largely, but not exclusively, associated with the state—and those who were, ideally, to be governed. Categories of collective identity, especially cultural categories like "indigenous," were fashioned into powerful logics of governance through law, moral rhetoric, and political activism. Further, categories like "indigenous" were formed into structures that could then be deployed actively to structure practices more generally, to invoke Giddens's (1984) sociological distinction.

Yet at the same time, the "strategic" face of collective identities like indígena was often met, perhaps always met, with a corresponding "tactical" response consisting of everyday practices of collective identity that could never be fully determined by broader structures-strategies (de Certeau 1984). Even more, as de Certeau emphasized, the gap between strategies and tactics at the level of everyday practices—in this case, around collective identity—created the ever-present conditions for resistance, creativity, and subversion. As we will see, this tension between the centripetal logics and the centrifugal practices of collective identity produced various frictions that came to define much of what was both productive and exclusionary within Bolivia's "indigenous state" (Postero 2017).

MOEMA: Some people say that you imply that with socialism all the
problems of women's liberation will be solved.

DOMITILA: What I think is that socialism, in Bolivia, like in any country, will be the tool which will create the conditions for
women to reach their level. And they'll do so through their
struggle, through their participation. And their liberation
will be their own work.

But I think that at this moment it's much more important to fight for the liberation of our people alongside the men. It's not that I accept machismo, no. But I think that machismo is a weapon of imperialism just like feminism is. Therefore, I think that the basic fight isn't between the sexes; it's a struggle of the couple. And when I say couple, I also include children and grandchildren, who have joined the struggle for liberation from a class position. I think that's fundamental now.

—Domitila Barrios de Chungara, in conversation
    with Moema Viezzer (1978)

From at least the colonial period, women have played a fundamental role in Bolivia within political and social movements, revolutionary mobilizations, and the articulation of moral cosmovisions. Even so, the place of women in public life has not been shared equally across social classes, ethnic backgrounds, and regions. For example, although men traditionally dominated national politics and *criollo* and mestizo affairs, the presence of peasant and indigenous women alongside men during key moments in Bolivian history was more striking. The most important example of this kind of sociopolitical complementarity was the case of Bartolina Sisa, the wife of the late eighteenth-century Indian rebel Julián Apasa Nina, who took the nom de guerre Túpac Katari. Like Katari, Sisa was eventually executed by the victorious Spanish colonial army after suffering the full brunt of symbol-laden brutality (see Ari Murillo 2003; Hylton and Thomson 2007; Thomson 2002). Sisa's death at the hands of the Spanish became a martyrdom and her legacy a source of inspiration for (especially highland indigenous) Bolivian women throughout the country's history.

During the early twentieth century, women took part in the first waves of union organizing. Although these movements were structured around pan-regional currents of anarcho-syndicalism, the problem of ethnic identity shaped its development in Bolivia. For example, in 1927 the Federación Obrera Femenina (FOF) was established to represent mostly indigenous women workers as a complement to the creation of the Federación Obrera Local (FOL) one year earlier. The FOF was an association that defended the interests of its constituent unions, which were made up of "women of popular Aymara background, commonly known as *cholas*," who worked in syndicates of "cooks, flower sellers, urban market vendors, and rural marketers" (Thomson et al. 2018: 339). The FOF, which was a key political and social institution for many working indigenous women until its suppression during the Barrientos dictatorship in 1964, faced resistance from its first years. Yet its early activists were determined to organize themselves in order to defend their collective interests both as workers and as members of an ethnic underclass.

In the 1980s, researchers with La Paz's Taller de Historia y Participación de la Mujer (Tahipamu) conducted oral histories with elderly former FOF members about their experiences in the 1930s and 1940s. As one aging Aymara sindicalista, Doña Peta, explained, the will to organize was a potent social force:

> Doña Peta: "What are we going to do?" We were talking in the market. Don José Mendoza, who would later be my partner, said to me, "You have to organize yourselves in a union. Get organized!" That afternoon it seemed easy to organize. We didn't have a place to meet; so we just met in the market, in the empty stalls. We did the impossible to get out of the houses [where we worked]. When the police came, they told us to get out. Some women comrades loaned us a room, but how could we all fit in there? There were loads and loads of us! That's how we founded the Union of Women Cooks (*Sindicato de Culinarias*), the 15th of August 1935. (quoted in Thomson et al. 2018: 340)

Another important historical example in which indigenous women in Bolivia organized themselves politically was in the mining centers, although the representation that emerged of women's empowerment in relation to men was somewhat ambiguous. In her classic 1979 study of Bolivian tin mines, based on research conducted in 1969 and 1970 in Oruro, June Nash wrote of the indigenous women in the mining camps:

> There is less opportunity for women [than for men] to gain self-expression and the community endorsement for it. A married woman is subjected to the limitation of the house, to almost unrestricted childbearing, and to dominance by the man whose needs she must dedicate herself to serve. Women who work as *palliris*, pulverizing ore and selecting out the metal, have some of the satisfaction that comes with independence, but they have a harder time maintaining a satisfactory domestic relation with a man of respect in the community. The very fact that a woman works is a threat to an industrious worker whose reason for being is to support a family. Male and female roles are dichotomized in the mining community, and there is still a mystique about women not entering the mine. (1993: 12–13)

In her groundbreaking 1978 *testimonio Let Me Speak!* Domitila Barrios de Chungara, an indigenous activist from the mining complex of Catavi-Siglo XX in the north of Potosí Department, gave a somewhat different account of women's political participation, especially through the establishment of the Housewives' Committee of Siglo XX, which played a role in many of the strikes and violent encounters with the government during the Banzer dictatorship of the mid-1970s. Nevertheless, in an indelible section entitled "How a Miner's Wife Spends Her Day," Barrios de Chungara described a grueling life of unacknowledged and unpaid work that began each morning at 4 AM making about a hundred *salteñas* to sell in the market.

Her workday only ended around midnight, after having throughout the day handwashed the laundry in cold water, purchased food for the family, supervised the children's schoolwork, and prepared the materials for the next morning's salteñas. Political organizing with the Housewives' Committee had to take place during brief pauses in this succession of unremitting labor. Even so, Barrios de Chungara viewed women's political militancy in the mining center as an essential act of resistance against the "common enemy"—the broader economic system in which "the bosses get richer and the workers' conditions get worse and worse" (1978: 35, 36).

Finally, in 1980, the most consequential indigenous women's organization in Bolivian history was established. In January of that year, during the short-lived and doomed presidency of Lidia Gueiler Tejada—Bolivia's only female head of state, who was overthrown in the Cocaine Coup of July 1980 by Luis García Meza (who was also her cousin)—the Federación Nacional de Mujeres Campesinas de Bolivia was formed.[3] The new women's federation was created as a constituent organization of the Confederación Sindical Única de Trabajadores Campesinos de Bolivia (CSUTCB), which was established in late June 1979 under the leadership of Genaro Flores. The founders of the Federación Nacional de Mujeres Campesinas de Bolivia included Lucila Mejía de Morales, Irma García, Isabel Juaniquina, and Isabel Ortega; Mejía de Morales was elected the organization's first executive secretary.

Like the CSUTCB, the Federación Nacional de Mujeres Campesinas de Bolivia affiliated itself immediately with the Central Obrera Boliviana (COB), a development that profoundly shifted the social and political orientation of Bolivia's national workers' association (see chapter 4). As a signal of its militant aspirations and sense of history, the Federación Nacional de Mujeres Campesinas de Bolivia added the name *Bartolina Sisa* to the organization, thereby becoming officially the Federación Nacional de Mujeres Campesinas de Bolivia "Bartolina Sisa" (FNMCB-BS). Colloquially, the federation was known after that as *Las Bartolinas*, a description that would come to evoke images of women activists at the very center of every political conflict and social transformation in Bolivian history for the next thirty-five years.

In November 2008, on the eve of the country's constitutional refoundation, the Bartolinas held a historic congress in the city of Santa Cruz. In part as a reflection of its expansion throughout the country and its internal division into departmental and provincial branches, and in part as a sign of the coming transformations under the new plurinational state, the Bartolinas reconstituted themselves as a confederation, adding "indígenas y originarias" to campesinas to bring their collective self-identification in line with the state's new hybrid ethnicity.[4] They thus became the Confederación Nacional de Mujeres Campesinas, Indígenas y Originarias de Bolivia "Bartolina Sisa" (CNMCIOB-BS).[5]

During the period 2006–15, the Bartolinas emerged as central protagonists in Bolivia's process of change. Even in relation to the other main organizations of the Pacto de Unidad,[6] the Bartolinas played a vanguard role as outspoken advocates who were ready and willing to defend the revolutionary process against all those who would oppose it. At the same time, their visibility on the front lines of conflict, and their institutional independence as a national women's social and political movement, gave the Bartolinas an aura of moral courage and made them a symbol for feminist empowerment throughout Latin America. In part, their organizational rhetoric drew from the broader history of Bolivia's worker and peasant movements. Nevertheless, at its core, the ideological logic of the Bartolinas was distinct, a singular contribution to the history of social movements, and an example of the power of culture in the present, to paraphrase James Dunkerley (2007a).

At a superficial level, the ideological history of the Bartolinas also reflected the influence of the wider transnational women's rights movement, particularly as this movement found expression in the 1979 Convention on the Elimination of All Forms of Discrimination against Women (CEDAW), which Bolivia signed (but did not ratify) in the same year in which the Bartolinas were established (Bolivia ratified CEDAW in 1990). Yet beyond the general historical similarities with other women's social movements in Latin America and beyond, what distinguished the Bartolinas was the way in which its members conceived of their sociopolitical roles as an organic extension of a deeper ontology that was ideally understood with reference to gender complementarity.

As Olivia Harris explained across a number of different studies (e.g., 1978, 2000), this conception of gender complementarity was one in which the active unity of the married couple crystallized the more basic underlying complementarity of an interconnected ontological system. As Frank Salomon described it, this system was one through which a "unified biological-technological productivity unfold[ed] seamlessly from human-telluric bonds through matrimonial alliance outward to very wide regional alignments and toward cosmological forces" (Salomon: 2001: 654).[7]

In this sense, the social and political activism of the Bartolinas during the period 2006–15 must be understood as an effort to align the civic and institutional imperative to build a new society through revolutionary mobilization with the underlying structure of the cultural universe itself. To place themselves at the leading edge of the process of change, therefore, was not a radical departure for the Bartolinas; rather, it was to participate in a project of public and militant complementarity through which—and *only* through which—the plurinational state could be made whole.

Moreover, because the Bartolinas viewed the task of constructing the plurinational state as a form of repair, a way to restore the political landscape to a condition in which the political "seamlessly" expressed the cosmological, they viewed any opposition to this task as a more fundamental attack on the "human-telluric bonds" of social life. This explains why the Bartolinas conducted zealous and unremitting campaigns against any perceived anti-government opposition across the entire span of the Morales era, including their denunciations of the Media Luna during the first Morales government, their condemnations of the Defensoría del Pueblo, their criticism of the Asamblea Permanente de Derechos Humanos de Bolivia (APDHB), and their support for the anti-NGO Law 351 in late August 2015.

For the Bartolinas, to struggle against the various critics of the MAS government was to struggle for a more basic ontological—and thus social—balance. This also explains why the Bartolinas could be such effective advocates for the process of change while at the same time maintaining a certain distance from particular members of the government—including, paradoxically, Evo Morales himself. More than any other among the prominent social and political movements during the period 2006–15, it was the Bartolinas who managed to radically depoliticize what they believed to be the historically inevitable—and socially necessary—turning point. In this sense, the MAS government and its (mostly male) leaders were merely the best instrument for overseeing this change—an imperfect instrument, to be sure, but by far the best among the alternatives.

In 2008, the charismatic and highly visible executive secretary of the Bartolinas was Patricia Choque Callisaya. Her term in office was 2006–9, during which she led the Bartolinas through some of the most important conflicts and confrontations of the epochal first Morales government. Choque's ascendance to the position of the leading indigenous female sociopolitical actor in Bolivia began in the important region of Jesús de Machaca (see above), where she rose through the ranks within the area's well-structured fiesta cargo system of indigenous leadership.

As in other regions of Bolivia's highlands, the ayllus of Jesús de Machaca had been reconstituted during the second part of the twentieth century after having been fragmented by the imposition of the rural peasant unions after the 1952 National Revolution. When identifying where she was from, Choque referred not to a specific hamlet or municipality, but to an ayllu: Ayllu Yauriri Unificada, one of nineteen ayllus in the region's "lower" moiety, or *marka*, which by 2008 had been organized into a political entity recognized by the state called MACOJMA—Marka de Ayllus y Comunidades Originarias de Jesús de Machaca.[8]

Each ayllu in Jesús de Machaca was led by a complementary husband and wife pair that were called Tata Mallku (father mallku) and Mallku Tayka (mother mallku); thus, there would be nineteen such pairs in MACOJMA and seven in MACOAS at any one time. At the highest level, each marka was led by one husband-and-wife pair that were called Jach'a Mallku and Jach'a Mallku Tayka. As Andrew Orta has explained, during their term of service, the Tata Mallku and Mallku Tayka "are, figuratively, the mother and father of the ayllu" (2004: 54). By extension, the maximal husband-and-wife pair of each of the two Jesús de Machaca markas was the mother and father to everyone in their moiety. However, despite this idealized conception of complementary sociopolitical leadership, in fact, the ayllu and especially the marka pairs tended to form around men on the rise rather than around women. In other words, when a man reached the highest and final levels of native leadership—in Jesús de Machaca and throughout the highlands—his wife became the maximal female leader by default.

Nevertheless, there was another route through which a talented woman could achieve success in organizational life: by leaving her home province to become part of the departmental and eventually national systems of federation and confederation leadership. This path was not formally dependent on the fortunes of a husband, although the marriage bond remained fundamental. This was precisely the means through which Patricia Choque had made her way to the top position in the Bartolinas. She had served as dirigente to the Mallku Tayka of her ayllu and, perhaps in recognition of the fact that her wider prospects were more promising than those of her husband, she was elected by the marka to represent it at the departmental level of the Bartolinas. She then became executive secretary of the departmental Bartolinas, whose offices were also in La Paz, which gave her a platform parallel to that of the national leaders. When she was elected executive secretary of the national confederation in 2006, she was only thirty-two years old.

I asked Choque whether it was difficult to pursue a life at the highest levels of organizational politics while maintaining a family that was disconnected from its provincial roots.

Yes, it is. I have a family, I have a husband and two daughters; my oldest daughter is already fourteen years old. For a woman who is also a political leader, this kind of life can be very difficult. First, you have to continue with the home, that never stops, the children continue with their lives, you have to prepare lunch every day, you have to deal with whatever happens each day. All of this is a huge worry for a mother, and, at the same time, there is the organization [the Bartolinas]. *I have to think about how I will manage it each day, all of the meetings that I have to preside over. I have to ask myself, What things do I need to do* [for the organization] *at every moment? What things do I have to bring home with me to work on at night?*

Was the housework shared with her husband, especially while she was serving in her capacity as leader of the Bartolinas?

Yes, when he has the time, because he is also working very hard for the family during the day. But when he has the time, he helps in the kitchen. We usually cook together, we wash the clothes together, at least on Saturdays and Sundays. Thus, from Monday to Friday, I work in the organization and my husband does his work, and that's how we keep our house together, no?

I asked Choque if this meant there was complementarity between her and her husband. If so, did she believe that complementarity was an important value—either in the home or in her organizational work? She drew a sharp distinction between the gendered structure of leadership in the ayllus and the peculiar system she had encountered in La Paz.

Yes, in general, I would say that there is complementarity between man and woman, especially in the provinces, for example, in my marka in Jesús de Machaca. . . . But the work there is very distinct from here [in La Paz]. *There, for example, we have meetings, there are* cabildos *and* ampliados [larger ayllu congresses], *in which all of the native leadership in the community* [la autoridad originaria de la comunidad] *must always strive for* chachawarmi.[9] *. . . So we are in a meeting, the husbands to one side, the native authorities in the middle, and the wives to another side. But in order to discuss certain points, in order to decide something important, the women have the word in order to decide* *things in the community, and in the cabildos as well. . . . Thus, that is how we learn to do things as women, how to express ourselves, how we are able to plan things, to propose important things in the cabildos, how to think for ourselves as women, how we are able to speak. We have the freedom to speak, no? On the contrary, here in the city, things are very different. We are still very powerful, but we don't act together with the men, they have their own organizations, there is something of a division between us. But as I said, there is no division like this in the provinces, there everything is chachawarmi. For example, look at me. I'm the executive secretary of the national organization* [of Bartolinas] *but my husband is not my co-leader.*

Like many leaders of indigenous social and political organizations, Choque was not an early or enthusiastic supporter of Evo Morales and MAS. On the contrary, the most important indigenous leader in those years before the historic elections of 2005 was Felipe Quispe, El Mallku. During the Gas War of 2003, Choque was the recording secretary for the Bartolinas, and she participated in the violent confrontations alongside her sisters in the organization.

In our organization, in our confederation, more than any other [in Bolivia], *we are living our objectives. We women are always struggling, always fighting for total change, it's been this way for decades. I have personally struggled, fought, in 2002, 2003, 2004, 2005, alongside my sisters. We have struggled both as leaders and as women. It is perhaps important to remember that this has also been a sad and painful history for us because we know that, within this process of change, we have been the pillars. As leaders, we must be the first ones on the street blockades, in the marches. If the leaders are not in the streets, the rank-and-file won't allow itself to be mobilized. But this also means that it is very risky to be a leader. For example, in 2003* [during Black October], *several of our leaders were severely injured and a few were killed.*

In late 2008, only a month before the triumphal national constitutional referendum, Choque was still unsatisfied with the pace of the process of change. She criticized the lack of revolutionary transformation within the economy and, in particular, within the hydrocarbon sector, which she blamed on corruption in the government and as the result of continuing entanglements with transnational corporations. But then her critical observations of certain members of the MAS government and Evo Morales took a curious turn. As Choque was explaining why the indigenous movements eventually encouraged their members to vote for Morales, despite the fact that El Mallku was their true leader, she said:

You need to understand something important—Evo Morales is neither in-digenous nor a peasant, and neither is he a miner as far as I know.

Are you talking about President Morales? I thought he was the first in-digenous president of Bolivia?

Well, he doesn't speak Aymara or Quechua, and frankly he doesn't speak Spanish perfectly either, right? . . . But there is something else that is even more difficult for us to accept, the fact that he is not married, he is not chachawarmi. When I was single, when I was young, I didn't think about the economy. My father and mother took care of me, they gave me my breakfast, my midday meal, I didn't know where money came from. This only happened when I got married and had my own children. But look at Brother Evo. It's true that he has children, but he's not with them, he doesn't live with them. I think they are in Oruro with their mothers, but I'm not sure.[10]

Why is the fact that Evo is not married important?

Because it means that he doesn't know how to run a family, what it takes to organize and sustain a family. What does the house need? Vegetables? Meat? Does something need to be fixed? How can he understand how to administer at the national level if he doesn't understand how to organize a house with a woman? He's going to miss many things that are important. He lacks important knowledge. For example, there are people right now who are dying of hunger but he can't see this because he doesn't know what it means to have to provide food for an entire family. When a mother or a father in a family has lived through these experiences, then they understand. There have been moments in my life in which I didn't have anything to give to my children [to eat]. This means that as a leader, there's nothing that I haven't already seen.

But what do you say to those who claim that Evo is married to the Boliv-ian people, that the whole country is now his family?

I don't understand that. It's not the same. When you don't have a family you don't have worries. Everything seems fine, peaceful, but that's not how people really live.[11]

THE LEGACY OF FAUSTO AND THE POLITICS OF WORLD-RENEWAL

In June 2005, the Guatemalan American investigative journalist Héctor Tobar published a fascinating account of the sense of crisis and possibility that was gripping Bolivia. June 2005 was an important moment, a period of transition within a transition. Carlos Mesa had recently resigned from the presidency after two fraught years in office following the resignation and exile of Gon-zalo Sánchez de Lozada in October 2003. After Mesa had left office, the next two constitutional successors refused to take up the post in the face of ongoing protests, leaving the chief justice, Eduardo Rodríguez Veltzé, the last person standing to assume the office of president with a mandate to prepare for early elections. Yet the historic campaign that would lead to the election of Evo Morales in December had not yet begun in earnest. Indeed, looking back, it is important to remember that Morales had not yet emerged as the leader of what Tobar describes as "Bolivia's Indian uprising." Instead, the most publicly militant and politically significant leaders were people like Abel Mamani, secretary general of the Federación de Juntas Vecinales de El Alto (FEJUVE), Roberto de la Cruz, secretary general of the Central Obrera Regional de El Alto, the radical ex-priest Wilson Soria, the Bartolinas, and Felipe Quispe, El Mallku.

In his analysis of Bolivia's "revolt on high," Tobar does not once refer to Morales. Álvaro García Linera, who is described by Tobar as a "political scientist who has studied Indian activism," is quoted on how the activists at the center of what Tobar calls Bolivia's "Indian-led rebellion" drew on cultural norms as part of their political mobilizations. As García Linera explains in Tobar's piece, "the logic of the agrarian community is brought to the urban world. . . . They say, 'We have to fix the streets because the water has washed everything away. . . . We have to build a soccer field for the young people.' It's all done with communal work, communal sharing and communal meeting" (quoted in Tobar 2005).

But it is not the absence of Evo Morales from Tobar's account that is most striking. Rather, it is the fact that Tobar, who was at the time the Buenos Aires bureau chief for the *Los Angeles Times*, discovered an intriguing ideological force at work behind Bolivia's "diverse social movement of anti-globalization." As he explains in a passage on the centrality of El Alto to the "Indian-led rebellion":

El Alto's schools and cafes, and its urban community centers, are where a new ideology of indigenous pride has flourished, thanks in large measure to Aymara writers such as Fausto Reinaga, whose 1970 book "The Indian Revolution" has become to this generation of activists what "The Autobiography of Malcolm X" was to a generation of African Americans. . . . Reinaga, who died in 1994, prophesied that his work would bring a violent revolution to Bolivia. The country would "cry out in pain and bleed thanks to my words," he wrote. (Tobar 2005)[12]

As Tobar continues:

One of those who read Reinaga as a young man was [Roberto] de la Cruz. Last week, he was on Bolivian TV, referring to the community's residents [in El Alto] as "our troops." "When you read 'La Revolución India,' the impact it has on you is very strong," De la Cruz said in an interview. "You have to put its arguments into practice if you want to liberate your race."

So who was this elusive guru of Indian revolution who predicted that his writings would pave the way for Bolivia's historical world-renewal? On the inside covers of the third edition of *La Revolución India*, which was published in 2007 by his indefatigable publicist, copy editor, and leading public advocate Hilda Reinaga (who was also his niece), we find more clues to this beguiling visionary. The "Mexican anthropologist and philosopher Ignacio Magaloni Duarte says: 'Whoever reads the incommensurable Fausto Reinaga becomes a new man'"; "Carlos Carrera, Ecuadorian . . . , says that 'In Fausto Reinga there is an American Gandhi'"; "the mercenary Latin American intelligentsia, in particular the Bolivian, continues to repeat the phrase today: 'Reinaga is insane. His books are an explosion of insanity'"; "Reinaga is no Nietzsche. . . . The philosophical rebellion of the Superman is restricted to the realm of thought, while Reinaga has given his thought the idea-force of a revolution. Four million Indians in Kollasuyu, eleven million in Peru, three million in Ecuador, one million in Argentina, one million in Chile, and millions in Mexico, Guatemala, Venezuela, Colombia, Brazil, Paraguay. . . . FIFTY MILLION INDIANS who are the spark on the shores of a volcanic ocean that will become a crater spewing fire and lava"; and, finally, "*La Revolución India* is a thunderous challenge to the West, a concrete expression of a social millenarian system that is hidden yet fundamental, it is an ideological instrument with which the Indian force will bury a rotting America and then sing the halleluiah of a New Society over its ruins."

Yet this thunderous challenge, this crater spewing fire and lava, could appear quite different at various moments during the period 2006–15, a kind of ideological shape-shifting that rendered the influence of Reinaga even more bedeviling. For example, in August 2015, what the Venezuelan philosopher and anthropologist Lucía Rincón Soto (2014a) has called Reinaga's "Indian Bible" figured prominently in the most unlikely of settings—a large and awkward gathering of government bureaucrats.

August 2 (a Sunday) was the third anniversary of one of the dozens of follow-on laws that were meant to implement the far-reaching provisions of the 2009 constitution. This date was important because Law 269, the "general law of linguistic rights and policies," contained a sharp-edged provision that was buried deep in the law's mandate. It specified that "all public servants who don't speak one of the languages of the native indigenous peasant peoples and nations must learn a regional language to a communicative level, in accordance with the principle of territoriality, within a maximum duration of three years." Although the meaning of "communicative level" was left ambiguous, the "principle of territoriality" was meant to recognize the dubious proposition that all 36 of Bolivia's official indigenous languages corresponded to nations with defined territorial boundaries—a proposition manifestly at odds with the country's actually existing linguistic diversity (see chapter 2).

Thus it was that in the early hours of a frigid winter morning, 2,520 government functionaries dragged themselves to La Paz's Coliseo Cerrado for a carefully staged event to mark the fact that they were the first group to have completed the language training specified by Law 269, which consisted of twenty-five hours of instruction in Aymara. As the event was scheduled to begin at 8 AM, with speeches by Vice Minister of Decolonization Félix Cárdenas and by Evo Morales, among others, the freshly multilingual multitude was required to arrive at around 7 AM so they could stand in long lines to receive a paper certificate of compliance with the law. At just after 8 AM, the ceremonies began with a greeting by the president, in apparently passable Aymara—*Aski urukipan jilanac kullacanak* (Good day, brothers and sisters).[13]

After that, the folkloric musical group Awatiñas played three songs in Aymara, to which the hundreds of government workers were expected to stand and sing along as a public demonstration of their linguistic capabilities. Needless to say, the effect was not one of a resounding chorus singing in the territorial indigenous language of La Paz. Rather, while the music of Awatiñas rang out through speakers, the people in the diverse crowd variously sang, mumbled, stared down at their certificates, or whispered with neighbors.

In his address, Cárdenas gave a fiery speech that momentarily awakened the sleepy morning assembly. He argued that Bolivia was a "political laboratory" that was yielding findings that would change the world. As he put it, "we are in the midst of an unstoppable process. We have told the world that identity and dignity are at the foundation of our revolution." At about 10:30, the ceremony ended, but before the government workers could return home they were obligated to queue up again to receive something else: a gift from the plurinational state to honor their accomplishment. Amid some grumbling, the 2,520 functionaries got in lines while large cardboard boxes were opened. Although I couldn't tell whether the gifts were received with gratitude, much less with millenarian rapture, each and every one of them was handed a copy of *La Revolución India*.

This use of Reinaga would become something of an official government policy over the next two years. Copies of *La Revolución India* were printed by the thousands by the Ministry of Communication and distributed as a text that effectively became the Morales government's symbolic—though certainly not programmatic—Little Red Book. For example, in August 2016, at events in Puerto Villarroel and Villa Tunari in Cochabamba Department, *seven thousand* copies of *La Revolución India* were distributed to thousands of secondary school students and teachers throughout the Chapare. During the ceremonies, Iván Canelas, the governor of the department, called *La Revolución India* "the work of a titan," and Félix Cárdenas, who was again present, told the students and teachers that "Fausto Reinaga is for us the fulcrum of our paradigm as a plurinational state." Finally, Lorenzo Cruz, the head of education for Cochabamba Department, thanked the national authorities for the massive distribution of *La Revolución India*, remarking that "education must become a fundamental pillar of social transformation in order to form new social beings with this revolutionary thought [of Reinaga]" (Autonomous Departmental Government of Cochabamba 2016; *Los Tiempos*, August 20, 2016).

Reinaga himself was born on March 27, 1906, most likely in the town of Macha in the north of Potosí's Chayanta Province. His given name was José Félix. Many years later, he would adopt the name *Fausto* after the protagonist of Goethe's masterpiece, since, like Faust, Reinaga considered himself a "man who didn't accept his fate such as it was and almost paid with his life for his aspirations" (quoted in Alvizuri 2012: 121). As Reinaga added, in a biographical passage from his 1978 book *El Pensamiento Amáutico*, "in 1957, in Leipzig . . . I found myself in front of the statue of Fausto and Mephistopheles. . . . On many occasions I contemplated the face of this man, which was furrowed with deep wrinkles, he who with a book and feathered quill in his hand had been devoured by the fire of knowledge, he who had sold his soul to the Devil" (1978: 65).

Reinaga claimed to be a direct descendent through his mother of the eighteenth-century Indian rebel Tomás Katari, who had been a native leader from Chayanta executed by the Spanish (like Túpac Katari) in 1781. Both of Reinaga's parents had participated in the Federal War of 1899 among the troops and supporters of Pablo Zárate, "El temible Willka." Throughout his life, Reinaga believed that this revolutionary genealogy flowed through his veins and infused his life and writings with a spirit of both historical destiny and duty to what he later came to understand as the Indian race (Kearney 2014).[14]

Reinaga became a Marxist during the 1930s and later entered politics during the regime of Gualberto Villarroel in the mid-1940s. Although he was a supporter of the Movimiento Nacionalista Revolucionario (MNR) and the 1952 National Revolution, he remained on the fringes of political power. In the early years of the National Revolution, Reinaga introduced to the Bolivian parliament a "radical indigenist program that proposed the Indian's integration into Bolivia's social and political life . . . and a proposal for a radical program of agrarian reform" (Escárzaga 2012), which were both rejected by MNR leaders.

Increasingly disenchanted with the corruption within the MNR government and frustrated with the way in which the MNR's policies were becoming unacceptably reformist despite the revolutionary ideology, Reinaga left Bolivia in 1957 to attend the Fourth World Trade Union Congress in Leipzig, then part of the communist GDR. From East Germany, Reinaga traveled to the Soviet Union, where he lived for three years. While in the Soviet Union, Reinaga "would publish in the Moscow weekly *Ogoniok*, speak on Soviet radio, and meet with Soviet intellectuals including Latin American history Professor Fasilio Ermolaer from the University of Moscow and Elena Romanova from the writer's union" (Kearney 2014: 169).

On visiting Lenin's tomb in Red Square, Reinaga fell into something like a mystical trance. As Reinaga described this experience in his later book on the "messianic sentiment of the Russian people" (Reinaga 1960):

The royal savior of the hungry and ignorant, the re-embodiment of Prometheus who had brought fire from the gods and given it to the Men of earth, the edifice of Russian power, the messiah of the exploited of the world, the demiurge of peace, liberty, and unity of Men, could not die. Lenin is aeviternal and immortal. In this instant, I awoke from my fascination. That astronomical eddy which had filled my head ceased instantly. I awoke from my trance. I saw and took note that I found myself still bathed in tears and facing Lenin. In this moment, just like a volcano that breaks mountains of solid rock, rips trees out by their roots, and vomits fire from its crater, I felt like [my disillusionment was] making my bones crack, my entrails burn, and my soul boil in flames, sick with doubt. Just like that, I felt a faith of light and of fire, from deep within, leave me. (quoted and translated by Kearney 2014: 170)

When Reinaga returned to South America from Europe and the Soviet Union in 1960, he went directly to Montevideo to attend a congress of the Uruguayan Communist Party. While there, the Uruguayan police arrested him and confiscated all of the copies of his 1960 book on the Russian people.

As Hilda Reinaga explained, this was the final moment in Fausto's definitive break with Marxism and European philosophy more generally, since "none of the communists attending the congress lifted a finger to help him," and he had to beg the Bolivian ambassador for assistance. The problem was that the ambassador at the time was the past (and future) Bolivian president Hernán Siles Zuazo, someone Reinaga had savagely criticized in writing and who had tried to bribe Reinaga to fall in line more obediently with the MNR program. Years before the humiliating experience of having to plead with Siles Zuazo for aid, the last words out of the ambassador's mouth to Reinaga, in the early years of the National Revolution, had been, "go fuck yourself, asshole!" (Kearney 2014: 175–76).

With his intellectual worldview imploding, Reinaga suffered a crisis of conscience once he finally returned to Bolivia. In a last attempt to find solace in the writings of European intellectuals, Reinaga began reading even more widely and even desperately, including the work of the Romanian pacifist philosopher and conscientious objector Eugen Relgis (then living in Uruguay) and the French dramatist and mystic Romain Rolland, who had won the 1915 Nobel Prize in Literature for his ten-volume *roman-fleuve* entitled *Jean-Christophe*. Yet "no amount of reading could solve his crisis" (Kearney 2014: 176).

Reinaga decided to make a pilgrimage to the Inca ruins at Machu Picchu. He traveled to Peru in the midst of a profound intellectual, spiritual, and political transformation. As Hilda Reinaga described it, "there was already the question in his mind: Why should the Indian have to follow other doctrines to be liberated, if he has his own principles? So then, it was already gestating in his mind, the issue that the Indian should take power. For this he needed a political party" (quoted in Kearney 2014: 176).

Fausto's journey to Machu Picchu provoked a radical shift in his approach to knowledge. Thenceforth, it would no longer be a question of attempting to synthesize largely Western philosophies or of adapting them, however creatively, to Bolivia's ethnic, economic, and political realities.[15] Rather, Reinaga realized that the foundation for a revolutionary worldview beyond both Marxism and the ideas of what he called the *"cholaje blanco-mestizo"* was to be found among what he considered the superior moral, scientific, and political histories of the Indian peoples of the Americas, even if these histories had been suppressed during centuries of colonialism, republicanism, and cholaje blanco-mestizo capitulation.[16]

To this end, in a ceremony at Tiwanaku, Reinaga was one of the founders of the Partido de Indios Aymaras y Keswas (PIAK) in 1962, a political party that became the less formally exclusionary Partido Indio de Bolivia (PIB) in 1966.

At the same time, Reinaga was hard at work throughout the 1960s creating the vast intellectual and political blueprint that would support both the ambitions of the PIB and its broader ideology, which he called indianismo, or Indianism. This ideology was developed across three sprawling volumes, published within two years: *La Revolución India* (1970), *Manifiesto del Partido Indio de Bolivia* (1970), and the *Tesis India* (1971).

As he put it, in one of the rousing final passages of *La Revolución India*:

> The politics of cholaje are a deadly pestilence for the Indian. They are the cholera, leprosy, that which flays his virginal humanity. For the Indian, Bolivia's political parties are a poison: they kill him like a dog. For this, the Indian doesn't have any other remedy but to form his own party, a party that is his and his alone, a party of his race, of his blood, and of his soul: the Indian Party of Bolivia (PIB). It is only the Indian Party that will liberate the Indian. The liberation of the Indian will be his own work; it will be from the Indian that a party of granite will be made, a party organized dialectically with the cells and the millenarian force of the Andean race. It will be a party that heralds to the entire world from the summit of Illimani, with the thunder of the pututu and the waving of the wiphala, the coming of the Indian Revolution in America. (2007a: 365–66)

Yet before the pututu could sound from the soaring heights of Mt. Illimani, the political situation in Bolivia was overturned by the dictatorship of Hugo Banzer, which effectively rendered impossible Reinaga's plans for Indian revolution throughout the next decade. Even more critically, Reinaga found himself at odds during these years of repression and cultural violence with another political movement that was in part inspired by his writings: katarismo, which was articulated through the 1973 Manifesto of Tiahuanaco and given political form through the Movimiento Revolucionario Túpac Katari (MRTK), founded in 1978. Reinaga came to believe that many of his katarista friends and allies were still much too devoted to principles derived from Western leftist doctrine rather than to the more radical rupture proposed by Indianism. He was also a much older figure than many of the emerging katarista leaders like Genaro Flores Santos, who was only thirty-seven years old when he helped to found the MRTK (by contrast, Reinaga was seventy-two in 1978).

Thus it was that, with his call for Indian revolution becoming more and more marginalized and his personal outlook becoming more resentful, Reinaga's life took a bizarre and ultimately tragic turn. In 1981, well into the brutal regime of Luis García Meza, Reinaga published *Bolivia y La Revolución de las*

FF.AA. (Bolivia and the Revolution of the Armed Forces). Although the circumstances surrounding the publication of this book are shrouded in some mystery (see Kearney 2014), the fact remains that the book appeared to many at the time to be a defense of García Meza's regime and an argument for how the Bolivian military, which was doing García Meza's bidding in the worst reign of terror in Bolivian history, should play a vanguard role in bringing Indians to power. The catastrophic reception of the book among many of Reinaga's former followers was magnified by the fact that Reinaga had accepted a payment from the García Meza regime accompanied by a document with the dictator's signature. Although the money was compensation for a loss that Reinaga had suffered years before, it was taken as yet further evidence that Reinaga had sold out, that he had come to embody his namesake to García Meza's Mephistopheles.[17]

As Kearney puts it, the publication of *FF.AA.* "was the political, social, and public death of Fausto Reinaga as an intellectual . . . [for] the remaining years of his life. His detractors would point to the book to destroy his reputation, marginalizing him for his alleged support of one of Bolivia's most brutal and complicated dictatorships" (2014: 236). As the Mexican intellectual Fabiola Escárzaga has described this dark twilight period for Reinaga: "he lived his final years in political marginalization and disenchantment, with a view that his ideas had been vanquished by the dominant tendency within the Indian organizations to subordinate themselves to the mestizo and neoliberal political projects" (quoted in Kearney 2014: 236).

Reinaga's final years were also spent in poverty, since he had always looked to the sales of his self-published books to eke out a meager living. Reinaga died in 1994, at the age of eighty-eight, not with Indian revolution in sight but in the midst of Bolivia's neoliberal apotheosis under Gonzalo Sánchez de Lozada and his reformist katarista vice president Víctor Hugo Cárdenas.

And yet, as we have seen, if Reinaga did, in fact, suffer a political, social, and public death as the leading and most radical Indianist intellectual during the last decades of his life; if his reputation was destroyed by his enemies from across the spectrum of Bolivian politics; and if he went to the grave with Bolivia held tightly in the grip of a neoliberal Washington Consensus that crystallized the dominance of a Western modernity that he once described as the "despoiler of the world's physical, artistic, and spiritual richness" (2007a: 83); nevertheless, within a decade, Reinaga's writings, particularly *La Revolución India*, would be rediscovered by a new generation and come to shape, more than any other line of thought, the ideological orientation of Bolivia's "native, indigenous, peasant" movements.

Moreover, it must also be recognized that despite the spiraling tragedy of his last years, and the almost absurd way in which Reinaga represented a kind of anti-Moses—instead of dying with the promised land in sight, Reinaga died in a "valley of tears" in a world that threatened to decimate his people, leaving "neither shadow nor dust" (2007a: 446, 447)—the force of his ideas had always been preserved among the grassroots, by Indianist university students, and by social leaders like Felipe Quispe, El Mallku, whose Movimiento Indígena Pachakuti (founded in 2000) was inspired by Reinaga's call for Indian revolution (see Escárzaga 2012). And among scholars of Bolivia, Reinaga had been fully rehabilitated by the early years of the period 2006–15. As Andrew Canessa has put it, in placing Reinaga within a broader context of movements for social justice for Bolivia's indigenous peoples, Reinaga was the "most influential Bolivian indigenous intellectual of the twentieth century . . . [the person] who for more than two decades was virtually the sole torch bearer for Indian rights" (2012: 9, 246).[18]

INDIGENISMO, INDIANISMO, NEOINDIANISMO: THE PRISM OF COLLECTIVE IDENTITY

Indigenism was a movement for revalorization. Indianism is a liberation movement. . . . Even more, indigenism was essentially a cholaje blanco-mestizo movement; by contrast, Indianism is a movement by and for Indians, a revolutionary Indian movement that doesn't want to be assimilated to anything or anyone. . . . In sum, indigenism is assimilation, integration into blanco-mestizo society. Indianism, by contrast, is based around two very different things: the Indian and his revolution. . . . [Moreover], it has been an unjustifiable historical embarrassment that the Indian has been disguised as a "peasant." The word *Indian* signifies the following: a race, a people, a nation, a civilization, and a culture. The word *peasant* signifies none of these. The Indian who latches on to the word *peasant* with both hands during the anti-sociological process of cholaje commits a stupidity. (Reinaga 2007a: 135–36)

At the heart of Fausto Reinaga's vision for revolution was the idea that liberation for Bolivia's indigenous populations depended on ideological autonomy. This is the reason that he consistently drew substantive distinctions between Indian, indigenous, and peasant. By recuperating "Indian" as the correct description for a "race, a people, [and] a nation," Reinaga was also arguing that liberation must necessarily be accompanied by an act of historical subversion, since "Indian" had served for centuries as the basic category of racial, legal, and social discrimination. By contrast, indigenous and peasant were categories that were dangerous for yet another reason: they were terms of collective identity that were introduced to Bolivia as part of supposedly emancipatory social movements that were derived from the same Western spectrum of ideas and geopolitical processes that had oppressed Bolivia's Indians since the colonial period.

Peasant was a political economic identity that was meant both to express certain central insights from Marxism and to overcome the racialized colonial "indio" at the same time. The "indigenous" of indigenism was more complicated, but for Reinaga no less insidious, no less susceptible to seducing his Indian brothers and sisters into acts of "stupidity." Reinaga understood indigenism as a Marxist-inflected literary and social movement that had emerged in Peru during the 1920s around writers such as Alejandro Peralta, Emilio Armaza, and Luis Valcárcel, and around social theorists such as José Carlos Mariátegui. It was a movement by and for urban elites in which the Indian was nothing more than a symbolic referent.

According to Reinaga, when indigenism, in this sense, arrived in Bolivia, it was likewise embraced by elites who used an apparent concern for Bolivia's Indians as a strategic mechanism of power and continued social control. As Reinaga conceptualized it, the parasitism of indigenism linked influential thinkers and political actors as diverse as Franz Tamayo and Víctor Paz Estenssoro, whose embrace of various forms of indigenism was ultimately a subtle form of enslavement (Reinaga 2007a: 137).[19]

By the time of Evo Morales's first election in 2005, "indigenous" had come to mean something quite different. Although this change took place in the very last years of Reinaga's life, there is no indication that his broader vision for Indian revolution would have changed because of it; indeed, many of the younger Indianist activists understood their contempt for this new incarnation of indigenism to be an extension of Reinaga's ideological critique. As we have seen at various points in this book, this new category of indigenous took shape in Bolivia by the late 1980s as part of the global development of a socio-juridical movement expressed most forcefully through International Labor Organization Convention 169, the "Indigenous and Tribal Peoples Convention," which Bolivia ratified in 1991 and implemented throughout the mid-1990s through social programs, legal clinics, and the devolution of some political and economic power to indigenous communities (see Goodale 2008a; Postero 2007).

And as I have argued elsewhere (Goodale 2008a), the convergence between indigenous demands for justice, rights as a dominant normative framework, and transnational social movement activism created the conditions in which enough urban "mestizos" were willing to throw their electoral support behind the charismatic and unprecedented Morales, who had already locked up the "indigenous" vote as the more viable alternative to the radical Indianist Felipe Quispe.

Yet it was precisely this fundamental linkage between indigenous rights discourse, the election of Evo Morales, and the increasing dominance of MAS that created a space for ideological differentiation. Particularly among younger intellectuals and activists, Morales's growing prominence and celebrity, especially outside of Bolivia, was evidence that the government's program for change was being shaped by the same kinds of foreign influences that he had campaigned against. Although these critics would never define themselves as "Indian" in order to mark this distinction with the president and the MAS government's policies, their criticism of the assimilationist and Western nature of the category "indigenous" was fundamentally Indianist; it was a reformulation of Reinaga's basic tenet that the "liberation of the Indian will be his own work."

Throughout the period 2006–15, an important, if often underground, center for the development of an Indianist ideological alternative to the MAS government's indigenist politics was the Centro de Estudiantes Campesinos (CEC), a student association at La Paz's Universidad Mayor de San Andrés (UMSA) that functioned as a catalyst for generations of radical thinkers and political militants. Although, as with the Movimiento Indígena Pachakuti, the CEC had not adopted the substantive "Indian" in its self-identification, there was no question that its ideological orientation was fundamentally Indianist.

Historically, the CEC's Indianist ideology had been framed in opposition to both the dominant Trotskyism of Bolivia's traditional revolutionary left and the orientation of student associations at UMSA like the Juventud Socialista (JS) and the Unión Revolucionaria de Universitarios Socialistas (URUS), which organized themselves around proletarian struggle.[20] But with the steady marginalization of Bolivia's traditional revolutionary left, a space was created for young Indianists to seek to undermine the Morales government on its own terms, that is, on the basis of ethnic identity rather than class. Influenced by both Reinaga's ethnocentric Indianist program and his millenarian vision of historical change, the CEC militants viewed Morales and the rest of the MAS leaders as pretenders and dangerous opportunists, politicians who had instrumentalized ethnic politics in order to gain access to the corridors of power and secure control over the country's natural resources.

The headquarters of the CEC was for decades housed in UMSA's principal building, the architect Emilio Villanueva's iconic 1947 Monoblock, but was

FIGURE 6.1 Headquarters of the Centro de Estudiantes Campesinos (CEC), which had been built against a crumbling wall on the urban campus of the Universidad Mayor de San Andrés (UMSA), La Paz, December 2008.

relocated sometime in the early 2000s to another more isolated, if distinct, location because of the CEC's demands to separate the organization from the other student associations to which they were fundamentally opposed. By late 2008, during the height of the ethnic and regional conflict in Bolivia, the CEC occupied a one-room building that had been haphazardly constructed as an annex to a crumbling outer wall at the end of one of UMSA's alleys, squeezed in between the Monoblock and another more permanent structure that contained university faculties, the cafeteria, and the branch of a national bank (see figure 6.2).

The outer walls of the CEC had been painted a soft shade of peach, and below the eaves of the corrugated metal roof, the letters "CEC" had been added in black above the door. On both sides of the entrance, the CEC militants had chosen to paint the symbolically rich honorific "Willka" (roughly, "sacred") below an Andean cross. Night and day, a ragged wiphala flew from a flagpole affixed to the outer wall of the CEC's windowless and cave-like building.

When I visited the CEC for the first time, my approach was warily observed from the doorway by the organization's elected general secretary, a graduate student in education sciences named Carlos.[21] He and the three other members of the CEC executive committee had little patience for an interposing anthropologist. At that moment, they were preoccupied with the demands of formulating an organizational position on the new constitution, one that did not reject it out of hand but rather would characterize it as a "reformist" document that was irrelevant to the deeper transformations that were coming. I asked Carlos how the ideological orientation of the CEC was different from that of the government.

Look, I think that we acknowledge that there are different types of ideology in the world. . . . But as Aymaras, as Quechuas, we speak of a Pachakuti, which means a kind of change that will return gradually, but inevitably. It's not a kind of change that will take place just from one night to the morning, just like that. Many historians . . . have already demonstrated that the change we are talking about takes place slowly but surely, every thousand years, or rather, a cycle of a thousand years. This process of change is neither vertical nor horizontal. We have to look for signs of the Pachakuti. . . . We are talking about Felipe Quispe in 2000, we are talking about the struggle of October 2003 in El Alto, all of these are signs that the Pachakuti is returning.

I asked them how they understood their role in this process of looking for signs of the coming world-renewal. Another CEC activist, Jhonny, responded:

How do we see ourselves? We see ourselves through the lens of Indianism, which doesn't mean, as some have said, that we are living in a utopian dream. But this also doesn't mean that we are going to leave the city and return to the countryside to buy some cattle. No, Indianism is more a contribution to the collective, it's a contribution to the world of ideas. Even though we come from different faculties and departments, for all of us the ultimate goal is the same: the reconstitution of the new Tawantinsuyu, the new Qollasuyu.

How much was CEC's vision of Indianism influenced by the writings of Fausto Reinaga? As Oscar, a history student, explained:

His work is absolutely fundamental, but there are subtle differences. In the past, our struggle was almost exclusively defined by the thirty-nine books of Fausto Reinaga.

Like La Revolución India?

La Revolución India, Europe: The Murderous Whore [1984], and many others we could name. But we think of Indianism in a different way, a new way. For example, look at Constantino Lima, one of the most radical deputies. He says we must exterminate all of the faces of the children [of colonialism, that is, mestizos].[22] *But in reality, no, we have thought about this approach and have rejected it for another way. We have deepened an approach based on what we know about our people through scientific studies. In fact, we* [Indians] *must protect them* [mestizos and Europeans], *they are also our brothers. What we emphasize in our culture is a love for life, a love for our culture, a love for our reality. It is about love and not hate. What we have discovered is that our ancestors always loved life, always loved their culture, they struggled for life and they didn't kill anyone. So this means that now, during this time of change, we can't isolate anyone, including North Americans and whites, not at all. So, what I would say is that our vision for the Pachakuti is one in which we will love everyone, whites, blacks, fat people, ugly people, people from different races, whoever, we all will have to care for life and Planet Earth. This is the* suma qamaña, *right?*[23]

But don't Evo Morales and the MAS government also promote the values of suma qamaña? Another member of the CEC executive committee, Pablo, responded:

Yes, but this is only strategic. In relation to Evo, he is not an Indianist in either style or substance.

Then how would you characterize him?

He is a reformist, an opportunist.... But nevertheless, we support the process of change more generally, no? The alternatives [those of the past] *would be much worse. There haven't been any structural changes yet, right? That's because we are all waiting for the day when the Pachakuti will arrive. On that day, only the Aymaras, the Quechuas . . . actually, the whole world, there will be light for the whole world. The Pachakuti will illuminate the whole world. The street blockades of Felipe* [Quispe] *were the beginning of this light upon the world. But about Evo? Even though what he says is not quite right* [that is, not Indianist], *there are connotations. What the world has seen is that a certain figure has been elected president, someone with an Aymara face, but ideologically, there is much that is lacking with this government. But the day of the Pachakuti is coming, it must come.*

By mid-2015, the political and social context in Bolivia had changed substantially, and the Indianists of CEC had likewise modified their approach to ideological differentiation. As we have seen, particularly after the TIPNIS conflict of 2011, the MAS government had put in motion a policy of strategic juridification that included targeted and drawn-out criminal prosecutions, the passage of national laws to placate critics, and the symbolic recourse to international courts as a form of juridical nationalism.

In October 2014, Morales had won the general elections again in a landslide, having crushed the nearest candidate (Samuel Doria Medina) by 37 percentage points. If in late 2008 the militants of CEC were convinced that the day of the Pachakuti was imminent, by mid-2015 the light of this new era had not become any brighter. As it turned out, the "reformist" and "opportunist" Morales and the MAS government had proven to be more resilient than anticipated, even as their policies, according to the CEC, had moved even farther away from the principles of Indian revolution.

One of the ways in which the activism of the CEC reflected these wider developments was in the increasing abstraction of its ideological interventions. In a curious way, this form of withdrawal mirrored that of Fausto Reinaga himself, whose very last works (e.g., *El Pensamiento Indio*, 1991) had become almost completely detached from the practical task of Indian revolution in Bolivia. In its place, Reinaga's writings took up mystical themes of global ecology, human interconnectedness, and cosmic knowledge. Indeed, Reinaga had signaled this growing detachment already by 1981, his annus horribilis. What he was working for by then was not Indian "power or death!" (2007a: 447), but something much more abstract, ethereal: "the victory of human thought made conscious by the Cosmos; . . . the reign of Truth and Liberty in all of the regions of the Earth" (2007b: 17).

Institutionally, the shift in orientation of the CEC during the third Morales government was marked by a transformation in its membership. Historically, the CEC had been dominated, both in its executive committee and in its rank-and-file, by students in education, social work, and agronomy, applied disciplines that encouraged practical engagement in community affairs, often under the influence of pedagogical theorists like Paolo Freire. But with the need to rearticulate its position regarding the Pachakuti and the eventual reversals that would bring Bolivia's Indians to power in a new age, the composition of CEC moved away from these disciplines toward the humanities, especially philosophy.

In this way, CEC leaders were able to explain the machinations of the government through a revolutionary philosophy of the longue durée in which the Pachakuti was understood as a global transformation, one that would take much more time and face many more obstacles. Yet, true to its underlying Indianist principles, the CEC continued to maintain, however philosophically, that the Pachakuti was inevitable, that the coming of a new structure of space-time was prefigured by the basic ontology of the cosmos itself.

Throughout 2015, the CEC was led by a charismatic philosopher who had withdrawn from his university classes to focus on theoretical writings and the development of an ideology that he—and others in the CEC at that time—described as "neo-Indianism." There were several key ideas that distinguished neo-Indianism from the Indianism of Reinaga and the earlier generations of the CEC. First, as he explained, Indianism no longer meant simply the liberation of Bolivia's Indians. Rather, "Indianism" was taken to be a more general philosophy of practice that embraced all human beings and the integrated cosmos that they "moved through," as he put it.

Second, perhaps reflecting the pervasive influence of the digital age, neo-Indianism did not reject modern technology in favor of traditional methods of harnessing energy and communication. As David Choquehuanca, the future power broker in all three Morales governments, had famously argued in 1992, Indians should stop reading books because they were instruments of colonialism. For the neo-Indianists of CEC, however, all forms of technology, including those produced by large Western corporations, could be adapted to the cause of transformation if used correctly. As the CEC philosopher explained, "we don't see Western technology as something that needs to be rejected since we don't believe any more in the total rupture between the West and the East."

And finally, he emphasized that the younger neo-Indianists were influenced by what he called "expansive criteria" for judging the coming of the Pachakuti, the signs for which must be found in changes taking place well beyond Bolivia's borders.

———

The ethnography of collective identity in Bolivia during the period 2006–15 revealed practices of ideological differentiation that took place in relation to broader changes in national politics and prevailing discourses of recognition. These shifting landscapes then produced a social context in which the meaning of ethnic identity itself was destabilized even as it remained deeply imbricated within Bolivia's histories of racial discrimination and ethnic mobilization. In this sense, the study of ethnic politics in Bolivia during the process of change suggested an alternative conception of collective identity and its consequences.

Rather than conceiving of the nuances between social movements or nations or ideologies of collective belonging (indigenismo, indianismo, neoindianismo) through their inclusions and exclusions, I think it more fruitful to view them as modes of refraction, as practices *through which* deeper cultural meanings were constructed and mobilized. Categories of collective identity—and the ideologies that articulated them—appeared, therefore, like prisms; they bent in ways that revealed the values that they apparently crystallized, but in a distorted fashion, and the ideological or cultural or historical light that passed through them always emerged both fractured and problematically luminous.

CONCLUSION: THE PACHAKUTI AND THE MILLENARIAN IMAGINATION

One afternoon, I walked from Maras to Misminay with an old man with whom I had become well acquainted. Midway along our walk, we stopped for a few minutes and sat down in a ditch to shelter ourselves from the cold wind. The inevitable bottle of trago was produced, and the wind became warmer. He asked how my work on astronomy was going, and I told him that I still felt completely ignorant. I then asked him if he thought that I would ever understand the sky and the stars. He thought for a minute, and indicating the land around us with a wide sweep of his arm, he asked me if I understood the land and the community yet. When I said that I did not, he drained another cup of trago and asked how, then, could I possibly hope to understand the sky.

—Gary Urton, *At the Crossroads of the Earth and the Sky* (1981)

To conclude, let me return to the problem with which I began this chapter. On the one hand, as we have seen, both particular categories of collective identity and collective identity itself were of foundational importance across the entire span of the period 2006–15. As the Vice Minister of Decolonization Félix Cárdenas had put it in an August 2015 speech in La Paz, identity and dignity were at the very foundation of the process of change. However, not all identities were meant to serve this emancipatory function. Even if it was the triumph of Bolivia's "native indigenous peasant" peoples and nations that was supposed to herald the new era of the plurinational state, in fact, even here, there were slippages and elisions. Despite the social and juridical commitment to ethnic diversity, a commitment expressed through the recognition of thirty-six native indigenous peasant nations in Article 5 of the constitution, and the inclusion of "ethico-moral" principles from both highland and lowland indigenous languages in Article 8, the practice of ethnic diversity was much more exclusionary.[24]

Indeed, one commonly heard this politics of ethnic sorting described as the emergence of an "Aymara oligarchy," given the dominance of self-identifying Aymaras throughout the national MAS power structure. And there is no question that the process of change privileged the preexisting social, union, and kinship networks of the Aymara-majority La Paz Department and the Lake Titicaca basin against native Quechua speakers who had settled in El Alto and who occupied important positions in the Morales governments. Yet it was in relation to lowland indigenous peoples, particularly the large and well-organized Guaraní, where the contradictions of the government's revolution-by-identity were sharpest.

Although the main organization of lowland indigenous peoples—the Confederación de Pueblos Indígenas de Bolivia (CIDOB)—had been a key early member of the pro-MAS Pacto de Unidad (until the TIPNIS conflict of 2011), its collective local and regional activism had comparatively little effect at the national level, since most of its members lived in communities in departments that formed the bedrock of the anti-government opposition. This political marginalization fed into a prevailing highland/lowland divide, except that instead of a division between indigenous Collas and "white" Cambas, the distinction became one between Aymaras, who largely held the reins of power in the seat of government, and all other "native indigenous peasant" peoples. To the extent that the constituent federations of CIDOB participated in the process of change, it was limited primarily to what could be accomplished in the new "autonomous" departmental assemblies.

But on the other hand, if the national politics of collective identity in Bolivia during the period 2006–15 could appear like an ideological Potemkin village, in which a radical ethnic pluralism masked currents of what might be thought of as *ethnopoly*, there was something else at work. Despite the best efforts of the MAS government to reduce collective identity to a category that could be discursively symbolized, embodied through recognizable artifacts (like the pututu), and juridified, that is, rendered into legal forms as a logic of governance, these efforts ultimately failed—but not because of a lack of governmental will or the inability to consolidate and project power in just the right ways.

Rather, the (state) ideology of collective identity confronted, in the end, certain cultural binds, certain cosmic ecologies that trapped the Morales administration within an inescapable governance paradox. Each time the highly effective MAS propaganda office identified Evo Morales with Túpac Katari and promoted his historic election as the dawning of the Pachakuti, it evoked a cultural ontology that it could not, by definition, control. Although the meaning of the Pachakuti was not fixed, what is clear is that it described the principle of millenarian renewal, a cyclic rotation that occurred at the level of the cosmos. If *kuti* can be translated more easily as "return" or "renewal," the meaning of *pacha* is more elusive and therefore underscores the scope of the dilemma. Although pacha is often translated as "Earth" or "land," this captures only a fraction of its ontological significance. Perhaps the best attempt at translation we have in English is the one given by Salomon and Urioste (1991: 14): "earth, world, time, place." Nevertheless, as they explain, *pacha* is "an untranslatable word that simultaneously denotes a moment or interval in time and a locus or extension in space—and does so, moreover, at any scale."

Thus we arrive at a finding with broader significance. To the extent to which the period 2006–15 in Bolivia was one in which the Morales government harnessed the power of a pervasive millenarian ideology in order to explain and justify its revolutionary ambitions, it also, at the same time, tacitly acknowledged its ultimate lack of control, its ultimate powerlessness as the cosmos renewed itself through upheaval and eventual equilibrium. In this sense, the Pachakuti represented a theory of millenarian change that merely accentuated the frailty and relative insignificance of human beings in relation to wider cosmic forces. Ironically, given the suppression of the traditional revolutionary left in Bolivia during the Morales years, Marxism at least created a space for an agentive vanguard within what was otherwise an equally millenarian doctrine of historical transformation.

Yet with each invocation of Túpac Katari's apocryphal words—"volveré y seré millones"—Evo Morales recognized, however unintentionally, that he too was destined to be carried away by the cosmic river that is called in Quechua the *Mayu*, that he too would pass from historical memory as the pacha was renewed and then renewed again.

Conclusion **THE POLITICS OF FOREVER**

Revolutions in the end would seem to have taken the sting out of the radical ideas and slogans of their early days. They achieved the necessary miracle of reconciling aspiring men to the substantial failure of their aspirations toward heaven on earth. They turned what were originally verbal instruments of revolt, means of moving men to social action against the existing order, into something we shall have to be up-to-date about and call myths, folklore, symbols, stereotypes, rituals.

—Crane Brinton, *The Anatomy of Revolution* (1965)

In mid-January 2009, two weeks before the historic referendum on the country's new constitution, Evo Morales was filled with the indignant fire of revolutionary change. At the seventh annual all-party congress of the Movimiento al Socialismo, which was held in the wind-swept altiplano city of Oruro, Morales issued a direct warning to those who would seek to thwart the momentum of the process of change, even—or especially—through legal means:

> Here comes the warning. If some member of Congress opposes or refuses to approve new laws in the national Congress, which will be based on the vote of the Bolivian people, I will just implement these norms by executive decree in order to put into practice the new constitution of the Bolivian state. . . . In that case, it won't only be the militancy of the Movimiento al Socialismo that will be important, but also the fundamental participation of the social movements.

Morales then briefly acknowledged the enormity of the task ahead, one in which law would form the basic architecture for the transformations to come.

> Look, I have given almost everything in order to have the new constitution approved. The question, however, will be how to apply it, how to implement it socially, economically, politically, and culturally. I want to be honest with you, I hope that the constitution is not a mistake. What worries me is the fact that certain constitutional experts have told me that we will need at least 100 new laws in order to implement the new Bolivian state constitution, that's a lot.

Morales then returned to the broader historical meaning of the country's impending refoundation. "We are not just passing through the palace, we are not just visiting it. We have arrived to stay. . . . I want to say to you all that we have taken back the palace. We are not just tenants, we have recovered what is rightly ours, brothers and sisters. That will be forever" (*La Razón*, January 13, 2009).

Well into the third Morales presidency, the government announced plans for a massive public works project that would render literal this spatialization of revolution. In mid-2015, construction began on the deep-set foundations of what was being called the "Great House of the People." Immediately behind the colonial Palacio Quemado, on the corners of Calles Bolívar and Potosí, the government had begun work in the busiest part of La Paz on a twenty-nine-floor building that was designed as a testament to the power and scope of its transformative vision. The ambition was to build the biggest structure in Bolivia, one with modern surveillance technology, bulletproof windows, and a helipad, all at the cost of over $40 million. Once completed, the new Great House of the People would be connected through underground corridors to the Palacio Quemado, which would be converted into a museum and tourist destination. Despite the fact that the municipal government of La Paz was firmly opposed to the massive new government building on the basis that it would clash with the historic architecture around the Plaza Murillo, the project was readily authorized through national legislation.

At the same time, the MAS government through its allies in the Plurinational Legislative Assembly were at work on yet another national referendum, this time in order to amend Article 168 of the constitution, which established presidential and vice presidential term limits of five years per term and two consecutive terms. By a slim margin—and amid a late-breaking and bizarre scandal over the president's former lover, the disputed death of an illegitimate child, and charges of nepotism involving a Chinese construction company—the referendum went down to defeat in February 2016. This result sent shockwaves through the MAS government and the Pacto de Unidad social movements most closely aligned with it.

The setback also came at a particularly inopportune moment for Morales personally, since work had already commenced on the extraordinary Museum of the Democratic and Cultural Revolution in Morales's birthplace, the small and impoverished Oruro town of Orinoca just south of Lake Poopó (which had been officially declared evaporated in December 2015). In February 2017, just a year after the constitutional referendum on term limits, the $7 million museum—where visitors could view Morales's honorary doctorates, his favorite soccer jerseys, and various mementos from state visits around the world—was inaugurated in an emotional ceremony.

Not to be deterred by the vicissitudes of *demos kratos* from its broader commitment to the principle that the process of change is forever, a group of MAS legislators filed a formal petition in September 2017 with the Plurinational Constitutional Tribunal (TCP) seeking to have Article 168—among various others—declared unconstitutional. The major legal arguments in the petition were based on references to the American Convention on Human Rights and the doctrine of intra-constitutionality, whereby certain provisions in a constitution cannot violate other provisions.

The claimants argued that Article 168 violated the fundamental rights of Bolivian citizens because by establishing term limits, the article restricted the "right to participate freely in the formation, exercise and control of political power" (Article 26). Moreover, Article 168 also violated Article 28 since term limits, according to the MAS claimants, represented a form of general and ongoing suspension of political rights, something only permitted in times of war, in cases of gross violations of public trust, and for treason.

On November 28, 2017, in a lengthy ruling, TCP President Macario Lahor Cortez Chávez, writing for the tribunal, accepted the reasoning of the MAS petition (TCP 0084/2017).[1] In striking down the term limits provision of Article 168, the TCP developed a novel doctrine of jurisprudence that it argued was fully consistent with the broader ideology of the country's process of change. In finding that Article 168 ran afoul of the constitution's more fundamental rights and obligations, the TCP was guided by a norm of interpretation that required its decision to be consistent with the "will of the people," as expressed through the Constituent Assembly of 2006–7. Since the constituyente did not intend to limit the scope of change in any way, the TCP argued, it was required to apply this interpretation to the question of presidential and vice presidential elections. The result was that term limits were ruled unconstitutional, clearing the way for Morales and García Linera to run again in the national elections of October 2019 and every five years thereafter, their success or failure dependent only on the "will of the people."[2]

Finally, in perhaps the most dramatic act of strategic juridification during the latter years of the third Morales government, it returned to the question of national economic development in the Territorio Indígena y Parque Nacional Isiboro-Sécure (TIPNIS). The 2011 conflict that followed on the government's proposal to build a series of highways through the protected bioreserve unleashed a wave of social resistance that threatened to undermine the MAS government's twin pillars of ideological commitment: first, to protect the rights of the country's indigenous peoples and make them the foundation for the new plurinational state; and second, to replace the Western capitalist imperative to consume greater and greater resources with the indigenous doctrine of living well, which emphasized an ecological orientation and long-term sustainability.

Yet in another move that was justified through a logic of legal fairness and commitment to the rule of law, the Morales government argued that the law that apparently resolved the 2011 TIPNIS conflict—Law 180 (see chapter 5)—had been based on a principle that violated the 2007 UN Declaration of the Rights of Indigenous Peoples, which Bolivia had adopted directly into national law in November 2007 (through Law 3760). With the support of UN officials in La Paz, the Morales government maintained that Law 180—a law that the government itself had drafted in order to resolve the 2011 conflict— was based on the principle of "intangibility," that is, the idea that the ecosystem of the bioreserve, which included human communities, was so unique and so fragile that it was legally exempt from any efforts to develop its resources through the conventional cost–benefit analyses of state planning.

According to the Morales government, however, intangibility was not an indigenous right recognized under international law. Based on this interpretation, and supported by what it claimed was several years of "free, prior, and informed consent" among the indigenous communities of TIPNIS, the Bolivian government adopted Law 266 in August 2017.[3] This law removed the references to intangibility in the 2011 TIPNIS law, thereby opening the region to wide-scale future infrastructure development and the likely expansion of coca production, something for which the president's former comrades in the Seis Federaciones del Trópico de Cochabamba had vigorously advocated.

Meanwhile, by the end of 2015, the most important currents of anti-government opposition in Bolivia had been absorbed, diverted, or, like Lake Poopó, officially declared evaporated. There were three major patterns in the rise and fall of resistance to the MAS government and the La Paz–centric "democratic and cultural revolution." First, among the indigenous and peasant social movements that had opposed the government at certain moments despite supporting it across the spectrum of historic elections and national referenda, the failure to coalesce into a more unified bloc was the result of internal fragmentation (particularly among the lowland federations); a basic unwillingness to mount a concerted movement against the country's first self-identifying indigenous president; and an active campaign directed from the highest levels in La Paz to divide and manage (if not conquer) Bolivia's social movements through the strategic use of organizational funding, community and regional improvement projects, and the extension of political patronage.

Despite the MAS government's position that Bolivia's process of change was building an "indigenous state" (Postero 2017), in fact, the practice of ethnic politics, especially during the third Morales presidency, revealed "indigenous" to be a categorical house of cards that could collapse with the slightest breeze. At the very least, the ethnography of this thoroughgoing centrifugality leads one to conclude that there wasn't an indigenous *movement* in Bolivia during the period 2006–15. Rather, there were various social movements that appropriated the socio-juridical concept of "indigenous" in different ways and to different ends, not all of which were consistent with the government's broader ideological and governing strategies.

Second, among the anti-government opposition movements of the former Media Luna, especially those whose resistance was grounded in the discourse of racial antagonism (even if it was articulated through the euphemistic language of regionalism), their plight was more easily tracked. The leaders who managed to escape before the juridical hammer came down went into exile in various countries in South America or in the United States. Although the government didn't engage in the kind of wide-scale confiscations of property or the imposition of civic penalties against remaining family members that are common in other countries that have passed through civil wars or civil conflicts with clear winners and losers, Bolivia's dozens of right-wing *exiliados* remained under standing criminal indictments.

However, as we have seen (in chapters 3 and 5), many of the leaders of the racialized strand of the anti-government opposition were disappeared into drawn-out criminal prosecutions that amounted to a form of what the Slovenian anthropologist Uršula Lipovec Čebron (2012) has called "legal erasure." The point was not to bring justice to the victims of the Porvenir Massacre or the Plaza de Rodillas of May 2008 through swift judgments and the public spectacle of long prison sentences. It was rather to denude the opposition of any remaining ideological will by slowly rendering its leaders invisible and impotent, in large part through the passage of time.[4]

And third, in perhaps the most significant if obscured development, the anti-government movements that had been animated by economic—rather than racial or ethnic—ideologies discovered that the Morales government, despite its confiscatory revolutionary rhetoric, was actually very good for business. With historic growth rates in the Bolivian macroeconomy and the IMF holding the country up as a paragon of fiscal discipline, private business interests from Santa Cruz's massive *agropecuario* sector to Sucre's lucrative tourism industry realized that Morales was no Robert Mugabe intent on breaking up and redistributing the country's capitalist infrastructure among the soldiers of the revolution. Instead, an implied bargain was struck. As long as the country's business elites did not resist what Victor Turner would have called the symbolic "condensation" of the process of change, they would be left alone to expand their capital investments, enter into transnational partnerships, and manage the risks to their assets through diversification.[5]

Indeed, during a follow-up research visit in July 2016, Luis Pedro Rodríguez Calvo, one of the most influential of Sucre's behind-the-scenes "blue bloods," told me that he had decided to invest again in yet another major expansion to his historic Hotel Parador Santa María La Real because the long-term economic prospects for the city were so promising. Whereas less than ten years before, the streets outside his sprawling landmark property had been filled with running street battles, crowds marching to the thunderous chant of "¡La sede, sí, se mueve! (The seat [of government], yes, it moves!), and the acrid smell of tear gas, now they were filled with wide-eyed tourists, guidebooks in hand, schoolchildren skipping along their way, and the rumble of modern buses bringing visitors to the center of town from Sucre's shining new airport, which opened in May 2016 through a public–private partnership (PPP) of which Rodríguez was a major supporter.

REVOLUTIONARY FRAGMENTS AT THE LIMITS OF RECOGNITION

By way of a more formal conclusion, let me try to draw together the diverse strands that have interwoven this study of scales of justice, ideology, and practice in Bolivia. Given the scope of the project, its longitudinal frame, and its grounding in a critical ethnography of a self-styled revolution that nevertheless sought to maintain a certain ambiguous methodological detachment, it would perhaps also be appropriate to consider its broader implications. At a general level, what does this study of the process of change in Bolivia reveal about the possibilities for radical change in the current conjuncture, the adequacy of law as a foundation for social and political transformation, and the outer limits to change imposed by wider political economies?

At a more concrete level, it is also inevitable that I would want to reflect on what this project's ethnographic longue durée suggests about how to interpret the process of change itself. Does it, in fact, represent a model for "alternative modernization" (Escobar 2010) based on "epistemologies of the South" (Santos 2014) that moves to the counter-ontological "rhythms of the Pachakuti" (Gutiérrez 2014)? Or, rather, should the revolutionary pretensions of the MAS government be unmasked, since they hide what is really a commitment to "neoliberalism with an Indian face," as Felipe Quispe put it (ABN 2009), an ideological subterfuge behind which lies an "explosion of extractivism that results in a new imperialism for extracting natural resources, pillaging the commons and degrading the environment . . . fuelled by the unprecedented global commodities boom" (Powęska 2017)?

To begin with the transversal theme of law and its discontents: What can be said about the ramifications of juristocracy, the broader post–Cold War imperative to make the ways and means of law the normative foundation for political transition and rights the "archetypal language" (Wilson 2001: 1) of justice-seeking and historical recompense? What emerges from the current study is a perspective on juristocracy that parses it into its ideological and empirical aspects. As ideology, juristocracy implies a certain progressivist teleology according to which the deepening of a culture of respect for and trust in law as the foundation for social, political, and economic organization is a precondition for specific changes: more equality, a fairer distribution of resources, wider political participation, the public recognition of historical injustices. As an empirical question, however, the rise of juristocracy as a state ideology and logic of governance is associated with a much more varied spectrum of practices and consequences.

On the one hand, the legalization of the process of change in Bolivia demonstrated yet again that the law is a superb mechanism through which to create, legitimate, and historically embed "key categories" (to paraphrase Raymond Williams). From the juridical birth of the "native indigenous peasant" to the making and unmaking of the TIPNIS bioreserve as "intangible," the law was wielded by government officials, jurists, social activists, and scholars as a forge in which the key categories of the "democratic and cultural revolution" were shaped and reshaped. From the perspective of these key categories only, Bolivia didn't simply pass through a period of historic change; under the guiding hand of the different MAS governments, it became a land of nearly unimaginable cultural, ecological, and moral transformation. As Article 8 of the 2009 constitution proclaimed, Bolivia was thenceforth a state of "unity, equality, inclusion, dignity, liberty, solidarity, reciprocity, respect, complementarity, harmony, transparency, balance, equality of opportunities, social and gender equity, respect for the common good, responsibility, [and] social justice."

Yet in practice, as we have also seen throughout this book, the juridification of politics in Bolivia was the mechanism for much more limited, exclusionary, and ambiguous shifts. At the same time that the new constitution articulated an unprecedented vision of a plurinational state in which power was diffused through a radical and post-Westphalian ideology of decentralism, it did so in terms of racialized categories of "peoples and nations." The result was a process of change in which exclusion was as deeply intertwined as inclusion—yet another governance paradox that was certain to undermine the emancipatory promise of the country's refoundation over time.

In the end, we must approach the question of law and change—and, *a fortiori*, law and revolution—with a certain Conradian amplitude. The rise and eventual apotheosis of law as a signal marker of the post–Cold War "seachange" (Wilson 2001: 1) proved to have its own historical trajectory, one in which the utopianism of juristocracy gave way to a more sober understanding of how law is mobilized in practice, and to what ends. Perhaps this is less a discovery and more of a return—that is, a return to the realization that law, in the end, is just law, nothing more but nothing less.

At the same time, the fragments that constituted Bolivia's "third revolution" were not merely those formed by the internal logics of the process of change itself. From the infusion of foreign direct investment by both private companies and massive state enterprises (in particular, Chinese) to the proliferation of cooperative agreements with state development agencies (with the exception of USAID, which was barred) to the growing importance of bilateral trade at the departmental level (notably involving Santa Cruz)—what is clear is that the strategy to fashion an "indigenous state" was always shaped by wider political economies, broader networks of finance, trade, and international relations that were structured by quite different norms and modes of action. In this sense, the MAS government's aspiration to refound Bolivia in an image solely of its own design, even with the support of about 60 percent of the country's citizens, was always quixotic.

At the most general level, therefore, what does the study of Bolivia have to tell us about the possibilities for radical change, or better yet, for the realization of what might be thought of as actually existing justice? Here I think the best frame of reference is the work of Nancy Fraser, who in 2008 augmented her earlier reflection on "dilemmas of justice in a 'post-socialist' age" (1995) as the giddy years of the early post–Cold War yielded to greater skepticism about the adequacy of the prevailing cosmopolitan verities.

To recall, Fraser had sensed danger in the transition away from questions of class and redistribution and their replacement by a politics of recognition, a shift that was examined and justified in a series of influential interventions by scholars such as Axel Honneth (1996) and Charles Taylor (1992).[6] Their argument was that identity violence represented a unique kind of harm, one that could not be reduced to or fully explained by underlying structures of economic inequality. The politics of recognition, and the vast legal armature that emerged to define and institutionalize it, was a way of expressing this alternative post-socialist account of justice.

Yet as Fraser rightly predicted in 1995, the rapid expansion of recognition politics as the new "moral grammar of social conflicts," as Honneth described it, would come to supplant—rather than coexist with—the redistributive politics that had shaped many radical and revolutionary movements over the preceding decades. As Fraser argued in 1995, comprehensive justice-seeking required attention to *both* identity harms and the injustices caused by pervasive and long-term economic inequality.

At the end of 2008, in the wake of both the globalization of the national security state after September 11, 2001, and the global financial crisis of 2007–8, Fraser returned to the problem of justice (Fraser 2008). She acknowledged that concern with both identity and economic harms remained necessary but was not sufficient in itself. What was also required was attention to the extent to which people were able to participate in political processes whose outcomes affected them. Thus, a politics of representation was added to her earlier framework for recognition and redistribution to round out an approach to justice that was adequate to what she argued were the "reimagined political spaces" to be found on a maturing post–Cold War landscape.

Nevertheless, this did not imply that concern was actually being divided between these three categories beyond the boundaries of vigorous debate over theories of justice. In fact, the disjuncture that Fraser had worried about in 1995 was only becoming more pronounced. The politics of recognition had evolved into a dominant, even discriminatory, justice framework at the same time that regional and global levels of economic inequality were growing at rates never seen before in the history of global capitalism (Piketty 2014). Yet the politics of recognition, articulated through the language of identity rights, had no answer for the political economic violence of a G-20 world (Moyn 2018; see also Goodale 2018c).

At a much smaller scale, however, one can read Bolivia's process of change as an experiment in implementing a justice framework that appeared to combine all three dimensions of Fraser's triad. If Fraser's 2008 revision can be taken as a philosophical hypothesis for how societies can achieve comprehensive justice in practice, then the period in Bolivia examined in this book can function as a test of sorts for this hypothesis—albeit one that unfolded at what Hardt and Negri would have described as the "capillary ends of . . . contemporary networks of power" (2000: 313). The findings are revealingly inconclusive.

There is no doubt that the process of change in Bolivia during the period 2006–15 brought an unprecedented degree of recognition justice to many populations whose historic exclusions had been based, in part, on identity. When people spoke with a deep sense of pride about how for the first time in their lives those at the highest levels of power had the same "face" as they did, this was evidence of recognition justice. When the preamble to the 2009 constitution placed the Pachamama in front of God, this was evidence of recognition justice. And when the government announced in 2015 that the new minister of justice was the Aymara lawyer and indigenous rights activist Virginia Velasco Condori, who posed for her official portrait in a magnificent black bowler hat and flowing powder-blue pollera, this was evidence of recognition justice.

The signs of representational justice in Bolivia, however, were more equivocal. As we have seen throughout this book, key turning points were marked by moments of political participation in the form of elections of public officials and a succession of direct democratic referenda, from the Referéndum revocatorio in August 2008 to the term limits referendum of February 2016. Even though voting in national elections and referenda was legally compulsory in Bolivia, the evidence suggests that political participation and even power expanded dramatically through the process of change; in particular, Bolivia's majority indigenous populations came to see formal political action, rather than either social action or everyday resistance, as their principal "weapon of the weak" (Scott 1985). Yet for those in the opposition, those who did not support the MAS government and its transformative policies, representational justice was more elusive. Although a form of representational justice could be found at lower levels, for example, through the perpetuation of opposition governance in Santa Cruz Department, this was a pale substitute for effective representation at the national level.

But it is in relation to the third pillar of Fraser's justice framework—the politics of redistribution—that the findings from research in Bolivia during the period 2006–15 present the greatest challenge. Although, as we have seen, Bolivia's macroeconomy entered a state of what the IMF described, approvingly, as "equilibrium," it did so largely on the basis of its massive foreign reserves-to-GDP ratio. In 2014, Bolivia surpassed China with the highest such ratio in the world: the $14 billion represented almost half of the country's GDP. Yet even though these earnings came through the development of the country's renationalized hydrocarbon sector, this did not lead to a policy of structural, nationwide redistribution.

It is true that social spending rose significantly in real terms during the period 2006–15 in the form of infrastructure projects and through the series of popular *bonos*—monthly payments to vulnerable segments of the population that amounted to a nascent social welfare system. But by many measures, Bolivia remained one of the poorest countries in South America, with high levels of infant mortality, one of the lowest human development indexes in Latin America, relatively low life expectancies, and, perhaps most critically, one of the highest levels of income inequality in the world. It is difficult to argue that the process of change led to redistributive justice in Bolivia when its Gini index value was 45.80 (in 2015).

Yet if we leave aside the problematic tools of quantitative indicators (see Merry 2016; Merry, Davis, and Kingsbury 2015), something different comes into focus. In a sense, one can say that two strands of justice in Fraser's terms came together during the period 2006–15 in Bolivia. That is, a more pervasive politics of redistribution *did* take place, but what was redistributed was the symbolic capital that came from the historic recognition of collective identities, primarily, but not exclusively, through law. In other words, it was recognition justice itself that was redistributed.

If so, the question becomes: Does the process of change in Bolivia represent a new model for revolution, one in which it is the radical recognition of categories of identity, rather than relations of production, that becomes the grounds on which the historic struggle is waged? In the end, the research over nine years that has led to this point reinforces the central thrust of Fraser's argument: that there are limits to how far the politics of recognition can be stretched over legacies of injustice, over chronic poverty, over structural violence. Indeed, to study Bolivia's historic, fraught, and remarkable process of change was in many ways to map these very outer limits and to imagine, at the same time, what might lie beyond.

POSTSCRIPT: SOARING ON THE WINGS OF THE INEFFABLE

On the morning of the *Willkakuti* in the year 5523 (according to the reimagined Andean-Amazonian calendar), I left my apartment in La Paz's Zona Sur on my way to El Alto. Having just arrived in Bolivia for the last full field season of the research project, I planned to spend part of the day simply walking through neighborhoods as a way to acclimatize myself (yet again) to the experience of living and working at altitude. Although I had walked and hiked over 1,000 km in the late 1990s while conducting doctoral research in the mountainous north of Potosí Department, I had found that the thin air affected me more notice-ably the older I became—more sleepless nights with a racing heart, longer pauses at the top of La Paz's steeper streets, more cups of restorative mate de coca. Since this was the beginning of the end, that is, the end of a research project that had unfolded over many years, with a number of fits and starts, many moments of doubt, and of course the ever-present anxiety of influence looming over it all, I stepped into the crisp morning air with a sense of keen anticipation mixed with something like nostalgia.

And yet on this morning, the swirl of emotions was heightened by some-thing else. Instead of taking a taxi to El Alto as I had done dozens, if not hun-dreds, of times before, a long slog in carbon monoxide–saturated air along one of several roads that climbed over 1,350 meters (about 4,500 feet), I was going to ride the Teleférico, the improbable cable car public transportation system that had opened the year before. Built by the Austrian-Swiss company Doppelmayr Garaventa, the world's largest manufacturer of high-technology gondolas, ski lifts, and "ropeways," the Teleférico had cost the Bolivian govern-ment a staggering $280 million.

As I approached the first station of the Teleférico's green line, my eyes followed the steady progress of cabins entering and leaving along a cable car line that climbed precipitously up the steep hill to the wealthy district of Bella Vista, where the cabins disappeared out of sight at the same time that others on the parallel cable plunged from the same height as they drew closer. After paying 3 bolivianos for the ticket (about 45 cents), I boarded the empty cabin in the gleaming and imposingly modern station assisted by young technicians in matching work uniforms that featured the system's official name: Mi Teleférico.

As the cabin swung smoothly into place, I noticed that mine was painted in a deep shade of royal blue; on its lower half was written "#MarParaBolivia" (a reference to the ongoing legal and political conflict with Chile over access to the sea); and below this, the system's slogan was repeated under a "T" that had been designed to resemble a structure one might find at Tiwanaku. In addition to Mi Teleférico, the cabin was painted with the second part of the system's slogan: "Uniting Our Lives."

With a distinct awareness that the Teleférico system had been built well within the boundaries of the seismic chaos of the Ring of Fire, my cabin shot out and up into the void, gaining hundreds of feet above the ground in sec-onds. It carried me up and down the hills of La Paz, stopping in the intermedi-ate stations of Aynacha Obrajes and Pata Obrajes. The green line ended at the station Chuqi Apu, where I was required to transfer to the yellow line for the rest of the thirty-minute trip to El Alto.

Because of the early hour, I made this first journey on the Teleférico alone, which was probably a good thing, since I don't know if I could have contained myself with others in the cabin. As the yellow line cabin passed through Supu Kachi (Sopocachi), it began the hair-raising ascent to La Ceja in El Alto. I spun around. I gazed down on the infinite variety of quotidian life below, transfixed, my heart pounding with fear and excitement. I had a lump in my throat for the entire ride and my eyes eventually filled with tears.

After finally arriving at the end of the yellow line, the El Alto station Qhana Pata, I got out of the cabin and simply stared out over the vastness of La Paz below. The Teleférico technician wanted me, at first, to move along, to leave with the rest of the arriving passengers, but I was grateful that he allowed me to stay for several minutes since I had been overwhelmed by the whole vertiginous experience. Soon after, however, a problematic sense of incredulity that such a system could have been built in La Paz gave way, perhaps inevitably, to questions about meaning—for example, how should the Teleférico be understood in relation to the country's process of change?

Not surprisingly, I soon learned that the Teleférico—which should certainly be included on any new list of the Seven Wonders of the (Post–Cold War) World—had been launched amid great controversy. The MAS government and its supporters viewed the massive public investment as an incomparable marker of the broader revolutionary transformations that were taking place under the Morales administration. Critics of the MAS government saw the Teleférico as a quite different symbol of the process of change, a vanity project of the president built at a relatively unimaginable cost that had produced almost no measurable improvement in standards of living, health care, education, or family incomes.

Over the course of the many weeks to follow, I would become something of a Teleférico frequent flyer. I would ride it on the way to meetings; I would take the Teleférico on the weekends, in which whole families from El Alto would pack into cabins to ride to La Paz's economically and culturally remote lower districts to eat ice cream; and sometimes, in the evenings, I would take the Teleférico to El Alto at sunset and return at night when the city below became a sea of little jewels of sparkling light. Among its other unexpected marvels, the cabins of the Teleférico were built with solar panels on the roof, which collected just enough energy throughout the day to illuminate a soft interior lamp.

Yet even though I continued to ponder the question of the Teleférico in relation to problems of meaning, ideology, and signs of transformation, it refused to yield anything of apparent ethnographic or analytical insight. Although I was certain that from the perspective of the research project, the Teleférico was good to think with, its broader significance continued to confound me. And then, toward the end of the end, during the last few days of research, I realized how the Teleférico was important.

Much like the first astonishing experience of soaring high above the architectural and social cacophony of the city, the symbolic meaning of the Teleférico was, ultimately, ineffable; its significance eluded reduction to demographic indicators or measurement along a defined spectrum of socioeconomic improvement. In this way, then, the Teleférico was the ideal embodiment of Bolivia's process of change, its contested refoundation, its enigmatic and fragmentary democratic and cultural revolution.

Notes

INTRODUCTION: MEANING AND CRISIS IN COSMIC TIME

1   See Nancy Postero (2017) for a rich discussion of the complexities of "refoundation" as an ordering logic.

2   For a similar argument for moving beyond the binary logics that can shape ethnographic writing, see Marisol de la Cadena's 2015 book, in which she develops a
compelling framework for understanding the mutual differences that coexist in
ethnographic description.

3   On the problems of identity, culture, and politics in Bolivia, see the important
work of Andrew Canessa (e.g., 2006, 2007, 2012a, 2012b); see also Postero (2017).
Classic and earlier analyses of identity beyond Bolivia can be found in, among
other sources, the various studies of Charles Hale (e.g., 2002, 2004).

4   For an exhilarating account of the importance of the Pachakuti within Bolivia's
process of change, see Gutiérrez Aguilar (2014).

5   For an innovative study that grapples with many of the same methodological
dilemmas, see Amal Hassan Fadlalla's "multifaceted" ethnography (2018) of the
production of transnational sovereignties in relation to the Sudanese and later
South Sudanese conflicts.

6   As I put it in a different study (Goodale 2008a: 187), "an *ayllu* is a macro-regional
fictive kinship category that was probably created to deal with the challenges of
living in the extreme ecological zones in the Andes (Murra 1972, 1975). The ayllu
has been an important unit of Andean social organization since pre-Hispanic
times. [In many parts of highland Bolivia], ayllus retain many of their historical features, including 'an internal organization based on dual and vertically
organized segments, communal distribution of resources, and a "vertical" land
tenure system which includes the use of noncontiguous *puna* (highland) and
valley lands' (Rivera Cusicanqui 1991; see also Platt 1982)."

7   Having made this point, I should underscore the importance of a work that
perhaps comes closest to providing a relatively unvarnished account of Bolivian history—the magisterial single-volume *Historia de Bolivia* produced by the
distinguished father, mother, and son team of Bolivian historians José de Mesa,
Teresa Gisbert, and Carlos D. Mesa Gisbert (who was also, during attenuated
terms of office, vice president and president of Bolivia). *Historia de Bolivia* was
released in its eighth edition in 2012, two years after the death of José de Mesa,
who had contributed—in addition to his scholarship—many of the elegant
hand-drawn black-and-white images up through the seventh edition. The eighth

edition analyzes Bolivian history to the end of 2010. I make frequent use of *Historia de Bolivia* throughout this book.

8 Factual material in this section is drawn from the *Historia de Bolivia* and from *The Bolivia Reader: History, Culture, Politics* (Thomson et al. 2018), of which I am one of the editors.

9 This excludes both the compromised election of 1964, in which Paz Estenssoro won with almost 98 percent of the vote as the only candidate, and the various elections during the years of the dictatorships.

10 See Eva Fischer's fascinating (2017) anthropological study of the "many lives of Túpac Katari," in which she analyzes the ways in which the collective memory of the late eighteenth-century Indian rebel was reinterpreted during different moments of cultural struggle in Bolivia.

11 For images of this political propaganda, see *The Bolivia Reader* (chapter 12).

12 Although "media luna" translates literally to "half moon," it is also used in Spanish to describe the form of the crescent moon.

13 This is not to say that opposition to the MAS government ended in 2009; far from it. As will be seen in different places in the book, but especially in chapters 3 and 5, the opposition underwent several important changes in the years after 2009, changes that themselves can be divided into several phases. But to give just one example of how some elements in Santa Cruz increasingly turned their attention to paramilitary options for resistance, Bolivian army and police units killed three men and wounded two others at the Hotel Las Américas in Santa Cruz on April 16, 2009, after a supposed plot to assassinate Morales had been discovered. The men who were killed were citizens of Hungary, Romania, and Ireland with purported links to Santa Cruz's virulently anti-government Comité Pro-Santa Cruz and its militant youth wing, the UJC. Although the circumstances surrounding the events of April 16 are still unclear, there is no question that opposition groups were preparing for armed resistance and engaging in paramilitary training during this period, as my research reveals (see chapter 3).

14 See Kohl and Farthing (2012), McNeish (2013, 2016a, 2016b), Postero (2013, 2017), various chapters in Wanderley (2011), and Webber (2015).

15 Regarding influential normative revolution theorists, perhaps none cast so long a shadow as Crane Brinton, whose *The Anatomy of Revolution* sat astride discussions of revolution from its first publication in 1938 to its third edition in 1965. Brinton, who was the McLean Professor of Ancient and Modern History at Harvard for over two decades, was skeptical of revolutions, having famously compared them to a fever that takes over a body politic with uncertain and often violent results. As he put it, the "tangible and useful results [of revolutions] look rather petty as measured by the brotherhood of man and the achievement of justice on this earth. The blood of the martyrs seems hardly necessary to establish decimal coinage" (1965: 259).

16 Applying these criteria to recent history, DeFronzo finds that the election of Evo Morales in 2005 ushered in a period of what DeFronzo calls "revolution through

democracy" in Bolivia. Regarding the fifth criterion, DeFronzo observes that the "replacement of [George W.] Bush by [Barack] Obama . . . likely reduced the threat of . . . U.S. military intervention against [the] democratically elected leftist revolutionary government" (2011: 446).

17 Nevertheless, the anthropologist Martin Holbraad is directing a five-year project sponsored by the European Research Council (Comparative Anthropologies of Revolutionary Politics [CARP], 2014–19) that promises to reorient the anthropological approach to revolution in fundamental ways. See www.ucl.ac.uk/anthropology/revolution.

18 Thomassen identifies three reasons why an "anthropology of revolution" never developed: first, revolutions involve structural transformations to the kinds of large-scale systems that have not been a traditional focus of anthropological research; second, at least since the 1980s, anthropologists have—following James Scott's study of "weapons of weak" (1985)—turned away from what Thomassen describes as "high politics" in favor of "ordinary and everyday forms of political behavior"; and third, since revolutions often "happen when nobody expects them," it is difficult to plan ethnographic research in such unpredictable circumstances. Moreover, to the extent to which revolutionary processes are violent, a putative anthropology of revolution confronts ethical impediments: "No responsible teacher would send a Ph.D. student into a war zone" (Thomassen 2012: 682–83).

19 As one might imagine, the effort to characterize the period 2006–15 in Bolivia has occupied various other scholars. For a cross section of some of the more influential of these other formulations (in English), see Burman (2016); Canessa (2006, 2012b, 2014); Dunkerley (2007a, 2007b); Fabricant (2012); Fabricant and Gustafson (2011); Farthing and Kohl (2014); Goldstein (2012); Gustafson (2009a, 2009b, 2010); Gutiérrez Aguilar (2014); Hylton and Thomson (2007); McNeish (2013); Postero (2010, 2013, 2017); Schilling-Vacaflor (2011); Thomson (2009); and Webber (2010, 2011, 2016).

20 For an important long-term study of the ways in which "Bolivia's coca growers reshaped democracy" and influenced in indelible ways the evolution of MAS as a ruling party, see Grisaffi 2019.

CHAPTER 1: HEARING REVOLUTION IN A MINOR KEY

1 For a study of the "limits of decolonization" based on research in Bolivia's hydrocarbon sector, see Anthias (2018).

2 For other work that examines the question of citizenship in Bolivia after the election of Evo Morales, see Albro (2010), Canessa (2012a, 2012b), and Farthing and Kohl (2014).

3 The Finnish critical development scholar Eija M. Ranta completed a PhD dissertation in 2014 precisely on the role of vivir bien in contemporary Bolivia. Her important study of vivir bien as both "discursive construction" and "contested practice" argues that it should be understood as a radical challenge to broader neoliberal contractions, which lead, in many cases, to the condition of what

the Portuguese sociologist Boaventura de Sousa Santos (2014) has described as "epistemicide." See also Ranta (2018).

4 This is not to say that the MAS government did not rely in practice on other forms of violence in the implementation of its policies, particularly after the resolution of the 2011 TIPNIS conflict. As will be seen in chapter 5, for example, the recourse to law emerged as an important strategy for consolidating state power and eliminating the threat posed by opposition figures in Santa Cruz and Sucre.

5 In 1995, the rising cocalero faction of the Confederación Sindical Única de Trabajadores Campesinos (CSUTCB) created the Asamblea por la Soberanía de los Pueblos (ASP) in order to field candidates in that year's municipal elections. Working under the "borrowed registration" (*sigla prestada*) of the legal Izquierda Unida (IU) party, the ASP captured eleven mayorships and forty-seven *concejales* in Cochabamba Department. In 1997, ASP-IU won four seats in the Bolivian Congress, including one for Morales, whose winning percentage in his Cochabamba district (70 percent) was the highest in the country (Assies 2009). After a dispute with leaders from the ASP, Morales and his supporters created a splinter party, the Instrumento Político por la Soberanía de los Pueblos (IPSP). In 1999, the IPSP allied with the Movimiento al Socialismo party (formerly the Movimiento al Socialismo-Unzaguista, founded in 1987 by the dissident *falangista* David Añez Pedraza) and MAS and IPSP—formally known as MAS-IPSP— thereby became a combined legally registered political party and sociopolitical movement.

6 As Herbert Klein observed, the War of the Chaco was the "most bitter conflict in Bolivia's history" (1982: 193). In this war between Bolivia and Paraguay, which was arguably fought as a resource proxy war between Standard Oil and Royal Dutch Shell for control over the potentially rich oil fields of the Gran Chaco, the Bolivians endured catastrophic losses. As Klein explains, "65,000 were killed, deserted, or died in captivity. . . . These out of a total population of just about 2 million persons created war losses equal to what the European nations had suffered in World War I" (1982: 194).

7 As the passage from Gogol's *Dead Souls* expresses the classic worry for countries in periods of uncertain transition: "Russia, where are you flying to? Answer! She gives no answer."

8 The phenotypic dimensions of Bolivia's process of change should not be avoided. One often heard political and ethnic divisions expressed in racialized terms that referred to skin color and one's "face" in ways that implied a biological relationship to culture, wealth, and worldview. For an important study of these linkages, especially the distinction between the Aymara categories of *q'ara*, *misti*, and *jaqi*, see Canessa (2012a).

9 Of course, one must acknowledge the extent to which revolutionary iconography was also fundamental in the years after the Russian Revolution. In echoes of contemporary Bolivia, at least for several decades up through World War II, the graphic poster in the Soviet Union was a principal medium for the trans-

mission of revolutionary ideology to a largely still illiterate population (Kenez 1985).

10 Oki Vega's father, Oscar Vega López, was a former president of Bolivia's Central Bank (1969–70) who was involved in a "mysterious case of arms trafficking" during his brief term at the head of the institution. According to Hugo Rodas Morales (2008: 338), Vega López, who had a family relation to the surprisingly reformist military dictator Alfredo Ovando Candia, permitted the Ovando government to secretly withdraw more than a million U.S. dollars to buy weapons from the Swiss Industrial Company (SIG). Between 1977 and 1980, according to Oki Vega, his father also played an important role in the founding of the Unidad Democrática y Popular (UDP), a left-wing alliance led by Hernán Siles Zuazo.

11 It should be emphasized that although the core of Comuna was formed by a small group of five or six intellectuals in 1999, the actual number of people who participated in the weekly meetings and contributed to the group's publications was fluid and often dependent on changing personal relationships among members. For example, the Aymara sociologist and later government minister and La Paz governor Félix Patzi Paco was an early and regular participant in Comuna. However, Patzi became alienated from Comuna in the early 2000s after a bitter falling out with García Linera, who had accused Patzi of thinking like a "pro-Indian, Trotskyite extremist" (quoted in Ranta 2014: 111).

12 One important early work that was not published with Muela del Diablo was *Bourdieu: Leído desde el Sur* [Bourdieu Read from the South] (Suarez et al. 2000), which was published through the combined support of the French Alliance, the Goethe Institute, the Embassy of Spain, the University of the Cordillera, and Plural editores, a major La Paz publishing house directed by José Antonio Quiroga, who was also a student-exile at UNAM in the early 1980s, though he was never a member of Comuna. In 2002, Quiroga—who was the nephew of the "mystical . . . symbol of the Bolivian left" (Mesa Gisbert 2008: 566), Marcelo Quiroga Santa Cruz (murdered in the offices of the Central Obrera Boliviana, or COB, on the day of García Meza's coup d'état)—was caught up in a minor scandal during the general election campaign when he refused Evo Morales's invitation to run as his candidate for vice president.

13 In addition to *El fantasma insomme* and *Bourdieu: Leído desde el Sur*, Comuna's most influential publications would include (in chronological order): *El retorno de la Bolivia plebeya* (García Linera et al. 2000), *Tiempos de rebélion* (García Linera et al. 2001), *Memorias de octubre* (Tapia, García Linera, and Prada 2004), *La transformación pluralista del Estado* (García Linera, Tapia, and Prada, 2007), and *El Estado: Campo de lucha* (García Linera et al. 2010).

14 For a fascinating ethnographic analysis of what he describes as "space-claiming protests" in Bolivia, see Bjork-James (2013).

15 I return to the role of Bolivia's miners within the country's revolutionary traditions in chapter 4, but here it must also be said that the exceptional mystique that surrounds them in relation to other notable categories of social actors is due in large part to the fact that they live what many consider heroic lives, in which

they do battle with "the Devil, or Tio, the Spanish term for the pre-conquest Supay or Huari" (Nash 1993: 7), in order to extract the minerals that will feed their families, their communities, and ultimately the nation. And as every Bolivian knows, this is a battle in which many miners will die, either in the mines themselves, or later, from the diseases that will slowly destroy their lungs. As June Nash described one such casualty of this historic battle, in her incomparable ethnography among tin miners, "Waldo was killed in an accident caused by dynamite falling out of its niche and blowing up in the paraje [station] he was in. He had worked thirty years in the mine. His body was discovered at 10:30 in the evening, after rigor mortis had set in. . . . The body was laid out in an elaborate casket with a window at his head. His mouth was open, his eyes closed, but the expression was of terror" (Nash 1993: 205).

16 For example, the province in which I conducted long periods of earlier research, Alonso de Ibáñez in the north of Potosí Department, voted to reelect the president in 2014 with 77 percent of the vote.

17 According to Article 152 of the Ley del Régimen Electoral that was in force in 2008, failure to vote without legal cause would result in a monetary fine and a range of onerous social penalties, including the inability to hold public office, make bank transfers, obtain a passport, or receive wages.

CHAPTER 2: LEGAL COSMOVISIONS

1 Morales was ultimately nominated for the 2007 Nobel Peace Prize in December 2006 by the 1980 recipient, Argentine human rights activist Adolfo Pérez Esquivel. Nevertheless, the 2007 prize was awarded jointly to former U.S. Vice President Al Gore and the Intergovernmental Panel on Climate Change.

2 See also Albro (2010).

3 For other analyses of the 2009 Bolivian constitution, see Canessa (2014), Fabricant (2013), Fabricant and Gustafson (2011), Gustafson (2009a, 2010), Hammond (2011), Postero (2017), and Schilling-Vacaflor (2011).

4 Almost immediately after Morales's speech, his minister of rural development, Carlos Romero, held a press conference in which he clarified that Article 398 would not, in fact, be retroactive, but would only apply to future acquisitions.

5 For a detailed consideration of Dabdoub's role in the anti-government opposition, see chapter 3.

6 Stavenhagen was also the first UN special rapporteur on the rights of indigenous peoples, serving between 2001 and 2008.

7 See, for example, Albó (1999); Ayllu Sartañani (1995); Calla (1999); CASDEL (1994); CIDOB (1992); Fernández Osco (2000); Léon (1997); Molina (1999); Orellana (1999); Ossio and Ramírez (1999); Ramírez and Ossio (1999); and Vacaflor (1999).

8 For a wide-ranging and compelling study of the relationship between indigenous mobilization, international law, and the "elusive promise" of development, see Engle (2010). For a pioneering analysis of the emergence of "indigenism" as a transnational discourse, see Niezen (2003).

9　Essays written by some of the participants at the 2004 seminar in Sucre, and a copy of the draft law on community justice, can be found in a 2005 publication by the IJB (Instituto de la Judicatura de Bolivia 2005).

10　For an early and especially insightful ethnographic study of challenges of liberal multiculturalism in Bolivia during this period, see Postero (2007).

11　The question of "autonomy" in post-2005 Bolivia is examined in more depth in chapter 5.

12　These thirty-six nations were the following: Aymara, Araona, Baure, Bésiro, Canichana, Cavineño, Cayubaba, Chácobo, Chimán, Ese Ejja, Guaraní, Guarasu'we, Guarayu, Itonama, Leco, Machajuyai-Kallawaya, Machineri, Maropa, Mojeño-Trinitario, Mojeño-Ignaciano, Moré, Mosetén, Movima, Pacawara, Puquina, Quechua, Sirionó, Tacana, Tapiete, Toromona, Uru-Chipaya, Weenhayek, Yaminawa, Yuki, Yuracaré, and Zamuco.

13　These quotations come from a symposium on arguments for and against the new constitution published on January 11, 2009, in *La Razón* (A9–A11).

CHAPTER 3: OPPOSITION AS A CULTURAL SYSTEM

1　For another study of the mytho-poetics of memory and violence in Bolivia whose approach resonates with the one taken in this chapter, see Canessa (2009).

2　In this chapter, I focus on the ethnography of the anti-government opposition in the years leading up to the ratification of the new constitution in January 2009 and the reelection of Evo Morales in December 2009. In both chapter 5 and in the conclusion, I examine the evolution of the right in Bolivia in later historical periods, up through 2015. For an insightful study of the relationship between revolutionary mobilization and right-wing opposition across Latin America, see Webber (2017b).

3　Indeed, during legal proceedings against leading members of the Sucre opposition movement in 2015, prosecutors threatened to confiscate my ethnographic notes from research conducted during 2008 and 2009. I offered to provide information on my research, if asked, but in the end prosecutors never contacted me as they made their case against the defendants. See chapter 5.

4　Other studies likewise explore the exceptional methodological and ethical dilemmas that are associated with the anthropology of right-wing politics, nativism, and the emergence of cultural identitarianism. See, for example, Holmes (2000), Shoshan (2016), and Teitelbaum (2017).

5　For a critical analysis of the historical constructions of the events of Ayo Ayo, which also examines the subsequent downfall of Zárate Willka and suppression by the victorious Liberals of the Aymara autonomy movement, see Kuenzli (2013). For other key treatments of the Aymara uprisings of the late nineteenth century, including debates over whether they should be considered a "race war" or an "ethnic autonomy movement," see Hylton and Thomson (2007) and Larson (2004).

6   The local lawyer, Gonzalo Durán, died during violent street protests on November 24, 2007, the day the Constituent Assembly finally approved the first draft of the new constitution; university students Juan Carlos Serrudo and José Luis Cardozo died on November 25 and 26.

7   Mujer de pollera is a description used for highland indigenous women who wear polleras, the traditional pleated skirts. Depending on context, it can have a slightly derogatory meaning or, as in the case of Cuéllar, it can be a term that reflects a certain sense of empowerment or social progress.

8   Although the prince and princess of the Principality of the Glorieta did not have any children, their blue blood lineage was passed on in Sucre through decades of intermarriages among members of their extended families and their descendants.

9   It must be said that the blue blood control of Sucre was weakened to a certain extent after the National Revolution of 1952, when some descendants from the old Sucre families left for a more uncertain future in Santa Cruz.

10   After one such press conference that I attended, on Christmas Eve 2008, the members present were heard greeting each other, and members of the press corps, with "¡Feliz Año No Evo!" a play on the traditional "¡Feliz Año Nuevo!" or "Happy New Year!"

11   Monteagudo is located in a verdant and hilly part of the Bolivian Chaco in southeastern Chuquisaca Department, about 280 km from the Paraguayan border.

12   The one notable exception to this general pattern was Fidel Herrera, president of the Municipal Council and a distant relation of the Marquises of Herrera.

13   Silvia Lazarte was the MAS union leader from the Chapare who was elected president of the Constituent Assembly in August 2006. She was a longtime ally of Evo Morales.

14   Although I was not present in Sucre on May 24, I was able to study the events through hours of raw video footage that I obtained from both the public prosecutor's office and the office of the Defensoría del Pueblo for Chuquisaca. Some of this raw footage formed the basis for the later prosecutions against Sucre's civic movement leaders. See chapter 5.

15   For a compelling attempt to "make sense" of the events of May 24, 2008, in Sucre against a background of the racialization of politics of Bolivia, see Calla (2011).

16   For reasons of space, ethnographic analyses and interpretation in this chapter focus on the major oppositional currents in Sucre and Santa Cruz. For a study of other important opposition movements in Bolivia, including the vaguely sinister forces of the Falange Socialista Boliviana (FSB), see Goodale (2018a, 2019).

17   For an important and early anthropological study of practices of Camba nationalism that examines the performative dimensions of violence, paramilitarism, and spectacle, see Fabricant (2009). See also Gustafson's analysis (2006) of "spectacles of autonomy and crisis," which also makes insightful linkages with forms of ritualized public performance, and Fabricant and Postero's later study of the relationship between embodiment and regional politics in Santa Cruz (2013).

18 For a historical overview of the creation of a cruceño elite, see Plata (2008).

19 These founders of Conalde were later joined by Savina Cuéllar (Chuquisaca) after her June 2008 election and Manfred Reyes Villa (Cochabamba) until he was recalled in the August 2008 Referéndum revocatorio.

20 For example, Dabdoub would at times decry the "MAS hordes" invading Santa Cruz at the behest of the government in La Paz; he adopted Antelo's "two Bolivias" understanding of the "closed" culture of the highland Aymaras; and he contrasted what he described as the "productive mentality" of the Camba nation with the "extractivist mentality" of "Andean" culture, the former being in harmony with the liberating potential of the free market, the latter requiring a debasing relationship of dependence on the government.

21 For an extended analysis of the relationship between economic and political history in Santa Cruz, see Soruco (2008).

22 Dunkerley's 1984 historical and critical study of Bolivia's 1952 National Revolution and its aftermath remains a foundational point of reference.

23 For a more sober historical account of the Santa Cruz uprising of 1957 and 1958, see Catoira Marín (1998).

24 As it turned out, the street that housed Santa Cruz's historic civic organizations was named after the most well known battle for Bolivians during the otherwise disastrous Chaco War (1932–35). The battle took place between Paraguayan troops and a contingent of Bolivian soldiers made up of volunteers from the La Paz professional soccer club The Strongest. The confrontation took place near a region called Cañada ("ravine") Esperanza, and the victory for the Bolivians was later called the Battle of Cañada Strongest (see Florentín 1986).

CHAPTER 4: A REVOLUTION WITHOUT REVOLUTIONARIES

1 All quotations from Almaraz are taken from Thomson et al. (2018).

2 There is a vast historical, testimonial, and critical literature on mining in Bolivia. The classic anthropological study remains June Nash's 1979 *We Eat the Mines and the Mines Eat Us*. For an extraordinary *testimonio* of life in the important Bolivian mining center of Siglo XX by a peasant woman who later became a central political figure in the fight against the Banzer dictatorship, see Domitila Barrios de Chungara's 1977 *"Si me permiten hablar . . .": Testimonio de Domitila, una mujer de las minas de Bolivia*, published in English in 1978 as *Let Me Speak!*

3 Here the impressive body of scholarship on Bolivia's left-wing traditions produced by the critical political scientist Jeffrey Webber should be more generally acknowledged. In addition to his 2011 book, see also Webber 2010, 2016, 2017a.

4 Exiled from the Soviet Union in 1929, Trotsky was murdered in Mexico City in 1940 by a Spanish-born Soviet intelligence agent acting on Stalin's orders, just two years after the Fourth International was established.

5 Trotsky's doctrine of permanent revolution and his emphasis on the anti-nationalist nature of socialist revolution was opposed to the policy of "socialism in one country," which became the Soviet Union's state ideology that justified the bureaucratization of the revolution and its identification with national interests.

6 These translated sections from the "Thesis of Pulacayo" are taken from Thomson et al. (2018).

7 See Albro (2005, 2006a, 2006b), Bjork-James (2013), Fabricant (2012), Gustafson (2009a, 2009b), Hylton and Thomson (2007), and Postero (2010, 2017).

8 Q'ara is a widely used pejorative term referring to people who are not originally from highland indigenous communities. As Bruce Mannheim explains, in relation to a similar usage in southern Peru, "to be q'ara, 'naked,' 'uncultured,' or 'uncivilized,' is to live outside of the [indigenous] moral order. Q'aras are outsiders . . . and as such maintain no ritual relationships with [the land]" (Mannheim 1991: 88; see also Canessa 2012a). It was in this sense that García Linera, for example, was often described as a q'ara by militants among the indigenous social movements and within the UMSA's Centro de Estudiantes Campesinos (CEC).

9 Mitma, the son of a well-known mining family from Huanuni, was later elected executive secretary of COB in January 2016 when he was forty years old.

10 In 1919, Lenin launched the "eradication of illiteracy" campaign, which required all Soviet citizens between the ages of eight and fifty years old to become literate in their native language. See Clark (2000).

11 These last two refer to the signal social policies of the first Goni government: Popular Participation and Educational Reform. For a detailed study of Popular Participation, see Postero (2007); for an extensive anthropological account of Educational Reform, which also addresses different ideological debates in the years after, see Gustafson (2009b).

12 See Fabricant (2012) and Fabricant and Gustafson (2011) for wide-ranging analyses of the land question in relation to the process of change during the early years of the period 2006–15.

13 This is an ironic reference to the indigenous "ethico-moral" principles formally adopted by the state in Article 8 of the new constitution (see chapter 1). Ama Llunk'u, which is not in Article 8, means "don't be servile." For a critical study of the role the articulation of these principles played within "indigenous politics," see Albro (2007).

14 The extent of Plata Arnez's loathing for the former minister of education in the Banzer government (1997–2001) was not tempered in the slightest by the fact that Hoz de Vila had been killed in a car crash only two weeks before, when he drove his SUV "into the void," as a newspaper put it at the time, on the treacherous Yungas Road. Before his death in 2015 at age sixty-six, Hoz de Vila had been one of Bolivia's leading political conservatives, with a long history as one of the country's most identifiable business power brokers.

15 This included (in 2016) an application to UNESCO to have the papers of Mauricio Hochschild declared an "intangible cultural heritage of humanity" since they established Hochschild's role in helping Jews escape to Bolivia during the Holocaust.

16 See, for example, Hindery (2013), Kohl and Farthing (2012), and McNeish (2013, 2016a, 2016b).

1   In September 2007, a group of Bolivian plaintiffs filed federal lawsuits in the United States against Sánchez de Lozada and his former minister of defense, José Carlos Sánchez Berzaín, under the Alien Tort Statute (ATS) and the Torture Victim Protection Act. The case, *Mamani et al. v. Sánchez de Lozada and Sánchez Berzaín*, wound its way slowly through the U.S. federal court system, culminating in a landmark jury verdict in April 2018, which found the two men legally liable for the human rights violations and extrajudicial killings of 2003. The jury awarded the Bolivian plaintiffs $10 million in damages. However, on May 30, 2018, federal judge James I. Cohn overturned the jury verdict on the basis that there was insufficient evidence to support it, a ruling that the plaintiffs' legal team promised to appeal.

2   For more on the consequences of the MAS government's strategic use of a "fiscal pact," especially during the post-TIPNIS years, see the conclusion.

3   Among its many activities, the ALICE Project team conducted a series of interviews on contemporary topics with a wide range of intellectuals, indigenous activists, and political leaders, normally at the project's home base at the Center for Social Studies at the University of Coimbra in Portugal, where Sousa Santos was a longtime professor. The first interview in the series of thirty-three was conducted with Xavier Albó in La Paz in March 2012. One of the last ALICE Project interviews was with the Greek Syriza Party economist Yanis Varoufakis in October 2015. As it so happens, I myself was interviewed (#13) by ALICE Project staff member Bruno Sena Martins in Coimbra in March 2014 (www.youtube.com/watch?v=ookpyCRZMFw).

4   At the end of January 2017, the Morales government quietly eliminated the Ministry of Autonomies by downgrading it to a vice ministry and folding it into the Ministry of Government. With this move, in which the formerly ideologically central Ministry of Autonomies ironically lost its own autonomy, the government tacitly signaled that it was forsaking the key legal and political mechanism behind the creation of a plurinational state.

5   Interviews were conducted at the TCP during a relatively brief period of follow-up ethnographic research in July 2016.

6   I asked Barrón if Morales was a good soccer player. *No, not really, but at least he played.*

7   The "martyrs of La Calancha" refers to the three sucrenses who died in the violence surrounding the Constituent Assembly in 2007. "La Calancha" is the name of the neighborhood near the military academy in Sucre where much of the worst violence took place.

8   To recall, I had reached Fernández in his prison cell in January 2009 with the assistance of his youngest daughter, Pamela, who made a direct call to her father while I was conducting an interview with opposition leaders in Santa Cruz. Fernández had invited me to interview him in San Pedro upon my return to La Paz later that month. On the appointed day, after receiving permission to enter the prison by the facility's director, I approached the gate filled with both excitement

and fear, since what I saw on the other side was dozens of men wandering in the open amid a troubling din with no prison guards in sight. Fernández had promised that he would send several bodyguards to escort me to his cell, but no one at the gate seemed to fit the description. However, several men pressed against the gate and eyed me with an anticipation that frightened me. After several minutes of conflicted contemplation—Would I be the first anthropologist to interview Fernández in San Pedro or would I be assaulted and taken as a potentially valuable hostage, or perhaps both?—I decided not to enter. This ethnographic failure was compounded several weeks later when I attempted to reach Bolivia's indigenous former vice president Víctor Hugo Cárdenas on his cell phone to arrange an interview. After explaining the purpose of my research to him in a long mini-speech that included something about the stunning emergence of racial violence against indigenous people directed by right-wing leaders like Leopoldo Fernández, I was suddenly interrupted: "I'm very sorry, but you must have the wrong number, this is Leopoldo Fernández."

9 For example, it wasn't until the end of 2015 that the court decided that it even had jurisdiction to hear the dispute. By the end of 2016, the court was still setting time limits and scheduling preliminary hearings. In its September 2016 order, the court set a time limit of March 2017 for the next series of pleadings by Bolivia and September 2017 for Chile's responses. However, as of December 2017, Bolivia had not filed any further pleadings with the court, leaving the status of the case unclear. Indeed, according to ICJ records, Bolivia's last pleading was filed in May 2015 (IJC 2017).

10 Even though the conflict with Chile over access to the sea remained one-sided, Bolivia's turn to international law did provoke various responses within Chile, some of which trafficked in troubling racial stereotypes. For example, in August 2015, a minor international row erupted over a commercial produced by the Chilean telecom company WOM in which an actor portrayed Evo Morales speaking with a rustic accent and acting like a buffoon during a fictional press conference. The Bolivian government made a formal complaint to the Chilean government on the basis that the commercial violated Chile's obligations under the 1969 Convention on the Elimination of All Forms of Racial Discrimination. In demanding that the Chilean government sanction WOM, the Bolivian government minister Carlos Romero said that "we hope that the Government of Chile will make a precedent of this telecom company for its aggressive, discriminatory, offensive, and fascist attitude, by bringing all possible legal sanctions to bear against it" (*Página Siete*, August 1, 2015). The Chilean government quickly brushed aside these demands, arguing that while "offensive and in bad taste," the commercial was protected by the "freedom of expression and the press."

11 In February 2016, Carlos Mesa was abruptly banished from Bolivia's ICJ legal team. Mesa, who was serving at the time as the team's most high-profile spokesperson, had angered the government by writing in an unrelated opinion piece that "President Morales owes more to Gonzalo Sánchez de Lozada than he is willing to recognize." This immediately led to "a wave of attacks by the

government against the spokesperson for the maritime claim" (*Correo del Sur*, February 10, 2016).

12 For a critical anthropological study of sociolegal practices in a regional Defensoría del Pueblo, see Wemyss (2016).

13 In May 2016, the MAS majority in the Plurinational Legislative Assembly elected David Tezanos Pinto as the new Defensor del Pueblo, with a six-year term in office. Tezanos Pinto had been unknown in Bolivia's human rights community before his election to the position. On the contrary, he had developed a career as a mid-level government functionary with close ties to high-ranking MAS officials, including Juan Ramón Quintana and García Linera. The appointment of Tezanos Pinto, who cut a striking figure with his shaved head, black patch over his left eye, and knee-length leather overcoat, arguably represented the functional end of Bolivia's independent NHRI.

CHAPTER 6: AND THE PUTUTU SHALL SOUND

1 The origins of intersectionality theory are usually traced to the writings of the American legal and critical race scholar Kimberlé Williams Crenshaw (e.g., 1989, 1991).

2 See also Canessa (2012a, 2012b).

3 In 1957, Gueiler had self-published an autobiography based on her experiences as a female revolutionary in a book entitled *La Mujer y la Revolución*.

4 On the often rancorous debates in the Constituent Assembly over the formulation of the state's new hybrid ethnicity, see Garcés (2011).

5 For the organization's political and institutional history, see the article "¿Quiénes somos?," written by Gustavo Adolfo Morales on the Bartolinas website, which featured the Bartolinas's motto: "Native indigenous peasant women building Bolivia's Plurinational State" (Morales 2009).

6 The Confederación de Pueblos Indígenas del Oriente Boliviano, the Consejo Nacional de Ayllus y Markas del Qullasuyu, the Confederación Sindical de Comunidades Interculturales de Bolivia (formerly the Confederación Sindical de Colonizadores de Bolivia), and the CSUTCB.

7 In a section on gender in her study of ecology and ritual in highland Peru, Billie Jean Isbell explains that "the clearest expression of [gender] complementarity is found in the belief that one is not an adult until one marries. Chuschinos say that a male and a female are not complete until they have been united with their 'essential other half'" (1978: 214). For other important works on gender in Bolivia, see Arnold (1997), Barragán (1999), and Gotkowitz (1997).

8 The region's "upper" moiety, or marka, which was composed of seven ayllus, was called MACOAS—Marka de Ayllus y Comunidades Originarias de Arax Suxta. For a detailed study of the indigenous social structures of Jesús de Machaca, see CEBEM (2009). See also Orta (2004).

9 Chachawarmi is the expression in Aymara used to describe the principle of complementarity. It can be translated as "man-woman." The corresponding phrase in Quechua is "tukuy ima qhariwarmi," or "everything is man-woman."

For a critique of how the principle of chachawarmi was at times problematically appropriated during the Morales period, see Burman (2011).

10 It should be clear from the central argument of the chapter—that the politics of recognition in Bolivia was interwoven with law, history, and a sense of justice to produce a potent strategy for both governance and the enactment of moral power—that I don't intend to enter into a debate over the status of Morales's indigeneity. Instead, what is relevant here are the ways in which categories of collective identity, including "indigenous," were mobilized, resisted, or projected in particular ways.

11 Morales's own views on gender seemed to confirm the belief that he was not chachawarmi. As he put it in an August 2015 interview, "From time to time, when men have problems, they can often resolve them over two beers. But with women, you can't do this" (*El Deber*, August 15, 2015).

12 The definitive anthropological study of El Alto during this period remains Sian Lazar's ethnography of what she calls the "rebel city" (2008).

13 An anonymous reviewer of this manuscript noted in relation to this greeting: "[this] is a neologism. For hundreds of years now, Aymara speakers have said 'buenos días' for 'good day.' This is *certainly* not a phrase Evo ever heard or used in his youth."

14 Patrick Kearney's 2014 study brought a fascinating perspective to the wider understanding of Reinaga's life, writings, and influence. Perhaps most remarkable of all, Kearney's 313-page opus was published as a master's thesis in Latin American studies under the direction of the anthropologist Nancy Postero at the University of California, San Diego. Kearney conducted extensive ethnographic interviews with members of Reinaga's family, most notably his niece Hilda, and these interviews uncovered a treasure trove of information about Reinaga's intellectual and political biography. In fact, Kearney focused so extensively on Hilda Reinaga in his thesis that she emerges as an important—if previously largely unacknowledged—thinker and intellectual historian in her own right.

15 Nevertheless, Reinaga continued to identity with various non-Bolivian and non-Indian intellectuals, especially Frantz Fanon (see, for example, Lucero 2008).

16 Cholaje blanco-mestizo was Reinaga's derogatory description for Bolivia's populations that were always in transition from their true natures, always searching for salvation through ideas, fashions, and modes of life that had not originally emerged from within Bolivia's essential autochthony. This description could not be reduced to a simple ethnic category; rather, it was a way of criticizing a set of interconnected historical, political, and psychological processes. Moreover, Reinaga applied this epithet largely to the Bolivian left. He considered Bolivia's trade unions, Trotskyists, socialists, and communists equally guilty of betraying the Indian race. It was for this reason that he rejected the category of campesino, or peasant, since it was associated with traditional (that is, Western) leftist movements. As he put it, "the Indian (or the 'peasant,' as he is called by the cholaje blanco-mestizo) . . . the Bolivian Indian in the struggle for his liberation

DOESN'T NEED TO WAIT, NO ONE HAS TO WAIT FOR THE COMMUNIST PARTIES
OF BOLIVIA" (Reinaga 2007a: 365).

17 The chapter in Kearney's thesis dedicated to Reinaga's transformation, at the end
of his life, into the "Bolivian Judas," includes a spirited effort to explain the intent
of the 1981 FF.AA. and to clarify Reinaga's relationship with García Meza in large
part based on Kearney's interviews with Hilda Reinaga.

18 See also Canessa's fascinating study of the relationship between Reinaga and
what Canessa (2010) describes as "indigenous masculinism."

19 For more expansive discussions of the differences between Peruvian and Bolivian currents of indigenismo, see Bigenho (2002); see also the classic article on
the "return of the Indian" by Albó (1991) and de la Cadena's study of "indigenous
mestizos" in Peru (2000).

20 On the relationship between Indianism and Marxism as "two revolutionary logics," see García Linera (2008).

21 The names of the CEC activists here are pseudonyms.

22 Constantino Lima was a legendary Indianist who had been elected to the
Bolivian Congress in 1985 as a member of the Movimiento Indio Túpac Katari
(MITKA), which he had helped to establish along with Felipe Quispe. Born in
1933 in a small hamlet in the arid region of Pacajes south of Lake Titicaca, Lima's
political worldview was formed at an early age. A journalist asked Lima once
why he had decided to enter political life. In his answer, Lima told a story: "It
was when I was 8 years old. I was with my mother, holding on to her, and we had
to walk 8 to 9 kilometers. My mother used to load wood onto the burros and sell
wood in the town to the q'aras so that we could buy sugar for tea. My mom took
me along so that I could look after the burros. When we arrived in town, a huge
dog came out of a house and attacked us. My mother defended herself as best
she could I while grabbed onto her pollera. But there were some kids, maybe five
or six years old, maybe older, and they shouted, 'Mom, mom, the dog wants to
eat these Indians, their meat must be really tasty!' But their mother didn't seem
to care. She wasn't even worried. Then these town kids started to kick my mother
in the ass and after they'd tied up the dog, they returned, they mocked us, they
called us 'little Indians.' Later, my mother complained to the corregidor [town
official]; she said that this happened every time we came into town with wood.
The corregidor was white and he made us go into an office where the same
group of boys was playing around and he sent for the white mom. Then the
corregidor began to scold my mother, 'Listen, goddammit, you better not insult
this little lady anymore, not one more time! Not one more complaint from you.'
He threatened her like that and my mom could only cry" (Zibechi 2009).
Lima was also credited with having rediscovered the wiphala in a book brought
from Peru in the late 1960s. According to Lima, the Bolivian version of the
flag was first exhibited in the town of Coro Coro in 1970 based on his
investigations.

23 Suma qamaña is the Aymara translation of "vivir bien," or "living well," in Article
8 of the 2009 Bolivian constitution. See Ranta (2014, 2018).

24 Without investing it with too much importance, it is perhaps worth noting that in the constitutional list of Bolivia's thirty-six newly recognized native indigenous peasant nations and peoples, a list that is alphabetical, the Aymara appear first, before the Araona.

CONCLUSION

1 Interestingly, the only TCP magistrate not to sign the decision was Efrén Choque Capuma, whose remarkable life and legal work are examined in chapter 2.

2 Despite the fact that the TCP devoted considerable attention to the ways in which Article 168 violated the American Convention on Human Rights, the secretary general of the Organization of American States, which oversees the convention, responded soon after the judgment that "the clause [of the American Convention] cited in the decision 'does not mean the right to perpetual power'" (Reuters, November 28, 2017).

3 For an insightful study of the politics of "free, prior, and informed consent" in what they describe as "Bolivia's extraction sector," see Schilling-Vacaflor and Eichler (2017).

4 A curious exception to this general approach to the main leaders of the racialized wing of the anti-government opposition involved Carlos Dabdoub Arrien. Despite the fact that he was arguably the most influential public intellectual behind the Santa Cruz autonomy movement, both as a widely published scholar of cruceño and Camba separatism, and as the inaugural head of the department's political office of "autonomy, decentralization, and democratic development," Dabdoub managed to avoid the sweeping searchlight gaze of strategic juridification (see chapter 5). Perhaps seeing the writing on the wall, he "retired" from politics in 2010 to return to his practice as a neurosurgeon at Santa Cruz's well-regarded Japanese University Hospital. As he told me in 2015, his decision to step away from the glare of public scrutiny was also motivated by more personal factors: with two sons in university in the United States, he was responsible for significant tuition costs. Finally, in a development that seemed to confirm Dabdoub's complete and utter reinvention, in 2015 he was named vice rector of the Santa Cruz campus of the Universidad Privada Franz Tamayo (UNIFRANZ), a relatively expensive institution that catered primarily to Brazilian students and children of the cruceño elite whose parents couldn't quite afford to send them to places like the University of Miami, Florida International University, or the University of South Florida.

5 For another use of the concept of "condensation" in anthropology, in this case through a fascinating study of slogans within the politics of neoliberalism, see Makovicky, Trémon, and Zandonai (2019).

6 For a fascinating anthropological study of justice-seeking and activism that likewise finds the work of Fraser illuminating, see Sapignoli (2018).

References

Adams, William, and Martin Mulligan. 2003. *Decolonizing Nature: Strategies for Conservation in a Post-Colonial Era*. London: Routledge.

Agencia Boliviana de Noticias (ABN). 2009. "Los verdaderos indígenas bolivianos comienzan a desmarcarse de Morales: Felipe Quispe lo califico de 'neoliberal con rostro de indio.'" https://abnoticias.wordpress.com/2009/02/26/los-verdaderos -indigenas-bolivianos-comienzan-a-desmarcarse-de-morales-felipe-quispe-lo -califico-de-%E2%80%9Cneoliberal-con-rostro-de-indio%E2%80%9D/.

Albó, Xavier. 1987. "From MNRistas to Kataristas to Katari." In *Resistance, Rebellion, and Consciousness in the Andean Peasant World, 18th to 20th Centuries*, edited by Steve J. Stern, 379–419. Madison: University of Wisconsin Press.

Albó, Xavier. 1991. "El retorno del indio." *Revista andina* 2, no. 9: 299–366.

Albó, Xavier. 1999. "Principales características del derecho consuetudinario." *Artículo Primero: Revista de Debate Social Jurídico* 7: 11–24.

Albó, Xavier, and Josep M. Barnadas. 1990. *La cara india y campesina de nuestra historia*. La Paz: UNITAS/CIPCA.

Albro, Roberto. 2005. "The Indigenous in the Plural in Bolivian Oppositional Politics." *Bulletin of Latin American Research* 24, no. 4: 433–53.

Albro, Roberto. 2006a. "Bolivia's 'Evo Phenomenon': From Identity to What?" *Journal of Latin American and Caribbean Anthropology* 11, no. 2: 408–28.

Albro, Roberto. 2006b. "The Culture of Democracy and Bolivia's Indigenous Movements." *Critique of Anthropology* 26, no. 4: 387–410.

Albro, Roberto. 2007. "Indigenous Politics in Bolivia's Evo Era: Clientelism, Llunkerío, and the Problem of Stigma." *Urban Anthropology* 36, no. 3: 281–320.

Albro, Roberto. 2010. "Confounding Cultural Citizenship and Constitutional Reform in Bolivia." *Latin American Perspectives* 37, no. 3: 71–90.

ALICE Project. 2016. "ALICE Background—'Reinventing Social Emancipation.'" http://alice.ces.uc.pt/en/index.php/about/where-does-alice-come-from/?lang=en.

Allende, Isabel. 1982. *La casa de los espíritus*. Barcelona: Plaza and Janés.

Almaraz Paz, Sergio. *Requiem para una república*. La Paz: Amigos del Libro.

Alvizuri, Verushka. 2012. *Le savant, le militant et l'Aymara: Histoire d'une construction identitaire en Bolivie (1952–2006)*. Paris: Armand Colin.

American Anthropological Association. 2016. "Anthropology Matters! 116th AAA Annual Meeting Call for Papers." *Anthropology News*, November 22.

Anaya, James. 1996. *Indigenous Peoples in International Law*. Oxford: Oxford University Press.

Antelo Gutiérrez, Sergio. 2003. *Los cruceños y su derecho de libre determinación.* Santa Cruz: Imprenta Landívar.

Antelo Gutiérrez, Sergio. 2017. *Los Cambas: Nación sin estado.* Santa Cruz: Instituto de Ciencia, Economía, Educación y Salud (ICEES).

Anthias, Penelope. 2018. *Limits to Decolonization: Indigeneity, Territory, and Hydrocarbon Politics in the Bolivian Chaco.* Ithaca, NY: Cornell University Press.

Ardaya Paz, Hernán. 1981. *Ñanderoga, el holocausto de un pueblo sojuzgado.* Santa Cruz: Imprint.

Arenas, Reinaldo. 1993. *Before Night Falls: A Memoir.* New York: Viking.

Arendt, Hannah. [1963] 2006. *On Revolutions.* New York: Penguin.

Arias, Enrique Desmond, and Daniel M. Goldstein, eds. 2010. *Violent Democracies in Latin America.* Durham, NC: Duke University Press.

Ari Murillo, Marina. 2003. *Bartolina Sisa: La generala aymara y la equidad de género.* La Paz: Editorial Amuyañataki.

Arnold, Denise. 1997. *Más allá del silencio: Las fronteras de género en los Andes.* La Paz: CIASE and Instituto de Lengua y Cultura Aymara.

Assies, Willem. 2009. "Cambio político: Pueblos indígenas y sus demandas en los sistemas políticos." *Revista CIDOB* 85–86 (May): 89–107.

Atahuichi Salvatierra, Ricardo Tito. 2007. *Asamblea constituyente y revolución boliviana.* La Paz: Author.

Autonomous Departmental Government of Cochabamba. 2016. *Gobierno inicia entrega de 7,000 libros de "Fausto Reinaga" a estudiantes y professores del trópico de Cochabamba.*

Ayllu Sartañani. 1995. *Perspectivas de decentralización en Karankas: La visión comunitaria.* La Paz: ILDIS.

Barragán, Rossana. 1999. *Indios, mujeres y ciudadanos: Legislación y ejercicio de la ciudadanía en Bolivia (siglo XIX).* La Paz: Fundación Diálogo.

Barrios de Chungara, Domitila, with Moema Viezzer. 1978. *Let Me Speak! Testimony of Domitila, a Woman of the Bolivian Mines.* New York: Monthly Review.

Barrón, Jaime. 2010. "Jaime Barrón es el electo alcalde de la ciudad de Sucre." EJU TV. http://eju.tv/2010/04/jaime-barrn-es-el-electo-alcalde-de-la-ciudad-de -sucre/.

Becker, Marc. 2011. "Correa, Indigenous Movements, and the Writing of a New Constitution in Ecuador." *Latin American Perspectives* 38, no. 1: 47–62.

Benedict, Ruth. [1946] 2005. *The Chrysanthemum and the Sword: Patterns of Japanese Culture.* New York: Houghton Mifflin.

Bennett, Tony, Lawrence Grossberg, and Meaghan Morris, eds. 2005. *New Keywords: A Revised Vocabulary of Culture and Society.* Malden, MA: Blackwell.

Berlin, Isaiah. 1979. *Concepts and Categories: Philosophical Essays by Isaiah Berlin.* New York: Viking.

Bigenho, Michelle. 1999. "Sensing Locality in Yura: Rituals of Carnival and of the Bolivian State." *American Ethnologist* 26, no. 4: 957–80.

Bigenho, Michelle. 2002. *Sounding Indigenous: Authenticity in Bolivian Music Performance.* New York: Palgrave.

Bjork-James, Carwil. 2013. "Claiming Space, Redefining Politics: Urban Protest and Grassroots Power in Bolivia." PhD diss., Department of Anthropology, City University of New York.

Bloch, Marc. 1953. *The Historian's Craft*. New York: Knopf.

Boulanger, Philippe. 2017. *Evo Morales ou le malentendu bolivien*. Paris: Editions Nuvis.

Brinton, Crane. 1965. *The Anatomy of Revolution*, 3rd ed. New York: Vintage.

Brunnegger, Sandra, and Karen Faulk, eds. 2016. *A Sense of Justice: Legal Knowledge and Lived Experience in Latin America*. Stanford, CA: Stanford University Press.

Brush, Stephen B. 1993. "Indigenous Knowledge of Biological Resources and Intellectual Property Rights: The Role of Anthropology." *American Anthropologist* 95, no. 3: 653–71.

Burgos-Debray, Elisabeth, ed. 1984. *I, Rigoberta Menchú: An Indian Woman in Guatemala*. London: Verso.

Burman, Anders. 2011. "*Chachawarmi*: Silence and Rival Voices on Decolonisation and Gender Politics in Andean Bolivia." *Journal of Latin American Studies* 43, no. 1: 65–91.

Burman, Anders. 2016. *Indigeneity and Decolonization in the Bolivian Andes: Ritual Practice and Activism*. Lanham, MD: Lexington.

Calla, Pamela. 2011. "Making Sense of May 24th in Sucre: Toward an Antiracist Legislative Agenda." In *Histories of Race and Racism: The Andes and Mesoamerica from Colonial Times to the Present*, edited by Laura Gotkowitz, 311–17. Durham, NC: Duke University Press.

Calla, Ricardo. 1999. *Justicia indígena y derechos humanos: Hacia la formulación de una política estatal de la diferencia*. La Paz: Ministerio de Justicia/World Bank.

Canessa, Andrew. 2000. "Fear and Loathing on the Kharisiri Trail: Alterity and Identity in the Andes." *Journal of the Royal Anthropological Institute* 6, no. 4: 705–20.

Canessa, Andrew. 2006. "'Todos somos indígenas': Towards a New Language of National Political Identity." *Bulletin of Latin American Research* 25, no. 2: 241–63.

Canessa, Andrew. 2007. "Who Is Indigenous? Self-Identification, Indigeneity, and Claims to Justice in Contemporary Bolivia." *Urban Anthropology* 36, no. 3: 195–237.

Canessa, Andrew. 2009. "Forgetting the Revolution and Remembering the War: Memory and Violence in Highland Bolivia." *History Workshop Journal* 68, no. 1: 173–98.

Canessa, Andrew. 2010. "Dreaming of Fathers: Fausto Reinaga and Indigenous Masculinism." *Latin American and Caribbean Ethnic Studies* 5, no. 2: 175–87.

Canessa, Andrew. 2012a. *Intimate Indigeneities: Race, Sex, and History in the Small Spaces of Andean Life*. Durham, NC: Duke University Press.

Canessa, Andrew. 2012b. "New Indigenous Citizenship in Bolivia: Challenging the Liberal Model of the State and Its Subjects." *Latin American and Caribbean Ethnic Studies* 7, no. 2: 201–21.

Canessa, Andrew. 2014. "Conflict, Claim and Contradiction in the New 'Indigenous' State of Bolivia." *Critique of Anthropology* 34, no. 2: 153–73.

Catoira Marín, Ricardo. 1998. *Las luchas sociales en Santa Cruz*. Santa Cruz: Editorial Universitaria.

Centro Boliviano de Estudios Multidisciplinarios (CEBEM). 2009. *Municipio Indígena originario aymara Jesús de Machaca*. La Paz: Centro Boliviano de Estudios Multidisciplinarios.

Centro de Asesoramiento Legal y Desarrollo Social (CASDEL). 1994. *Rodeo Chico: Una expresión de pluralismo jurídico*. Cochabamba: CASDEL.

Centro de Investigación y Promoción del Campesinado (CIPCA). 2017. "35 años de historia." http://www.cipca.org.bo/index.php/quienes-somos/historia-cipca.

Chodor, Tom. 2015. *Neoliberal Hegemony and the Pink Tide in Latin America: Breaking Up with TINA?* Basingstoke, UK: Palgrave Macmillan.

Choque Canqui, Roberto. 1986. *La masacre de Jesús de Machaca*. La Paz: Ediciones Chitakolla.

Choque Canqui, Roberto, and Esteban Ticona. 1996. *Jesús de Machaca: La marka rebelde*. La Paz: CEDOIN.

Clark, Charles E. 2000. *Uprooting Otherness: The Literacy Campaign in NEP-Era Russia*. Selinsgrove, PA: Susquehanna University Press.

Clarke, Kamari Maxine. 2009. *Fictions of Justice: The International Criminal Court and the Challenge of Legal Pluralism in Sub-Saharan Africa*. Cambridge: Cambridge University Press.

Clarke, Kamari Maxine, and Mark Goodale, eds. 2010. *Mirrors of Justice: Law and Power in the Post-Cold War Era*. New York: Cambridge University Press.

Clifford, James. 1986. "Partial Truths." In *Writing Culture: The Poetics and Politics of Ethnography*, edited by James Clifford and George E. Marcus, 1–26. Berkeley: University of California Press.

Colloredo-Mansfeld, Rudi. 1999. *The Native Leisure Class: Consumption and Cultural Creativity in the Andes*. Chicago: University of Chicago Press.

Colloredo-Mansfeld, Rudi. 2002. "'Don't Be Lazy, Don't Lie, Don't Steal': Community Justice in the Neoliberal Andes." *American Ethnologist* 29, no. 3: 637–62.

Comaroff, John L., and Jean Comaroff. 2006. "Law and Disorder in the Postcolony: An Introduction." In *Law and Disorder in the Postcolony*, edited by Jean Comaroff and John L. Comaroff, 1–56. Chicago: University of Chicago Press.

Comparative Constitutionalism Project. 2017. "Informing Constitutional Design." www.comparativeconstitutionsproject.org.

Condarco Morales, Ramiro. 1983. *Zárate, el "Temible" Willka: Historia de la rebelión indígena de 1899*, 2nd ed. La Paz: Ed. Renovación.

Confederación Indígena del Oriente Boliviano (CIDOB). 1992. *Proyecto de ley indígena*. La Paz: CIDOB.

Contreras, Manuel. 1993. "Estaño, ferrocarriles y modernización, 1900–1930." In *Los bolivianos en el tiempo*, edited by Alberto Crespo. La Paz: Universidad Andina Simón Bolivar-INDEAA.

Convention on the Elimination of All Forms of Discrimination against Women (CEDAW). 1979. http://www.ohchr.org/EN/ProfessionalInterest/Pages/CEDAW.aspx.

Corte Nacional Electoral de Bolivia (CNE). 2009. *Las elecciones generales bolivianas de diciembre de 2009*. La Paz: CNE.

Couso, Javier, Alexandra Huneeus, and Rachel Sieder, eds. 2010. *Cultures of Legality: Judicialization and Political Activism in Latin America*. Cambridge: Cambridge University Press.

Crenshaw, Kimberlé Williams. 1989. "Demarginalizing the Intersection of Race and Sex: A Black Feminist Critique of Antidiscrimination Doctrine, Feminist Theory and Antiracist Politics." *University of Chicago Legal Forum* 1: 139–67.

Crenshaw, Kimberlé Williams. 1991. "Mapping the Margins: Intersectionality, Identity Politics, and Violence against Women of Color." *Stanford Law Review* 43, no. 6: 1241–99.

Cronon, William. 1996. "The Trouble with Wilderness or, Getting Back to the Wrong Nature." *Environmental History* 1, no. 1: 7–28.

Dabdoub, Carlos. 2009. "El Holocausto de Terebinto." EJU TV. http://eju.tv/2009/05/el-holocausto-de-terebinto/.

Dangl, Benjamin. 2019. *The Five Hundred Year Rebellion: Indigenous Movements and the Decolonization of History in Bolivia*. Chico, CA: AK Press.

Davis, Kevin E., Angelina Fisher, Benedict Kingsbury, and Sally Engle Merry, eds. 2012. *Governance by Indicators: Global Power through Classification and Rankings*. Oxford: Oxford University Press.

de Certeau, Michel. 1984. *The Practice of Everyday Life*. Berkeley: University of California Press.

DeFronzo, James. 2011. *Revolutions and Revolutionary Movements*. Boulder, CO: Westview.

de la Cadena, Marisol. 2000. *Indigenous Mestizos: The Politics of Race and Culture in Cuzco, Peru, 1919–1991*. Durham, NC: Duke University Press.

de la Cadena, Marisol. 2010. "Indigenous Cosmopolitics in the Andes: Conceptual Reflections beyond 'Politics.'" *Cultural Anthropology* 25, no. 2: 334–70.

de la Cadena, Marisol. 2015. *Earth Beings: Ecologies of Practice across Andean Worlds*. Durham, NC: Duke University Press.

Deleuze, Gilles. 1994. *Difference and Repetition*. Translated by Paul R. Patton. New York: Columbia University Press.

Domingo, Pilar. 2010. "Novel Appropriations of the Law in the Pursuit of Political and Social Change in Latin America." In *Cultures of Legality: Judicialization and Political Activism in Latin America*, edited by Javier Couso, Alexandra Huneeus, and Rachel Sieder, 254–78. New York: Cambridge University Press.

Donham, Donald L. 1999. *Marxist Modern: An Ethnographic History of the Ethiopian Revolution*. Berkeley: University of California Press.

Draper, Melissa Crane, and Jim Shultz. 2008. "Introduction." In *Dignity and Defiance: Stories from Bolivia's Challenges to Globalization*, edited by Jim Shultz and Melissa Crane Draper, 1–6. Berkeley: University of California Press.

Dunkerley, James. 1984. *Rebellion in the Veins: Political Struggle in Bolivia, 1952–1982*. London: Verso.

Dunkerley, James. 2007a. *Bolivia: Revolution and the Power of History in the Present.* London: Institute for the Study of the Americas.

Dunkerley, James. 2007b. "Evo Morales, 'the Two Bolivias,' and the Third Bolivian Revolution." *Journal of Latin American Studies* 39, no. 1: 133–66.

Ehrlich, Eugen. [1913] 2001. *Fundamental Principles of the Sociology of Law.* New Brunswick, NJ: Transaction.

Ellison, Susan Helen. 2018. *Domesticating Democracy: The Politics of Conflict Resolution in Bolivia.* Durham, NC: Duke University Press.

Engle, Karen. 2010. *The Elusive Promise of Indigenous Development: Rights, Culture, Strategy.* Durham, NC: Duke University Press.

Escárzaga, Fabiola. 2012. "Comunidad indígena y revolución en Bolivia: El pensamiento indianista-katarista de Fausto Reinaga y Felipe Quispe." *Política y cultura* 37: 185–210.

Escobar, Arturo. 2010. "Latin America at a Crossroads: Alternative Modernizations, Postliberalism, or Post-Development?" *Cultural Studies* 24, no. 1: 1–65.

Fabian, Johannes. 1983. *Time and the Other: How Anthropology Makes Its Object.* New York: Columbia University Press.

Fabricant, Nicole. 2009. "Performative Politics: The Camba Countermovement in Eastern Bolivia." *American Ethnologist* 36, no. 4: 768–83.

Fabricant, Nicole. 2012. *Mobilizing Bolivia's Displaced: Indigenous Politics and the Struggle over Land.* Chapel Hill: University of North Carolina Press.

Fabricant, Nicole. 2013. "Good Living for Whom? Bolivia's Climate Justice Movement and the Limitations of Indigenous Cosmovisions." *Latin American and Caribbean Ethnic Studies* 8, no. 2: 159–78.

Fabricant, Nicole, and Bret Gustafson, eds. 2011. *Remapping Bolivia: Resources, Territory, and Indigeneity in a Plurinational State.* Santa Fe: SAR.

Fabricant, Nicole, and Nancy Postero. 2013. "Contested Bodies, Contested States: Performance, Emotions, and New Forms of Regional Governance in Santa Cruz, Bolivia." *Journal of Latin American and Caribbean Anthropology* 18, no. 2: 187–211.

Fadlalla, Amal Hassan. 2018. *Branding Humanity: Competing Narratives of Rights, Violence, and Global Citizenship.* Stanford, CA: Stanford University Press.

Farthing, Linda, and Benjamin Kohl. 2014. *Evo's Bolivia: Continuity and Change.* Austin: University of Texas Press.

Ferguson, James. 2006. *Global Shadows: Africa in the Neoliberal World Order.* Durham, NC: Duke University Press.

Fernández Osco, Marcelo. 2000. *La ley del ayllu: Práctica de jach'a justicia y jisk'a justicia (justicia mayor y justicia menor) en comunidades aymaras.* La Paz: PIEB.

Fischer, Eva. 2017. "From Rebellion to Democracy: The Many Lives of Túpac Katari." *History and Anthropology* 29, no. 4: 493–516. doi: 10.1080/02757206.2017.1401536.

Florentín, Heriberto. 1986. *La Batalla de Strongest: Apuntes para la historia de la Guerra del Chaco,* 2nd ed. Buenos Aires: Editorial el Foro.

Foran, John. 2005. *Taking Power: On the Origins of Third World Revolutions.* Cambridge: Cambridge University Press.

Fraser, Nancy. 1995. "From Redistribution to Recognition? Dilemmas of Justice in a 'Post-Socialist' Age." *New Left Review* 212 (June/August): 68–93.

Fraser, Nancy. 2008. *Scales of Justice: Reimagining Political Space in a Globalizing World*. Cambridge: Polity.

French, Jan Hoffman. 2004. "Mestizaje and Law Making in Indigenous Identity Formation in Northeastern Brazil: 'After the Conflict Came the History.'" *American Anthropologist* 106, no. 4: 663–74.

French, Jan Hoffman. 2006. "Buried Alive: Imagining Africa in the Brazilian Northeast." *American Ethnologist* 33, no. 3: 340–60.

Galeano, Eduardo. 1971. *Las venas abiertas de América Latina*. Mexico City: Siglo XXI Editores.

Garcés, Fernando. 2011. "The Domestication of Indigenous Autonomies in Bolivia: From the Pact of Unity to the New Constitution." In *Remapping Bolivia: Resources, Territory, and Indigeneity in a Plurinational State*, edited by Nicole Fabricant and Bret Gustafson, 46–67. Santa Fe: SAR.

García Linera, Álvaro. 2008. "El desencuentro de dos razones revolucionarias: Indianismo y marxismo." *Kuri Muyu: Revista del Arte y la Sabiduría de las Culturas Originarias* 5: 19–28.

García Linera, Álvaro, Raquel Gutiérrez, Raúl Prada, Felipe Quispe, and Luis Tapia, eds. 2001. *Tiempos de rebélion*. La Paz: Muela del Diablo.

García Linera, Álvaro, Raquel Gutiérrez, Raúl Prada, and Luis Tapia, eds. 2000. *El retorno de la Bolivia plebeya*. La Paz: Muela del Diablo.

García Linera, Álvaro, Raúl Prada, Luis Tapia, and Oscar Vega Camacho, eds. 2010. *El estado: Campo de lucha*. La Paz: Muela del Diablo.

García Linera, Álvaro, Luis Tapia, and Raúl Prada, eds. 2007. *La transformación pluralista del estado*. La Paz: Muela del Diablo.

Geertz, Clifford. 1983. *Local Knowledge: Further Essays in Interpretive Anthropology*. New York: Basic Books.

Giddens, Anthony. 1984. *The Constitution of Society: Outline of the Theory of Structuration*. Berkeley: University of California Press.

Gold, Marina. 2015. *People and State in Socialist Cuba: Ideas and Practices of Revolution*. New York: Palgrave Macmillan.

Goldstein, Daniel M. 2003. "'In Our Own Hands': Lynching, Justice, and the Law in Bolivia." *American Ethnologist* 30, no. 1: 22–43.

Goldstein, Daniel M. 2004. *The Spectacular City: Violence and Performance in Urban Bolivia*. Durham, NC: Duke University Press.

Goldstein, Daniel M. 2010. "Toward a Critical Anthropology of Security." *Current Anthropology* 51, no. 4: 487–517.

Goldstein, Daniel M. 2012. *Outlawed: Between Security and Rights in a Bolivian City*. Durham, NC: Duke University Press.

Goldstone, Jack, ed. 1994. *Revolutions: Theoretical, Comparative, and Historical Studies*. Fort Worth, TX: Harcourt Brace College.

Goldstone, Jack. 2001. "Toward a Fourth Generation of Revolutionary Theory." *Annual Review of Political Science* 4 (June): 139–87.

Goodale, Mark. 2006. "Reclaiming Modernity: Indigenous Cosmopolitanism and the Coming of the Second Revolution in Bolivia." *American Ethnologist* 33, no. 4: 634–49.

Goodale, Mark. 2008a. *Dilemmas of Modernity: Bolivian Encounters with Law and Liberalism.* Stanford, CA: Stanford University Press.

Goodale, Mark. 2008b. "Legalities and Illegalities." In *A Companion to Latin American Anthropology*, edited by D. Poole, 214–29. Malden, MA: Blackwell.

Goodale, Mark. 2017. *Anthropology and Law: A Critical Introduction.* New York: NYU Press.

Goodale, Mark. 2018a. "God, Fatherland, Home: Notes for an Anthropology of Prejudice." https://www.researchgate.net/publication/326606332_God_Fatherland _Home_Notes_for_an_Anthropology_of_Prejudice/download.

Goodale, Mark. 2018b. "The Legibility of Fausto Reinaga." *The Paris Review* (December). www.theparisreview.org/blog/2018/12/17/the-legibility-of-fausto -reinaga/.

Goodale, Mark. 2018c. "What Are Human Rights Good For?" *Boston Review* (July). http://bostonreview.net/global-justice/mark-goodale-what-are-human-rights -good.

Goodale, Mark. 2019. "Toward an Anthropology of the Broken Twig: Reflections on Rightwing Mobilization in Bolivia." In *Dark Shadows: Anthropology, Ideology, Violence*, edited by M. Goodale. New York: Berghahn.

Goodale, Mark, and Nancy Postero, eds. 2013. *Neoliberalism Interrupted: Social Change and Contemporary Governance in Contemporary Latin America.* Stanford, CA: Stanford University Press.

Gotkowitz, Laura. 1997. "Within the Boundaries of Equality: Race, Gender, and Citizenship in Bolivia (Cochabamba, 1880–1953)." PhD diss., Department of History, University of Chicago.

Gotkowitz, Laura. 2007. *A Revolution for Our Rights: Indigenous Struggles for Land and Justice in Bolivia, 1880–1952.* Durham, NC: Duke University Press.

Greenberg, Jessica. 2014. *After the Revolution: Youth, Democracy, and the Politics of Disappointment in Serbia.* Stanford, CA: Stanford University Press.

Greene, Thomas H. 1990. *Comparative Revolutionary Movements: Search for Theory and Justice*, 3rd ed. Prentice-Hall Contemporary Comparative Politics. Englewood Cliffs, NJ: Prentice-Hall.

Gregory, Derek. 2001. "(Post)Colonialism and the Production of Nature." In *Social Nature: Theory, Practice, and Politics*, edited by Noel Castree and Bruce Braun, 84–111. Oxford: Blackwell.

Grisaffi, Thomas. 2019. *Coca Yes, Cocaine No: How Bolivia's Coca Growers Reshaped Democracy.* Durham, NC: Duke University Press.

Gueiler Tejada, Lydia. 1957. *La mujer y la revolución.* La Paz: Author.

Guise, Anselm Verener Lee. [1922] 1997. *Six Years in Bolivia: The Adventures of a Young Mining Engineer.* West Lafayette, IN: Purdue University Press.

Gumucio Dagron, Alfonso. 2017. "La memoria organizada." http://gumucio.blogspot .ch/2017/04/la-memoria-organizada.html.

Gupta, Akhil, and James Ferguson, eds. 1997. *Anthropological Locations: Boundaries and Grounds of a Field Science.* Berkeley: University of California Press.

Gurr, Ted Robert. 1970. *Why Men Rebel.* Princeton, NJ: Princeton University Press.

Gustafson, Bret. 2006. "Spectacles of Autonomy and Crisis: Or, What Bulls and Beauty Queens Have to Do with Regionalism in Eastern Bolivia." *Journal of Latin American and Caribbean Anthropology* 11, no. 2: 351–79.

Gustafson, Bret. 2009a. "Manipulating Cartographies: Plurinationalism, Autonomy, and Indigenous Resurgence in Bolivia." *Anthropological Quarterly* 82, no. 4: 985–1016.

Gustafson, Bret. 2009b. *New Languages of the State: Indigenous Resurgence and the Politics of Knowledge in Bolivia.* Durham, NC: Duke University Press.

Gustafson, Bret. 2010. "When States Act Like Movements: Dismantling Local Power and 'Seating' Sovereignty in Bolivia." *Latin American Perspectives* 37, no. 4: 48–66.

Gutiérrez Aguilar, Raquel. 2014. *Rhythms of the Pachakuti: Indigenous Uprising and State Power in Bolivia.* Durham, NC: Duke University Press.

Gutiérrez Aguilar, Raquel, Raúl Prada, Álvaro García Linera, and Luis Tapia, eds. 1999. *El fantasma insomne: Pensando el presente desde El manifiesto comunista.* La Paz: Muela del Diablo.

Hale, Charles R. 1997. "Cultural Politics of Identity in Latin America." *Annual Review of Anthropology* 26, no. 1: 567–90.

Hale, Charles R. 2002. "Does Multiculturalism Menace? Governance, Cultural Rights and the Politics of Identity in Guatemala." *Journal of Latin American Studies* 34, no. 3: 485–524.

Hale, Charles R. 2004. "Rethinking Indigenous Politics in the Era of the 'Indio Permitido.'" NACLA *Report on the Americas* 38, no. 2: 16–21.

Hale, Charles R. 2006. "Activist Research v. Cultural Critique: Indigenous Land Rights and the Contradictions of Politically Engaged Anthropology." *Cultural Anthropology* 21, no. 1: 96–120.

Hale, Charles R. 2010. Comments at the symposium "Reflections on Engaged Anthropology," sponsored by the Department of Anthropology, Rutgers University, New Brunswick, NJ, February 12.

Hammond, John L. 2011. "Indigenous Community Justice in the Bolivian Constitution of 2009." *Human Rights Quarterly* 33, no. 3: 649–81.

Hardt, Michael, and Antonio Negri. 2000. *Empire.* Cambridge, MA: Harvard University Press.

Harris, Olivia. 1978. "Complementarity and Conflict: An Andean View of Women and Men." In *Sex and Age as Principles of Social Differentiation*, edited by J. S. LaFontaine, 21–40. London: Academic Press.

Harris, Olivia. 1995. "Ethnic Identity and Market Relations: Indians and Mestizos in the Andes." In *Ethnicity, Markets, and Migration in the Andes: At the Crossroads of History and Anthropology*, edited by Brooke Larson, Olivia Harris, and Enrique Tandeter, 351–90. Durham, NC: Duke University Press.

Harris, Olivia. 2000. *To Make the Earth Bear Fruit: Ethnographic Essays on Fertility, Work and Gender in Highland Bolivia.* London: Institute of Latin American Studies.

Harvey, David. 2003. *The New Imperialism*. Oxford: Oxford University Press.

Hayden, Robert M. 1992. "Constitutional Nationalism in the Formerly Yugoslav Republics." *Slavic Review* 51, no. 4: 654–73.

Hindery, Derrick. 2013. *From Enron to Evo: Pipeline Politics, Global Environmentalism, and Indigenous Rights in Bolivia*. Tucson: University of Arizona Press.

Hirschl, Ran. 2004. *Towards Juristocracy: The Origins and Consequences of the New Constitutionalism*. Cambridge, MA: Harvard University Press.

Holmes, Douglas R. 2000. *Integral Europe: Fast Capitalism, Multiculturalism, Neofascism*. Princeton, NJ: Princeton University Press.

Honneth, Axel. 1996. *The Struggle for Recognition: The Moral Grammar of Social Conflicts*. Cambridge, MA: MIT Press.

Hylton, Forrest, and Sinclair Thomson. 2007. *Revolutionary Horizons: Past and Present in Bolivian Politics*. London: Verso.

Ibarra, Hernán. 2010. *Visión histórico política de la constitución del 2008: Estudios y análisis*. Quito: Centro Andino de Acción Popular (CAAP).

Instituto de la Judicatura de Bolivia. 2005. *Justicia comunitaria en los pueblos originarios de Bolivia*. Sucre: Editorial Túpac Katari.

International Court of Justice (ICJ). 2017. "Obligation to Negotiate Access to the Pacific Ocean (Bolivia v. Chile)." http://www.icj-cij.org/en/case/153.

International Institute for Democracy and Electoral Assistance (IDEA). 2017. "IDEA Constitution Building Primers." www.constitutionnet.org/primers.

Iorga, Romana. 2000. *Auz simplu*. Bucharest: Editura Semne.

Isbell, Billie Jean. 1978. *To Defend Ourselves: Ecology and Ritual in an Andean Village*. Austin: University of Texas Press.

John, S. Sándor. 2009. *Bolivia's Radical Tradition: Permanent Revolution in the Andes*. Tucson: University of Arizona Press.

Kapferer, Bruce. 1988. *Legends of People, Myths of State: Violence, Intolerance, and Political Culture in Sri Lanka and Australia*. Washington, DC: Smithsonian Institution Press.

Kapferer, Bruce. 2015. "Introduction." In *In the Event: Toward an Anthropology of Generic Moments*, edited by Lotte Meinert and Bruce Kapferer, 1–28. New York: Berghahn.

Kearney, Patrick Louis Williams. 2014. "Insurgent Legacy: Fausto Reinaga and the Indian Revolution." MA thesis, Latin American Studies, University of California, San Diego.

Kenez, Peter. 1985. *The Birth of the Propaganda State: Soviet Methods of Mass Mobilization, 1917–1929*. Cambridge: Cambridge University Press.

Kirsch, Stuart. 2012. "Juridification of Indigenous Politics." In *Law against the State: Ethnographic Forays into Law's Transformations*, edited by Julia Eckert, Brian Donahoe, Christian Strümpell, and Zerrin Özlem Biner, 23–43. Cambridge: Cambridge University Press.

Klein, Herbert S. 1982. *Bolivia: The Evolution of a Multi-Ethnic Society*. New York: Oxford University Press.

Klein, Naomi. 2007. *The Shock Doctrine: The Rise of Disaster Capitalism*. New York: Metropolitan.

Klug, Heinz. 2000. *Constituting Democracy: Law, Globalism and South Africa's Political Reconstruction*. Cambridge: Cambridge University Press.

Kohl, Benjamin, and Linda Farthing. 2006. *Impasse in Bolivia: Neoliberal Hegemony and Popular Resistance*. London: Zed.

Kohl, Benjamin, and Linda Farthing. 2012. "Material Constraints to Popular Imaginaries: The Extractive Economy and Resource Nationalism in Bolivia." *Political Geography* 31, no. 4: 225–35.

Kohn, Eduardo. 2013. *How Forests Think: Toward an Anthropology beyond the Human*. Berkeley: University of California Press.

Küchler, Susanne. 2004. "Re-Visualising Attachment: An Anthropological Perspective on Persons and Property Forms." In *Law, Anthropology, and the Constitution of the Social: Making Persons and Things*, edited by Alain Pottage and Martha Mundy. Cambridge: Cambridge University Press.

Kuenzli, E. Gabrielle. 2013. *Acting Inca: National Belonging in Early Twentieth-Century Bolivia*. Pittsburgh: University of Pittsburgh Press.

Larson, Brooke. 2004. *Trials of Nation Making: Liberalism, Race, and Ethnicity in the Andes, 1810–1910*. Cambridge: Cambridge University Press.

Lazar, Sian. 2008. *El Alto, Rebel City: Self and Citizenship in Andean Bolivia*. Durham, NC: Duke University Press.

Lenin, Vladimir. [1902] 1975a. "What Is to Be Done? Burning Questions of Our Movement." In *The Lenin Anthology*, edited by Robert C. Tucker, 12–114. New York: W. W. Norton.

Lenin, Vladimir. [1917] 1975b. "Enemies of the People." In *The Lenin Anthology*, edited by Robert C. Tucker, 305–6. New York: W. W. Norton.

Lenin, Vladimir. [1919] 1975c. "The Dictatorship of the Proletariat." In *The Lenin Anthology*, edited by Robert C. Tucker, 489–91. New York: W. W. Norton.

Léon, Rosario. 1997. *Justicia comunitaria: Los quechuas de Tapacarí*. La Paz: Ministerio de Justicia/World Bank.

Lindsay, Reed. 2004. "Bolivian Peasants Turn to Lynch Law. Corrupt Officials Face Brutal Village Justice That Goes Back to Inca Times." *Guardian*, September 19.

Lipovec Čebron, Uršula. 2012. "Exclusion politique et sanitaire : Le corps des 'effacés' slovènes." *Ethnologie française* 42, no. 2: 241–49.

Low, Setha M., and Sally Engle Merry. 2010. "Engaged Anthropology: Diversity and Dilemmas: An Introduction to Supplement 2." *Current Anthropology* 51, no. S2: S203–26.

Lucero, José Antonio. 2008. "Fanon in the Andes: Fausto Reinaga, Indianismo and the Black Atlantic." *International Journal of Critical Indigenous Issues* 1, no. 1: 13–22.

Makovicky, Nicolette, Anne-Christine Trémon, and Sheyla S. Zandonai, eds. 2019. *Slogans: Subjection, Subversion, and the Politics of Neoliberalism*. London: Routledge.

Malagón Barceló, Javier. 1961. "The Role of the *Letrado* in the Colonization of America." *The Americas* 18, no. 1: 1–17.

Mannheim, Bruce. 1991. *The Language of the Inka since the European Invasion*. Austin: University of Texas Press.

Marcus, George E. 1995. "Ethnography in/of the World System: The Emergence of Multi-Sited Ethnography." *Annual Review of Anthropology* 24, no. 1: 95–117.

Marcus, George E. 1999. "What Is at Stake—and Is Not—in the Idea and Practice of Multi-Sited Ethnography." *Canberra Anthropology* 22, no. 2: 6–14.

Mariátegui, José Carlos. 1928. *Siete ensayos de interpretación de la realidad Peruana*. Lima: Biblioteca "Amauta."

Marof, Tristán. 1926. *La justicia del Inca*. Brussels: Librería Falk Fils.

Mauss, Marcel. [1925] 1967. *The Gift: Forms and Functions of Exchange in Archaic Societies*. New York: W. W. Norton.

McNeish, John-Andrew. 2013. "Extraction, Protest and Indigeneity in Bolivia: The TIPNIS Effect." *Latin American and Caribbean Ethnic Studies* 8, no. 2: 221–42.

McNeish, John-Andrew. 2016a. "Extracting Justice? Colombia's Commitment to Mining and Energy as a Foundation for Peace." *International Journal of Human Rights* 4: 500–516.

McNeish, John-Andrew. 2016b. "Voting to Derail Extraction: Popular Consultation and Resource Sovereignty." *Third World Quarterly* 38, no. 4: 1128–45.

Medeiros, Carmen. 2001. "Civilizing the Popular? The Law of Popular Participation and the Design of a New Civil Society in 1990s Bolivia." *Critique of Anthropology* 21, no. 4: 401–25.

Mendieta, Pilar. 2010. *Entre la alianza y la confrontación: Pablo Zárate Willka y la rebelión indígena de 1899 en Bolivia*. La Paz: Institut français d'études andines.

Merry, Sally Engle. 2006a. *Human Rights and Gender Violence: Translating International Law in Local Justice*. Chicago: University of Chicago Press.

Merry, Sally Engle. 2006b. "Transnational Human Rights and Local Activism: Mapping the Middle." *American Anthropologist* 108, no. 1: 38–51.

Merry, Sally Engle. 2016. *The Seductions of Quantification: Measuring Human Rights, Gender Violence, and Sex Trafficking*. Chicago: University of Chicago Press.

Merry, Sally Engle, Kevin E. Davis, and Benedict Kingsbury, eds. 2015. *The Quiet Power of Indicators: Measuring Governance, Corruption, and Rule of Law*. New York: Cambridge University Press.

Mertus, Julie. 2009. *Human Rights Matters: Local Politics and National Human Rights Institutions*. Stanford, CA: Stanford University Press.

Mesa, José de, Teresa Gisbert, and Carlos D. Mesa Gisbert, eds. 2008. *Historia de Bolivia*. La Paz: Editorial Gisbert.

Mesa Gisbert, Carlos D. 2008. "1997–2006: La crisis del estado." In *Historia de Bolivia*, edited by José de Mesa, Teresa Gisbert, and Carlos D. Mesa Gisbert, 607–39. La Paz: Editorial Gisbert.

Mignolo, Walter. 2007. "Delinking: The Rhetoric of Modernity, the Logic of Coloniality, and the Grammar of De-Coloniality." *Cultural Studies* 21, no. 2: 449–514.

Molina Rivero, Ramiro. 1999. *El derecho consuetudinario en Bolivia.* La Paz: Ministerio de Justicia/World Bank.

Molina Saucedo, Carlos Hugo. 2012. *Andrés Ibáñez, un caudillo para el siglo XXI: La Comuna de Santa Cruz de la Sierra de 1876.* La Paz: Plural Editores.

Morales, Gustavo Adolfo. 2009. "¿Quiénes somos? Breve y cronológica historia de la C.N.M.C.I.O.B." https://web.archive.org/web/20120102170104/http://www.bartolinasisa.org: 80/sitio.shtml?apc=&s=b.

Mossop, Brian. 2014. "1974: The Weimar Republic Comes to Gay Toronto." In *Translation Effects: The Shaping of Modern Canadian Culture*, edited by Kathy Mezeik, Sherry Simon, and Luise von Flotow, 399–415. Montreal: McGill-Queen's University Press.

Moyn, Samuel. 2018. *Not Enough: Human Rights in an Unequal World.* Cambridge: Belknap Press of Harvard University Press.

Murra, John. 1972. "El control vertical de un máximo de pisos ecológicos en la economía de las sociedades andinas." In *Visita de la provincia de Léon Huánuco en 1562, por Iñigo Ortiz de Zúñiga*, edited by John Murra, 427–68. Huánuco, Peru: Universidad Nacional Hermillo Valdizan.

Murra, John. 1975. *Formaciones económicas y políticas del mundo andino.* Lima: Instituto de Estudios Peruanos.

Nash, June. [1979] 1993. *We Eat the Mines and the Mines Eat Us: Dependency and Exploitation in Bolivian Tin Mines.* New York: Columbia University Press.

Niezen, Ronald. 2003. *The Origins of Indigenism: Human Rights and the Politics of Identity.* Berkeley: University of California Press.

Niezen, Ronald. 2013. "The Law's Legal Anthropology." In *Human Rights at the Crossroads*, edited by Mark Goodale, 185–97. New York: Oxford University Press.

Olivera, Oscar. 2004. *¡Cochabamba! Water War in Bolivia.* Cambridge, MA: South End.

Orellana Halkyer, René. 1999. "Repensando proposiciones y conceptos sobre el derecho consuetudinario." *Artículo Primero: Revista de Debate Social Jurídico* 7: 41–54.

Orellana Halkyer, René. 2004. "Interlegalidad y campos jurídicos: Discurso y derecho en la configuración de órdenes semiautónomos en comunidades quechuas en Bolivia." PhD diss., Faculty of Law, University of Amsterdam.

Orta, Andrew. 2004. *Catechizing Culture: Missionaries, Aymara, and the "New Evangelization."* New York: Columbia University Press.

Ortner, Sherry. 1973. "On Key Symbols." *American Anthropologist* 75, no. 5: 1338–46.

Ossio, Lorena, and Silvina Ramírez. 1999. *Análisis jurídico.* La Paz: Ministerio de Justicia/World Bank.

Partido Obrero Revolucionario (POR). 2013. *Por la revolución y dictadura proletaria: Declaración política.* Cochabamba: Ediciones MASAS.

Piketty, Thomas. 2014. *Capital in the Twenty-First Century.* Cambridge: Belknap Press of Harvard University Press.

Plata, Wilfredo. 2008. "El discurso autonomista de las élites de Santa Cruz." In *Los barones del Oriente: El poder en Santa Cruz ayer y hoy*, edited by Ximena Soruco, Wilfredo Plata, and Gustavo Medeiros, 101–71. Santa Cruz: Fundación Tierra.

Platt, Tristan. 1982. *Estado boliviano y ayllu andino: Tierra y tributo en el norte de Potosí.* Lima: Instituto de Estudios Peruanos.

Postero, Nancy. 2005. "Indigenous Responses to Neoliberalism." *Political and Legal Anthropology Review* 28, no. 1: 73–92.

Postero, Nancy. 2007. *Now We Are Citizens: Indigenous Politics in Postmulticultural Bolivia.* Stanford, CA: Stanford University Press.

Postero, Nancy. 2010. "Morales's MAS Government: Building Indigenous Popular Hegemony in Bolivia." *Latin American Perspectives* 37, no. 3: 18–34.

Postero, Nancy. 2013. "Bolivia's Challenge to 'Colonial Neoliberalism.'" In *Neoliberalism, Interrupted: Social Change and Contested Governance in Contemporary Latin America*, edited by Mark Goodale and Nancy Postero, 25–52. Stanford, CA: Stanford University Press.

Postero, Nancy. 2017. *The Indigenous State: Race, Politics, and Performance in Plurinational Bolivia.* Berkeley: University of California Press.

Postero, Nancy Grey, and Leon Zamosc. 2006. "The Struggle for Indigenous Rights in Latin America." *Journal of Latin American and Caribbean Anthropology* 11, no. 1: 208–10.

Pottage, Alain. 2004. "Introduction: The Fabrication of Persons and Things." In *Law, Anthropology, and the Constitution of the Social*, edited by Alain Pottage and Martha Mundy, 1–39. Cambridge: Cambridge University Press.

Powęska, Radosław. 2017. "State-Led Extractivism and the Frustration of Indigenous Self-Determined Development: Lessons from Bolivia." *International Journal of Human Rights* 21, no. 4: 442–63. doi: 10.1080/13642987.2017.1284446.

Price, David H. 2016. *Cold War Anthropology: The CIA, the Pentagon, and the Growth of Dual Use Anthropology.* Durham, NC: Duke University Press.

Ramírez, Silvina, and Lorena Ossio. 1999. *Propuesta normativa para el reconocimiento de la justicia comunitaria.* La Paz: Ministerio de Justicia/World Bank.

Ramos, Alcida Rita. 1994. "The Hyperreal Indian." *Critique of Anthropology* 14, no. 2: 153–71.

Ranta, Eija M. 2014. "In the Name of Vivir Bien: Indigeneity, State Formation, and Politics in Evo Morales' Bolivia." PhD diss., University of Helsinki.

Ranta, Eija M. 2018. *Vivir Bien as an Alternative to Neoliberal Globalization: Can Indigenous Terminologies Decolonize the State?* Abingdon, UK: Routledge.

Razsa, Maple. 2015. *Bastards of Utopia: Living Radical Politics after Socialism.* Bloomington: Indiana University Press.

Reed, John. 1919. *Ten Days That Shook the World.* New York: Boni and Liveright.

Reinaga, Fausto. 1960. *El sentimiento mesiánico del pueblo ruso.* La Paz: Ediciones SER.

Reinaga, Fausto. 1970. *Manifiesto del partido indio de Bolivia.* La Paz: Ediciones PIB.

Reinaga, Fausto. 1971. *Tesis India.* La Paz: Ediciones PIB.

Reinaga, Fausto. 1978. *El pensamiento amáutico.* La Paz: Author.

Reinaga, Fausto. 1981. *Bolivia y la revolución de las FF. AA.* La Paz: Ediciones Comunidad Amáutica Mundial.

Reinaga, Fausto. 1984. *Europa prostitute asesina: Congreso mundial de los intelectuales del tercer mundo.* La Paz: Comunidad Amaútica Mundial.

Reinaga, Fausto. [1970] 2007a. *La Revolución India*. La Paz: Author and Hilda Reinaga.

Reinaga, Fausto. [1981] 2007b. *La Revolución Amáutica*. La Paz: Author and Hilda Reinaga.

Riles, Annelise. 1998. "Infinity within the Brackets." *American Ethnologist* 25, no. 3: 378–98.

Riles, Annelise. 2000. *The Network Inside Out*. Ann Arbor: University of Michigan Press.

Rincón Soto, Lucía. 2014a. "Fausto Reinaga y su pensamiento amáutico: Su crítica a la filosofía occidental." *Revista Latinoamericana de Derechos Humanos* 25, no. 2: 15–31.

Rincón Soto, Lucía. 2014b. "Pensar y hacer: Una reflexión desde Nuestroamérica." *Revista Comunicación* 23, no. 2: 95–107.

Rivera Cusicanqui, Silvia. 1991. "Liberal Democracy and Ayllu Democracy in Bolivia: The Case of Northern Potosí." *Journal of Development Studies* 26, no. 4: 97–121.

Rodas Morales, Hugo. 2008. *Marcelo Quiroga Santa Cruz: El socialismo vivido, Tomo II (1969–1977)*. La Paz: Plural Editores.

Roy, Arundhati. 2003. *War Talk*. Boston: South End.

Saint-Just, Louis Antoine de. [1791] 2004. "L'esprit de la Révolution." In *Saint-Just, Oeuvres complètes*, edited by Miguel Abensour and Anne Kupiec. Paris: Gallimard.

Salomon, Frank. 2001. "Review of *To Make the Earth Bear Fruit: Ethnographic Essays on Fertility, Work and Gender in Highland Bolivia*." *Journal of Latin American Studies* 33, no. 3: 654–56.

Salomon, Frank, and George L. Urioste, eds. 1991. *The Huarochirí Manuscript: A Testament of Ancient and Colonial Andean Religion*. Austin: University of Texas Press.

Santos, Boaventura de Sousa. 1987. "Law: A Map of Misreading. Toward a Postmodern Conception of Law." *Journal of Law and Society* 14, no. 3: 279–302.

Santos, Boaventura de Sousa. 1995. *Toward a New Common Sense: Law, Science and Politics in the Paradigmatic Transition*. New York: Routledge.

Santos, Boaventura de Sousa. 2014. *Epistemologies of the South: Justice against Epistemicide*. London: Routledge.

Sapignoli, Maria. 2018. *Hunting Justice: Displacement, Law, and Activism in the Kalahari*. Cambridge: Cambridge University Press.

Schelchkov, Andrey. 2011. *Andrés Ibáñez y la Revolución de la Igualdad en Santa Cruz: Primer ensayo de federalismo en Bolivia, 1876–1877*. Santiago: Universidad de Santiago de Chile.

Schilling-Vacaflor, Almut. 2011. "Bolivia's New Constitution: Towards Participatory Democracy and Political Pluralism?" *European Review of Latin American and Caribbean Studies* 90: 3–22.

Schilling-Vacaflor, Almut, and Jessika Eichler. 2017. "The Shady Side of Consultation and Compensation: 'Divide-and-Rule' Tactics in Bolivia's Extraction Sector." *Development and Change* 48, no. 6: 1–25.

Scott, James C. 1985. *Weapons of the Weak: Everyday Forms of Peasant Resistance.* New Haven, CT: Yale University Press.

Shimose, Pedro. 1968. *Poemas para un pueblo.* La Paz: Editorial y Librería "Difusión."

Shoshan, Nitzan. 2016. *The Management of Hate: Nation, Affect, and the Governance of Right-Wing Extremism in Germany.* Princeton, NJ: Princeton University Press.

Shultz, Jim. 2008. "Conclusion: What Bolivia Teaches Us." In *Dignity and Defiance: Stories from Bolivia's Challenge to Globalization,* edited by Jim Shultz and Melissa Crane Draper, 291–96. Berkeley: University of California Press.

Sieder, Rachel. 2010. "Legal Cultures in the (Un)Rule of Law: Indigenous Rights and Juridification in Guatemala." In *Cultures of Legality: Judicialization and Political Activism in Latin America,* edited by Javier Couso, Alexandra Huneeus, and Rachel Sieder, 161–81. New York: Cambridge University Press.

Sieder, Rachel, and John-Andrew McNeish, eds. 2013. *Gender Justice and Legal Pluralities: African and Latin American Perspectives.* London: Routledge.

Skocpol, Theda. 1979. *States and Social Revolutions: A Comparison of France, Russia, and China.* Cambridge: Cambridge University Press.

Soruco, Ximena. 2008. "De la goma a la soya: El proyecto histórico de la élite cruceña." In *Los barones del Oriente: El poder en Santa Cruz ayer y hoy,* edited by Ximena Soruco, Wilfredo Plata, and Gustavo Medeiros, 1–100. Santa Cruz: Fundación Tierra.

Speed, Shannon. 2008. *Rights in Rebellion: Indigenous Struggle and Human Rights in Chiapas.* Stanford, CA: Stanford University Press.

Stanton, Gregory H. 2013. "The Ten Stages of Genocide." Genocide Watch. http://www.genocidewatch.org/genocide/tenstagesofgenocide.html.

Starn, Orin. 1991. "Missing the Revolution: Anthropologists and the War in Peru." *Cultural Anthropology* 6, no. 1: 63–91.

Starn, Orin. 1994. "Rethinking the Politics of Anthropology: The Case of the Andes." *Current Anthropology* 35, no. 1: 13–38.

Stavenhagen, Rodolfo. 1988. *Derecho indígena y derechos humanos en América Latina.* Mexico City: Instituto Interamericano de Derechos Humanos, Colegio de México.

Stavenhagen, Rodolfo. 1990. "Derecho consuetudinario indígena en América Latina." In *Entre la ley y la costumbre: El derecho consuetudinario indígena en América Latina,* edited by Rodolfo Stavenhagen and Diego Iturralde, 27–46. Mexico City: Instituto Indigenista Interamericano/Instituto Interamericano de Derechos Humanos, Colegio de México.

Stocking, George W., ed. 1985. *Observers Observed: Essays on Ethnographic Fieldwork.* Madison: University of Wisconsin Press.

Suarez, Hugo José, Raquel Gutiérrez, Álvaro García Linera, Claudia Benavente, Félix Patzi, and Raúl Prada, eds. 2000. *Bourdieu: Leído desde el Sur.* La Paz: French Alliance, Goethe Institute, Embassy of Spain, University of the Cordillera, Plural Editores.

Tapia, Luis, Álvaro García Linera, and Raúl Prada, eds. 2004. *Memorias de octobre.* La Paz: Muela del Diablo.

Taussig, Michael. 1980. *The Devil and Commodity Fetishism in South America.* Chapel Hill: University of North Carolina Press.

Taylor, Charles. 1992. *Multiculturalism and "The Politics of Recognition."* Princeton, NJ: Princeton University Press.

Teitelbaum, Benjamin. 2017. *Lions of the North: Sounds of the New Nordic Radical Nationalism.* New York: Oxford University Press.

Tellería, Loreta. 2015. "La hegemonía verde: Control de los recursos naturales en Bolivia bajo el discurso medioambienta." *La Migraña: Revista de Análisis Político* 14: 25–41.

Thomassen, Bjørn. 2012. "Notes towards an Anthropology of Political Revolutions." *Comparative Studies in Society and History* 54, no. 3: 679–706.

Thompson, E. P. 1977. *Whigs and Hunters: The Origin of the Black Act.* London: Penguin.

Thomson, Sinclair. 2002. *We Alone Will Rule: Native Andean Politics in the Age of Insurgency.* Madison: University of Wisconsin Press.

Thomson, Sinclair. 2009. "Bull Horns and Dynamite: Echoes of Revolution in Bolivia." *NACLA Report on the Americas* 42: 21–27.

Thomson, Sinclair, Rosanna Barragán, Xavier Albó, Seemin Qayum, and Mark Goodale, eds. 2018. *The Bolivia Reader: History, Culture, Politics.* Durham, NC: Duke University Press.

Tobar, Héctor. 2005. "Revolt on High: The Indians of Bolivia's El Alto Lead a Drive for Social Change That Has Toppled Two Presidents." *Los Angeles Times,* June 16.

Tribunal Constitucional Plurinacional (TCP). 2017. "Acción de inconstitucionalidad abstracta." *Gaceta Constitucional Plurinacional,* November 28. Docket Number 0084/2017.

Trotsky, Leon. 1938. "The Death Agony of Capitalism and the Tasks of the Fourth International: The Mobilization of the Masses around Transitional Demands to Prepare the Conquest of Power." Leon Trotsky Internet Archive. https://www.marxists.org/archive/trotsky/1938/tp/index.htm#contents.

Trujillo, Julio C. 2013. *Constitucionalismo contemporáneo: Teoría, procesos, procedimientos y retos.* Quito: Universidad Andina Simón Bolivar.

Turner, Terence. 1997. "Human Rights, Human Difference: Anthropology's Contribution to an Emancipatory Cultural Politics." *Journal of Anthropological Research* 53, no. 3: 273–91.

Turner, Victor. 1967. *The Forest of Symbols: Aspects of Ndembu Ritual.* Ithaca, NY: Cornell University Press.

UNASUR. 2008. *Informe de la Comisión de UNASUR sobre los sucesos de Pando: Hacia un alba de justicia para Bolivia.* Quito: Unión de Naciones Suramericanas.

Urton, Gary. 1981. *At the Crossroads of the Earth and the Sky: An Andean Cosmology.* Austin: University of Texas Press.

Vacaflor, Jorge. 1999. *Los derechos indígenas en la constitución política de siete países latinoamericanos.* La Paz: ILDIS.

Varnoux Garay, Marcelo. 2005. "La ciencia política en Bolivia: Entre la reforma y la crisis de la democracia." *Revista de Ciencia Política* 25, no. 1: 92–100.

Vega, Oscar. 2011. *Errancias: Aperturas para vivir bien*. La Paz: CLASCO and Muela del Diablo.

Volkan, Vamik. 1997. *Bloodlines: From Ethnic Pride to Ethnic Terrorism*. Boulder, CO: Westview.

Wanderley, Fernanda, ed. 2011. *El desarrollo en cuestión: Reflexiones desde América Latina*. La Paz: CIDES-UMSA.

Wanderley, Fernanda, and José Peres-Cajías, eds. 2018. *Los desafíos del desarrollo productivo en el siglo XXI: Diversificación, justicia social y sostenibilidad ambiental*. La Paz: Universidad Católica Boliviana.

Webber, Jeffery R. 2010. "Bolivia in the Era of Morales." *Latin American Research Review* 45, no. 3: 248–60.

Webber, Jeffery R. 2011. *From Rebellion to Reform in Bolivia: Class Struggle, Indigenous Liberation, and the Politics of Evo Morales*. Chicago: Haymarket.

Webber, Jeffery R. 2015. "The Indigenous Community as 'Living Organism': José Carlos Mariátegui, Romantic Marxism, and Extractive Capitalism in the Andes." *Theory and Society* 44, no. 6: 575–98.

Webber, Jeffery R. 2016. "Evo Morales and the Political Economy of Passive Revolution in Bolivia, 2006–2015." *Third World Quarterly* 37, no. 10: 1855–76.

Webber, Jeffery R. 2017a. "Evo Morales, Transformismo, and the Consolidation of Agrarian Capitalism in Bolivia, 2006–2016." *Journal of Agrarian Change* 17, no. 2: 330–47.

Webber, Jeffery R. 2017b. *The Last Day of Oppression, and the First Day of the Same: The Politics and Economics of the New Latin American Left*. Chicago: Haymarket.

Wemyss, Martyn. 2016. "Human Rights and Legal Subjectivity in Highland Bolivia." PhD diss., Department of Anthropology, London School of Economics.

Williams, Raymond. 1976. *Keywords: A Vocabulary of Culture and Society*. London: Croom Helm.

Williamson, John. 1992. "The Eastern Transition to a Market Economy: A Global Perspective." Centre for Economic Performance, Occasional Paper, Series 2: 1–44.

Wilson, Richard A. 2001. *The Politics of Truth and Reconciliation in South Africa*. Cambridge: Cambridge University Press.

Wood, Gordon S. 1993. *The Radicalism of the American Revolution*. New York: Vintage.

Worsley, Peter. 1957. *The Trumpet Shall Sound: A Study of "Cargo" Cults in Melanesia*. London: MacGibbon and Lee.

Xiang, Biao. 2013. "Multi-Scalar Ethnography: An Approach for Critical Engagement with Migration and Social Change." *Ethnography* 14, no. 3: 282–99.

Zibechi, Raúl. 2009. "Constantino Lima: La otra política nace de lo cotidiano." Upside Down World, September 15. http://upsidedownworld.org/noticias-en-espa /noticias-en-espa-noticias-en-espa/bolivia-constantino-lima-la-otra-polca-nace -de-lo-cotidiano/.

Index

AAA (American Anthropological Association), 31–32
Achacachi, 67
Acta del Pueblo, 170–71
agency and ascription, with collective identity, 203–4
agricultural economy, in Santa Cruz, 118–19, 123, 125
Aguas del Tunari, 20
ALICE Project team, 177, 259n3
Allende, Salvador, 11
allochrony, politics of, 5
Almaraz Paz, Sergio, 135, 146–47
alternative modernization, 240
Álvarez, José Luis, 151–56, 160
American Convention of Human Rights, 236
Anatomy of Revolution (Brinton), 59, 234
Andean anthropology, critique of, 7
Andean radicalism, 120
lo andino (ideal Andean), 7
Andrés Ibáñez Law of Autonomies and Decentralization (Law of Autonomies), 172–74, 176–81, 184
Antelo Gutiérrez, Sergio, 119–20
anthropological approach, to ideology, 37–38
anthropologists, 17, 27, 57, 98, 251n17
anthropology, 7, 11; engagement with, 12–14, 98; goal of, 100; history and, 9; of transformation, 32; in world of meaning and crisis, 31–32
anti-democratic, constitutionalism as, 73

anti-Indian and anti-highland rhetoric, 97
APDHB (Permanent Assembly of Human Rights of Bolivia), 42, 75, 210
APG (Asamblea del Pueblo Guaraní), 179
Arendt, Hannah, 26
Arquiri Apu Mallku, 13
arrest and trial: of Barrón, 184–86; of Leopoldo Fernández, 186–87, 259n8
Article 168: term limits on president and vice president, 236; unconstitutionality of, 236–37, 264n1
articles, in constitution, 77, 78, 82, 87–90, 167, 232, 254n4
artifact, constitution as, 74, 80, 81, 83
Asamblea Constituyente, 22
Asamblea del Pueblo Guaraní (APG), 179
At the Crossroads of the Earth and Sky (Urton), 231
Autodeterminación, 49
autonomous municipalities, 172, 173–74
autonomy, 10, 22, 24, 43, 77, 84, 255n11; concept of, 167; decolonization and, 169–81; Flores Condori on, 166, 167; Ibáñez on, 170–72; model of, 122; native indigenous peasant, 176–80, 231; Santa Cruz struggle of, 122–23, 124–25; statute of, 118. *See also specific autonomies*
autonomy, separatism and, 119–29, 131–32; mytho-history relating to, 97, 118, 130, 256n16; oppositional ideology relating to, 118; regional identification relating to, 118

ayllus, 14, 168, 249n6
ayllus, of Jesús de Machaca: husband
and wife pairs in, 211; Mallku Tayka,
211; Tata Mallku, 211
Ayllu Yauriri Unificada, 211
Aymaras, 93, 217, 227, 228, 232, 262n13

Baldomar Salgueiro, Luis, interview
with, 98–99, 133
Banzer Suárez, Hugo, 2, 87, 141, 163,
208, 221
Barbie, Klaus (Butcher of Lyon), 2
Barrios de Chungara, Domitila, 205–6,
208
Barrón, Jaime: as academic, 182–83;
arrest and trial of, 184–86; interview
of, 183, 185–86; as mayor of Sucre,
183–84; Morales supported by, 182–83
Bartolinas, power of complementarity
and, 205–8, 213–15; Choque Callisaya
with, 210–12; with historic congress,
209; ideological history of, 209; in interconnected ontological system, 210,
261n7; plurinational state relating
to, 209, 210; in social and political
movement, 209
base and superstructure relationship,
reconfiguration of, 7
Battle of the First Cross, 102
Battle of the Mangroves, 129
Benedict, Ruth, 100–101
Black October of 2003, 20, 86, 174,
259n1
Bolivia, 22, 86, 122, 134, 138–43; in
1998–99, 6–7; during 2006–15, 5, 9,
10, 18, 59, 65, 142, 210, 233; oppression
1964–82, 2, 5; in post-2005, 5, 7, 10
Bolivia and the Revolution of the
Armed Forces (Bolivia y La Revolución de las (FF.AA.), 221–22
bourgeois private property, 153–54
bourgeois reform, 153
Brinton, Crane, 59, 234
Burnt Palace, 41

El Cacique, Leopoldo Fernández, as,
193, 195
CAINCO (Cámara de Industria, Com-
ercio, Servicios y Turismo de Santa
Cruz), 119, 124
calibrated pragmatism, 5
Cámara Agropecuaria del Oriente
(CAO), 98, 118–19, 124, 125, 133
Cámara de Industria, Comercio,
Servicios y Turismo de Santa Cruz
(CAINCO), 119, 124
Camba nationalism, 119–21, 130, 131,
232, 256n17
Canessa, Andrew, 223, 263n18
CAO (Cámara Agropecuaria del
Oriente), 98, 118–19, 124, 125, 133
capitalism, 17, 152, 243
Carrasco Condarco, Mary, 193
Carry Albornos, Alfredo, 177–78
Cava, Jhon, 108, 110–13
CCP (Comparative Constitutions
Project), 76
CEC (Centro de Estudiantes Campesi-
nos), 225–27, 229–30, 263n21
CEDAW (Convention on the Elimina-
tion of All Forms of Discrimination
against Women), 8–9, 19, 209
CEDIB (Centro de Información y Docu-
mentación Bolivia), 189
Central America, 48
Central Obrera Boliviana (COB), 69, 137,
143, 146, 208; blockades used by, 144,
145; hunger strikes used by, 144, 155;
leadership of, 157; mobilization in
streets used by, 144
Central Obrera Regional de El Alto, 215
Centro de Estudiantes Campesinos
(CEC), 225–27, 229–30, 263n21
Centro de Información y Document-
ación Bolivia (CEDIB), 189
César, Julio, 54–55
CGTFB (Confederación General de
Trabajadores Fabriles de Bolivia), 143
chachawarmi, 212–13, 261n9

Charagua autonomy, 178

Chile, Bolivia dispute with, 190–91, 260nn9–10

"cholaje blanco-mestizo," 220, 223, 262n16

cholas, women as, 206

Choque Callisaya, Patricia: with Bartolinas, 210–12; interview with, 212–14; on Morales, 213–14, 262nn10–11

Choque Capuma, Efrén, 91–94

CIC (Comité Interinstitucional por la Capitalidad), 104–5, 106–7, 114, 182

CIDOB (Confederación de Pueblos Indígenas de Bolivia), 232

city of white, darkness in, 101–18

CNMCIOB-BS (Confederación Nacional de Mujeres Campesinas, Indígenas y Originarias de Bolivia "Bartolina Sisa"), 209

COB (Central Obrera Boliviana), 69, 137, 143–46, 157, 208

cocalero movement, 40, 141, 252n5

Cochabamba Department, 20, 24, 128, 129

Cochabamba Manifesto (2000), 20

CODEINCA (Comité Cívico de Intereses de Chuquisaca), 105

Code of Criminal Procedure, 87–88

coevalness, 4–5, 76

Cold War, 11, 16, 32, 47, 65, 74

Coliseo Cerrado Julio Borelli Viterito: MAS groups in, 33–35; new constitution celebrated at, 35–36; revolutionary slogans and banners in, 34–35; rituals at, 34–35; "Yes!" campaign at, 34–35, 36, 96

Colla, Camba and, 131, 232

Colla bourgeoisie, 126

collective belonging, 167

collective identity, 205–22; agency and ascription relating to, 203–4; categories of, 204, 231; contention with, 203, 204; ethnography of, 230–31; foundational importance of, 203; ideology of, 232–33; intersectionality with, 203–4, 261n1; national politics of, 232; prism

of, 223–31; relationality with, 203–4; strategic face of, 204; terms of, 224

collectivist transformation, of economy, 97

Colque Gutiérrez, Adolfo, 40–41

COMCIPO (Comité Cívico Potosinista), 57–58, 157

COMIBOL (Corporación Minera de Bolivia), 18, 163

Comité Cívico de Intereses de Chuquisaca (CODEINCA), 105

Comité Cívico Potosinista (COMCIPO), 57–58, 157

Comité Interinstitucional por la Capitalidad (CIC), 104–5, 106–7, 114, 182

Comité pro Santa Cruz, 119, 121, 128, 178

Communications Ministry, 45, 252n9

communicative level, of regional language, 200, 214–16

Communist Manifesto (Marx), 50, 147, 158

community justice, 66–67, 78–79; Code of Criminal Procedure relating to, 87–88; concept of, 167; indigenous customary law, 86–89, 254n6, 254n8, 255n9; pluralism relating to, 86–92

compañeros fallecidos en la vigilia, 3

Comparative Constitutions Project (CCP), 76

complementary sociopolitical leadership, concept of, 205–15, 261n7

Comuna: founders and members of, 47–51; García Linera with, 46–47; origins of, 47, 49–50, 253n11; publications of, 50–51, 253n13

CONALDE (Consejo Nacional Democrático), 22, 121, 257n19

CONAMAQ (Consejo Nacional de Ayllus y Markas del Qullasuyu), 13, 25, 66, 144, 145, 167

Confederación de Pueblos Indígenas de Bolivia (CIDOB), 232

Confederación de Trabajadores de la Educación Urbana de Bolivia (CTEUB), 149

Confederación General de Trabajadores Fabriles de Bolivia (CGTFB), 143
Confederación Nacional de Mujeres Campesinas, Indígenas y Originarias de Bolivia "Bartolina Sisa" (CNMCIOB-BS), 209
Confederación Sindical Única de Trabajadores Campesinos de Bolivia (CSUTCB), 21, 69, 144, 145, 208
Consejo Nacional de Ayllus y Markas del Qullasuyu (CONAMAQ), 13, 25, 66, 144, 145, 167
Consejo Nacional Democrático (CONALDE), 22, 121, 157n19
Conservative party, 101
Conservative Sucre Battalion, 102
Constituent Assembly of 2006–2007, 70, 73, 79, 81, 110, 167, 237; advisory role for, 11, 29; formation of, 7; protests relating to, 103, 112, 182, 196
constitution, 5, 28–31, 72–73; articles in, 77, 78, 82, 87–90, 167, 232, 254n4; as artifact, 74, 80, 81, 83; at Coliseo Cerrado Julio Borelli Viterito, 35–36; ethical-moral principles in, 39, 181, 232; Flores Condori on, 167–69; ideology of structural change in, 39; as Magna Carta, 75–76, 97; with Morales, 7, 13, 21–23, 24–25, 35; national mobilization for, 34; as an organ of democratic power, 70–71; preamble to, 38, 76, 203, 243; as talisman, 74–85; thirty-six nations and people in, 90, 167–68, 231–32, 255n12; as uncompromising framework for plurinational state cosmovisión, 65; "Yes!" campaign support of, 34–35, 36, 96
constitutionalism, 71, 73
constitutional law, realities of, 71–72
constitutional revolution, 68–74, 153–54
Constitution-Building Processes Programme, 70
constitution-making, 70

Convención Progresista Universitaria (CPU), 54
Convention on the Elimination of All Forms of Discrimination against Women (CEDAW), 8–9, 19, 209
Corporación Minera de Bolivia (COMIBOL), 18, 163
"The Corruption of MAS: Ama Sua, Ama Llulla, Ama Llunk'u, Ama Ke'lla," 158, 258n13
Corte Electoral Departamental, 61
cosmic time, meaning and crisis in, 1–5; anthropology in world of, 31–32; (not) missing the revolution, 6–15, 249n2; revolution from inside out, 26–28; revolution in fragments, 28–31; VOLVERÉ Y SERÉ MILLONES, 15–26
cosmovisions, 32, 64–74, 89, 94, 133, 203
counterrevolution, 10, 96
CPU (Convención Progresista Universitaria), 54
cruceño sentiment, 130–31, 172
CSUTCB (Confederación Sindical Única de Trabajadores Campesinos de Bolivia), 40, 69, 144, 145, 208
CTEUB (Confederación de Trabajadores de la Educación Urbana de Bolivia), 149
Cuéllar, Savina, interview with, 107–10, 111
cultural identity, 203
cultural logics, process of change in, 96
cultural norms, process of change around, 65
cultural revolution, 26, 241
cultural space-time, 9
cultural system, 95–133
cultural taxonomy, 5
cultural transformation, 241

Dabdoub Arrien, Carlos, 120–23, 171, 257n20

darkness, in city of white, 101–18
Daza Groselle, Hilarión, 170–71
deaths, 222–23, 263n17; in Sucre, 103–4;
    survivors, 3, 5–6
decentralism, 241
Declaration of the Rights of Indigenous
    Peoples, 237
decolonization, 169–81
Decree 21060, 18
Defensoría del Pueblo, 19, 196–98, 210,
    261n13
DeFronzo, James, 27, 250n16
democracy, revolution through, 29
democratic and cultural revolution,
    26, 241
democratic norms, 65
democratic power, 70–71
democratic self-governance, FSTMB
    promotion of, 148
departmental autonomy, 172, 173
destabilizing manipulation, of coeval-
    ness, 4–5
detention and torture, of Mamani, 3–6
dictatorships, 2, 3, 5, 6, 140, 144
disaster capitalism, 17

The Echo of Equality, 170
eclecticism, in formulation of principles,
    46
ecological transformation, 241
economic axis, of national life, miners
    as, 139
economy, 7, 18, 25, 97, 101, 137; develop-
    ment of, 156; ideologies of, 239–40;
    in Santa Cruz, 123, 125
egalitarian movement, 171, 172
EGTK (Ejército Guerrillero Túpac Ka-
    tari), 39, 48, 49
Ehrlich, Eugen, 92–93
Ejército Guerrillero Túpac Katari
    (EGTK), 39, 48, 49
El Alto, 18–19, 20, 34, 60–63, 112, 227
elections, 60, 126, 183, 215, 233; 2002, 88,
    120; 2005, 37, 42, 65, 69, 70, 88, 120,

173, 213, 227–25; 2009, 58, 151; 2014,
    156, 229; 2019, 237
El Prado, 1, 2–3, 5
La emancipación de los trabajadores
    será obra de ellos mismos, 143–48
emancipation, preservation and, 97, 147
emancipatory politics, 73, 98
empowerment, for indigenous people,
    141, 224–25
engagement: with anthropology, 12–14,
    98; with ethnographic study, 11
Engels, Friedrich, 150
English Black Act of 1723, 73, 74
enslavement, 224
Episteme, 49
Equality Club, 170
escudo, 149
ethical dilemmas, with ethnographic
    study, 101, 255n4
ethical-moral principles, 39, 181, 232
ethnic identity, 202–4
ethnic valorization, 10–11
ethnographic analysis, 37
ethnographic data, on process of
    change, 29–30
ethnographic research: in El Alto, 60–63;
    in La Paz, 60–63, 96, 102; in Santa
    Cruz, 96–97, 101; in Sucre, 97–98,
    101; of 2006–2015, 18, 97, 249n7
ethnographic study, 6, 7, 11, 30–31,
    249n2; ethical dilemmas with, 101,
    255n4; ethics with, 4; methodology
    for, 8–10, 13–14; of revolution, 27;
    trust relationships needed for, 98
ethnographic truths, 10
ethnography: of clashing ideologies,
    140; of collective identity, 230–31; of
    constitutional revolution, 74; include
    and negate with, 5; longitudinal, 9,
    10, 240; of mirages, 133; multisited,
    8–9; of resistance to MAS ascendency,
    in La Paz, 97; of revolution and
    counterrevolution, 96; of right-wing
    mobilization, 97, 255n2

"Evo Remains, My Revolution Advances"
("Evo Se Queda, Mi Revolución
Avanza"), 201
exploitation, of miners, 136–37, 138, 188

Fabricant, Nicole, 256n17
Falange Socialista Boliviana (FSB),
114, 129
false consciousness, 37
El fantasma insomne, 50
far-right propaganda, in Santa Cruz, 96
Fausto. *See* Reinaga, Fausto
Fausto legacy, politics of world-renewal
and, 218–23, 262n15; Aymara greeting
with, 217, 262n13; communicative
level of regional language with, 200,
214–16; Law 269 relating to, 216–17;
Tobar relating to, 214–16, 262n12
FDTEULP (Federación Departamental
de Trabajadores de Educación Ur-
bana de La Paz), 149, 151
Federación de Empresarios Privados de
Santa Cruz (FEPSC), 119, 124
Federación de Juntas Vecinales de El
Alto (FEJUVE), 215
Federación Departamental de Traba-
jadores de Educación Urbana de La
Paz (FDTEULP), 149, 151
Federación Nacional de Mujeres
Campesinas de Bolivia-Bartolina Sisa
(FNMCB-BS), 21, 69, 145, 208–9
Federación Obrera Femenina (FOF),
206–7
Federación Sindical de Trabajadores
Mineros de Bolivia (FSTMB),
138–39; democratic self-governance
promoted by, 148; emancipation
promoted by, 147; with revolutionary
left, 146, 148
federalism, 101, 120
federal state, Bolivia as, 122
Federal War of 1899, 101–2, 218
federation and confederation leadership, women in, 211

Federation of Neighborhood Councils
of El Alto, 34
FEJUVE (Federación de Juntas Vecinales
de El Alto), 215
Félix, interview with, 193–95
FEPSC (Federación de Empresarios
Privados de Santa Cruz), 119, 124
Fernández, Leopoldo: arrest and trial
of, 186–87, 259n8; as El Cacique, 193,
195; interview with, 23, 98–100
Fernández, Pamela, 99–100
Fexpocruz, 124
FF.AA. (*Bolivia y La Revolución de las*),
221–22
fieldwork, 13
Fiscal Pact, 174
Flores Condori, Petronilo: on au-
tonomy, 166, 167; on constitution,
167–69; on indigenous movement,
66–69, 166–69
FNMCB-BS (Federación Nacional de
Mujeres Campesinas de Bolivia-
Bartolina Sisa), 21, 69, 145, 208–9
FOF (Federación Obrera Femenina),
206
Fourth International, 138, 140, 142, 257n3
fragments: at limits of recognition,
240–45; revolution in, 28–31; unifica-
tion of, 44–51
framing devices, 4–6, 9–10
Fraser, Nancy, on justice, 242–45
FSB (Falange Socialista Boliviana),
114, 129
FSTMB (Federación Sindical de Trabajadores Mineros de Bolivia), 138–39,
146, 147, 148
Fundación Tierra, 189
*Fundamental Principles of the Sociology
of Law* (Ehrlich), 92–93

García Linera, Álvaro: in Comuna,
46–47; in prison, 39; as vice president, 43, 49, 58, 133, 142–43, 156, 158,
179, 188–90, 215, 237

García Meza, Luis, 2, 47, 109, 163, 187, 208, 222
Gas War of 2003, 20, 213
global financial crises of 2007–8, 242
Gobierno Autónomo Indígena Guaraní Charagua Iyambae, 178
Goethe, Johann Wolfgang von, 52
Gold, Marina, 37–38
Goldstein, Daniel, 12–13, 79
Goni. See Sánchez de Lozada, Gonzalo
government: of MAS, 23, 26, 28–29, 30–31, 36, 41, 42–43, 113–14; MNR, 125, 129, 140. See also Morales government
Great House of the People, 235–36
Grupo Comuna. See Comuna
Guaraní Nation of Charagua Iyambae, 177, 178, 232
Guarayo Aruquipa, Samuel, 16, 35, 72
Gueiler Tejada, Lidia, 208, 261n3
guerrilla warfare, 154–55
Guevara, Che, 3, 16, 21, 28, 40, 164
Gustafson, Bret, 19, 251
Gutiérrez Aguilar, Raquel, 47, 48, 49

"Hasta Siempre, Comandante," 134
highlands, lowlands division with, 95, 232
Hirschl, Ran, 69–70, 93
Historia del movimiento obrero boliviano (Lora), 148
historical observation, 4, 9–10
historic congress, Bartolinas with, 209
"Holocaust of Terebinto," 129, 132
Honneth, Axel, 242
Housewives' Committee of Siglo XX, 208
"How a Miner's Wife Spends Her Day," 208
human rights, 19; Morales government on, 195–97; tragic dissonance of, 192–98
hunger strikes, 144, 155–56
hydrocarbon industries, nationalization of, 21

Ibáñez, Andrés: on autonomy, 170–72; on egalitarianism, 171, 172; Equality Club founded by, 170; political and social movement in Santa Cruz led by, 169–71
ideal Andean (lo andino), 7
ideal indigenous person (lo indígena), 7
identity: ethnic, 202–4; multicultural, 19; politics of, 10–11, 19, 203. See also collective identity
ideological alliance, with peasantry, 139
ideological commitment, of MAS, 237
ideological differences, between revolutionary left and peasant movements, 141
ideological force, consistency, and strength, 156–61
ideological framework, of pluralistic belonging, 5
ideological guidance, of Lenin, 45
ideological history, of Bartolinas, 209
ideological innovations, 38
ideological logics, 96
ideological permutations, 56
ideological traditions, 139–40
ideology, 38, 140; of collective identity, 232–33; of economy, 239–40; of MAS, 10–11, 23, 37, 45, 46, 142, 159–60; multiscalar longitudinal ethnography relating to, 9; oppositional, 118; with process of change, 36–37, 39, 44–45, 252n8; of structural change, 39; of Trotsky, 139, 142, 144, 149
IJB (Instituto de la Judicatura de Bolivia), 86, 93
ILO (International Labor Organization) Convention 169, 24, 86
IMF (International Monetary Fund), 17, 75, 239
imperialism, fight against, 6
Indian, 223–24, 225
Indianism, 223, 225, 227–28, 263n20
Indianist, 144, 188, 222–25, 228–29, 230

Indian revolution, 216, 221, 222, 223, 224, 229
"The Indian Revolution" ("La Revolución India") (Reinaga), 200, 216, 228
Indians, 168
indian uprising, 215
lo indígena (ideal indigenous person), 7
indigenism, 223–24, 263n19
indigenismo, 142
indigenismo, indianismo, neoindianismo: enslavement relating to, 224; Indian, 223–24, 225; Indianism, 223, 225, 227–28, 263n20; Indianist, 144, 188, 222–25, 228–29, 230; indigenism, 223–24, 263n19; indigenous, 223–24, 225; MAS relating to, 225, 228, 229; Morales relating to, 223–24, 225, 228, 229, 230; peasant, 223–24; social movements relating to, 224, 231
indigenous, 223–24, 225
"Indigenous and Tribal Peoples Convention," 86–87, 224
indigenous-bourgeois pro-transnational government, of Morales, 160
indigenous customary law, 86–89, 254n6, 254n8, 255n9
indigenous Guaraní, in Santa Cruz, 126
indigenous people, 7, 19, 53, 90–91, 244; conflict march of, 25; confrontation with, 14–15; constitution and, 78–79; empowerment for, 141, 224–25; justice for, 67–68; in La Paz, 13–14; movement of, 66–69, 166–69, 238; native indigenous peasant autonomy, 176–80; rights laws of, 24
indigenous state, 97, 204, 238, 242
indigenous world-reversal, 29, 141
inequality, 7
infrastructure, 11, 24–25
inhumane life, of miners, 135–36, 146–48
Instituto de la Judicatura de Bolivia (IJB), 86, 93
Instrumento Político por la Soberanía de los Pueblos (IPSP), 40

intangibility, principle of, 237–38, 241
interconnected ontological system, 210, 261n7
intermediate approach, to revolution, 28
International Criminal Court, 32
International IDEA, 70
International Labor Organization (ILO) Convention 169, 19, 24, 86, 224
international law, 190
International Monetary Fund (IMF), 17, 75, 239
interpretative coherence, 9–10
intersectionality, with collective identity, 203–4, 261n1
IPSP (Instrumento Político por la Soberanía de los Pueblos), 40
Isiboro-Sécure National Park and Indigenous Territory. *See* TIPNIS

Jean-Christophe (Rolland), 220
Jiliri Apu Mallku, 13
JS (Juventud Socialista), 53, 225
judicialization, of mega-politics, 70
juridification, 7, 25, 66, 101, 241
jurisdicción indígena originaria campesina, 78–79
juristocracy, 240–41
justice, 240; Fraser on, 242–45; indigenous, 67–68; multiscalar longitudinal ethnography relating to, 9; process of change and, 243; recognition, 243; representational, 243–44; rights-based forms of, 19. *See also* community justice
La justicia del Inca (Marof), 138
Juventud Socialista (JS), 53, 225

Katari, Túpac, 21, 35, 76, 206, 233
knowledge breaks chains of enslavement, 148–56, 258nn10–11

labor associations, 137
Laguna Paniagua, Héctor "Chiqui" Renato, interview with, 98–99, 125–26

La Higuera, 3

Lanza, Álvaro, 4

La Paz Department, 8, 16, 24; Coliseo Cerrado Julio Borelli Viterito in, 33–35, 36, 96; ethnographic research in, 60–63, 96, 102; indigenous people in, 13–14; massive protest in, 11, 25, 57; survivors in, 1, 3, 4; union in, 149

latifundia, 77, 123, 125

Latin American New Left, 140

law, 24, 190; change and, 241; constitutional, realities of, 71–72; discontents of, 240; indigenous customary, 86–89, 254n6, 254n8, 255n9; living, 92–94; logic of, 68–74; major consequences in understanding role of, 71–74; process of change through, 65–66; revolutionary vision reconciled with, 66; transformation and, 66

law, unstable assemblage of, 166–68; conclusion to, 198–99; human rights, tragic dissonance of, 192–98; plurinationalism, through autonomy and decolonization, 169–81

Law 180 (TIPNIS Protection Law), 188–89, 237–38

Law 266, 238

Law 269, 216–17

Law 351 (Ley de Otorgación de Personalidades Jurídicas), 58, 187–89, 192, 210

Law 1818, 19

lawfare, 191

Law of Autonomies (Andrés Ibáñez Law of Autonomies and Decentralization), 181, 184; autonomous municipalities, 172, 173; departmental autonomy, 172, 173; native indigenous peasant autonomy, 176–80; regional autonomy, 172, 174

Law of Bilingual Education, 19

Law of Granting Legal Statuses, 187–88

Law of Popular Participation (1994), 19, 173

Lazarte, Silvia, 112, 256n13

legal cosmovisions, 64–74

legal decolonization, 179, 180–81

legalization, of process of change, 241

legal pluralism, 181

Lenin, Vladimir, 45, 46, 150

Ley de Otorgación de Personalidades Jurídicas (Law 351), 58, 187–89, 192, 210

Liberal party, 101, 102

Lima, Constantino, 228, 263n22

living law, 92–94

living well, 39, 51, 251n3

Llorenti, Sacha, 114, 202; interview with, 44; in MAS government, 41, 42–43

longitudinal ethnography, 9, 10, 240

longue durée, 10, 229, 240

Lora, Guillermo, 139, 140, 148, 150

Machaca Quispe, Felipe, 143–46

Machicado, Mangel, 149–50

MACOJMA (Marka de Ayllus y Comunidades Originarias de Jesús de Machaca), 211, 261n8

Magna Carta, 75–76, 97; of Santa Cruz, 118, 121

El Mallku. *See* Quispe, Felipe

Mallku Tayka, 211

Mamani, Alejandro: detention and torture of, 3–6; reparation claims of, 2, 5–6; as survivor spokesman, 3

Manifesto of Tiahuanaco (1973), 221

Manifiesto del Partido Indio de Bolivia (Reinaga), 211

marginalization, 5, 90

Marka de Ayllus y Comunidades Originarias de Jesús de Machaca (MACOJMA), 211, 261n8

Marof, Tristán, 138

martyrs of Calancha, 183, 259n7

Marx, Karl, 45, 50, 150

Marxist response, 36–38, 48, 49, 50, 147, 169, 224; revolution relating to, 39, 51, 53

MAS. *See* Movement to Socialism
Masas, 157, 158
MAS *asembleístas*, 103
MAS Bolsheviks, *cruceño* White army vs., 97
MAS-IPSP, 40
Massacre of Ayo Ayo, 102–3, 105, 113, 128
Massacre of Porvenir, 23–24, 42, 99, 186, 192–95, 239
Mauss, Marcel, on constitution, 80–81
Media Luna, 22–23, 35, 118, 121, 210, 238, 250n12
mega-politics, 70, 93
Merry, Sally Engle, 8–9, 12
Mesa, Carlos, 86, 162, 191, 214–15, 260n11
methodologies: for anthropology, 11–12; for ethnographic study, 8–10, 13–14
Mexico, 47–49
militant street mobilizations, in Santa Cruz, 118–19
Military-Peasant Pact, 69, 141
millenarian imagination, Pachakuti and, 231–33
miners, 3, 18, 40, 42, 48, 253n15, 257n2; as economic axis of national life, 139; exploitation of, 136–37, 138, 188; inhumane life of, 135–36, 146–48; lifespan of, 136; mining congresses of, 152; movement of, 138–39; potosino, 57–58
mining camps, women in, 207–8
mining congresses, 152
Ministry of Autonomies, 176, 177, 179, 259n4
Ministry of Communication, 82, 203, 218
Ministry of Community Justice, 167
Ministry of Culture and Tourism, 179
Ministry of External Relations, 202
Ministry of Justice, 1, 2, 64–66
Ministry of Water, 34
MIR (Movimiento de Izquierda Revolucionaria), 90

"Missing the Revolution" (Starn), 7
MNR (Movimiento Nacionalista Revolucionario government of Hernán Siles Zuazo), 125, 129, 140, 219
mobilization, in streets, 34, 56, 97, 118–19, 144, 255n2
Mojocoya, autonomy of, 177
Morales, Evo, 2, 5, 9, 16, 43, 56; alliance of, 21; Álvarez on, 153–54, 156; Barrón support of, 182–83; Choque Callisaya on, 213–14, 262nn10–11; critics of, 23, 24; ethnic identity of, 202–4; inauguration ritual performed by, 11; indigenismo, indianismo, neoindianismo relating to, 223–24, 225, 228, 229, 230; new constitution with, 7, 13, 21–23, 24–25, 35; scandal of, 25–26; transformative vision of, 235–36; violent treatment of supporters of, 23; warning of, 235
Morales government, 21–25, 56–60, 113–14, 250n13; Defensoría del Pueblo and, 19, 196–98, 261n13; on human rights, 195–97; indigenous-bourgeois pro-transnational government, 160; on international law, 190; lawfare relating to, 191; Law of Granting of Legal Statuses as tool of, 187–88; NGOs relating to, 188–89; scandal of, 189; sea question of, 190; TIPNIS Protection Law of, 188–89, 237–38
moral transformation, 241
movements: of indigenous people, 66–69, 166–69, 238; of miners, 138–39; political and social, in Santa Cruz, 169–71; to socialism, 171; of workers, 152–53, 156, 160. *See also specific movements*
Movement to Socialism (MAS) party, 2, 13, 16; bourgeois reform promoted by, 153; at Coliseo Cerrado Julio Borelli Viterito, 33–35; cultural taxonomies mobilized by, 5; government of, 23, 26, 28–29, 30–31, 36, 41, 42–43,

113–14; ideological commitment of, 237; ideology of, 10–11, 23, 37, 45, 46, 142, 159–60; indigenismo, indianismo, neoindianismo relating to, 225, 228, 229; Llorenti relating to, 41, 42–43; Potosí support for, 58; resistance to, 97, 238–39, 264n4; revolutionary project of, 56, 69; student branch of, 54

Movimiento al Socialismo, 235

Movimiento de Izquierda Revolucionaria (MIR), 90

Movimiento Indígena Pachakuti, 223

Movimiento Nacionalista Revolucionario (MNR) government of Hernán Siles Zuazo, 125, 129, 140, 216

Movimiento Originario Popular, 8

Movimiento Revolucionario Túpac Amaru (MRTA), 54, 221

Muela del Diablo, 50, 253n12

mujer de pollera, 105, 108, 256n7

multicultural identity, 19

multiscalar longitudinal ethnography, 9

multisited ethnography, 8–9

Museum of the Democratic and Cultural Revolution, 236

mytho-histories, 97, 118, 130, 256n16

"Nación Camba/Nación Aymara Quechua" map, 130

National Agrarian Tribunal, 86

National Human Rights Institution (NHRI), 196

nationalism, Camba, 119–21, 130, 131, 232, 256n17

nationalization, of hydrocarbon industries, 21

national mobilization, for constitution, 34

national politics, of collective identity, 232

National Revolution (1952), 129, 139, 140, 171, 181, 211, 219, 220, 257n22

native indigenous peasant autonomy, 176, 180, 231; of Guaraní Nation of Charagua Iyambae, 177, 178; of Mojocoya, 177; of Totora Marka, 177, 179; of Uru Chipaya, 177

Nava Andrade, Aydée, on constitution, 83–84

Nelson Huayllas, Rudy, 179–81, 259n5

neo-Indianism, 230

neoliberalism, 11, 17, 19, 38, 47, 155; with Indian face, 240

neoliberal rights-infused cosmopolitanism, 29

neoliberal world order, 11, 20

New Political Economy, 18

NGOs (nongovernmental organizations), 58, 67, 70, 86, 188–89

NHRI (National Human Rights Institution), 196

Nicaraguan revolution, 11

nobility, of Sucre, 105–7, 111, 256n12, 256nn8–9

nongovernmental organizations (NGOs), 58, 67, 70, 86, 188–89

normative approach, to revolution, 26–27, 28, 250n15

(not) missing the revolution, 6–15, 249n2

Office of Constitutional Development, 92

open university, to unification of fragments, 44–51

opposition, as cultural system, 95–100; conclusion to, 132–33; darkness in city of white, 101–18; thin green line between autonomy and separatism, 118–32, 256n16

oppositional ideology, 118

opposition movement: in Santa Cruz, 36, 61, 77, 84, 85, 98, 127; in Sucre, 31, 36, 61, 77, 79–80, 83, 98, 255n3

oppression 1964–1982, 2, 5

organic revolutionary left, creation of: with Fourth International, 138, 140, 142, 257n3; with FSTMB, 138–39; with ideological traditions, 139–40; Military-Peasant Pact relating to, 69, 141

Orientalism, 16

Pachakuti, 5, 9, 141, 227–30, 240; millenarian imagination and, 231–33

Pachamama, 24, 77–78, 81, 243

Pacto de Unidad, 21–22, 69, 157, 204; members of, 25, 31, 209, 232, 261n6

pact of reciprocity, 174

Palacio Quemado, 13, 22, 35, 141, 150, 157, 235–36; attack on, 41–42

Pando Department, 23–24, 98, 119, 122, 186, 192–93

Partido de Indios Aymaras y Keswas (PIAK), 220

Partido Indio de Bolivia (PIB), 220–21

Partido Obrero Revolucionario (POR), 138, 140, 142–43, 148, 158–61

Patzi, Félix, 34, 35–36

Paz Estenssoro, Víctor, 18, 20, 150, 250n9

Paz Zamora, Jaime, 87, 121, 155

peasantry, 90–91, 139, 140, 141, 142, 223–24; native indigenous peasant autonomy, 176–80

El Pensamiento Amáutico (Reinaga), 218

Peredo, Antonio, 2, 28–29, 49, 65, 68

Permanent Assembly of Human Rights of Bolivia (APDHB), 42, 75, 210

permanent revolution, 138, 140, 155

permanent struggle, to balance sheets of government, 56–60

Peta, Doña, 207

phenomenological approach, to revolution, 26–27, 28, 251n17

PIAK (Partido de Indios Aymaras y Keswas), 220

PIB (Partido Indio de Bolivia), 220–21

PIEB (Programa de Investigación Estratégica en Bolivia), 86

Plata Arnez, Vilma, interview with, 158–61, 159n14

Plaza 25 de Mayo, in Sucre, 23, 34, 113–14, 256n14

Plaza de Rodillas, 23–24, 117, 118, 239

pluralism, 11, 68, 79, 83, 86–92

pluralistic belonging, ideological framework of, 5

Plurinational Constitutional Tribunal (TCP), 91, 178, 180–81, 199, 236–37, 264n2

plurinationalism, 89; through autonomy and decolonization, 169–81

Plurinational Legislative Assembly, 70, 187, 236

plurinational state, 166, 241; Bartolinas relating to, 209, 210; legal pluralism in, 86–92

political, social, public death, of Reinaga, 222–23, 263n17

political and social movement, in Santa Cruz, 169–71

Political Constitution of State, 176

political debate, 51

political parties, rural, 8

political patronage, 156

political power, redistribution of, 11, 242–44

politics, 7; of allochrony, 5; emancipatory, 73, 98; of identity, 10–11, 19, 203; mega-politics, 70, 93; national, of collective identity, 232; of recognition, 243–45; of representation, 243; of revolution, 242

politics, of forever, 234–39; revolutionary fragments at limits of recognition, 240–45; soaring on wings of ineffable, 245–48

POR (Partido Obrero Revolucionario), 138, 140, 142–43, 148, 158–61

Porvenir. See Massacre of Porvenir

Postero, Nancy, 19, 31, 38, 97, 142, 174, 179, 204, 224, 238

posters, 148–51

postneoliberal subjects, 38–39, 51

Potosí Department, 16, 58, 66, 78, 80, 179; mining town of, 101, 106, 162–63; research in, 7, 8, 14, 15, 57–58, 254n16

potosino miners, 57–58

practice: multiscalar longitudinal ethnography relating to, 9; study of scales of justice, ideology, and, 240

Prada Alcoreza, Raúl ("Chato"), 47, 49

preamble, to constitution, 38, 76, 203, 243

The Preexistence of the Native Indigenous Peasant Peoples and Nations, 176

process of change, 29–30, 62–65, 140, 240; Almaraz Paz on, 135; constitutional law, realities of, 71–72; in cultural, historical, and ideological logics, 96; ideology relating to, 36–37, 39, 44–45, 252n8; juridification relating to, 7, 25, 66, 101; justice relating to, 243; legalization of, 241; major consequences in understanding role of law with, 71–74; Teleférico as, 246–48

Programa de Investigación Estratégica en Bolivia (PIEB), 86

proletarian revolution, 137, 138, 139

protests, 11, 25, 57, 103, 112, 182, 196

Provincial Agrarian Federation of Communities of Caranavi, 15–16

publication: of Comuna, 50–51, 253n13; of constitution, 81–82

public resources, redistribution of, 11, 45, 76

public transportation system, of Teleférico, 245–48

Puebla, Carlos, 134

pututu, 57, 140, 177, 200–204; Bartolinas and power of complementarity, 205–14; collective identity, 203, 223–31; Fausto legacy and politics of world-renewal, 214–23; Pachakuti and millenarian imagination, 231–33

q'aras, 145, 258n8

Quispe, Felipe (El Mallku), 67, 213, 215, 223, 225, 227–28, 240

Rabocheye Dyelo, 45

racial antagonism, 238–39

racial discrimination, 230

racially inflected violence, in Santa Cruz, 96

racism, with taxi driver, 201–2

Radokov, Alexei, 148–49

Ramírez Santiesteban, Edgar, 162–65, 258n15

recognition, politics of, 243–45

recognition demands, of survivors, 2

recognition justice, 243

redistribution, 10; of political power, 11, 242–44; of public resources, 11, 45, 76

Referéndum revocatorio, 22–23, 60–61, 113, 243–44, 254n17

refoundation, 6, 169, 174, 209, 235, 241, 248; in 2009, 24, 26, 36–41, 70, 89, 97, 122, 154, 167, 181, 242; process of, 7, 10, 30, 118, 179, 195, 202

regional autonomy, 172, 174–75

regional identification, 118

regional trade organizations, in Santa Cruz, 124

reglamentación, 187

Reinaga, Fausto: background of, 218–19, 262n14; crisis of conscience suffered by, 220; final years of, 222–23; PIAK founded by, 220; political, social, public death of, 222–23, 263n17; revolution vision of, 223–24; travels of, 219–21; works of, 200, 211, 216–18, 221, 227–28, 229

relationality, with collective identity, 203–4

reparation claims, 2, 5–6

representation, politics of, 243

representational justice, 243–44

Requiem for a Republic (Alamaraz Paz), 135

research project, 10–11, 19

resistance, to MAS, 97, 238–39, 264n4

resistance movements: academic and critical studies of, 17–18; during ethnographic research of 2006–2015, 18, 97, 249n7; inequality relating to, 20; interdisciplinary writing about, 17–18

Resistencia Universitaria de Trabajo Autónomo (RUTA), 54

"La Revolución India" ("The Indian Revolution") (Reinaga), 200, 216, 228

revolution: alternative, 97; approaches to, 26–27, 28, 250n15; constitutional, 68–74, 153–54; cultural, 26, 241; democratic, 26, 29, 241; fragments, 28–31; from inside out, 26–28; legacy of, 142; Marxist response to, 39, 51, 53; (not) missing the revolution, 6–15; need for, 53; politics of, 242; process of change relating to, 62–63; spatialization of, 235; utopian promise of, 57; of workers, 137–41, 144–47. *See also specific revolutions*

revolution, heard in minor key, 33–35; burning all boats after bridges are built, 41–44; conclusion to, 60–63; open university to unification of fragments, 44–51; permanent struggle to balance sheets of government, 56–60; reinscribing the subject, refounding the state, 36–41; sorrows, of young revolutionary, 52–56

revolution, without revolutionaries: conclusion to, 161–65; La emancipación de los trabajadores será obra de ellos mismos, 143–48; knowledge breaks chains of enslavement, 148–56; strength is ideological force and consistency, 156–61

revolutionary fragments, at limits of recognition, 240–45

revolutionary idealism, 59

revolutionary left, 141, 146, 148, 164, 169. *See also* organic revolutionary left, creation of

revolutionary mobilization, 56

revolutionary movement, 54

revolutionary pragmatism, 59

revolutionary project, of MAS, 56, 69

revolutionary slogans and banners, at Coliseo Cerrado Julio Borelli Viterito, 34–35

revolutionary theory, of Lenin, 45

revolutionary transformation, 74, 145, 154, 213, 247–48

revolutionary violence, 39, 252n4

revolutionary vision, law reconciled with, 66

revolution vision, of Reinaga, 223–24

rights, 19, 24, 29, 96, 192–98

rights-based constitutional law, 74

rights-based forms, of justice, 19

right-wing mobilization, ethnography of, 97, 255n2

rituals: at Coliseo Cerrado Julio Borelli Viterito, 34–35; inauguration, of Morales, 11

Roberto, interview with, 193–94

Rodríguez Calvo, Luis Pedro, interview with, 106–8

Rodríguez Veltzé, Eduardo, 191, 215

Rojas Vaca, Victor Hugo, 130–32

Rolland, Romain, 220

rural political parties, 8

RUTA (Resistencia Universitaria de Trabajo Autónomo), 54

Salar de Uyuni, 16

Sánchez de Lozada, Gonzalo (Goni), 18–19, 88, 174, 193; exile of, 214; government of, 49, 144, 150, 196, 222

San Pedro Prison, 23, 33, 98, 100, 186–87, 192

Santa Cruz, 8, 11, 13, 22, 23, 24, 177; agricultural economy in, 118–19, 123, 125; autonomy struggle of, 122–23,

124–25; economy in, 123, 125; ethnographic research, 96–97, 101; far-right propaganda in, 96; indifference in, 126; indigenous Guaraní in, 126; Magna Carta of, 118, 121; opposition movement in, 36, 61, 77, 84, 85, 98, 127; political and social movement in, 169–71; racially inflected violence in, 96; regional trade organizations in, 124; separatist policies in, 96; servitude in, 126, 133; violence in, 126–29

Santa Cruz, opposition to autonomy statute of: with militant street mobilizations, 118–19; Secretariat of Autonomy, Decentralization, and Development relating to, 118, 123

scales, with multiscalar longitudinal ethnography, 9

scandal, of Morales, 25–26

Secretariat of Autonomy, Decentralization, and Development, 118, 123

Seis Federaciones del Trópico de Cochabamba, 238

self-governance, 19

self-identification, 167, 168, 176

separatism, autonomy and, 118–32, 256n16

separatist policies, in Santa Cruz, 96

servitude, in Santa Cruz, 126, 133

Shimose, Pedro, 132

Shining Path Maoist movement, 7, 54

SIAH (Sistema de Archivo Histórico de Comibol), 161–62

Sindicato de Culinarias (Union of Women Cooks), 207

Sisa, Bartolina, 40, 76, 206

Sistema de Archivo Histórico de Comibol (SIAH), 161–62

social and political movement, of Bartolinas, 209

social change, 7, 10–11

socialism, 164; movement to, 171; as road to communism, 157. See also Movement to Socialism

social movements, 224, 231

social spending, 244

social transformation, 59, 71, 93, 190, 209

Soledad, interview with, 54–56, 59

sorrows, of young revolutionary, 52–56

de Sousa Santos, Boaventura, 50, 177

sovereign power, 71, 73

spaces, places and, 8

spatialization, of revolution, 235

Starn, Orin, 7

state bureaucracy, 29

strategic juridification, 182–92, 237

structural change, 39, 73

structural transformation, 30, 31, 54, 74, 144, 235

student branch, of MAS, 54

study, of scales of justice, ideology, practice, 240

Sucre, 8, 11, 68, 171, 183–84; constituent assembly in, 21, 22; deaths in, 103–4; ethnographic research in, 97–98, 101; nobility of, 105–7, 111, 256n12, 256nn8–9; opposition movement in, 31, 36, 61, 77, 79–80, 83, 98, 255n3; Plaza 25 de Mayo in, 23, 34, 113–14, 256n14; violence in, 103–5, 112–18, 256n6

suma qamaña, 228, 263n23

survivors: death of, 3, 5–6; in La Paz, 1, 3, 4; Mamani as spokesperson for, 3; of oppression between 1964 and 1982, 2, 5; recognition demands of, 2; reparation claims of, 2, 5–6; violence and harassment of, 2, 6

synchronic and diachronic approaches, to ethnographic study, 9, 10

Tahipamu (Taller de Historia y Participación de la Mujer), 207

talisman, constitution as, 74–85

Taller de Historia y Participación de la Mujer (Tahipamu), 207

Tapia, Luis, 47, 48, 49

Tata Mallku, 211

TCP (Plurinational Constitutional Tribunal), 91, 178, 180–81, 199, 236–37, 264n2

teachers: hunger strike of, 155–56; union of, 156

Teleférico: cable car public transportation system of, 245–48; process of change relating to, 246–48; symbolic meaning of, 247–48

term limits, on president and vice president, 236

Tesis India (Reinaga), 211

theoretical arguments, 4

"Thesis of Pulacayo" (Lora), 139, 148, 152, 158, 162

third revolution, 29, 37, 74, 142, 241–42, 251n19

thirty-six nations and people, in constitution, 90, 167–68, 231–32, 255n12

Thomassen, Bjørn, 27, 28, 251n18

Thompson, E. P., on logic of law, 73–74

Thomson, Sinclair, xii

TIPNIS (Isiboro-Sécure National Park and Indigenous Territory), 188; area of, 24–25, 238, 241; conflict of 2011, 30, 31, 46, 51, 52, 56, 62, 72, 73, 99, 120, 151, 156–57, 160, 237; impact of, 52, 59, 73, 157, 178, 187; post, 25, 56, 58, 59, 93, 191–92, 196–99, 229; resolution of, 30–31

TIPNIS Protection Law (Law 180), 188–89, 237–38

Tobar, Héctor, 214–16, 262n12

Totora Marka, autonomy of, 177, 179

transformation: anthropology of, 32; of constitution, 80, 82; cultural, ecological, moral, 241; ideology of, 20, 147; law and, 66; process of, 5, 8, 9, 11, 17–18, 23, 27, 28, 29, 51, 62, 82, 97, 126, 141, 175, 180, 195, 197, 204; revolutionary, 74, 145, 154, 213, 247–48; social, 59, 71, 93, 190, 209; structural, 30, 31, 54, 74, 144, 235

"The Transformation of Bolivia's Plurinational State and the Autonomy Process," 175

transformative promise, of general law and rights-based constitutional law, 74

transformative vision, of Morales, 235–36

Treaty of Peace and Friendship, 190

Tribunal Constitucional Plurinacional. *See* Plurinational Constitutional Tribunal

Trotsky, Leon, 257nn4–5; doctrine of permanent revolution, 140; ideology of, 134, 138–44, 149; influence of, 140; peasantry relating to, 139, 140

Trotskyist movement, 30, 40, 53, 148, 151–52, 155–56, 225

Trotskyized country, Bolivia as, 134, 138–43

Trump, Donald, 31–32

trust relationships, for ethnographic study, 98

UCB (Universidad Católica Boliviana), 201

UDHR (Universal Declaration of Human Rights), 75, 202

UJC (Unión Juvenil Cruceñista), 13, 85, 119, 128, 130–32, 257n24

UMSA (Universidad Mayor de San Andrés), 48, 49, 52, 53, 225–26

UNAM (Universidad Nacional Autónoma de México), 47, 48

UNASUR (Unión de Naciones Suramericanas), 23, 194–95

Uncle Sam, 150, 258n11

unconstitutionality, of Article 168, 236–37, 264n1

UNDP (United Nations Development Programme), 75

Unión de Naciones Suramericanas (UNASUR), 23, 194–95

Unión Juvenil Cruceñista (UJC), 13, 85, 119, 128, 130–32, 257n24

Union of Russian Social-Democratics Abroad, 45
Union of Women Cooks (*Sindicato de Culinarias*), 207
union organizing, by women, 206
Unión Revolucionaria de Estudiantes Normalistas, 152
Unión Revolucionaria de Universitarios Socialistas (URUS), 53, 152, 225
unions, 144, 149, 156
unitary Republic, 87, 88, 89
Unitary Social State of Plurinational Communitarian Law, 169
United Nations Development Programme (UNDP), 75
Universal Declaration of Human Rights (UDHR), 75, 202
Universidad Católica Boliviana (UCB), 201
Universidad Mayor, Real y Pontificia de San Francisco Xavier de Chuquisaca, 102
Universidad Mayor de San Andrés (UMSA), 48, 49, 52, 53, 225–26
Universidad Nacional Autónoma de México (UNAM), 47, 48
university revolution, in 1970, 53
Urquieta, Cecilia, on constitution, 83
Uru Chipaya, autonomy of, 177
URUS (Unión Revolucionaria de Universitarios Socialistas), 53, 152, 225
USAID, 242
utopian promise, 57, 71–72

Vega Camacho, Oscar ("Oki"), 47–48, 49, 50, 253n10
vernacularization, 71
Vice Ministry of Community Justice, 66
Vice Ministry of Decolonization, 179, 217, 231
Viezzer, Moema, 205–6

vigil, at El Prado shack, 2–3
village-based ethnohistorical and ethnographic research, impact of, 7
Villarroel, Gualberto, 41–42
Villa Tunari–San Ignacio de Moxos Highway, crisis of, 56–57
Villena Villegas, Rolando, 75, 197–98
violence, 96; harassment and, of survivors, 2, 6; revolutionary, 39, 252n4; in Santa Cruz, 126–29; in Sucre, 103–5, 112–18, 256n6
violent treatment, of Morales supporters, 23
Volveré y seré millones, 15–26, 233

War of the Chaco, 41, 137, 252n6
War of the Pacific, 190
Washington Consensus, 19, 47
Water War in Cochabamba in 1999 and 2000, 20, 144
Webber, Jeffrey, 142, 144
"What Is to Be Done?" (Lenin), 45
White army, MAS Bolsheviks, *cruceño vs.*, 97
Williams, Raymond, 36–37
women: as *cholas*, 206; in federation and confederation leadership, 211; fundamental role of, 206; in mining camps, 207–8; union organizing of, 206
Wood, Gordon, on constitutional revolution, 72–73
workers: movement of, 152–53, 156, 160; revolution of, 137–41, 144–47
World Bank, 25, 75
World Trade Organization, 17

"Yes!" campaign, 34–35, 36, 96

Zapatista revolt, 11
Zárate Willka, Pablo, 102, 218